# Measuring the Tax Burden on Capital and Labor

# Measuring the Tax Burden on Capital and Labor

edited by Peter Birch Sørensen

CESifo Seminar Series

The MIT Press
Cambridge, Massachusetts
London, England

This book was set in Palatino on 3B2 by Asco Typesetters and was printed and bound in
the United States of America.

Library of Congress Cataloging-in-Publication Data

Measuring the tax burden on capital and labor / edited by Peter Birch Sørensen.
    p.   cm. — (CESifo seminar series)
Includes bibliographical references and index.
ISBN 0-262-19503-8 (alk. paper)
1. Taxation—Case studies. 2. Taxation—Econometric models. I. Sørensen, Peter Birch.
II. Series.

HJ2305.M426   2004
336.2'001'51—dc22                                                    2003066826

10 9 8 7 6 5 4 3 2 1

# Contents

# CESifo Seminar Series in Economic Policy

The CESifo Seminar Series in Economic Policy aims to cover topical policy issues in economics from a largely European perspective. The books in this series are the products of papers presented and discussed at seminars hosted by CESifo, an international research network of renowned economists supported jointly by the Center for Economic Studies at Ludwig-Maximilians-Universität, Munich, and the Ifo Institute for Economic Research. All publications in this series have been carefully selected and refereed by members of the CESifo research network.

Hans-Werner Sinn

# Preface

The ongoing process of globalization has generated renewed interest in summary measures of effective tax burdens. Faced with rising international mobility of capital and labor, policy makers have become more eager to know how the level of tax in their country compares with tax levels in other countries with which they are competing for mobile tax bases. Academic researchers have also been looking for tractable empirical summary measures of taxation to investigate whether taxes affect the international location of economic activity, whether tax policy in one country interacts with tax policy in other countries, and whether tax competition does indeed tend to reduce the relative tax burden on the more mobile factors of production.

As a result the recent years have seen a revival of studies of effective tax rates, and a concomitant proliferation of alternative measures of effective taxation. Unfortunately, the ultimate users of these studies—in academe as well as in policy-making circles—do not always seem to appreciate the strengths and weaknesses of the many different methods for calculating effective tax rates. Indeed, many users of effective tax rate measures seem unaware that different methods may yield quite different results and hence may suggest very different policy conclusions.

Against this background the present volume seeks to provide an overview of the most important approaches currently used to measure effective tax rates. The aim is to highlight the advantages and disadvantages of the different approaches and to illustrate their practical use by specific empirical case studies. The contributions are by academic researchers and by practitioners with extensive experience in the production and use of effective tax rate measures. All derive from papers presented at the CESifo Venice Summer Institute workshop on

Measuring the Tax Burden on Capital and Labor in July 2002. After the workshop the papers were refereed and edited for publication.

It is my hope that this volume will become a useful reference and tool for academics and practitioners seeking an overview of the state of the art of measuring effective tax rates. I am grateful to the discussants at the CESifo Summer Institute whose insightful comments helped the authors in revising their papers, and I am much indebted to the referees whose careful evaluations of the revised papers were a great help in the editing process. Thanks are also due to CESifo President Hans-Werner Sinn who encouraged this project right from the start, to Roisin Hearn and Nicola Papaphilippou from the CESifo office whose efficient organization of the Summer Institute created such a pleasant environment for the workshop, and to Silke Übelmesser and Marko Köthenbürger from the CES who assisted me on practical matters during the editing process.

Finally, the authors, the editor, and the publisher are indebted to the editors of the OECD Economic Studies for permission to use, in chapter 7, the article by David Carey and Josette Rabesona, which was originally published in the *OECD Economic Studies* 35 (2002): 129–174.

Peter Birch Sørensen

# Contributors

*David Carey*
Economics Department
OECD

*W. Steven Clark*
Centre for Tax Policy and
Administration
OECD

*Kirk A. Collins*
University of Ottawa

*James B. Davies*
University of Western Ontario

*Michael P. Devereux*
University of Warwick

*Roger Gordon*
University of California, San
Diego

*Harry Grubert*
Office of Tax Policy
US Treasury Department

*Jakob de Haan*
University of Groningen

*Christopher Heady*
Centre for Tax Policy and
Administration
OECD

*Laura Kalambokidis*
University of Minnesota

*Alexander Klemm*
Institute for Fiscal Studies,
London

*Josette Rabesona*
Economics Department
OECD

*Joel Slemrod*
University of Michigan, Ann
Arbor

*Jan-Egbert Sturm*
University of Munich
and CESifo

*Peter Birch Sørensen*
University of Copenhagen

*Bjørn Volkerink*
Maastricht University

# Measuring the Tax Burden on Capital and Labor

# 1    Measuring Taxes on Capital and Labor: An Overview of Methods and Issues

Peter Birch Sørensen

## 1.1   Introduction

### 1.1.1   Why Study Effective Tax Rates?

The tax systems of modern economies are highly complicated. They reflect the complex pattern of economic activities, the numerous different forms in which incomes accrue, and the many delicate political compromises underlying the tax laws. When trying to understand and model how taxes affect the economy, economists must inevitably resort to simplified descriptions of the tax system. To be able to see the big picture, policy makers have further a need for summary measures capturing the net effects of the many different provisions of the tax code.

Studies of so-called effective tax rates seek to provide such summary measures. An effective tax rate measures the net amount of tax levied on a certain economic activity, in accord with rules defining the tax base and the statutory tax rate imposed on that base. By estimating effective tax rates, tax economists are trying to answer questions such as: What is the overall burden of taxes on capital and labor, on average and at the margin? How do the net tax burdens vary across different sectors of the economy, across different types of investment, and across different groups of taxpayers? How have the tax burdens on different activities and factors of production evolved over time? And how would net tax burdens change if the tax laws were changed in certain ways?

Equipped with estimates of effective tax rates, analysts may study empirically whether and to what extent taxes affect economic behavior, and policy makers may evaluate whether the net outcome of all the different tax laws accords with their intentions, and how specific changes in the tax code would affect the incentives and net tax burdens faced by taxpayers.

### 1.1.2   Some Milestones in Effective Tax Rate Analysis

The study of effective tax rates on income from capital received a major stimulus from the work of King and Fullerton (1984), which in turn built on earlier research by Hall and Jorgenson (1967) and King (1974). The many studies initiated by King and Fullerton indicated that the tax systems of most OECD economies were characterized by serious non-neutralities in the early and mid-1980s; this was reflected in large differences in marginal effective tax rates on capital across different asset types, modes of finance, and investor groups. The studies also suggested that the overall marginal effective tax burden on capital was quite high, in part because of the failure to adjust the nominal income tax base for inflation. Thus the King-Fullerton studies left the impression of a highly distortionary system of capital income taxation. Because of their impact on professionals within national and international policy-making bodies, there is hardly any doubt that these studies helped to pave the way for the wave of tax reforms sweeping through the OECD area in the second half of the 1980s and the early 1990s. An important element in most of the reforms was the attempt to achieve greater neutrality of capital income taxation by eliminating tax priviliges for particular types of investment and by bringing depreciation for tax purposes more in line with true economic depreciation. At the same time research from this period also left a puzzle (addressed in chapter 4 of this volume): a study by Gordon and Slemrod (1988) estimated that in 1983 the US tax system collected no net revenue from taxing capital income. How could this be reconciled with the many studies indicating a high marginal tax burden on income from capital?

The original King-Fullerton studies focused on domestic investments financed by domestic savings. But as international capital flows were liberalized during the 1980s, the tax burden on cross-border investment attracted growing attention. Alworth (1988) and Keen (1991) showed how the King-Fullerton methodology could be extended to the study of taxation of multinational companies, and Michael P. Devereux and his collaborators at the Institute for Fiscal Studies in London made a major effort to generalize the King-Fullerton method to allow estimation of marginal effective tax rates on foreign direct investment. This work became an important input into an OECD study on "Taxing Profits in a Global Economy," which provided internationally comparable estimates of marginal effective tax rates on domestic and foreign direct investment in all the OECD countries at the start of the 1990s (OECD 1991).[1]

The same methodology was subsequently used by the Ruding Committee in its study of company taxation in the European Community (European Commission 1992). Some years later Michael Devereux and his IFS colleagues developed a further extension of the King-Fullerton framework, enabling estimation of average as well as marginal effective tax rates on domestic and foreign direct investment.[2] This method was applied in the European Commission's recent report on company tax problems in the European Union (European Commission 2001). A common theme running through these international studies of effective tax rates is that foreign investment tends to be overtaxed relative to domestic investment, due to incomplete alleviation of international double taxation. Hence these studies have helped to keep the removal of tax obstacles to cross-border investment on the policy agenda of international organizations like the OECD and the European Commission. But they have also attracted criticism that the open-economy King-Fullerton framework tends to overestimate the tax burden on international investment because it does not allow for all of the possibilities for tax planning available to multinational companies (see chapter 5 in this volume).

While most studies of effective tax rates have focused on taxes on capital, the recent years have witnessed a growing interest in measuring the tax burden on labor. In part this reflects a suspicion that high and rising taxes on labor have contributed to the stubbornly high rates of unemployment in several European countries. The increased focus on labor taxation may also reflect a perceived need to stimulate labor supply in order to counter the demographic trend toward a growing number of retirees relative to workers. In an influential study, Mendoza, Razin, and Tesar (1994) proposed a simple method for estimating average effective tax rates on labor, capital, and consumption, by combining the Revenue Statistics of OECD Member States with data from the OECD National Income Accounts. This method was applied in a provocative econometric study by Daveri and Tabellini (2000) suggesting that a large part of the rise in unemployment in Continental Europe over the period 1965 to 1995 could be explained by the rising tax burden on labor.

A similar method of estimating average effective tax rates on the basis of aggregate data was used by the European Commission (1997) to argue that international tax competition has caused a shifting of the tax burden away from mobile capital toward less mobile labor. As a supplement to these methodologies based on macro data, the OECD secretariat has developed its "Taxing Wages" approach to measuring average and marginal tax rates on labor, applying the key parameters from current tax rules to hypothetical model households with a specified level and composition of income.

## 1.2  Measuring Taxes on Capital

In this chapter I provide a summary of the main points made in this volume, within an organizing framework that should help the reader see how the various chapters fit together and complement each other.[3] In section 1.2, I deal with the measurement of effective tax rates on investment in physical capital, and in section 1.3, I focus on the measurement of taxes on labor and on human capital investment.

There are two main approaches to the measurement of effective tax rates on income from capital. One approach uses parameters from current tax laws to calculate the expected future tax burden on hypothetical investment projects, given specific assumptions about asset types, modes of finance, and the tax status of the investor. This may be termed the forward-looking approach. Another methodology uses data on capital taxes collected from firms and their owners and relates these revenue data to estimates of the before-tax income from capital. For reasons which will become clear below, this may be called the backward-looking approach.

### 1.2.1  Measures Using Parameters of Tax Legislation

*The Basic Forward-Looking Measures*
The forward-looking measures of effective tax rates on capital are grounded in the neoclassical theory of investment, as set out in detail in the survey by Michael Devereux in chapter 2. This section is a simplified restatement of some of Devereux's main results. To focus on basic methodological issues, we will initially abstract from risk, debt finance, and personal taxes. We will also simplify by abstracting from inflation throughout the analysis.[4]

Consider a corporate firm investing one dollar in some real asset at time zero. If the asset depreciates at the exponential rate $\delta$, and if we treat time as a continuous variable, the *gross* return from the asset at time $u$ will be $(p + \delta)e^{-(p+\delta)u}$, where $p$ is the firm's discount rate, and $p$ is the *net* rate of return before tax. Hence the net present value of the corporation tax collected over the lifetime of the asset will be

$$NPVT = \int_0^\infty \tau(p + \delta)e^{-(p+\delta)u}\, du - A = \frac{\tau(p + \delta)}{p + \delta} - A, \qquad (1.1)$$

where $\tau$ is the statutory corporate income tax rate, and $A$ is the present value of the future reduction in tax due to all deductions from the corporate tax base associated with the investment. For simplicity, let us assume that the only deductions are ordinary depreciation allowances granted at the rate $\phi$ (which may deviate from $\delta$) on a declining balance basis. We then have

$$A = \int_0^\infty \tau\phi e^{-(p+\phi)u}\, du = \frac{\tau\phi}{p + \phi}. \qquad (1.2)$$

Net of depreciation, the investment will generate a flow of *pre-tax* income with a present value equal to

$$NPV = \int_0^\infty p e^{-(p+\delta)u}\, du = \frac{p}{p + \delta}. \qquad (1.3)$$

The forward-looking measure of the *average effective tax rate* proposed by Michael Devereux in chapter 2 is

$$AETR^f = \frac{NPVT}{NPV} = \frac{(\tau - A)(p + \delta) + \tau(p - p)}{p}. \qquad (1.4)$$

Thus the average effective tax rate measures the proportion of the value of the project which is paid in tax. As the reader may verify from (1.2) and (1.4), we have $AETR^f = \tau$ when $\phi = \delta$. However, when taxable income deviates from true economic income ($\phi \neq \delta$), the average effective tax rate will deviate from the statutory tax rate.

The average effective tax rate may be calculated for any value of the pre-tax rate of return $p$. Of particular interest is the amount of tax collected on the *marginal* investment project with a net-of-tax value equal to zero. Gross of tax and depreciation, the present value of the revenue from an extra unit of investment is $PVG = (p + \delta)/(p + \delta)$, so a marginal investment project requiring an initial investment outlay of one dollar satisfies $PVG - NPVT - 1 = 0 \Leftrightarrow (1 - \tau)(p + \delta)/(\rho + \delta) = 1 - A$, where we have used (1.1). Solving this expression for $p$, we obtain the required before-tax rate of return on the marginal investment, denoted by $\hat{p}$ and referred to as the *cost of capital*:

$$\hat{p} = \frac{(1 - A)(\rho + \delta)}{1 - \tau} - \delta. \tag{1.5}$$

Setting $p = \hat{p}$ in (1.4) and inserting (1.5) into the numerator, we obtain a forward-looking measure of the *marginal effective tax rate*:

$$METR^f = \frac{(\tau - A)(\rho + \delta)}{(1 - \tau)\hat{p}}. \tag{1.6}$$

A more familiar expression for the marginal effective tax rate is

$$METR^f = \frac{\hat{p} - \rho}{\hat{p}}, \tag{1.7}$$

which says that the $METR^f$ is the difference between the before-tax and the after-tax rate of return, measured relative to the before-tax return. As the reader may check, one arrives at (1.6) by inserting (1.5) into the numerator of (1.7). Hence (1.6) and (1.7) are just alternative ways of expressing the same measure. Note from (1.2) that if the tax code allows immediate expensing of investment ($\phi \to \infty$), we have $A = \tau$. Equation (1.6) then reproduces the well-known result that the marginal effective tax rate is zero under a cash-flow tax with full expensing of investment.

Equations (1.5) and (1.7) summarize the standard King-Fullerton method of estimating the marginal effective tax rate in the absence of personal taxes. The preceding analysis shows that the King-Fullerton marginal effective tax rate is just the borderline measure of the average effective tax rate proposed by Devereux and used in various recent studies such as the one by the European Commission (2001). Indeed, by using (1.6) and (1.7) in (1.4), one can express the average effective tax rate as a weighted average of the $METR^f$ and the statutory tax rate:

$$AETR^f = \left(\frac{\hat{p}}{p}\right) METR^f + \left(1 - \frac{\hat{p}}{p}\right) \tau. \tag{1.8}$$

For the marginal investment project where $p = \hat{p}$ we thus have $AETR^f = METR^f$, but for projects with very high rates of return the average effective tax rate approaches the statutory rate.

When firms earn an above-normal rate of return and must choose between mutually exclusive investment projects, their investment decisions are likely to be influenced by the average as well as by the marginal effective tax rate. For example, suppose that a company can locate production in two different countries. If it faces a high fixed setup cost in each location, it may only be able to make positive profits if it concentrates all activity in one country. In deciding where to locate, a profit-maximizing firm will then start by calculating the optimal scale of investment in each location. This will depend on the *marginal* effective tax rate. The firm will then calculate the total after-tax profit generated by the optimal scale of investment in the two locations. This will be influenced by the *average* effective tax rate. Finally, the firm will locate in the country offering the highest total after-tax profit. Thus both measures of effective taxation are relevant, albeit for different types of investment decision. In particular, there is evidence that the $AETR^f$ has a significant effect on the international location of foreign direct investment, as Devereux explains in chapter 2.

### The Role of Debt Finance and Personal Taxes

A main contribution of King and Fullerton (1984) was the extension of the framework of Hall and Jorgenson (1967) to allow for debt finance and personal taxes. These factors may influence the value of an investment project and the cost of capital via their impact on the firm's discount rate.

In the absence of risk and personal taxes, the firm's discount rate under equity finance is simply equal to the risk-free market interest rate, denoted by $r$. When investment is financed by *debt*, the relevant discount rate is the firm's *after-tax* interest rate, since interest payments are deductible from the corporate tax base:

$$\rho = r(1 - \tau). \tag{1.9}$$

The return to the firm's debt-financed investment will accrue to financial investors in the form of interest income. Suppose now that the marginal investor is subject to personal tax on interest income at the rate $m$. His after-tax return $(s)$ will then be

$$s = r(1 - m). \tag{1.10}$$

The expression for the marginal effective tax rate in (1.7) must now be modified in the following way to account for taxes collected at the personal as well as at the corporate level:

$$METR^f = \frac{\hat{p} - s}{\hat{p}}. \tag{1.11}$$

Equation (1.10) also gives the net marginal return to saving in the case of equity finance if stock prices adjust to ensure that personal investors obtain the same after-tax return on shares and corporate bonds, that is, if[5]

$$r(1 - m)V = (1 - m^D)D + (1 - z)(\Delta V - N). \tag{1.12}$$

In this arbitrage condition $V$ is the market value of outstanding shares in the firm at the start of the period, $\Delta V$ is the increase in the total market value of the firm's shares over the period, $D$ is the dividend paid out at the end of the period, $N$ is new equity injected by shareholders at the end of the period, $m^D$ is the personal tax on dividends net of any dividend tax relief, and $z$ is the effective personal tax rate on accrued capital gains on shares. The left-hand side of (1.12) is the opportunity cost of holding shares rather than bonds, and the right-hand side is the after-tax return on shares, consisting of after-tax dividends and after-tax capital gains (note that $\Delta V - N$ is the capital gain on the shares outstanding at the start of the period).

Equation (1.12) may be used to derive the firm's discount rate under equity finance. Suppose that the firm has already designed an optimal investment plan which has maximized its initial market value $V$. By definition, a marginal increase in its investment will then leave $V$ unaffected in the current period. If shareholders inject a unit of *new equity* into the firm to finance a unit increase in investment, it then follows from (1.12) that $\Delta V = N = 1$, since $r(1 - m)V$ as well as $(1 - m^D)D$ will be unchanged. From the start of the next period, the value of $V$ will thus be one unit higher than before, so shareholders will require an increase in their income from shares equal to the opportunity cost $r(1 - m)$. If the return to the extra investment is paid out as dividends, equation (1.12) implies that the corporation must be able to generate an extra dividend $\rho$ satisfying

$$\rho(1 - m^D) = r(1 - m) \Leftrightarrow \rho = r\left(\frac{1 - m}{1 - m^D}\right). \tag{1.13}$$

Alternatively, the firm may decide to finance the unit increase in investment by *retained profits*, that is, by reducing its dividends $D$ by one unit in the current period. Since the *initial* market value $V$ is still unaffected (given that investment had already been optimized), this unit reduction in dividends must generate a capital gain equal to $(1 - m^D)/(1 - z)$ to maintain the financial market equilibrium condition (1.12). In the subsequent periods shareholders will require a rate of return $r(1 - m)$ on this increase in their wealth. Assuming again that the return to the marginal corporate investment is paid out as dividends, the additional dividend $\rho$ must therefore be sufficient to ensure that

$$\rho(1 - m^D) = r(1 - m)\left(\frac{1 - m^D}{1 - z}\right) \Leftrightarrow \rho = r\left(\frac{1 - m}{1 - z}\right). \tag{1.14}$$

The discount rates in (1.9), (1.13), and (1.14) are derived on the assumption that any differences in the after-tax returns to debt and equity instruments will be eliminated by the arbitrage behavior of financial investors. But it seems equally plausible that the attempts of corporations to minimize their cost of finance would eliminate any differences in discount rates across the different modes of finance. Given the asymmetric tax rules prevailing in most countries, these two equilibrium conditions cannot be met simultaneously. King and Fullerton (1984) sidestepped this difficulty by considering two alternative scenarios. One scenario (the so-called fixed-$r$ case) assumed that the arbitrage behavior of financial investors was dominant, enforcing the discount rates in (1.9), (1.13), and (1.14). In this case the after-tax return to saving is given by (1.10) regardless of the form of corporate finance, but the cost of corporate capital differs across modes of finance. In the alternative scenario (the fixed-$p$ case) King and Fullerton assumed that the financial arbitrage of corporations will equalize the cost of the different types of finance, implying identical discount rates for debt, retained earnings, and new equity. In this case the cost of capital will be the same across all modes of finance, but savers will end up with different after-tax returns to debt and equity.

Thus, because it assumes perfect substitutability between debt and equity instruments combined with asymmetric tax rules, the King-Fullerton framework cannot explain why corporations would want to use both types of financing instruments at the same time as financial investors would want to hold both asset types. As a consequence studies in the King-Fullerton tradition take financing and portfolio decisions to be exogenous and typically calculate effective tax rates for each single mode of finance. To estimate an average value for the effective tax rate, it is normally assumed that the marginal debt–equity mix corresponds to the average proportions of debt, new equity and retained earnings observed in the data. As is pointed out by Devereux in chapter 2, one problem with this approach is that the firm's marginal source of finance may change over the lifetime of the investment project considered.

### Accounting for Risk

An alternative way of dealing with personal taxes is to introduce a risk premium in the firm's borrowing rate of interest, which depends on its debt-to-asset ratio, and to allow for a risk premium on shares that depends on the firm's dividend payout ratio. It is customary to assume that the firm's cost of credit is rising in the debt–asset ratio, reflecting an increased risk of bankruptcy as leverage goes up. Moreover it is sometimes assumed that the risk premium on shares is decreasing in the dividend payout ratio, as shareholders have a (non-tax) preference for dividends over capital gains. This may be because shareholders attach a positive "signaling" value to dividends, or because they have difficulties monitoring whether managers make efficient use of the firm's internal funds.

In these circumstances the weighted average cost of corporate finance ($WACF$) would be given as

$$WACF = d[r + a(d)] + (1 - d)\rho, \qquad 0 \le d \le 1, \tag{1.15}$$

and the cost of equity finance $\rho$ would be given by the arbitrage condition

$$r(1 - m) + b(\omega) = \rho[\omega(1 - m^D) + (1 - \omega)(1 - z)], \qquad 0 \le \omega \le 1. \tag{1.16}$$

The variable $d$ is the debt–asset ratio, $a$ is the risk premium on the firm's debt, $b$ is the risk premium on its shares, and $\omega$ is the fraction of the return on shares taking the form of dividends, with the remaining fraction $1 - \omega$ accruing as capital gains. Via its dividend policy the corporation can control $\omega$. A value-maximizing corporation will choose $d$ and $\omega$ so as to minimize its weighted average cost of finance, subject to (1.15) and (1.16). In such an optimum debt and equity will be equally costly *at the margin*, due to the endogenous adjustment of the risk premia, and the split between new equity and retained profits will be determined by the optimal value of $\omega$. Once the optimal financial policy has been identified, the resulting value of $WACF$ (the overall discount rate) can be used to determine a unique cost of corporate capital, and the optimal values of $d$ and $\omega$ can be used to calculate the overall after-tax return to the savers who finance corporate investment.

This approach to corporate finance and investment is in the spirit of Boadway, Bruce, and Mintz (1984). In principle, it allows for optimizing financial behavior of corporations as well as the arbitrage behavior of financial investors. For purposes of calculating the effective tax rate, the researcher may assume that the empirically observed values of $d$, $\omega$, $p$, and $r + a$ reflect this optimizing behavior. These are attractive features of a methodology for estimating effective tax rates. But the modelling of risk embodied in equations (1.15) and (1.16) is somewhat rudimentary and ad hoc. A more satisfactory theory must relate the risk premium in the cost of capital to the risk characteristics of the firm's real assets.

Such a theory is outlined by Devereux in chapter 2. His analysis implies that the risk premium varies positively with the covariance between the stochastic asset return and the investor's future income from other sources. An important issue is how taxes affect the risk premium in the required before-tax rate of return. Devereux shows that this question can only be answered by specifying the entire probability distribution of the before-tax return to the real asset considered. Depending on the specific assumptions made, the risk premium may or may not be affected by the tax system. Since complete knowledge of the distribution of before-tax asset returns is rarely available, it is difficult to estimate the impact of taxes on the cost of capital in the presence of risk. This would seem to favor an approach where the analyst simply calculates the effective tax rate for alternative exogenous levels of the before-tax return, in line with the method for calculating the forward-looking average effective tax rate given in (1.4).

### Should Measures of Effective Tax Rates Allow for Personal Taxes?

The formulas presented above (equations 1.9 to 1.13) assume that the marginal financial investor is subject to domestic personal income tax. However, the marginal investor could also be a tax-exempt or tax-privileged institution such as a pension fund acting on behalf of household savers, or a foreign household or institutional investor. Uncertainty regarding the identity and tax status of the marginal investor makes it hard to estimate the marginal tax bill collected at the investor level, as Devereux points out in chapter 2.

The high international mobility of capital also makes it questionable whether it is meaningful to add up corporate and personal taxes to get an overall measure of the effective tax rate. To see the problem, note that equation (1.11) may be rewritten as

$$METR^f = \frac{\hat{p}-s}{\hat{p}} = \frac{\overbrace{(\hat{p}-r)}^{\substack{\text{Tax on}\\\text{investment}}} + \overbrace{(r-s)}^{\substack{\text{Tax on}\\\text{saving}}}}{\hat{p}}. \qquad (1.17)$$

In a small open economy with perfect capital mobility and residence-based personal income taxation, the before-tax interest rate $r$ will be exogenously given from the world capital market. In the absence of taxation and risk, this interest rate would also represent the cost of capital. Thus the "investment tax wedge" $(\hat{p} - r)$ in (1.17) reflects the extent to which the tax system distorts domestic investment, while the "savings tax wedge" $(r - s)$ measures the degree to which the personal tax system distorts domestic savings. By reducing domestic investment, a rise in the investment tax wedge will tend to *reduce* capital imports, whereas a rise in the savings tax wedge will tend to *increase* the inflow of capital by discouraging domestic saving. Hence the two tax wedges should not be added together in a single measure of the marginal effective tax rate if one wants to study how the tax system affects international capital flows, as Sinn (1988) pointed out several years ago. Moreover, if the purpose is to investigate how taxes affect domestic investment, one should focus entirely on the investment tax wedge and leave out the personal tax wedge $(r - s)$ from the measure of the marginal effective tax burden. On the other hand, if one wants to study the impact of taxation on domestic saving, one may neglect the corporation tax reflected in the investment tax wedge, as was in fact done in the report by the OECD (1994) on taxation and saving.

The prevalence of institutional and foreign shareholders and a predominant focus on investment incentives explain why many recent studies of effective tax rates have abstracted from personal taxes. However, even if one only wants to estimate the investment tax wedge $(\hat{p} - r)$, it may not be appropriate to neglect personal taxes altogether. The reason is that the cost of capital $\hat{p}$ depends on the firm's discount rate $\rho$, which is affected by personal taxes if the controlling shareholder is subject to personal income tax. Thus there is no easy way out of the problem of allowing for personal taxes in the estimation of effective tax rates.

### Measuring Taxes on Foreign Direct Investment
The forward-looking King-Fullerton framework for effective tax rate analysis allows the researcher to specify all the institutional details that are relevant for the hypothetical investment project considered. In par-

ticular, although cross-border direct investment may involve more complicated patterns of finance and greater complexity of tax rules, the King-Fullerton framework can in principle be amended to allow for these complications, as pointed out by Devereux in chapter 2.

However, in practice, analysts have rarely tried to account for all of the intricate tax planning practices used by multinational companies to reduce their tax burden. These practices include the financing of foreign investment via finance subsidiaries located in tax havens, the shifting of debt from low-tax to high-tax jurisdictions, the shifting of taxable profits through transfer pricing, the exploitation of special tax rules applying to royalties, and the exploitation of special tax regimes offered by host governments to attract particularly mobile or valuable activities.

In chapter 5, Harry Grubert analyzes the implications of such practices for the measurement of effective tax rates on foreign direct investment. In the first part of the chapter he sets up a simple simulation model of a multinational company to illustrate how the effective tax rate on FDI may be affected by the most important forms of tax planning. This simulation analysis highlights the importance of how royalties are taxed and whether companies can use tax haven finance subsidiaries. It also shows that shifting debt to high-tax foreign locations can have a notable effect on the effective tax rate.

In the second part of chapter 5, Grubert supplements these hypothetical calculations by using tax return and survey data to analyze the determinants of the actual average effective tax rate on overall US manufacturing investment abroad. Among the most important determinants are the shifting of real assets and debt to low-tax jurisdictions, other forms of income shifting, the share of royalties in total foreign source income, and home country repatriation taxes. This part of Grubert's analysis indicates that compared to the average local company, the US subsidiaries operating abroad face a 5 percentage point lower average effective tax rate as a result of the tax benefits they enjoy by being part of a multinational enterprise. This finding clearly goes against the perception that cross-border direct investment tends to be overtaxed due to incomplete relief of international double taxation.

In the final part of chapter 5, Grubert presents an econometric analysis to suggest that host governments tailor their tax rules for inward FDI so as to increase their national welfare. Specifically host governments offer tax concessions to highly mobile foreign companies in the electronics and computer industry, and to foreign companies that sell a large share of their output offshore (presumably because offshore sales tend to improve the terms of trade of the host country). In contrast, subsidiaries of other R&D-intensive companies face relatively high effective tax rates, apparently because they tend to earn high local rents that can be appropriated by the host government.

Grubert's thought-provoking analysis raises some fundamental methodological questions. For example, if income can be shifted from a low-tax to a high-tax subsidiary, to which one should the tax benefit be attributed when estimating the average effective tax rates in each location? Clearly, the reduction in the global tax burden can only be obtained if the company operates in both jurisdictions simultaneously. More generally, given that many tax-planning strategies are fundamentally multilateral in nature, the assignment of the resulting tax benefits to the individual entities in a multinational group may require more or less arbitrary assumptions. Grubert's analysis also shows that the tax burden on a subsidiary in a multinational group of companies will generally depend on the activities and location of other entities in the group. This means that the effective tax rate on foreign direct investment will tend to be *company-specific*. Hence one cannot estimate the incentive for FDI by only looking at the parameters of tax legislation in the host and home countries, as previous studies have assumed. While these observations may seem somewhat pessimistic, Grubert's contribution also offers some constructive suggestions on alternative ways of estimating the tax burden on foreign direct investment.

### 1.2.2   Measures Using Data on Taxes Collected

#### *The Basic Backward-Looking Measures*
The use of tax return data in section 5.2 of Grubert's chapter is an example of the second main approach to effective tax rate analysis. This method uses data on capital income taxes paid and relates the observed tax bill to some estimate of the before-tax income from capital. By definition, the total income from capital before tax is $pK$, where $K$ is the total capital stock, and where we recall that $p$ is the average before-tax rate of return. If the total capital income tax bill in period $t$ is $T_t$, the so-called backward-looking definition of the *average* effective tax rate on capital income in period $t$ is

$$AETR^b = \frac{T_t}{p_t K_t}.$$

(1.18)

To focus on the basic methodology, we will once again simplify by abstracting from debt and personal taxes. If the tax savings from depreciation allowances in year $t$ amount to $D_t$, the corporate income tax bill (representing the entire capital income tax bill) will then be

$$T_t = \tau_t(p_t + \delta)K_t - D_t. \tag{1.19}$$

When the rate of depreciation for tax purposes $(\phi)$ differs from the true depreciation rate $(\delta)$, the book value of assets in the firms' tax accounts $(K^T)$ will deviate from the true replacement value of the capital stock. If the firms' gross investment in the past period $t - u$ was $I_{t-u}$ and the rate of depreciation for tax purposes has varied over time, we have

$$K_t^T = \int_0^\infty I_{t-u} \cdot e^{-\int_u^t \phi_{t-s}\,ds}\,du \tag{1.20}$$

and

$$D_t = \tau_t \phi_t K_t^T. \tag{1.21}$$

Equations (1.18) through (1.21) make clear that the average effective tax rate estimated for the current period $t$ will generally depend on the history of investment as well as on historical tax rules. Indeed, we might have subtracted an additional term from the right-hand side of (1.19) to allow for the current tax savings stemming from deductions for losses carried over from the past. These observations explain why the measure in (1.18) is referred to as a "backward-looking" effective tax rate.

However, under certain stylized assumptions the average effective tax rate in (1.18) will coincide with the forward-looking measure of the average effective tax rate given in (1.4). Specifically, suppose that the economy has followed a golden rule path where the capital stock has grown at a constant rate equal to the real interest rate $r$ so that

$$I_{t-u} = (r + \delta)K_{t-u}. \tag{1.22}$$

Suppose further that the rate of depreciation for tax purposes has been constant in the past. Since (1.22) implies that $I_{t-u} = I_t e^{-ru}$, equation (1.20) then simplifies to

$$K_t^T = \int_0^\infty I_t \cdot e^{-(r+\phi)u}\,du = \frac{I_t}{r + \phi}. \tag{1.23}$$

From (1.2), (1.21), and (1.23) we get $D_t = A_t I_t$, which may be inserted into (1.19) along with (1.22) to give

$$T_t = [(\tau_t - A_t)(r + \delta) + \tau(p_t - r)]K_t. \tag{1.24}$$

Substituting (1.24) into (1.18), we get $AETR^b = [(\tau_t - A_t)(r + \delta) + \tau(p_t - r)]/p_t$. Comparing this to (1.4), and remembering that $\rho = r$ in the absence of personal taxes, we see that $AETR^b = AETR^f$ under the assumptions made. In other words, with an unchanging tax law and steady golden rule growth, the backward-looking and the forward-looking measures of the average effective tax rate are identical. Moreover, if we add the assumption of constant returns to scale so that $p_t = \hat{p}_t$, the result $AETR^b = AETR^f$ implies $AETR^b = METR^f$, since we have seen previously that $AETR^f = METR^f$ when $p = \hat{p}$. Thus the *backward-looking average* effective tax rate will also equal the *forward-looking marginal* effective tax rate under stable tax laws, golden rule growth and constant returns, as Roger Gordon, Laura Kalambokidis, and Joel Slemrod point out in chapter 4.

But to the extent that these restrictive assumptions are violated, the three measures of effective tax rates will deviate from each other. In particular, the existence of pure profits $(p > \hat{p})$ means that the backward-looking average effective tax rate will deviate from the forward-looking marginal effective tax rate governing the incentive to invest. In chapter 4, Gordon, Kalambokidis, and Slemrod (henceforth GKS) therefore propose an alternative measure of the marginal effective tax rate which may be estimated from data on tax revenue and income. The backward-looking marginal effective tax rate measure suggested by GKS is

$$METR^b = \frac{(T - E)/K}{(T - E)/K + r(1 - \tau)}, \tag{1.25}$$

where $T$ is still the actual capital income tax revenue observed, while $E$ is the estimated revenue which would be collected under a so-called R-base cash flow tax that excludes financial income and replaces depreciation allowances by expensing for new investment (all variables in equation 1.25 refer to time $t$, but for convenience we drop the time subscripts). To understand the rationale for (1.25), recall that $A = \tau$ under full expensing. According to (1.24) the tax revenue accruing under a cash-flow tax would therefore be

$$E = \tau(p - r)K, \tag{1.26}$$

so from (1.24) and (1.26) we have

$$\frac{T-E}{K} = (\tau - A)(r + \delta),  \tag{1.27}$$

where $A$ now indicates the present value of the tax savings from depreciation allowances under current tax laws. In the absence of personal taxes we have $\rho = r$. It then follows from (1.5) that

$$\hat{p} - r = \frac{(\tau - A)(r + \delta)}{1 - \tau},  \tag{1.28}$$

so from (1.7), (1.27), and (1.28) we get

$$METR^f \equiv \frac{\hat{p} - r}{\hat{p}} = \frac{(\tau - A)(r + \delta)}{\hat{p}(1 - \tau)} = \frac{(T - E)/K}{(T - E)/K + r(1 - \tau)}.  \tag{1.29}$$

The result in (1.29) shows that the backward-looking GKS measure of the marginal effective tax rate is indeed equal to the forward-looking marginal effective tax rate, given the assumptions of constant tax laws and golden rule growth underlying equation (1.24) (which was used in deriving this equation).

Note the intuitive appeal of the GKS measure: we know from theory that a cash flow tax does not impose any tax burden on investment at the margin. Hence it is tempting to estimate the marginal effective tax burden on capital income by calculating the additional revenue generated by the current income tax compared to a cash-flow tax. As indicated in (1.29), which abstracts from personal taxes, this additional revenue stems from the fact that the income tax only allows depreciation (implying $A < \tau$) rather than full expensing (which would imply $A = \tau$).

### Backward-Looking versus Forward-Looking Measures

Since investment decisions depend on current and expected future tax rules, a measure of the effective tax rate should in principle be forward-looking if it is meant to capture the effects of taxation on the incentive to invest. However, in practice, it is very difficult to incorporate the effects of all the complex details of the tax code in a forward-looking model of the effective tax rate. The main advantage of backward-looking measures is that the impact of all the special provisions in the tax law will tend to be reflected in the revenue data used to construct these measures. If the tax laws are relatively stable over time and the economy does not deviate too much from its golden rule growth path, a backward-looking effective tax rate may therefore be a good proxy for the ideal forward-looking measure. But the greater the historical instability of tax laws and of investment and profits, the less one should rely on a backward-looking effective tax rate as an indicator of incentives for future investment. In particular, a backward-looking measure cannot be used to evaluate the effects of tax reform proposals on the incentives for capital formation and on the distribution of income.

Gordon, Kalambokidis, and Slemrod analyze in chapter 4 the extent to which different effective tax rate measures will provide a biased indicator of the "true" marginal effective tax rate on investment, once various complicating factors are taken into account. They compare the forward-looking King-Fullerton marginal effective tax rate ($METR^f$) to the backward-looking average effective tax rate ($AETR^b$) and to their own GKS measure ($METR^b$). As we have seen above, all of these measures will generate the correct marginal effective tax rate in a simple setting with golden rule growth, constant tax laws, and constant returns. Maintaining the assumptions of golden rule growth and constant tax laws, the authors consider a number of complications such as risk, pure profits, debt finance, and resale of assets with the purpose of stepping up the basis for (accelerated) depreciation. They find that their own GKS measure is the only indicator that consistently equals the theoretically correct marginal effective tax rate even if the researcher does not have explicit knowledge of the amount of risk, pure profit, use of debt finance, and frequency of asset resales. Gordon, Kalambokidis, and Slemrod then proceed to show that all of the three measures yield biased estimates of the marginal effective tax rate in the presence of tax-motivated choice of organizational form and tax-motivated debt arbitrage. Nevertheless, they conclude that in many cases where the $METR^f$ and the $AETR^b$ will overestimate the true marginal effective tax rate, the GKS measure will yield a lower and more realistic estimate of the marginal tax burden. In this way the analysis in chapter 4 helps to resolve the puzzle that conventional measures such as $METR^f$ often imply very high effective tax rates whereas the actual net revenue from capital income taxes seems to be very low in many countries.

Gordon, Kalambokidis, and Slemrod are concerned with finding the best possible indicator of the tax distortion to investment decisions. Sometimes analysts and policy makers may also be concerned with the impact of tax on the current distribution of factor income between capital and labor. In that case it seems most appropriate to use a backward-looking average effective tax rate to measure the tax burden on capital income, since such a measure records the actual taxes collected from intramarginal as well as marginal investment projects. Backward-looking average tax rates, measured using actual revenue figures, take into account the effects of tax planning, tax relief provided by lax or discretionary administrative practice, as well as noncompliance. If we only want to study the effect on today's income distribution, it is no problem that the backward-looking average tax rate may partly reflect past tax laws and the historical behavior of investment and profits.

However, a problem with backward-looking as well as forward-looking measures is that taxes formally levied on capital income may not represent a true burden on capital owners if taxes are shifted via changes in relative prices induced by a change in investment behavior. In particular, it may be misleading to add up the revenue from source-based and residence-based capital income taxes in an open economy, since the incidence of the two types of taxes will be very different. With high capital mobility, a source-based capital income tax will tend to be shifted onto workers in the form of lower real wages because it generates a capital outflow. By contrast, a residence-based capital income tax will tend to be fully reflected in a lower net return to the capital owner because it cannot be avoided by moving capital abroad (on the optimistic assumption that tax enforcement is effective). This suggests that the revenues from source-based and residence-based capital income taxes should not be lumped together in a single measure of the overall effective tax rate if the purpose is to study the effect of taxation on the distribution of after-tax incomes.

### Estimating Backward-Looking Average Effective Tax Rates: Macro Data versus Micro Data

Backward-looking average effective tax rates can be estimated either from macro data or from micro data. The most well-known measure of the average effective tax rate on capital income derived from *macro data* is the one proposed by Mendoza, Razin, and Tesar (1994). These authors combine the OECD tax revenue statistics with statistics on aggregate before-tax factor incomes taken from the OECD National Income Accounts. According to their method (henceforth referred to as the MRT method), the average effective tax rate on capital income is calculated as the total reveneue from taxes deemed to fall on capital, divided by the economy's net operating surplus (which is the national accounts measure of aggregate pre-tax capital income net of depreciation).

In chapter 7, David Carey and Josette Rabesona provide a detailed discussion of the MRT method and propose a number of modifications to it. The advantage of the method is that it is relatively simple and allows a comparison of effective tax rates across countries and over time, based on readily available OECD data. However, as Carey and Rabesona point out, the MRT method relies on some very restrictive assumptions. For example, to estimate the capital income tax component in total personal income tax revenue, MRT assume that the effective *personal* tax rates on labor income and capital income are identical. This neglects the tax favors granted to many important forms of capital income such as the imputed return to owner-occupied housing, the return to pension saving, and dividends. It also neglects the fact that several countries operate a dual income tax system that systematically taxes capital income at a lower rate than labor income. Ceteris paribus, the neglect of these factors means that the MRT method tends to overestimate the effective tax rate on capital, but some other features of the method work in the opposite direction. First, the MRT method excludes certain taxes on movable property from the estimated capital income tax revenue. Second, the method assumes that all of the income of the self-employed represents capital income, even though it partly reflects the reward to the labor input of the selfemployed. Third, by categorizing all of the personal income tax revenue either as labor taxes or capital income taxes, the method neglects the fact that part of personal tax revenue may stem from taxes on government transfers.

Via successive modifications of the basic MRT measure, Carey and Rabesona try to account for these and other complications. They find that more realistic estimates of the average effective tax rate on capital income often deviate substantially from the crude meausures implied by the MRT method. In particular, whereas the simple MRT measures suggest that the rising overall tax burden in Europe in recent decades has been concentrated on labor income, the modified effective tax rate measures offered by Carey and Rabesona do not support this conclusion. On this basis they conclude that macro-based measures of average effective tax rates must be used with great care and should be supplemented by other tax indicators that can corroborate the story they tell.

Such alternative tax indicators could be average effective tax rate measures based on *micro-level data* drawn from tax returns. In chapter 10 Steven Clark discusses and illustrates the use of micro-based estimates of average effective tax rates. One theme running through this chapter is that micro-based measures can account for differences in tax treatment across (groups of) taxpayers and can be used to construct more precise estimates of average economywide tax rates, compared to measures based only on aggregate revenue data. In the area of capital income taxation, Clark's paper highlights the critical importance of adjusting for cyclical effects and business losses in measuring an economywide average effective corporate tax rate. He reviews various ways of adjusting for business losses by means of micro data, and certain issues encountered with each technique. He also uses micro data to document significant variations in effective tax rates by firm size and across industries, thereby underscoring the relevance of going beyond aggregate summary measures of the effective tax rate on corporate income.

### 1.2.3   Using Alternative Measures of Taxes on Capital: What Difference Does It Make?

Do the various measures of the effective capital income tax rate yield very different quantitative estimates in practice? The previous sections have already touched upon this important issue. In chapter 3 it is considered more systematically by Michael Devereux and Alexander Klemm. They calculate six different measures of the effective capital income tax rate for the United Kingdom over the last thirty years. Besides considering the forward-looking average and marginal effective tax rates ($AETR^f$ and $METR^f$) and the backward-looking GKS measure of the marginal effective corporate tax rate ($METR^b$), they also construct a time series for the backward-looking MRT measure of the overall average effective capital income tax rate, and two backward-looking series for the average effective corporate tax rate; one based on aggregate data for the corporate sector, and another based on individual company accounts.

Devereux and Klemm show how forward-looking effective tax rate measures depend crucially on assumptions regarding personal taxes, the source of finance, and whether underlying economic parameters such as the rate of inflation and the market rate of interest are allowed to vary over time. They also demonstrate how use of alternative definitions of taxation from company accounts can give a markedly different impression of the evolution of effective tax rates over time. Further they show how macro-based backward-looking measures of taxes on capital depend crucially on what taxes are included in capital income tax revenue.

Overall, Devereux and Klemm find that the different measures give a very different picture of the level and evolution of the effective tax rate on capital. They conclude that appropriate choice of methodology and careful use of data are vital in the construction and use of effective tax rates. Empirical researchers cannot simply pick the most convenient measure and assume that alternative measures would yield more or less the same results. Correspondence with theory as well as correspondence with real-world institutional details are criteria that may be used in choosing between alternative measures.

### 1.3 Measuring Taxes on Labor

We now turn to the measurement of effective tax rates on labor income. Again, we may distinguish between average and marginal effective tax rates, and between measures based on the parameters of tax legislation versus measures using data on taxes paid. In addition a distinction can be made between direct taxes collected from employers and employees and indirect taxes on consumption that drive a further wedge between the labor cost of the employer and the real disposable wage of the employee. In the following section we will specify these measures and indicate how they are likely to affect behavior in the labor market.

#### 1.3.1 Basic Measures of Effective Tax Rates on Labor Income

One main approach to the estimation of effective tax rates on labor income is to specify the labor income and other relevant characteristics of a hypothetical representative taxpayer (individual or household) and calculate the average or marginal tax burden implied by current tax laws.

To give a stylized example of this fairly straightforward methodology, let $w$ be the wage paid to the worker *after* deduction for taxes levied on the employer but *before* deduction for taxes levied on the employee. In many countries the payroll tax and social security tax levied on the employer ($T^{se}$) and the social security tax collected from the employee ($T^{sw}$) both depend on $w$, that is, $T^{se} = T^{se}(w)$ and $T^{sw} = T^{sw}(w)$ (quite often the tax schedules $T^{se}(w)$ and $T^{sw}(w)$ are purely proportional, but sometimes they include an absolute maximum and/or a tax-exempt minimum value of $w$). The personal tax on labor income is usually levied on $\hat{w} \equiv w - T^{sw}(w)$, representing the worker's income after deduction for social security taxes. The personal labor income tax schedule $T^p(\hat{w})$ captures the progressivity of the personal income tax and may depend on the taxpayer's family status. To the extent that the taxation of labor income is integrated with the taxation of nonlabor income $y$, the labor income tax bill must be specified as $T^p = T^p(\hat{w}, y)$, and the analyst must make some assumption on $y$. In simple applications $y$ is usually set equal to zero, so below we will just abstract from nonlabor income.

The *average effective direct tax rate on labor income* ($\tau^{ad}$) is defined as the total direct labor tax bill relative to the employer's total labor cost $w + T^{se}(w)$:

$$\tau^{ad} = \frac{T^{se}(w) + T^{sw}(w) + T^p(w - T^{sw}(w))}{w + T^{se}(w)}. \tag{1.30}$$

The numerator on the right-hand side of equation (1.30) measures the total direct tax wedge between the employer's labor cost and the net wage received by the employee. The *marginal effective direct tax rate on labor income* ($\tau^{md}$) measures the increase in this tax wedge induced by a unit increase in the employer's labor cost:

$$\tau^{md} = \frac{\dfrac{dT^{se}}{dw} + \dfrac{dT^{sw}}{dw} + \dfrac{dT^p}{d\hat{w}}\left(1 - \dfrac{dT^{sw}}{dw}\right)}{1 + \dfrac{dT^{se}}{dw}}. \tag{1.31}$$

With knowledge of $w$ and of the current tax schedules $T^{se}(w)$, $T^{sw}(w)$, and $T^p(\hat{w})$, the analyst can calculate the effective direct tax rates in (1.30) and (1.31).

An alternative approach that has been widely used to estimate the *average* effective direct tax rate on labor income is to use *macro data* on aggregate labor income tax revenues and aggregate labor income. According to this method, pioneered by Mendoza, Razin, and Tesar (1994), the average effective direct tax rate on labor income is calculated as

$$\tau^{ad} = \frac{S^e + S^w + \alpha^{se}S^{se} + \alpha^w R^p}{W + S^e + S^w + \alpha^e Y^e}, \tag{1.32}$$

where $S^e$ are aggregate payroll taxes and social security taxes paid by employers, $S^w$ and $S^{se}$ are aggregate social security taxes paid by employees and by the self-employed, respectively, $R^p$ is the total personal income tax revenue, $\alpha^w$ is the fraction of personal taxes estimated to fall on labor income, $\alpha^{se}$ is the share of $S^{se}$ estimated to represent a tax on the labor income of the self-employed, $W$ is the total compensation of employees net of payroll taxes and social security contributions, $Y^e$ is total income from self-employment, and $\alpha^e$ is the estimated labor income share of $Y^e$. Thus the numerator of (1.32) is a measure of the aggregate taxes on labor, and the denominator is a measure of the aggregate before-tax labor income earned by wage earners and by the self-employed.

The macro-based effective tax rate in (1.32) is sometimes referred to as an *implicit tax rate on labor* or as a *labor tax ratio*. While data for $S^e$, $S^w$, $S^{se}$, and $R^p$ can be obtained directly from the revenue statistics of the OECD, existing studies of labor tax ratios differ from each other in the particular method or data source used to estimate the variables $\alpha^{se}$, $\alpha^w$, $W$, $\alpha^e$, and $Y^e$. The difficulties involved are discussed by Carey and Rabesona in chapter 7 and by de Haan, Sturm, and Volkerink in chapter 9.

Macro data have also been used by Mendoza, Razin, and Tesar (1994) and others to estimate an average effective indirect tax rate on consumption ($c$). By reducing the net reward to work, indirect consumption taxes are part of the overall tax burden on labor. Based on aggregate revenue data and national income accounts, the average effective indirect tax rate on consumption can be calculated as follows:

$$c = \frac{\text{Revenue from indirect consumption taxes}}{\text{Private consumption} + \text{Government nonwage consumption}}. \tag{1.33}$$

The measure of aggregate consumption in the denominator of (1.33) is somewhat broader than the actual consumption tax base in OECD countries. The motivation for including government nonwage consumption in the denominator is that part of the VAT and excise taxes included in the numerator end up being paid by the government itself via higher prices of privately produced inputs used in the production of government services. Again, empirical studies differ in the exact way in which they define and measure the magnitudes in the numerator and the denominator in (1.33). In chapter 7, Carey and Rabesona discuss the issues involved.

For the individual worker the effective tax rate on consumption will depend on his particular consumption pattern, given that commodity taxation is nonuniform across commodities. In principle, micro data may provide information on individual consumption patterns, but quite often the analyst may have to resort to a macro-based average measure of $c$ like the one given in (1.33), even if he uses the parameters of tax legislation to estimate the *direct* effective tax rate on labour.

Armed with an estimate of the effective indirect tax rate on consumption, one can calculate a *total* averate effective tax rate on labor income that includes direct as well as indirect taxes. Suppose that the consumption expenditure in the denominator of (1.33) is measured in producer prices (i.e., excluding indirect taxes), and suppose we normalize the producer price level at unity. With the notation in (1.30), the worker's after-tax real wage rate measured in producer prices may then be written as $[w - T^{sw}(w) - T^p(w - T^{sw}(w))]/(1 + c)$, whereas the employer's total real labor cost is $w + T^{se}(w)$. The total direct and indirect tax wedge on labor income is the difference between these two magnitudes. Using (1.30), we may therefore express the *total average effective tax rate on labor income* $(\tau^a)$ as

$$\tau^a = \frac{w + T^{se}(w) - [w - T^{sw}(w) - T^p(w - T^{sw}(w))](1 + c)^{-1}}{w + T^{se}(w)} = \frac{\tau^{ad} + c}{1 + c}.$$

(1.34)

The *total marginal effective tax rate on labor income* $(\tau^m)$ is the increase in the total direct and indirect tax wedge induced by a unit increase in the employer's total labor cost. Differentiating in the numerator and denominator of (1.34) and using (1.31), we thus have

$$\tau^m = \frac{1 + \dfrac{dT^{se}}{dw} - \left[1 - \dfrac{dT^{sw}}{dw} - \dfrac{dT^p}{d\hat{w}}\left(1 - \dfrac{dT^{sw}}{dw}\right)\right](1 + c)^{-1}}{1 + \dfrac{dT^{se}}{dw}} = \frac{\tau^{md} + c}{1 + c}.$$

(1.35)

In analyzing the effects of taxation on labor market behavior, one should in principle focus on total effective tax rates. The total *average* effective tax rate is likely to influence decisions on participation in the formal labor market, and it also has an income effect on the number of working hours supplied by labor market participants. In addition a higher total average effective tax rate may have a tax-push effect on wage setting in imperfect labour markets, such as by provoking more aggressive union wage claims. Furthermore the total average tax rates for workers in different income groups provide information on the way the tax system affects the after-tax distribution of labor incomes. The total *marginal* effective tax rate will have a substitution effect on the number of hours worked, and for a given average tax rate, a higher marginal tax rate may dampen wage claims in imperfect labor markets.[6] Thus both measures of the effective tax rate are needed for a complete analysis of the impact of tax on labor market performance.

### 1.3.2   Measures Based on Tax Legislation: The "Taxing Wages" Approach

The leading example of a labor tax measure derived from the parameters of tax legislation is the Taxing Wages approach applied by the OCED. In chapter 8, Christopher Heady describes and discusses this approach, which is used to calculate the average and marginal direct tax burden on the labor income of eight "typical" taxpayer types in each OECD country. The method assumes that each taxpayer's annual income from employment equals some fraction of the average gross wage earnings of a full-time worker in the manufacturing sector of each OECD economy (the so-called average production worker, APW). Additional assumptions are made regarding other relevant personal circumstances such as family status and number of dependent children. The taxes considered are personal income tax, social security taxes by employers and employees, and payroll taxes. Universal family benefits paid in respect of dependent children are also taken into account, to facilitate comparison between countries that provide family support through deductions from the tax base and countries that support families via cash benefits. Apart from this, taxpayers are assumed to have no other nonlabor income.

  Given these assumptions plus information on current labor income tax rules, the total and marginal direct tax wedges can be calculated for the eight household types, using the procedure summarized in equations (1.30) and (1.31) above. The strength of the Taxing Wages methodology is that it allows international comparisons of labor tax burdens for workers of similar types. In contrast to macro-based measures, the Taxing Wages approach allows estimation of marginal tax burdens, and its measures are not affected by cross-country differences in population structures and income distributions. Heady also points out the limitations of the approach. For example, it only considers workers within a fairly narrow income range, and so does not capture the entire tax burden on labor. In chapter 10, Steven Clark illustrates how micro data collected from tax returns can provide a more complete picture of the level and distribution of labor income taxes across the entire population of taxpayers.

The most important methodological limitation of the Taxing Wages approach is the exclusion of indirect taxes on the goods that workers consume. As Heady explains, this reflects that OECD member states have not yet agreed on a common framework for estimating the effective indirect tax rate on consumption.

The final part of Heady's chapter investigates the extent to which the taxing wages measure of the average effective direct tax rate on the average production worker correlates with the macro-based estimate of the average effective direct labour income tax rate offered by Carey and Rabesona in chapter 7. A cross-country analysis for the year 2000 shows a high correlation coefficient of 0.85, but time series correlations for individual countries give a very mixed picture, with a weak or even a negative correlation between the two tax rate measures for some countries. Thus the choice between a macro-based measure and the popular Taxing Wages measure seems to matter and must be made with a view to the purpose of the study and the questions being asked.

### 1.3.3 Alternative Measures of Labor Tax Burdens: What Difference Do They Make?

In chapter 9, Jakob de Haan, Jan-Egbert Sturm, and Bjørn Volkerink provide a systematic analysis of the implications of choosing different measures of the average effective tax rate on labor income. They start by surveying the alternative ways in which effective labor tax rates have been measured in recent cross-country macroeconomic studies of the effects of taxation on unemployment and growth. Almost all of these studies have used average effective tax rates; the great majority has been based on macro data, and only few have included indirect taxes. De Haan, Sturm, and Volkerink find that although the different tax indicators imply significant differences in the estimated *level* of taxation, the various measures are generally quite highly correlated over time. The authors then run a number of regressions to test whether the

statistical significance of the labor tax rate in some well-known empirical models of unemployment and investment is affected by the choice
between the different tax rate measures. They find that this is generally
not the case, which is in line with the reported high correlations for
most tax rate indicators. Thus de Haan, Sturm, and Volkerink arrive at
a more optimistic conclusion than Chris Heady: for the purpose of
macroeconomic time series analysis, the choice of indicator for the average effective labor income tax rate does not seem to matter too much,
although the levels of these indicators differ a lot across countries.

This finding is consistent with the analysis of Carey and Rabesona in
chapter 7. Carey and Rabesona propose a number of reasonable modifications to the macro-based measure of the average effective direct tax
rate on labor income introduced by Mendoza, Razin, and Tesar (1994).
They show that the estimated level of the effective tax rate can be significantly affected by these modifications, but they also find that their
own preferred measure of the labor income tax rate is in most cases
highly correlated over time with the measure of Mendoza, Razin, and
Tesar.

Coupled with the findings of Devereux and Klemm in chapter 3, this
suggests that the estimation of effective tax rates on capital income
involves greater uncertainties than the estimation of effective tax rates
on income from labor. This seems plausible, given that capital income
tends to be harder to measure and to be subject to more complex tax
rules.

### 1.3.4   Measuring Taxes on Human Capital

While studies of effective tax rates on investment in physical and financial capital abound, there have been very few attempts to estimate
effective tax rates on the return to investment in *human* capital. Both
forms of investment involve the sacrifice of present for future consumption, but whereas the net return to investment in nonhuman capital depends on the rules for taxing capital income, the net return on
human capital investment is governed by the taxation of labor income
and by public subsidies for education.

Giving the growing importance of education and training in the
knowledge-based "new" economy, it seems increasingly important to
develop a method for estimating the effective tax burden on the return
to human capital investment. In chapter 6, Kirk Collins and Jim Davies
offer such a methodology. This section outlines the main features of

their approach, which is based on a forward-looking effective tax rate measure using parameters from current laws on taxation and education subsidies.

Collins and Davies define the effective tax rate on the return to a specified education program (the effective tax rate on human capital, $ETR^h$) as

$$ETR^h = \frac{r_g - r_n}{r_g}, \tag{1.36}$$

where $r_g$ is the internal rate of return to the education program in the absence of tax, and $r_n$ is the internal rate of return in the presence of tax. The taxpayer is assumed to enroll in the education program in period $t$ and to retire from the labor market in the later period $T$. If he did not enroll in the program, he could expect to earn the amount of before-tax labor income $E_t^*$ in period $t$; if he completes the program, he will actually earn the before-tax income $E_t$ in that period. His direct (before-tax) cost of education in year $t$ is denoted $C_t$ while his opportunity cost is the forgone labor income $E_t^*$. Hence the internal before-tax return to the education program is given by the equation

$$\sum_{t=1}^{T} \frac{E_t - E_t^* - C_t}{(1 + r_g)^{t-1}} = 0. \tag{1.37}$$

Replacing the before-tax variables in (1.37) by the corresponding after-tax variables $E_t^a$, $E_t^{a*}$ and $C_t^a$, the after-tax return to education can be found from

$$\sum_{t=1}^{T} \frac{E_t^a - E_t^{a*} - C_t^a}{(1 + r_n)^{t-1}} = 0. \tag{1.38}$$

The earnings variables $E_t$ and $E_t^*$ can be estimated from cross-sectional micro data for individuals with different ages and education levels, and $E_t^a$ and $E_t^{a*}$ can be calculated from current tax laws, given data for $E_t$ and $E_t^*$. The variables $C_t$ and $C_t^a$ can be estimated from data on tuition fees plus current rules regarding public education grants, subsidized student loans, and so on.

Note that if the labor income tax were levied at a flat constant rate $\tau$ and allowed deduction for the direct cost of education $C_t$, we would have $(E_t^a - E_t^{a*} - C_t^a) = (1 - \tau)(E_t - E_t^* - C_t)$, and $r_n$ would be equal to $r_g$, implying a zero effective tax rate on human capital investment. In other words, a purely proportional labor income tax with full deduction for all private costs of education is neutral toward investment in human capital, so a positive effective tax rate on such investment derives from the progressivity of the labor income tax and/or from nondeductibility of the direct costs of education.

Notice also that since most meaningful education programs are "lumpy" investments involving a substantial amount of forgone current earnings, it is difficult in practice to distinguish between the marginal and the average effective tax rate on human capital investment. For this reason Collins and Davies only refer to the effective tax rate on the return to particular education programs.

To measure how the fiscal system affects the overall incentive for human capital investment, one must also account for the fact that the government bears a substantial part of the direct costs of education by paying salaries to teachers and professors, by maintaining the buildings of schools and universities, and so on. These costs are part of the direct *social* costs of education $(C_t^p)$, so the social (or public) return to human capital investment $(r_p)$ should be calculated as[7]

$$\sum_{t=1}^{T} \frac{E_t - E_t^* - C_t^p}{(1+r_p)^{t-1}} = 0. \tag{1.39}$$

Given this estimate of $r_p$, Collins and Davies define the *effective subsidy rate on human capital* $(ESR^h)$ as

$$ESR^h = \frac{r_g - r_p}{r_g}, \tag{1.40}$$

and they define the *net effective tax rate on human capital* as $ETR^h - ESR^h$.

Collins and Davies apply this methodology to a study of effective tax and subsidy rates on human capital investment in Canada. For individuals with median earnings, they find that effective tax rates on human capital formed in first-degree university study are sizable, although not as high as for physical capital. When the expenditure side and its direct subsidies are taken into account, the net effective tax rate on human capital becomes negative. The authors also find that the taxation of human capital is far from uniform. Effective tax rates depend on income level, gender, part-time versus full-time study, whether students have loans, number of dependants, and use of tax-sheltered savings plans. Workers at higher levels of the lifetime earnings distribution may face substantially higher effective tax rates than low-income workers, as a result of progressive labor income taxation.

This case study of Canada illustrates how the framework proposed by Collins and Davies can be used to quantify the impacts of a wide range of tax and subsidy provisions on the incentive to invest in human capital. Their innovative analysis should stimulate further studies in this somewhat neglected area of effective tax rate analysis.

## 1.4   Concluding Remarks

Economic behavior is constrained by the intricate web of institutions shaped by the private and public sectors. The tax system is one such important and complex institution. In trying to understand how taxes affect economic incentives—which is arguably the most important purpose of effective tax rate analysis—the analyst must therefore pay attention to institutional detail. At the same time there is a need for summary measures capturing the main effects of the complex tax laws, to help analysts and policy makers from getting lost in the jungle of special provisions. The art of effective tax rate analysis is to provide such summary measures without obscuring important details that are seriously at odds with the generalizations and simplifications needed to derive them.

The present introduction cannot do justice to the many insights contained in the following chapters. I nevertheless hope that it has provided a useful roadmap that will encourage the reader to study the contributions of this volume to the state of the art of effective tax rate analysis.

## Notes

1. One of the scholarly articles emerging from this work was Devereux and Pearson (1995).

2. Examples of this line of research are Chennels and Griffith (1997), Devereux and Griffith (1998), and Devereux, Griffith, and Klemm (2002).

3. For a complementary overview of the methods and problems of effective tax rate analysis, see OECD (2000).

4. In chapter 2 Devereux shows explicitly how effective tax rates are influenced by inflation.

5. For a moment it will be convenient to treat time as being divided into discrete periods.

6. The effects of taxation on wage formation in alternative models of imperfect labor markets are analyzed in detail in Sørensen (1999).

7. Equation (1.39) abstracts from positive externalities from education. Alternatively, these could be deducted from the estimate of $C_t^p$.

# References

Alworth, J. 1988. *The Finance, Investment and Taxation Decisions of Multinationals*. New York: Basil Blackwell.

Boadway, R. W., N. Bruce, and J. M. Mintz. 1984. Taxation, inflation and the marginal tax rate on capital in Canada. *Canadian Journal of Economics* 15: 278–93.

Chennells, L., and R. Griffith. 1997. *Taxing Profits in a Changing World*. London: Institute for Fiscal Studies.

Daveri, F., and G. Tabellini. 2000. Unemployment, growth and taxation in industrial countries. *Economic Policy* 30: 47–104.

Devereux, M. P., and M. Pearson. 1995. European tax harmonisation and production efficiency. *European Economic Review* 39 (9): 1657–82.

Devereux, M. P., and R. Griffith. 1998. The taxation of discrete investment choices. Institute for Fiscal Studies Working Paper 98/16.

Devereux, M. P., R. Griffith, and A. Klemm. 2002. Corporate income tax reforms and international tax competition. *Economic Policy* 35: 449–96.

European Commission. 1992. *Report of the Committee of Independent Experts on Company Taxation*. Luxembourg: Office for Official Publications of the European Communities.

European Commission. 1997. Towards tax co-ordination in the European Union: A package to tackle harmful tax competition. COM(97) 495 final.

European Commission. 2001. Company taxation in the internal market. Commission Staff Working Paper SEC(2001) 1681.

Gordon, R. H., and J. B. Slemrod. 1988. Do we collect any revenue from taxing capital income? *Tax Policy and the Economy* 2: 89–130.

Hall, R. E., and D. W. Jorgenson. 1967. Tax policy and investment behaviour. *American Economic Review* 57: 391–414.

Keen, M. J. 1991. Corporation tax, foreign investment and the single market. In L. A. Winters and A. J. Venables, eds., *The Impact of 1992 on European Trade and Industry*. Cambridge: Cambridge University Press.

King, M. A. 1974. Taxation, investment and the cost of capital. *Review of Economic Studies* 41: 21–35.

King, M. A., and D. Fullerton. 1984. *The Taxation of Income from Capital: A Comparative Study of the United States, the United Kingdom, Sweden, and West Germany*. Chicago: University of Chicago Press.

Mendoza, E. G., A. Razin, and L. Tesar. 1994. Effective tax rates in macroeconomics: cross-country estimates of tax rates on factor incomes and consumption. *Journal of Monetary Economics* 34 (3): 297–323.

OECD. 1991. *Taxing Profits in a Global Economy: Domestic and International Issues*. Paris.

OECD. 1994. *Taxation and Household Saving*. Paris.

OECD. 2000. *Tax Burdens—Alternative Measures*. OECD Tax Policy Studies, no. 2. Paris.

Sinn, H.-W. 1988. The 1986 US tax reform and the world capital market. *European Economic Review* 32: 325–33.

Sørensen, P. B. 1999. Optimal tax progressivity in imperfect labour markets. *Labour Economics* 6: 435–52.

# 2    Measuring Taxes on Income from Capital

Michael P. Devereux

## 2.1    Introduction

This chapter reviews a number of different approaches that have been taken in what is now a large literature on measuring the taxation of income from capital. It is not the intention to summarize all approaches but rather to set out a general framework in which the advantages and disadvantages of alternative approaches can be assessed.

Before beginning to discuss measurement, however, it is useful to identify the purpose of such measurement. What are the economic questions to which a particular measure might provide an answer? This preliminary issue is discussed in section 2.2. Two important issues stand out. First, what *is* a tax on capital income? For example, is it a tax that is formally levied on a specific income stream received by owners of capital, or would it include any tax that reduces the income of the owners of capital? Second, is it a measure designed to shed light on the distribution of taxes among individuals, or to indicate how the tax might affect the size and composition of the capital stock?

In practice, there have been two main lines of research on the measurement of taxes on income from capital. One line has been based on the original theoretical approach of Jorgenson (1963), which attempts to identify the impact of taxes on the cost of capital—the real required pre-tax rate of return on an investment project. The well-known approach of King and Fullerton (1984) in developing measures of the effective marginal tax rate follows this line of research, although there are several examples of alternative approaches. This general approach is based on the use of parameters enshrined in tax legislation, notably statutory tax rates and the ways in which taxable income is defined.

Recently this approach has been extended to consider discrete investment decisions that may affect the composition of the capital stock (Devereux and Griffith 1998a,b, 2003). The effective marginal tax rate is not directly relevant in such decisions. Instead, such decisions depend on an effective average tax rate. However, such a measure can also be derived using the parameters of tax legislation itself.

An alternative line of research has been to use data on tax revenues, or the tax liabilities of firms. Data on individual firm tax liabilities are available from company accounting (or tax) records, while data on aggregate tax revenues are available for many countries. To use such data in the creation of tax rates, the tax liability or revenue must be scaled by some measure of the underlying income that is taxed. The result is typically a measure of an average tax rate. In the case of company tax liabilities, usually some measure of firm profit is chosen. Various scaling factors have been used in the case of aggregate revenue data. The most widely known is the approach of Mendoza et al. (1994), in which revenue from taxes on capital is divided by a measure of the operating surplus of the economy.

Recently too this type of measure has been developed in a new direction. Gordon et al. (chapter 4 of this volume) propose a measure of the effective marginal tax rate that can be derived from such data, rather than the usual approach of using the parameters of tax legislation. This approach is based on the comparison of actual tax revenue with the revenue that would be collected by a hypothetical tax based solely on economic rent (and have a zero effective marginal tax rate).

In section 2.3, I proceed to set out the main approaches of economic theory and examine how taxes on capital income affect investment decisions. Using a simple model, I derive two broad measures of effective tax rates: a marginal rate that affects the scale of investment, and an average rate which affects discrete choices. In section 2.4, I consider some further issues that arise in making such effective tax rates operational. In particular, I consider the role of personal taxes, the impact of using alternative sources of finance, cross-border direct investment, risk, and the extent to which more complex models of the firm can be used. In section 2.5, I then consider an alternative form of effective tax rate, based on observable data on tax payments. The central question here is the extent to which such measures can be used to shed light on the economic decisions set out in section 2.3. In the concluding section 2.6, I provide some reflections on the use of the different measures.

## 2.2   What Are Taxes on Income from Capital, and Why Do We Want to Measure Them?

Before addressing the question of how to measures taxes on the income from capital, it is useful to consider why we might be interested in such measurements. In other words, what questions might be answered by measuring such taxes? Only when we have identified the questions should we attempt to provide the answers.

In general, taxes raise two types of concern: the distribution of the burden of the tax across individuals, and the impact of the tax on economic behavior. Clearly, in attempting to discover distributional effects, we should be concerned with the effective incidence of the tax. Of course, this is very difficult. For example, the effective incidence of a corporation tax may be shared among a large number of individuals, depending on the conditions in a number of markets.

But consideration of effective incidence also raises a question about what might be considered to be a tax on the income from capital. That is because the income stream received by owners of capital might be lower in the presence of many taxes, not just those levied directly on that income stream. For example, a wage tax could reduce the income to capital owners if workers were able to bid up the gross wage in order to pass on the tax. An origin-based VAT might give firms located in one country a disadvantage relative to their competitors elsewhere; this too might reduce the net income stream to the owners of capital.

For these reasons this chapter does not address the effective incidence of taxes that may affect the income from capital. As such, it has nothing to say about the distribution of such taxes. Instead, it focuses only on efficiency aspects. Even here, though, similar questions arise. Fundamentally, social welfare is likely to depend on the size and composition of the capital stock located in a jurisdiction. Any taxes that affect decisions that determine these may therefore reduce social welfare (or possibly increase it, in the presence of negative externalities).

But again there is no obvious classification of taxes that may affect the size and composition of the capital stock. Certainly the link between effective incidence and distortions to the capital stock is tenuous. In a standard model of a small open economy, for example, owners of capital do not bear the effective incidence of taxes on capital income. But their capital investment decisions are affected by such taxes, which may suggest considering only taxes that are formally incident on capital. But the fact that a tax is formally incident on income from capital is neither necessary nor sufficient for it to affect the size or composition of the capital stock. For example, in a small open, capital-importing economy, individual, residence-based taxes on income from capital are likely to affect savings but unlikely to affect domestic investment. Further, as noted above, wage taxes that are partly passed on to capital owners may affect investment.

In section 2.3, I review two types of decision concerning investment. The first is the scale of investment undertaken. This is the traditional approach of economic theory, and typically the impact of a tax is measured by its impact on the before-tax required real rate of return—the cost of capital. If a tax raises the cost of capital, then it is likely to result in lower investment; conversely, if it lowers the cost of capital, then it is likely to result in higher investment. The second is the composition of capital, which can be affected by discrete investment choices—for example, which of two mutually exclusive investments to undertake. The theory indicates that such a decision depends on how taxes affect the after-tax profit of the investments, which can be measured by an effective average tax rate.

But neither of these approaches provides a clear-cut definition of which taxes are relevant in affecting investment decisions. In keeping with most of the literature, this chapter focuses only on taxes that are formally incident on income from capital. More specifically, it is primarily concerned with source-based taxes. This approach is most easily justified in the context of a small open economy, which takes the world rate of return (after source-based taxes) as given. This provides convenient no-arbitrage conditions in which the impact of taxes formally on capital income can be clearly identified.

It may be the case that other taxes also affect investment decisions.[1] However, in principle, the impact of such taxes on investment decisions depends also on assumptions regarding market conditions. Here I make the simplest assumption that such taxes do not affect investment decisions. Any alternative should require us to spell out precisely the route by which investment decisions are affected.

Finally, it should be noted that the chapter focuses almost exclusively on measuring taxes on capital income derived from the corporate sector. This approach is taken mainly for simplification. Clearly, it is also possible to attempt to measure the taxation of income earned outside the corporate sector. Indeed, the extent to which taxes affect the choice of legal form may be an important issue. However, while the tax treatment of noncorporate enterprises differs from that of companies, most of the principles addressed below apply also to investment undertaken by either form of enterprise.

## 2.3 Theory of Investment Decisions

The discussion of the previous section set out alternative economic questions relating to taxes on the income from capital, and also raised the issue of which taxes should be incorporated in any analysis. As noted above, I narrow my questions and the taxes examined as follows:

1. To the impact of taxes on the composition and size of the capital stock in a particular jurisdiction.

2. To only taxes that are formally incident on the return to capital owned by a corporation, although they may be levied on the corporation or its shareholders.

### 2.3.1 The Basic Model

The traditional approach to examining the impact of taxes on the level of investment by firms was originally set out by King (1974), drawing notably on earlier contributions by Jorgenson (1963) and Hall and Jorgenson (1967).

The approach used by King is based on a dynamic model of the firm in the context of a risk-neutral shareholder. Specifically, a capital market arbitrage condition requires that the market value of the equity of the firm at the end of period $t$, denoted $V_t$, be determined by the condition

$$\{1 + (1 - m)i\}V_t = \frac{1 - m^D}{1 - c}D_{t+1} - N_{t+1} + V_{t+1} - z(V_{t+1} - N_{t+1} - V_t).$$

(2.1)

The appendix at the end of this chapter gives definitions of the variables used here.

The right-hand side of equation (2.1) is the after-tax payoff—earned at the end of period $t + 1$—to an individual owning the equity of a firm from the end of period $t$. It consists of net income from dividends, $D_{t+1}$, after personal tax at rate $m^D$ and a tax credit at rate $c$, less new equity contributed to the firm, $N_{t+1}$, plus the value of the firm at the

end of period $t + 1$, $V_{t+1}$, net of capital gains tax at an effective rate
$z$ due on any change in the value of the firm. The left-hand side is the
post-tax return from investing an amount $V_t$ in a deposit paying interest at a nominal rate $i$, on which tax is paid at rate $m$. For a risk-neutral
investor, these must be equal, and this implies that $V_t$ must also be the
market value of the equity of the firm at the end of period $t$. Solving for
$V_t$ implies

$$V_t = \frac{\gamma D_{t+1} - N_{t+1} + V_{t+1}}{1 + \rho}, \tag{2.2}$$

where $\rho = (1 - m)i/(1 - z)$ is the tax-adjusted nominal discount rate
and $\gamma = (1 - m^D)/(1 - c)(1 - z)$ is a tax discrimination variable, which
captures the impact of tax on a round-trip of paying one unit of dividends financed by one unit of new equity. The role played by $\gamma$ is discussed further in section 2.4.2.

$V_t$ is related to real investment by the firm through the equality of
sources and uses of funds within the firm in each period:

$$D_t = F(K_{t-1})(1 - \tau) - q_t I_t + B_t - [1 + i(1 - \tau)]B_{t-1}$$
$$+ \tau\phi(q_t I_t + K_{t-1}^T) + N_t. \tag{2.3}$$

By accounting identity, dividends in period $t$ are equal to net revenue
$F(K_{t-1})$, where $K_{t-1}$ is the capital stock at the end of period $t - 1$, after
corporation tax at rate $\tau$, less new investment $I_t$, at price $q_t$, plus new
one-period borrowing $B_t$, less the repayment of last period's borrowing
at interest rate $i$ (deductible from tax), less tax allowances for new and
past investment at rate $\phi$, where $K_{t-1}^T$ is the value of the capital stock
for tax purposes at the end of period $t - 1$, plus new equity $N_t$. I
assume that the price of output rises by the inflation rate $\pi$ in each
period, and normalize its price at the end of period $t$ to unity. I also
normalize the price of the capital stock in period $t$ to be unity.

Two further expressions reflect the evolution over time of the capital
stock and the valuation of the capital stock for tax purposes:[2]

$$K_t = (1 - \delta)K_{t-1} + I_t \tag{2.4}$$

and

$$K_t^T = (1 - \phi)K_{t-1}^T + (1 - \phi)q_{t-1}I_{t-1}. \tag{2.5}$$

Assume that the firm chooses the capital stock in any period to maximize the wealth of its shareholder, $V_t$, given by (2.2), subject to (2.3),

(2.4), and (2.5). Within this framework I examine two separate types of decisions that the firm may need to make.

### 2.3.2 The Optimal Scale of the Capital Stock

The first decision is the traditional one as to the optimal size of the capital stock. To find this, combine the four expressions, and then differentiate with respect to $K_t$. This yields the first-order condition for the optimal capital stock:

$$(1 - \tau)(1 + \pi)F'(K_t) = (1 - A)\{\rho + q_{t+1}\delta - (q_{t+1} - 1)\}, \tag{2.6}$$

where

$$A = \frac{\tau\phi(1 + \rho)}{\rho + \phi}. \tag{2.7}$$

The left-hand side of (2.6) is the after corporation tax net revenue generated in period $t + 1$ from increasing $K_t$. Note that the change in the capital stock is only for one period: $K_{t+1}$ is unaffected. The right-hand side of (2.6) represents the cost of increasing $K_t$. This reflects the financial cost of tying funds up in the higher capital stock for one period, $\rho$, the fall in the value of the asset over the period due to depreciation, $\delta$, less any increase in the relative price of capital goods over the period, $(q_{t+1} - 1)$.

For a given cost of increasing $K_t$ for one period then, (2.6) can be thought of determining the minimum acceptable real rate of return, $F'(K_t)$. All projects earning a return greater than this should be accepted; all those earning a rate of return less than this should be rejected. It is common to split this required rate of return into two components, reflecting the cost of depreciation and the remaining cost. That is, define $p$ to be the before-tax rate of return on a project, over and above the rate of depreciation, so that $F'(K) = p + \delta$. The cost of capital is defined as the minimum acceptable value of $p$, denoted $\hat{p}$, where

$$\hat{p} = \frac{(1 - A)}{(1 - \tau)(1 + \pi)}\{\rho + \delta(1 + \pi^K) - \pi^K\} - \delta, \tag{2.8}$$

and where $\pi^K$ is the increase in the price of the capital stock, and so $q_{t+1} = 1 + \pi^K$.

This is the basic expression for the cost of capital in much of the investment literature.[3] It is straightforward to see that a rise in the rate of allowances $A$ reduces the cost of capital, and a rise in the tax rate $\tau$ increases the cost of capital (although such an increase also raises $A$). Personal taxes are relevant only to the extent to which they affect the discount rate $\rho$. In the special case where the shareholder's tax rate on interest income is equal to his effective tax rate on capital gains, the discount rate is independent of personal taxes.

In the absence of tax, the cost of capital is simply the real interest rate $r$. One natural measure of the effective marginal tax rate is therefore the proportionate increase in the cost of capital that arises as a result of taxation:

$$e = \frac{\hat{p} - r}{\hat{p}}. \tag{2.9}$$

There are a number of issues that must be explored further, however, before this measure can be used to assess how taxes affect the incentive to invest. One is the role of personal taxes. A second concerns how the perturbation to the capital stock is financed. So far the analysis has not allowed the use of debt or new equity to change. The first-order condition on the capital stock held both constant; implicitly the incremental investment is therefore financed by a reduction in dividends, and the return is paid to shareholders in the form of dividends. However, there are clearly other possibilities. A third issue is the role of international taxes in the context of foreign direct investment. A fourth is the impact of introducing risk. I will consider each of these in turn in section 2.4.

There are, of course, other issues that are not addressed here due to lack of space. One of these is the possibility that tax rates may be expected to change over time. This can arise because, for example, the government has already announced a reform, or it has specific measures that generate changes in the tax parameters for a certain investment over time, such as a tax holiday.[4] Tax rates could also change because of the asymmetric nature of most taxes; when taxable income is negative, typically it does not generate an immediate tax rebate, but it must be carried forward to some future period to offset against subsequent positive income. If a firm is in such a position in either period $t$ or period $t + 1$, this can generate large effects on the cost of capital.[5]

### 2.3.3  The Optimal Composition of Capital

The approach so far is based on a model in which firms simply choose the optimal size of the capital stock. In effect, the capital stock is assumed to be continuously divisible, so that investment can be undertaken up to the point where it becomes unprofitable.

However, it is possible to consider other types of decision that firms make concerning their capital. One important distinction is to consider a firm that has two types of capital. These may reflect different continuously divisible assets used in the production process, in which case the approach above can still be used. However, they may also represent mutually exclusive choices. For example, one type of capital may represent setting up a new plant in the firm's country of residence. Another may represent setting up a plant in some other country. Depending on the cost structure involved in the investment, it may be unprofitable for the firm to build both plants. Instead, it must choose between them.[6] This type of decision may therefore affect the composition of the firm's capital stock. And in the case where that composition represents capital located in different jurisdictions, it can also affect the total capital located in each jurisdiction.

This suggests a two-stage decision-making process. At stage 1, the firm makes the discrete choice between mutually exclusive options. At stage 2, it chooses the optimal level of the type of capital chosen at stage 1.[7] In analyzing this, suppose that $\hat{V}_t^A$ and $\hat{V}_t^B$ represent the maximized wealth of the shareholder if either option A or option B is undertaken (i.e., where in either case the firm chooses the optimal level of the capital stock). Then, consistent with the firm aiming to maximize the wealth of the shareholder, the firm should choose option A if $\hat{V}_t^A > \hat{V}_t^B$, and vice versa.

The role of tax at the stage 1 decision cannot be captured by its impact on the cost of capital, however. To examine the stage 1 decision, I abstract from the stage 2 decision by assuming that the investment is of a fixed size. More specifically, I consider the case of a unit increase in the capital stock in period $t$ only, as above, but where the unit increase can be in one of two types of capital. As above, assume for now that there is no issue of new equity or debt associated with the investment.

It is useful to define the value to the shareholder of a project $i$ in the absence of tax as $R^*$, where the asterisk denotes values in the absence of tax:

$$R^* = -1 + \frac{1}{1+i}\{(1+\pi)(p+\delta) + (1+\pi^K)(1-\delta)\}. \tag{2.10}$$

This is also the net present value in the absence of tax of the economic rent of the project. In the simpler case where $\pi = \pi^K$, and $1 + i = (1+r)(1+\pi)$, (2.10) reduces to

$$R^* = \frac{p - r}{1 + r}. \tag{2.11}$$

In the absence of tax, the firm would choose project A over project B if $R^{*A} > R^{*B}$, and vice versa.

In the presence of tax, the choice would be based on the comparison of after-tax values, $R^A$ and $R^B$. Following the same approach, the after-tax value can be written as

$$R = -\gamma(1 - A) + \frac{\gamma}{1 + \rho} \{(1 + \pi)(p + \delta)(1 - \tau) + (1 + \pi^K)(1 - \delta)(1 - A)\}. \tag{2.12}$$

One measure of the impact of tax is to consider a form of effective average tax rate, $\hat{\alpha}$, such that $R = (1 - \hat{\alpha})R^*$, or

$$\hat{\alpha} = \frac{R^* - R}{R^*}. \tag{2.13}$$

In effect such a tax rate measures the proportion of the economic rent that is taken in tax. The higher is $\hat{\alpha}$, the less likely a project is to be chosen. An alternative measure, which captures the same idea, is to base the effective average tax rate on total income rather than on economic rent. Such a measure is more akin to those commonly based on accounting and aggregate data (described in section 2.5). It is defined as

$$\alpha = \frac{R^* - R}{p/(1 + r)} = \hat{\alpha}\left(\frac{p - r}{p}\right). \tag{2.14}$$

Clearly, these two measures reflect the same information, as one is a simple transformation of the other. However, they have rather different properties. In particular, it is possible to show that $\alpha$ is a weighted average of the effective marginal tax rate $e$ and the statutory tax rate adjusted for personal taxes, denoted $t$:[8]

$$\alpha = \left(\frac{\hat{p}}{p}\right)e + \left(1 - \frac{\hat{p}}{p}\right)t, \tag{2.15}$$

where

$$t = 1 - \gamma(1 - \tau)\left(\frac{1+i}{1+\rho}\right). \tag{2.16}$$

The weights in (2.15) reflect the profitability of the investment. For a marginal investment, $p = \hat{p}$ and so $\alpha = e$. As the profitability of the investment rises, the weight on $e$ falls and the weight on $t$ rises. As $p \to \infty$, $\alpha \to t$.

As with the effective marginal tax rate, there are several further important issues that need to be raised. These are discussed in section 2.4.

### 2.3.4 Financial Constraints

There is another way in which taxes can affect firms' investment, and that is through the availability of finance. Suppose that the cost of external finance rises with the amount used. In this case, investment can exceed after-tax retained earnings, but a lower tax liability would increase the available internal funds, and thereby reduce the need for external funds. In turn this would reduce the cost of external funds, and at the margin, investment would be higher.

In the extreme case where external finance is prohibitively expensive, investment is constrained to be no greater than after-tax earnings. From (2.3), in the absence of debt and new equity finance, the condition that $D_t \geq 0$ implies

$$q_t I_t \leq (1 - H)F(K_{t-1}), \tag{2.17}$$

where

$$H = \tau\left\{\frac{(1 - \phi)F(K_{t-1}) - \phi K_{t-1}^T}{(1 - \tau\phi)F(K_{t-1})}\right\}. \tag{2.18}$$

Here $H$ is a rather different form of average tax rate. In the absence of tax, $H = 0$ and investment is constrained by the before-tax net revenue. In the presence of tax, it is constrained by after-tax net revenue, with $H > 0$. This type of effect is quite different from the effects on incentives described above. Although there is now a vast literature examining the possibility of financial constraints on investment (e.g., see Hubbard 1998 for a survey), this role of tax has been largely ignored. We will not discuss it in any detail here, except to note that it is closely related to the measures of taxation based on observed tax liabilities or revenue (described in section 2.5).

## 2.4   Other Issues

Much of the basic analysis in section 2.3 is uncontroversial, and is shared by many different approaches to measuring taxes on the income from capital. Where approaches differ tends to be in specific detailed assumptions. I now address the more important issues involved in translating the theory into practical measures of taxation. I discuss a number of issues in turn.

### 2.4.1   Personal Taxes

The model set out in section 2.3 makes two important assumptions:

• The market value of the corporation is determined by the no arbitrage condition (2.1).

• The managers of the corporation aim to maximize this market value.

Both assumptions are strong and open to question.[9] I address them in turn.

The first problem is not that there may be arbitrage opportunities in financial markets but rather that it is very difficult—and in practice, impossible—to identify for which economic agent or agents the arbitrage condition holds. To see this, consider a very simple case in which there are two individuals, $i = A, B$, and two assets, $j = 1, 2$. $A$ and $B$ could be residents of different countries, but need not be. The return from each asset is $r_j$. Let the tax rate for individual $i$ on the income from asset $j$ be $m_{ij}$. Then, in the absence of risk, individual $i$ will hold both assets only if her after-tax rates of return are the same:

$$s_i = (1 - m_{i1})r_1 = (1 - m_{i2})r_2. \tag{2.19}$$

If the tax rates vary across $i$ and $j$, then this can only hold by chance for both individuals. If it does not hold for both, then one individual—say $A$—will be at a corner solution, holding only one asset. In this case the return required on each asset—and hence their price—will be determined by $B$. That is, $B$ is the "marginal investor," and the personal tax rates in (2.1) are those that apply to the marginal shareholder $B$.

There have been many attempts to identify the tax rates of marginal shareholders. One common approach, dating back to Elton and Gruber (1970), is to identify the change in the share price at the moment when a dividend is paid, and the share moves from cum-div to ex-div. In principle, the fall in the value of the share should reflect the size of the dividend payment and the tax rates of the marginal investor.

However, there may not be a single marginal investor, or even a class of marginal investors with the same tax rates. In practice, we observe investors with different tax rates holding a broad range of assets. One possible explanation involves risk. Suppose, for example, that investor $i$ faces a low tax rate on asset 1 but that all other tax rates are identical. This would induce investor $i$ to hold a greater proportion of asset 1 in her overall portfolio. In fact she should increase her holding of the asset up to the point where the tax advantage is exactly offset by the greater risk she has taken on by reducing the overall diversification of her portfolio. In this case the lower tax rate asset 1 is matched by a higher required return by investor $i$ from that asset. If this point is reached, then she may continue to hold other assets as well, just as other investors do. In this case there may be many "marginal" investors who may face different tax rates.

Even if there is only one (class of) marginal investor, she would be virtually impossible to identify. There is no reason, for example, why she should be a resident of the same country as the corporation—and so she may face taxes set in any country. But if there is no single (class of) marginal investor, then it is not reasonable to assume that companies are able to take account of the personal characteristics, including personal tax rates, of all marginal investors.

The second assumption is equally problematic. It is not necessarily the case that the marginal shareholder has the majority vote among the shareholders. In fact it is unlikely; if there is an investor who only invests in one type of asset, then it is quite plausible that he would have a majority vote.

Consider this case a little further. Suppose that the existing structure of taxes leaves $B$ as the marginal shareholder but $A$ holding the majority of the shares of company 1. $A$ can therefore instruct the managers of the company to act in his interest. Suppose then that $A$'s tax rate changes in such a way that he would prefer more investment at the cost of a lower marginal rate of return. This might mean that $B$ would no longer want to hold shares in company 1. However, given an almost infinite set of possible investors in a world capital market, it is plausible that there is a least one investor who would buy $B$'s shares and who would become the new marginal investor. The market value of the firm would probably change, but it would still not reflect the valuation of the controlling shareholder $A$.

The relevant personal tax rates are in this case those of the majority owner of a firm, and not the marginal shareholder. However, it may not even be possible to identify the majority owner—indeed there may be no majority owner. This takes us to two different considerations. The first is the nature of voting power—how large a stake is necessary to control decisions? The second concerns corporate governance more generally—to what extent do boards of directors take into account the personal taxes of any shareholder? Arguably, if directors maximize anything, it is after-corporation tax profit.

In attempting to define effective rates of tax on capital income, it is necessary to make some assumptions about the relevant personal tax rates. But this discussion calls into question all such assumptions. In particular, with a world capital market, it is not necessarily sensible to assume that the relevant shareholder is a domestic resident. In any case, the marginal shareholder may determine the share price but not affect investment decisions.

If boards of directors really wanted to maximize the after-tax wealth of a given shareholder, they would be faced with the same difficulties as outlined here. One plausible assumption is simply that managers do not take personal taxes into account in their investment decisions, either because they do not know whose personal tax rates to take into account or because no shareholder is sufficiently powerful to require them to do so.

### 2.4.2  Sources of Finance

How firms finance their activities has been an active area of research for many years, but it is probably fair to say that many issues in this area have yet to be resolved. The modern literature on this topic began with the Modigliani and Miller (1958) irrelevance theorems, and has since continued with contributions taking account of agency costs, signaling, property rights, and financial constraints. There is no space to survey this literature here.[10]

In measuring taxes on the income from capital, four main issues arise. First, what forms of finance are available to the firm? Second, should an incremental investment project be assumed to be financed from a single source of finance, or from a mixture of sources? Third, should the underlying cost of finance be allowed to differ according to its source? Fourth, if a single source of finance is assumed, should it be assumed that all positive and negative cash flows in all periods of the investment are identified with the same source? We discuss these issues in turn.

The traditional distinction between sources of finance is that between equity and debt. This distinction is important for tax purposes since they are generally treated differently. Typically interest payments are deductible in determining corporate profit; they may or may not be taxed when received by lender. Dividend payments differ in that they are typically not deductible in determining corporate profit, although there have been many forms of integration of corporate and personal taxes.

A further important distinction in measuring the impact of taxes on capital income is between two classes of equity finance: new equity and retained earnings. These differ again due to taxation. Consider an investment in an asset that costs the firm \$1. If financed by new equity, this costs the shareholder \$1. However, if cash dividends paid by the firm are reduced by \$1, then the net cost to the shareholder depends on the personal tax that would have been paid had the cash dividend not been reduced. In the model above, this is measured by $\gamma$. If $\gamma < 1$, then the net cost is lower with retained earnings. If the proceeds of the investment are paid to shareholders as dividends, then this difference in cost is reflected in a difference in effective tax rates.

In principle, there are many other forms of financial contract that have elements of debt and equity finance by which a firm can raise finance. These include, for example, swaps and various forms of option that the literature on measuring effective tax rates has not yet incorporated. If the set of cash flows associated with a form of financing is well defined, and a clear set of tax rules applies to these cash flows, then there is no reason why any form of financing could not be modeled. However, below I discuss only the more standard forms of finance.

The second issue is whether it is preferable to consider an investment financed by a single source of finance, or by a mix of sources. The former approach is used by studies in the King and Fullerton (1984) tradition. The latter is exemplified by, for example, Boadway, Bruce, and Mintz (1984). Both approaches can easily be incorporated into measures of effective tax rates. The choice between them depends on which underlying model of corporate finance is used.

One common approach to analyzing sources of finance used by a firm is to begin by allowing costs to differ according to sources of finance. For example, for $\gamma < 1$, it is typically assumed that new equity finance is more expensive than retentions. Debt may initially be the cheapest form of finance due to interest deductibility. To formulate a model, it is commonly assumed that the interest rate paid by the firm increases as the proportion of debt increases. (Several other factors could also be taken account of in a complete model.)

This type of model favors the King and Fullerton approach. That is, as the firm increases its investment in any period, the marginal source of finance changes. It may begin with debt, switch to retained earnings (until dividends reach zero), switch back to debt, and as the interest rate increases, eventually switch to new equity. (This model underlies most studies that incorporate financial constraints.) Ex post, the firm may therefore use all three sources of finance. However, any given increment to investment is likely to be financed from a single source.

An alternative approach is to assume the existence of some other costs, or some general equilibrium, that makes an individual firm indifferent to its choice of finance. A well-known example of such a model is that of Miller (1977). This model essentially derives an equilibrium in which individual investors hold either equity or debt, depending on their personal tax rate. There is a unique aggregate equilibrium that determines the required return on equity, but the cost of finance to any individual firm is independent of its source of finance.

In principle, this might justify an assumption that the firm uses all three sources of finance for a marginal project. However, this model would imply that the costs of all three were the same. The problem in measuring effective tax rates is to make assumptions that allow this to be true. For example, this may include a higher underlying rate of return required on debt, which is offset by tax deductibility of interest. What this model does not justify, however, is a weighted average of sources of finance which have different costs.

The Boadway et al. (1984) approach is, however, based on a weighted average where the costs differ according to sources of finance. They use actual costs of debt and equity as observed in the market: the cost of debt finance is the observed interest rate, while the cost of equity finance is calculated using price-earnings ratios from stock market data. They justify this using a model in which both the cost of equity and the cost of debt rise with the debt–equity ratio (see Boadway 1987). In this model the firm first selects the debt–equity ratio that minimizes the average cost of financial capital. This debt–equity ratio is then used to choose the optimal capital stock.

The fourth issue raised above is whether it should be assumed that the same source of finance is marginal for the whole lifetime of the investment. This question has two aspects, which we consider in turn. First, in considering a one-period perturbation in the capital stock, what is an appropriate assumption about the marginal source of finance when the asset is purchased (in period $t$) and when the return is earned (in period $t + 1$)? In the context of equity finance, the answer to this was most clearly specified by Edwards and Keen (1984), drawing on Auerbach (1979).

We have already argued that the cost to the shareholder of a \$1 investment is \$1 if the investment is financed by new equity, and \$$\gamma$ if it is financed by retained earnings. Conversely, a return of say \$$1 + p$ paid out as a dividend is worth \$$\gamma(1 + p)$ to the shareholder, while the same return used to reduce new share issues is worth \$$1 + p$. This implies that it is important to specify the marginal source of finance in both periods. Suppose, for example, that new equity is the marginal source of finance in both periods. Then the dividend tax, represented by $\gamma$, is irrelevant; dividend payments are not affected by the investment. On the other hand, suppose that retained earnings are the marginal source of finance in both periods. Then both the cost of the investment and the return depend on $\gamma$; in deriving the cost of capital, these two effects cancel out so that the cost of capital is again independent of $\gamma$. This is reflected in the analysis in section 2.3.

The dividend tax therefore only affects the cost of capital if the marginal source of finance changes between the two periods. The most common case analyzed is that in which the marginal source of finance in period $t$ is new equity, while in period $t + 1$ it is retained earnings. In this case the dividend tax tends to raise the cost of capital. But the opposite is equally plausible, and in this case the dividend tax tends to reduce the cost of capital.

The second aspect of this issue is how cash flows in subsequent periods are financed. Such cash flows can arise even with a one-period perturbation of the capital stock, since there may be some effect on depreciation allowances indefinitely. In effect, this determines the discount rate to be applied in obtaining the present value of such allowances. In the model above the shareholder's discount rate $\rho$ should be used for all discounting. However, if all cash flows subsequent to period $t + 1$ are assumed to be reflected in changes in debt issued and repaid, then it can be shown that the net effect is equivalent to the appropriate discount rate being the net of tax nominal interest rate, $(1 - \tau)i$. This is equivalent to the approach taken by King and Fullerton (1984), who treat this as the firm's discount rate.[11] However, it is more difficult to take this approach for new equity finance, since it is necessary to define in each period the impact on new equity and dividends. It turns out that only in very extreme cases can the approach of King and Fullerton be justified in this case (such an approach is followed in Sorensen 1990 and OECD 1991).

An alternative approach is to assume that the marginal source of finance is retained earnings in all periods other than period $t$. Devereux and Griffith (1998b, 2003) explicitly make this assumption. In this case the definition of $R$ in (2.12) holds only for investment financed by retained earnings. If either debt or new equity is used, then an additional term must be added to reflect the tax consequences. This is defined as

$$F = \gamma \, dB_t \left\{ 1 - \frac{1 + i(1 - \tau)}{1 + \rho} \right\} - (1 - \gamma) \, dN_t \left\{ 1 - \frac{1}{1 + \rho} \right\}, \tag{2.20}$$

where $dB_t$ is the change in debt in period $t$, $dN_t$ is the change in new equity in period $t$ and all other terms are as defined above.

This approach allows the whole of the cost of investment to be met from a single source of finance, or for up to all three sources to be used. Clearly, $F$ becomes relevant in determining both the cost of capital and the effective average tax rate.

### 2.4.3   Foreign Direct Investment

The analysis so far has considered only the case where the firm invests domestically. In practice, multinational companies may produce in other countries. This raises an extra layer of complication in calculating effective tax rates. The extra complication arises from taxes that may be levied by either the host or home country on cash flows between the parent company and the affiliate. Such taxes may include withholding taxes levied by the host country on dividends and interest paid to the parent, and also additional taxes levied by the home country on receipts of income from the host country.

This taxation can also be complicated by complex international transactions, possibly designed to take advantage of specific tax rules. For example, profits may be repatriated through an intermediary company in a country with a beneficial tax regime, or profits from high- and low-taxed countries may be mixed to avoid paying any home country tax.

In principle, as with the domestic case, effective tax rates can be calculated for any investment with well-defined cash flows and a well-defined tax system. However, in practice, the vast array of alternative means of organising cross-border investment flows means that it is very difficult to provide a comprehensive analysis. Analyses of effective tax rates in such a setting have been carried out by Alworth (1988), Keen (1991), OECD (1991), and Devereux and Griffith (2003). Devereux, Lammersen, and Spengel (2000) extend the analysis to consider more complex cross-border financial arrangements. The general approach is to consider a parent company in country $i$ that has a wholly owned subsidiary in country $j$. The subsidiary can be financed by the parent in the same three ways as the parent. This approach permits the effective tax rates of multinational firms to be compared with those of purely domestic firms.

There are relatively few issues of principle that arise in extending the approach set out in section 2.3 to cross-border investment. Clearly, the more complex structure calls for additional assumptions to be made regarding, for example, the ways in which the affiliate is financed. Further, as the structure of the tax regime is more complex, allowance should be made for the different ways in which foreign source income is taxed by the home country. However, these extensions arise only from making the form of investment more complex. As noted elsewhere, the basic framework described here can be extended almost indefinitely to encompass more complex models. But as there are few general points of principle involved, I do not discuss this extension any further.

### 2.4.4   Risk

Most of the literature on measuring taxes on income from capital has ignored risk. This is an important omission, as historically the return on risky assets has far exceeded that on safe assets, implying that the risk premium is large.

The analysis of the impact of taxes in the presence of risk here draws on Devereux (2003). We begin with a general way of pricing risky assets, using the fundamental asset pricing approach of Cochrane (2001). This defines the current market value of a stochastic cash flow $\tilde{x}$ arising in one period's time as

$$V[\tilde{x}] = E(\tilde{m}\tilde{x}). \tag{2.21}$$

The tilde indicates a stochastic variable. In this expression, $\tilde{m}$ is a stochastic discount factor that can be generated from a simple two-period model of consumption, in which the investor optimally allocates consumption over periods $t$ and $t + 1$. Given a utility function $u(c)$, where $c$ is consumption, and a rate of time preference, $\beta$, we have

$$\tilde{m} = \beta \frac{u'(\tilde{c}_{t+1})}{u'(c_t)}. \tag{2.22}$$

If there were no uncertainty and no inflation, then $\tilde{m}$ would simply reflect the risk-free rate of interest $r$; that is, $\tilde{m} = 1/(1+r)$. More generally, $E(\tilde{m}) = 1/(1+r)$. Using this, and expanding the expected value of the product of $\tilde{m}$ and $\tilde{x}$, we can also write

$$V[\tilde{x}] = E(\tilde{m})E(\tilde{x}) + \text{cov}(\tilde{m}, \tilde{x})$$

$$= \frac{E(\tilde{x})}{1+r} + \text{cov}(\tilde{m}, \tilde{x}). \tag{2.23}$$

The first term on the RHS of this expression is the value of receiving a certain $E(\tilde{x})$ next period. The second term captures the effect of risk. Note that due to the strict concavity of the utility function, $\text{cov}(\tilde{m}, \tilde{x})$ has the opposite sign to $\text{cov}(\tilde{c}_{t+1}, \tilde{x})$. Hence, if $\tilde{x}$ is positively correlated with $\tilde{c}_{t+1}$, then $\text{cov}(\tilde{m}, \tilde{x}) < 0$, implying a lower $V[\tilde{x}]$.

Now return to the investment considered in section 2.3 and make both the financial return and economic depreciation stochastic. To simplify, assume that there is no inflation and ignore personal taxes. Then, in the absence of tax, the NPV of the project is

$$R^* = -1 + V[1 + \tilde{p}]$$

$$= -\frac{r}{1+r} + \frac{E(\tilde{p})}{1+r} + \text{cov}(\tilde{m}, \tilde{p}), \tag{2.24}$$

as the nonstochastic part of the return in period $t + 1$ can be discounted at the risk-free rate $r$. The cost of capital in the absence of tax is then

$$c^* = r + \lambda, \tag{2.25}$$

where $\lambda = -(1+r)\,\text{cov}(\tilde{m}, \tilde{p})$ is the risk premium (which is positive if $\tilde{p}$ is positively correlated with $\tilde{c}_{t+1}$).

In the presence of tax, the NPV of the project, given in (2.12), becomes

$$R = -(1-A) + (1-\tau)V[\tilde{p}^T + \tilde{\delta}] + (1-A)V[1-\tilde{\delta}], \tag{2.26}$$

where, for reasons explained below, we use $\tilde{p}^T$ to denote the stochastic financial return in the presence of tax. Assume that the tax system is known and constant. Using the formulation (2.23), $R$ can be written as

$$R = -\frac{r(1-A)}{1+r} + \frac{(1-\tau)E(\tilde{p}^T)}{1+r} - \frac{(\tau - A)E(\tilde{\delta})}{1+r}$$

$$+ (1 - \tau)\,\mathrm{cov}(\tilde{p}^T, \tilde{m}) + (\tau - A)\,\mathrm{cov}(\tilde{K}, \tilde{m}), \tag{2.27}$$

where $\tilde{K} = 1 - \tilde{\delta}$ is the value of the asset in period $t + 1$. Now find the cost of capital, namely the value of $E(\tilde{p})$ for which $R = 0$. Solving (2.27) for $R = 0$ yields

$$R = 0 \Rightarrow E(\tilde{p}^T) = \frac{(1-A)}{(1-\tau)}\{r + E(\tilde{\delta})\} - E(\tilde{\delta}) + \lambda^T + \frac{(\tau - A)}{(1-\tau)}\mu, \tag{2.28}$$

where $\lambda^T = -(1+r)\,\mathrm{cov}(\tilde{p}^T, \tilde{m})$ and $\mu = -(1+r)\,\mathrm{cov}(\tilde{K}, \tilde{m})$. Apart from the last two terms of the RHS, this is equivalent to the definition of the cost of capital in the absence of risk (2.8). Clearly, the last two terms represent the risk premium in the presence of tax. For $\mathrm{cov}(\tilde{c}_{t+1}, \tilde{p}^T) > 0$, the additional risk associated with the financial return increases the required expected return, as in the absence of tax. If $\mathrm{cov}(\tilde{c}_{t+1}, \tilde{K}) > 0$, then $\mu > 0$, and this implies that the last term, generated by the capital risk, also increases the required expected return.

Leaving this last term aside, consider the relationship between $\lambda$ and $\lambda^T$. This depends on the relationship between $\tilde{p}$ and $\tilde{p}^T$, where each is defined for a marginal investment; that is, an investment earning $\tilde{p}$ is marginal in the absence of tax, and an investment earning $\tilde{p}^T$ is marginal in the presence of tax. In the absence of risk, these are scalars that can easily be compared. However, in the presence of risk, any comparison must take into account the whole distribution of each return.

To see this, consider the case of a simple linear relationship:

$$\tilde{p}^T = a + b\tilde{p}, \tag{2.29}$$

where $a$ and $b$ are scalars. For any value of $b$ it is possible to find a value of $a$ such that $\tilde{p}$ represents a marginal investment in the absence of tax, and $\tilde{p}^T$ represents a marginal investment in the presence of tax. Specifically this holds for any combination of $a$ and $b$ for which

$$b = \frac{(1-A)}{(1-\tau)} - \frac{a}{r} + \frac{(1+r)}{r}\frac{(\tau - A)}{(1-\tau)}V[\tilde{\delta}]. \tag{2.30}$$

This implies that $b$ can take any value. This is important, as the implication of (2.29) is that in the presence of tax the risk premium is

$$\lambda^T = b\lambda. \tag{2.31}$$

To see the implications of this, consider two special cases. To simplify, let the depreciation rate be nonstochastic so that $\mu = 0$; this has no impact on the main results:

(a)   $b = 1 \Rightarrow a = \left(\dfrac{\tau - A}{1 - \tau}\right)\{r + (1 + r)\delta\}.$

In this case the cost of capital is

$$R = 0 \Rightarrow E(\tilde{p}^T) = \frac{(1 - A)}{(1 - \tau)}\{r + \delta\} - \delta + \lambda. \tag{2.32}$$

Here the risk premium is identical that in the absence of tax. The risk-free element of the cost of capital is grossed up by the factor $(1 - A)/(1 - \tau)$, but the risk premium is unchanged. Since the risk premium is likely to be considerably larger than the risk-free rate of interest, the tax has only a small impact on the overall cost of capital.[12]

(b)   $b = \dfrac{1 - A}{1 - \tau} \Rightarrow a = \left(\dfrac{\tau - A}{1 - \tau}\right)(1 + r)\delta.$

In this case the cost of capital is

$$R = 0 \Rightarrow E(\tilde{p}^T) = \frac{(1 - A)}{(1 - \tau)}\{r + \lambda + \delta\} - \delta. \tag{2.33}$$

This is a quite different case, since the risk premium is grossed up by the same factor as the risk-free rate, $(1 - A)/(1 - \tau)$.

In analyzing the impact of taxes on the cost of capital in the presence of risk, it is therefore vital to specify the distribution of returns from available investments. Expression (2.32) says that only the risk-free rate of return need be grossed up as long as the risk of the marginal project in the presence of tax is the same as the risk of the marginal project in the absence of tax. However, this is a special case. Expression (2.33) presents another special case in which both the risk-free rate of return and the risk premium must be grossed up by the same factor.

There is no obvious way to choose between these approaches, or indeed, between these and any other assumption made about the value of $b$. Given that the impact of tax as measured by the effect on the cost of capital depends on an arbitrary assumption about the distribution of returns for investments that are marginal in the presence and absence of tax, then arguably it would be better to use another approach altogether.

In principle, we need a measure that is independent of the relative risk of the two projects, which are marginal either in the presence or absence of tax. One possibility, proposed by Devereux (2003), is to consider the current market value of the before-tax stochastic cash flows of a marginal investment project.[13] Suppose that in the absence of tax, a marginal project has stochastic cash flows with a current market value of $V^*$. In the presence of tax, a project with the same initial costs has before-tax stochastic flows with a current market value of $V$. There is an infinite set of pairs of expected before-tax rates of return and risk premia that generate a current market value of $V$. However, if the project is marginal, then the current market value of its after-tax stochastic flows must be equal to $V^*$. An effective marginal tax rate can therefore be defined from $V(1 - e) = V^*$, or $e = (V - V^*)/V$. This measure is independent of the risk characteristics of the two projects. However, while this approach is helpful in identifying the characteristics of various tax systems, it is not easily applied in empirical work.

### 2.4.5   A Model Firm Approach

One criticism of the approach set out in section 2.3, and discussed at length in this section is that it typically makes very simple assumptions regarding the nature of the firm's activities. For example, it typically deals with only the most rudimentary elements of the tax regime, and it does not model other costs involved in making an incremental investment.

Of course, this is a criticism of practice rather than theory. In principle, there is no reason why any well-specified investment project could not be modeled, with the ensuing tax liabilities—calculated at any chosen level of sophistication—used to generate estimates of effective tax rates. There is a trade-off, however; the more specialized the investment project, and the more specialized the nature of the tax regime, then the less general will be the ensuing effective tax rates.

An example of an approach that takes the literature in this direction is the European Tax Analyser model (Jacobs and Spengel 1996, 2002), which extends the model firm approach of OECD (1985). The basic idea is to generate a detailed model of a hypothetical firm that incorporates a large number of accounting items from the balance sheet and profit and loss account. For example, the assets in the model include intangible assets, three types of tangible fixed assets, three types of financial assets, inventories, and trade debtors. As well as the elements of the tax mentioned above, this model incorporates the rules for valuing inventories, the taxation of corporate capital gains, employee pension schemes, provisions for bad debts, and loss relief.

Within this framework, one approach would be to explicitly model an incremental investment of the form described in section 2.3, though in rather more detail. The basic approach in section 2.3 could be used to generate the same measures of effective marginal and average tax rates.

This is quite similar to the approach actually taken by the authors. However, they make assumptions about the whole range of activities of the hypothetical firm over a ten-year life span. In effect they compute the NPV of net income generated in the presence and absence of tax.[14] They use the difference between these two values to generate a measure akin to the effective average tax rate described in section 2.3. The main difference, in principle, between the two approaches is that the ensuing effective tax rate is the relevant effective tax rate only if the whole ten-year life of the firm is seen as a specific investment decision, that is, one of a number of mutually discrete opportunities available to the firm at the outset. For example, if the firm had a specific ten-year investment, which could be undertaken in one of two countries, then the effective tax rate computed would be the relevant measure in the decision of in which country to locate.

While this approach, in principle, takes into account much more detailed analysis of the firm, it also necessarily needs to make some very specific assumptions. One, for example, is the role of the cost of labor, and specifically the incidence of wage taxes and relief for pension contributions. Holding the gross wage cost to be constant across countries implies strong assumptions about effective incidence.

## 2.5   Other Approaches

While the previous two sections have set out many of the issues arising in attempting to construct measures of effective tax rates based on the basic theoretical model, much of the empirical literature has taken a completely different approach. This approach is not to identify cash flows associated with any specific type of investment but rather to look at the ratio of tax payments to some measure of capital income in a single period.

Such an approach can take many forms. Empirical work using individual firms, for example, has used accounting ratios as a measure of an effective tax rate. For example, Kemsley (1998), Altshuler et al. (2001), and Grubert and Mutti (2000), all follow this type of approach in considering cross-border investment. At a more aggregated level, a similar approach has been used with industry or national level data. For example, Grubert and Mutti (1991), Hines and Rice (1994), and Swenson (1994) all use US data on the aggregate activities of affiliates of multinational companies. Such data permit the derivation of a measure of an effective tax rate for, say, the affiliates of US firms operating in another country.

At a more aggregated level still, measures have been derived using aggregate tax revenue in a given year as a ratio of some measure of capital income. The most well-known work advocating such an approach is that by Mendoza et al. (1994). This approach splits all tax revenues in a country into three categories: taxes on consumption, labor, and capital. The last of these is divided by the operating surplus of the economy to generate a form of effective tax rate on capital.

Such measures certainly have some advantages over the measures discussed in previous sections. Given data on tax payments and some measure of capital income, they are relatively easy to compute. Such data are fairly readily available for a large number of countries and time periods; by contrast, it is much harder to collect reliable data on provisions of the tax regimes in some countries.

In addition data specifically on tax payments (or liabilities) automatically weight different activities according to their contribution to taxable income—for example, investment in different types of asset and using different forms of finance. They also reflect a wide range of provisions of tax regimes that cannot easily be taken into account in basing measures on tax rules. These include a large number of special features of tax regimes, as well as features of the international tax system. There is a problem with international activity, however. That is, company accounts may record the worldwide profits and tax liabilities of the firm; these may not reflect the tax regime of any one country.[15]

However, an important question in using such measures is what they are actually measuring. To begin to answer this, consider this form of tax rate applied to the simple model of the firm analysed in section 2.3. Expression (2.3) implies that the taxes paid by the firm in period $t$ are

$$T_t = \tau\{F(K_{t-1}) - iB_{t-1} - \phi_t K_{t-1}^T\}. \tag{2.34}$$

A typical measure of accounting profit would be

$$\Pi_t = F(K_{t-1}) - iB_{t-1} - \delta K_{t-1}, \tag{2.35}$$

where $\delta$ is here assumed to be the accounting rate of depreciation as well as the true economic rate of depreciation. It is also assumed here, for simplicity, that assets cannot be depreciated for tax purposes in the year in which they are purchased.

A typical accounting measure of an average tax rate is $Z_t = T_t/\Pi_t$. It is clear from (2.34) and (2.35) that in the special case where the allowance rate in the tax system is equal to that in the accounts (and always has been, so that $K_{t-1} = K_{t-1}^T$), this rate is equal to the statutory rate, $Z_t = \tau$. In a sense this is obvious; tax revenue is defined by multiplying taxable profit by the statutory rate; dividing tax revenue by taxable profit (as in this case) yields the statutory rate.

But this observation begs two important questions. The first concerns the measure of income that is used to scale the tax liability. The second concerns the relationship with either of the measures generated from the theory and described above. We discuss each of these in turn.

### 2.5.1   An Alternative Measure of Income

First, suppose $Z_t \neq \tau$. What does this tell us? In the simple model outlined here, and with a stable tax system, this implies that $\phi \neq \delta$ and hence $K_{t-1} \neq K_{t-1}^T$. In countries where the capital allowance rate is fixed by legislation, this is quite likely to be the case.

But the interpretation is important. Using $Z_t$ as an effective tax rate implicitly assumes that $\Pi_t$ is, in some sense, a "true" measure of profit. If $Z_t \neq \tau$, then the implication is that the tax base is deliberately too large or too small. This clearly may be the case. But another interpretation is possible. Suppose that the government designs its tax system to identify the right level of profit as precisely as possible. It defines capital allowance rates in legislation precisely because accounting profits can be manipulated: a firm may use low depreciation rates in order to boost profits. In this case, the measure of taxable profit might be more reliable. If $Z_t \neq \tau$, then accounting profits may be incorrectly measured.

In the context of effective tax rates based on company accounts, such an argument may not be completely convincing. Each firm is different, and each has a different mix of assets. Given proper accounting standards, it is hard for firms to consistently manipulate their profits. A tax regime that does not allow a great deal of flexibility in determining profits may be more likely to incorrectly assess profit. However, the argument may be more convincing for other data sources. For example, national accounts typically use arbitrary measures of depreciation. Here the tax regime might define the level of profit in the economy more accurately than official statisticians.

But the general point is clear: unless we are confident of the base of the effective tax rate measure, it is hard to interpret the case where $Z_t \neq \tau$. To some extent, similar problems arise in computing the effective tax rates defined in sections 2.3 and 2.4. They too depend on assumptions about the true economic depreciation rate, and where no depreciation rate is observed, the researcher must choose a value. However, these measures at least provide a more reliable basis for comparison across countries and time. That is, the hypothetical investment studied above can be held constant across different tax regimes, in order to compute effective tax rates. If the tax rate is based on an observed valuation of profit, then there may be differences in measurement practices, say between countries (e.g., because of differences in accounting standards), that result in a misleading comparison of effective tax rates.

### 2.5.2   Comparison with Effective Rates Implied by Theory

The second important question is, even if we trust the base of the effective tax rate measure, do we learn anything about investment incentives? There are two parts to this question, corresponding to analysis based on the cost of capital and marginal investment projects, and analysis of discrete choices.

#### An Observable Effective Average Tax Rate?

We begin with a comparison with the effective average tax rate of section 2.3, on the ground that the tax rates described here seem more akin to an average rather than a marginal rate. Taking the definition of $\alpha$ in (2.14), and ignoring personal taxes and inflation, we can write the effective average tax rate[16]

$$\alpha = \tau + \frac{\tau(\delta - \phi)}{p} \times \frac{r}{r + \phi}. \tag{2.36}$$

To make a direct comparison with $Z$ as defined above, ignore debt, normalize the end of period $t - 1$ capital stock to unity, and write $F(K_{t-1}) = p + \delta$. In this case

$$Z_t = \tau + \frac{\tau(\delta - \phi)}{p} K_{t-1}^T. \tag{2.37}$$

There is a special case where these two measures are identical: $\phi = \delta$, which implies that $K_{t-1}^T = r/(r + \phi)$ and hence $\alpha = Z_t = \tau$. However, this simply returns us to the case where taxable profit is equal to accounting profit; this case is so special, in fact, that the effective marginal tax rate is also equal to $\tau$.

In general, however, these definitions are very different from each other, despite the strong assumptions used to make them this comparable. In particular, $K_{t-1}^T$ depends on the past history of investment. For example, if the firm's investment has grown at rate $g$ in every period, then (continuing to set $K_{t-1} = 1$)

$$K_{t-1}^T = \frac{g + \delta}{g + \phi}. \tag{2.38}$$

Even in the simplest conditions, without debt or personal taxes, then, these two concepts of the average tax rate are very different from each other. For there to be a positive value of $g$ that makes these two measures equal to each other, $\delta$ would need to be much smaller than $r$.

This should not be surprising. The effective average tax rate defined in section 2.3 is a forward-looking concept applied to a well-specified investment project. The average tax rate defined as the ratio of current tax liabilities to current profit depends on both the history of investment and the history of the tax system.

### An Observable Effective Marginal Tax Rate?
In general, it should be clear that $Z_t$ does not correspond to an effective marginal tax rate. For one thing, it can be applied to any project, and not just a marginal one. However, Gordon et al. (in chapter 4 of this volume) propose a new method of generating a measure of an effective marginal tax rate based on the use of observable tax revenues. The

basic idea is to compare revenue generated under the actual tax regime with revenue that would have been generated under a regime that taxed only economic rent.[17]

To understand this approach, it is useful to return to the simple investment analyzed in section 2.3. Ignoring personal taxes and inflation, for simplicity, write the value in period $t + 1$ of all taxes associated with the investment as[18]

$$T = \tau(p + \delta) - A(r + \delta). \tag{2.39}$$

By contrast, a tax based solely on economic rent would generate tax payments with a period $t + 1$ value of

$$E = \tau(p - r). \tag{2.40}$$

This would be true of any tax based on economic rent generated over the life of the project. The difference between these two is

$$T - E = (\tau - A)(r + \delta). \tag{2.41}$$

Returning to the expression for the cost of capital in (2.8), in the absence of inflation and personal taxes, we can easily show that

$$\hat{p} - r = \frac{(\tau - A)(r + \delta)}{1 - \tau} = \frac{T - E}{1 - \tau}. \tag{2.42}$$

As a result we can construct an effective marginal tax rate as

$$\varepsilon = \frac{\hat{p} - r}{\hat{p}} = \frac{T - E}{T - E + (1 - \tau)r}. \tag{2.43}$$

The proposal by Gordon et al. (chapter 4 of this volume) is to construct this measure of the effective marginal tax rate as follows: (1) observe actual tax revenues $T$ in some period, (2) construct an estimate of $E$ for the same period, and (3) adjust using $\tau$ and $r$ as in (2.43). Their proposal is more detailed than described here though; it allows for personal taxes and taxes on unincorporated businesses.

An important advantage of such a measure is that it uses the observable data discussed above. However, there is a disadvantage to using data in any given period—even if an average is taken over several years. To see this, it is only necessary to observe that the derivation above used all the tax payments generated by the investment discounted to their period $t + 1$ value. But in this measure the timing of tax payments matters. To see this, compare the tax profiles of two tax systems, both levied on economic rent. A cash flow tax generates tax payments of

Period $t$:        $T_t^{CF} = -\tau,$

Period $t + 1$:   $T_{t+1}^{CF} = \tau(1 + p).$

A tax based on economic rent as it accrues would generate tax payments of

Period $t$:        $T_t^{AR} = 0,$

Period $t + 1$:   $T_{t+1}^{AR} = \tau(p - r).$

Although these two systems generate the same net present value of tax payments, they have very different profiles. Suppose, for example, that the actual tax is a cash flow tax but that the tax on accrued economic rent is used as the benchmark tax. Then, in the absence of any other activity within the firm, the Gordon et al. (chapter 4 of this volume) measure would generate an effective tax rate of $\tau/(1 - \tau)r$ in period $t$ and $-\tau(1 + r)/(1 - \tau)r$ in period $t + 1$. After discounting, these sum to zero, as expected. This result suggests that, in practice, careful use should be made of the measure, in particular, in the way in which the effective tax rate varies over time.

## 2.6   Conclusions and Reflections on the Use of Alternative Measures

In this chapter I have reviewed alternative approaches to measuring the taxation of income from capital. The discussion focused on measures designed to capture the effects of taxation on economic decisions that determine the size and composition of the capital stock. I have not discussed issues of effective incidence, except to the extent of making assumptions as to which specific taxes to study.

The main focus of the chapter has been on the measures derived from economic theory. In empirical work, these tend to be based on the legal parameters of tax regimes, rather than on observed tax revenues or tax liabilities (the GKS measure is arguably an exception). My basic model yields two measures, reflecting two alternative forms of investment decision. An effective marginal tax rate is relevant for decisions concerning the scale of the capital stock, and an effective average tax rate is relevant for discrete investment choices.

As with any economic model, a central question is whether measures derived from the model accurately reflect the complexities of the real world. Section 2.4 was devoted to extensions of the basic model setup in section 2.3, in order to investigate some of the more complex characteristics both of investments and of tax regimes. Particular attention was paid to the role of personal taxes, the source of finance of the investment, the extent to which taxes on foreign direct investment are modeled, the risk of the investment, and the extent to which more complex models of firm behavior are incorporated.

A review of the basic modeling approaches, however, cannot ultimately decide how useful different measures are. Such a question can only be answered empirically. Since we do not know the "true" values of these measures, it is difficult to assess the measures simply by examining the estimated series. Some progress might be made through empirical evidence that actual investment behavior responds to changes in particular measures.

In the last section of the chapter, I examined the popular approach of deriving empirical measures of effective tax rates based on observed tax revenues or tax liabilities. Typically these measures are not based on a theoretical model of investment. Researchers have used such measures in part because they are relatively easily available. But easy availability is not a very good criterion for selecting a measure—especially a measure not derived from a theoretical model. The usefulness of such measures therefore depends on whether they end up being at least as correlated with the underlying "true" measure as the more sophisticated measures based on economic theory.

In some instances this may be the case. For example, in examining tax rates on cross border investment, measures based on the parameters of the legal tax regime may not capture the possibilities available for shifting profit between jurisdictions. In this case, it is possible that measures based on observed tax revenues could be closer to "true" values.

But, in general, such ad hoc measures should be treated with considerable caution. A typical "average" tax rate is likely to be a poor approximation of an effective marginal tax rate, as it is does not capture investment incentives at the margin. It is even likely to be a poor approximation to an effective average tax rate because it is based on historic data, rather than matching the forward-looking nature of an investment project. The performance of such measures in empirical models of investment is also more difficult to assess. This is because the measures themselves depend on the scale and nature of investment and are hence endogenous. Dealing with such endogeneity can prove to be very difficult.

It is not even clear that such measures dominate using the statutory tax rate, at least as an approximation to an effective average tax rate. The measure of the effective tax rates derived in section 2.3 varies according to the rate of profit earned on the investment project, but in the absence of personal taxes, it converges to the statutory corporation tax rate as the rate of profit rises. We might therefore expect the effective average tax rate to be positively correlated with the statutory tax rate. This may not always be true of ad hoc measures.

One important empirical issue is whether the measures described in this chapter yield very different measures of taxation. Suppose that the differences examined here turn out to be small empirically. Then we might generate the reassuring conclusion that any of these measures is likely to be a good approximation of "true" tax rates. If this were true, we could simply use the most convenient measure. This question is explored by Devereux and Klemm (chapter 3 of this volume). Unfortunately for empirical researchers, there is little evidence in favor of this reassuring conclusion. It *does* matter how measures of tax rates are constructed. Choosing between them is then ultimately a matter of judgment, taking into account the correspondence with theory, and the correspondence with the real world.

### Appendix: Definitions of Variables

| | |
|---|---|
| $V_t$ | Market value of the equity of the firm at the end of period $t$ |
| $D_t$ | Cash dividends paid by the firm at the end of period $t$ |
| $N_t$ | New equity issued by the firm at the end of period $t$ |
| $K_t$ | Capital stock at the end of period $t$ |
| $I_t$ | Investment in period $t$ |
| $F(K_{t-1})$ | Net output generated at the end of period $t$ |
| $B_t$ | One-period debt issued at the end of period $t$ |
| $r$ | Real rate of interest |
| $i$ | Nominal rate of interest |
| $\pi$ | Inflation rate in price of output |
| $\pi^K$ | Inflation rate in price of capital |
| $q_t$ | Relative price of capital goods at the end of period $t$ |
| $\delta$ | Economic depreciation rate |

| | |
|---|---|
| $\tau$ | Statutory corporation tax rate |
| $\phi$ | Capital allowance rate |
| $K_t^T$ | Value of the capital stock for tax purposes at the end of period $t$ |
| $A$ | Present value of allowances per unit of investment |
| $\rho$ | Nominal, tax adjusted, discount rate |
| $\gamma$ | Tax discrimination variable |
| $m$ | Personal tax rate on interest income |
| $m^D$ | Personal tax rate on dividend income |
| $c$ | Tax credit on dividend income |
| $z$ | Personal effective capital gains tax rate |
| $p$ | Pre-tax rate of return on investment |
| $\hat{p}$ | Cost of capital |
| $e$ | Effective marginal tax rate |
| $R^*$ | Net present value of investment project in the absence of tax |
| $R$ | Net present value of investment project in the presence of tax |
| $\alpha$ | Effective average tax rate |
| $\hat{\alpha}$ | Alternative measure of effective average tax rate |
| $t$ | Statutory corporation tax rate, adjusted for personal taxes |
| $H$ | One-period average tax rate |
| $F$ | Net present value of financial flows |
| $\tilde{m}$ | Stochastic discount factor |
| $\tilde{x}$ | Stochastic cash flow |
| $c_t$ | Consumption in period $t$ |
| $u(c_t)$ | Utility in period $t$ |
| $\beta$ | Rate of time preference |
| $c^*$ | Cost of capital in the absence of tax, but in the presence of risk |
| $\tilde{p}^T$ | Stochastic financial return in the presence of tax |
| $\lambda$ | Risk premium in the absence of tax |
| $\lambda^T$ | Risk premium in the presence of tax |
| $\mu$ | Premium for capital risk |
| $\Pi_t$ | Accounting profit in period $t$ |
| $Z_t$ | Average tax rate based on accounting data |
| $T$ | Tax payments associated with investment project |
| $E$ | Tax payments on investment project generated by a tax on economic rent |
| $\varepsilon$ | Measure of effective marginal tax rate; see Gordon et al. (chapter 4 of this volume) |

# Notes

I thank participants at the CESifo conference, two anonymous referees, and Peter Birch Sørensen for helpful comments and advice. The chapter draws on joint research, especially with Rachel Griffith.

1. Some attempts have been made to incorporate other taxes into the type of measures discussed here. See, for example, McKenzie, Mintz, and Scharf (1997).

2. Note that the formulation (2.5) applies only to a specific form of depreciation allowances. Other forms are also used; in addition there may be investment tax credits. However, all of these can be incorporated into a more general formulation of $A$, and do not change the general formulation (2.6).

3. Note that this is not the only possible formulation of the impact of taxes on the marginal investment decision. An alternative approach, and equivalent in theory, is to work with marginal $q$. See, for example, Poterba and Summers (1983).

4. See Mintz (1990) for an analysis of tax holidays.

5. This is explored, for example, by Devereux (1987) and Robson (1989). Cross-sectional variation in the cost of capital resulting from such asymmetries is exploited in models of investment in Devereux (1989) and Devereux et al. (1994).

6. A number of models of multinational firm behavior are based on this type of approach. See, for example, Horstman and Markusen (1992) and Motta (1992).

7. The company may decide at some preliminary stage to build, for example, a factory. However, the size of the factory may depend on the tax regime in the country in which it is built.

8. More details can be found in Devereux and Griffith (2003). Note that in the absence of personal taxes, $t = \tau$.

9. Of course, it is also possible to consider investment in noncorporate form. This is not pursued in this chapter.

10. The literature is too vast to give even a representative flavor. However, some useful references are Harris and Raviv (1991), Hart (1995), and Hubbard (1998).

11. They consider an investment that lasts forever, although with an exponentially declining product.

12. This is the result found by Gordon (1985) and Bulow and Summers (1984). Implicitly, then, they assume that the underlying risk of the two marginal projects is the same.

13. An alternative would be to use the certainty equivalent of the return.

14. Actually the end-of-year-10 value is computed, but this is effectively the same.

15. Further discussion of this point is contained in Devereux and Klemm (chapter 3 of this volume).

16. This uses $A = \tau\phi/(r + \phi)$ and represents the case where there is no inflation and where no depreciation allowance is permitted in the year in which the investment is incurred. I assume this here in order to make a simpler comparison between the two forms of tax rate.

17. Gordon and Slemrod (1983) and Gordon et al. (2003) use this approach to analyse the extent to which the United States collects more revenue that it would under such a tax.

18. This includes any allowances claimed in any other period, converted into a period $t + 1$ value.

# References

Altshuler, R., H. Grubert, and T. S. Newlon. 2001. Has US investment abroad become more sensitive to tax rates? In J. R. Hines, ed., *International Taxation and Multinational Activity*. Chicago: University of Chicago Press.

Alworth, J. 1988. *The Finance, Investment and Taxation Decision of Multinationals*. Cambridge, MA: Blackwell.

Auerbach, A. J. 1979. Wealth maximization and the cost of capital. *Quarterly Journal of Economics* 21: 107–27.

Boadway, R. W. 1987. The theory and measurement of effective tax rates. In J. M. Mintz and D. D. Purvis, eds., *The Impact of Taxation on Business Activity*. Kingston, Ontario: John Deutsch Institute for the Study of Economic Policy, pp. 61–98.

Boadway, R. W., N. Bruce, and J. M. Mintz. 1984. Taxation, inflation and the marginal tax rate on capital in Canada. *Canadian Journal of Economics* 15: 278–93.

Bulow, J. I., and L. H. Summers. 1984. The taxation of risky assets. *Journal of Political Economy* 92: 20–39.

Cochrane, J. H. 2001. *Asset Pricing*. Princeton: Princeton University Press.

Devereux, M. P. 1987. Taxation and the cost of capital: The UK experience. *Oxford Review of Economic Policy* 3: 17–32.

Devereux, M. P. 1989. Tax asymmetries, the cost of capital and investment. *Economic Journal* 99: 103–12.

Devereux, M. P. 2003. Taxing risky investment. Discussion Paper 4053. London: CEPR.

Devereux, M. P., and R. Griffith. 1998a. Taxes and the location of production: Evidence from a panel of US multinationals. *Journal of Public Economics* 68(3): 335–67.

Devereux, M. P., and R. Griffith. 1998b. The taxation of discrete investment choices. Institute for Fiscal Studies Working Paper 16.

Devereux, M. P., and R. Griffith. 2003. Evaluating tax policy for location decisions. *International Tax and Public Finance* 10: 107–26.

Devereux, M. P., M. J. Keen, and F. Schiantarelli. 1994. Corporation tax asymmetries and investment: Evidence from UK panel data. *Journal of Public Economics* 53: 395–418.

Devereux, M. P., L. Lammersen, and C. Spengel. 2000. *The Effective Levels Of Company Taxation In The Member States Of The EU*. Brussels: European Commission.

Edwards, J. S. S., and M. J. Keen. 1984. Wealth maximization and the cost of capital: A comment. *Quarterly Journal of Economics* 98: 211–14.

Gordon, R. H. 1985. Taxation of corporate capital income: Tax revenues versus tax distortions. *Quarterly Journal of Economics* 100: 1–26.

Gordon, R., and J. Slemrod. 1988. Do we collect any tax revenue from taxing capital income? *Tax Policy and the Economy* 2: 89–130.

Gordon, R., L. Kalambokidis, and J. Slemrod. 2003. Do we *now* collect any tax revenue from taxing capital income? *Journal of Public Economics* 88: 981–1009.

Grubert, H., and J. Mutti. 1991. Taxes, tariffs and transfer pricing in multinational corporate decision making. *Review of Economics and Statistics* 73: 285–93.

Grubert, H., and J. Mutti. 2000. Do taxes influence where US corporations invest? *National Tax Journal* 37: 475–88.

Hall, R. E., and D. Jorgenson. 1967. Tax policy and investment behavior. *American Economic Review* 57: 391–414.

Harris, M., and A. Raviv. 1991. The theory of capital structure. *Journal of Finance* 46: 297–355.

Hart, O. 1995. *Firms, Contracts and Financial Structure*. Oxford: Oxford University Press.

Hines, J. R., and E. Rice. 1994. Fiscal paradise: Foreign tax havens and American business. *Quarterly Journal of Economics* 109: 149–82.

Horstmann, I., and J. Markusen. 1992. Endogenous market structures in international trade (*natura facit saltum*). *Journal of International Economics* 32: 109–29.

Hubbard, R. G. 1998. Capital market imperfections and investment. *Journal of Economic Literature* 36: 193–225.

Jacobs, O. H., and C. Spengel. 1996. *European Tax Analyser*. Baden-Baden: Nomos.

Jacobs, O. H., and C. Spengel. 2002. *Effective Tax Burden in Europe*. ZEW Economic Studies 15. Heidelberg: Phyica-Verlag.

Jorgenson, D. W. 1963. Capital theory and investment behaviour. *American Economic Review* 53: 247–59.

Keen, M. J. 1991. Corporation tax, foreign direct investment and the single market. In L. A. Winters and A. J. Venables, eds., *The Impact of 1992 on European Trade and Industry*. Cambridge: Cambridge University Press.

Kemsley, D. 1998. The effect of taxes on production location. *Journal of Accounting Research* 36: 321–41.

King, M. A. 1974. Taxation, investment and the cost of capital. *Review of Economic Studies* 41: 21–35.

King, M. A., and D. Fullerton. 1984. *The Taxation of Income from Capital: A Comparative Study of the United States, the United Kingdom, Sweden and West Germany*. Chicago: University of Chicago Press.

McKenzie, K. J., J. M. Mintz, and K. A. Scharf. 1997. Measuring effective tax rates in the presence of multiple inputs: A production based approach. *International Tax and Public Finance* 4: 337–59.

Mendoza, E. G., A. Razin, and L. L. Tesar. 1994. Effective tax rates in macroeconomics: Cross-country estimates of tax rates on factor incomes and consumption. *Journal of Monetary Economics* 34: 297–323.

Miller, M. H. 1977. Debt and taxes. *Journal of Finance* 32: 261–75.

Mintz, J. M. 1990. Corporate tax holidays and investment. *World Bank Economic Review* 4: 81–102.

Modigliani, F., and M. H. Miller. 1958. Cost of capital, corporation finance and the theory of investment. *American Economic Review* 48: 261–97.

Motta, M. 1992. Multinational firms and the tariff-jumping argument: A game theoretic analysis with some unconventional conclusions. *European Economic Review* 36: 1557–71.

OECD. 1985. *Two Reports by the Committee on Fiscal Affairs on Quantitative Aspects of Corporate Taxation*. Paris: OECD.

OECD. 1991. *Taxing Profits in a Global Economy: Domestic and International Issues*. Paris: OECD.

Poterba, J. M., and L. H. Summers. 1983. Dividend taxes, corporate investment and Q. *Journal of Public Economics* 22: 135–67.

Robson, M. H. 1989. Measuring the cost of capital when taxes are changing with foresight. *Journal of Public Economics* 40: 261–92.

Sørensen, P. B. 1990. Issues in the theory of international tax coordination. Bank of Finland Discussion Paper 4.

Swenson, D. L. 1994. The impact of US tax reform on foreign direct investment in the United States. *Journal of Public Economics* 54: 243–66.

# 3 Measuring Taxes on Income from Capital: Evidence from the United Kingdom

Michael P. Devereux and
Alexander Klemm

## 3.1 Introduction

Devereux (in chapter 2 of this volume) discusses a number of theoretical issues that arise in the measurement of taxes on income from capital. This chapter illustrates some of these issues in the context of the development of taxes in the United Kingdom over the last three decades. In particular, we provide estimates for the United Kingdom for many of the measures discussed in chapter 2 by Devereux. In some cases we also provide alternative estimates of the same measure, based on differences in the underlying assumptions. For example, we provide estimates of effective tax rates with and without personal taxes, for alternative sources of finance, and for investments in different assets. We also deconstruct measures of average tax rates based on accounting data and tax revenue data, by investigating in more detail the factors that determine their values.

Since this is, in effect, a companion paper to chapter 2, we do not repeat the analysis there. The focus here is on quantitative differences between alternative measures. The central question is simple to state, although less simple to answer: How important, in practice, are differences between measures? That is, can empirical researchers pick a measure that is relatively easy to construct, secure in the knowledge that different measures typically generate similar values? Or, to put it another way, is the discussion of alternative ways of measuring taxes on income from capital simply an arcane debate, of little practical interest or use?

The evidence presented below indicates that different measures do indeed generate very different values. We do not go as far as testing alternative measures in, say, an econometric model of investment.[1] However, given the results presented below, it seems highly unlikely that similar econometric results would be generated by using the different measures; not only do the measures take different values, their movement over time is also quite different.

It is not surprising that some of these measures differ—after all they do not all attempt to measure the same thing. It is well known, for example, that a given tax regime may have high average rates but low marginal rates. What may be more surprising is that measures designed to capture the same aspect of the tax system can also vary widely. For example, average tax rates differ depending on whether they are constructed using aggregate tax revenue data, accounting data, or tax legislation. Such differences reflect, for example, whether the measure is forward-looking and whether, and how, different investment projects or firms are aggregated. This suggests that empirical work investigating the taxation of income from capital should take careful account of how those taxes are measured. Measures should be chosen on the basis of how well they conform to the underlying economic theory, and to taxation in practice. A measure chosen on the basis of how easy it is to construct may give misleading results.

We proceed in section 3.2 by presenting a summary of a number of different measures, corresponding to the main measures discussed in chapter 2. After comparing these broad measures, we investigate some of them in more detail. In particular, in section 3.3 we examine the impact of alternative assumptions on measures of effective marginal and average tax rates, derived for a hypothetical investment project along the lines of Devereux and Griffith (2003). In section 3.4, we turn to measures based on accounting data, using data on UK listed companies from Thomson Financial Datastream. In section 3.5, we analyze measures based on aggregate data on tax revenues and develop a measure based on income generated in the corporate sector of the economy only. We present brief conclusions in section 3.6.

## 3.2 A Brief Summary of Measures

We begin with a brief summary of alternative approaches, based on the analysis and classifications in chapter 2. Figure 3.1 presents a summary of five main approaches and table 3.1 presents pairwise correlation coefficients for the measures. Detailed descriptions of the derivation of each measure are provided in the appendix.

This figure reveals enormous variation across alternative measures of the tax rate on capital income. This is supported by the correlation

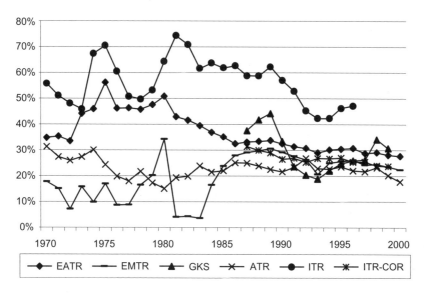

**Figure 3.1**
Overview of tax measures. *EATR*: Effective average tax (economic profit rate 20%; assets: weighted average of plant & machinery and land & buildings; source of finance: weighted average of equity and debt; interest and inflation rates: actual values). *EMTR*: Effective marginal tax rate (assets: weighted average of plant & machinery and land & buildings; source of finance: weighted average of equity and debt; interest and inflation rates: actual values). *GKS*: Effective marginal tax rate based on macroeconomic data, calculated as suggested by Gordon et al. (chapter 4 of this volume). *ATR*: Average tax rate based on company accounts data. *ITR*: Implicit tax rate for capital based on macroeconomic data as calculated by Mendoza et al. *ITR-COR*: Implicit tax rate based on macroeconomic data for corporate sector only.

coefficients, which are insignificantly different from zero for most pairs of measures, and even negative for some.[2] Some variation is due to fundamental differences in the approach taken, and some is due to differences in data. Before further analyzing these differences, we briefly explain assumptions used in figure 3.1.

• Effective marginal tax rate (EMTR)
• Effective average tax rate (EATR)

These two measures are shown for a general investment, using the approach set out in Devereux and Griffith (2003). Each effective tax rate reflects an investment that is partly in plant and machinery and partly in buildings, and it financed partly by new equity or retained earnings and partly by debt.[3] For the EATR we assume a rate of economic profit of 20 percent.[4] At this stage we exclude personal taxes; in effect this

**Table 3.1**
Coefficients of correlation between tax measures

|         | EATR      | EMTR     | GKS      | ATR      | ITR     | ITR-COR |
|---------|-----------|----------|----------|----------|---------|---------|
| EATR    | 1         |          |          |          |         |         |
|         | *31*      |          |          |          |         |         |
| EMTR    | −0.4386*  | 1        |          |          |         |         |
|         | *31*      | *31*     |          |          |         |         |
| GKS     | 0.6530*   | 0.7210*  | 1        |          |         |         |
|         | *13*      | *13*     | *13*     |          |         |         |
| ATR     | −0.1858   | −0.0787  | −0.1870  | 1        |         |         |
|         | *31*      | *31*     | *13*     | *32*     |         |         |
| ITR     | 0.4896*   | −0.2566  | 0.9334*  | −0.1894  | 1       |         |
|         | *27*      | *27*     | *10*     | *27*     | *27*    |         |
| ITR-COR | 0.8129*   | 0.6374*  | 0.5073   | 0.3833   | 0.7011* | 1       |
|         | *13*      | *13*     | *13*     | *13*     | *10*    | *13*    |

Notes: Numbers in italics indicate the number of observations. Starred values are significant at the 5 percent level. The data used start from 1970. Tax measures are the same as in figure 3.1.

could be seen as an overall effective tax rate for a non-tax-paying shareholder who does not receive any tax credit associated with dividend payments by UK companies. To make the effective tax rate measures more comparable to the others in figure 3.1, we allow the economic parameters to vary over time. That is, the values of the real interest rate and the inflation rate are based on actual values observed in each year. In addition the weights attributed to alternative assets and sources of finance also vary over time.[5] However, we assume a constant economic depreciation rate for each asset.[6]

• Average tax rate, based on company accounting records (ATR)

This measure is based on individual company accounting records taken from Datastream (more details are provided in section 3.4). The measure shown here is the UK corporation tax liability of the company expressed as a proportion of total before-tax profit (after interest payments and depreciation).

• Overall average tax rate on capital income, based on aggregate tax revenue data (ITR)

• Average tax rate of the corporate sector (ITR-COR)

The first of these is the measure proposed by Mendoza et al. (1994). It is based on the ratio of revenues from all taxes deemed to be on capital to a measure of the operating surplus of the economy. The second is a related measure developed in section 3.5. It uses a similar methodology but is restricted to the corporate sector of the economy; this makes it more comparable to the other measures. It is defined as corporation tax revenues divided by corporate income, including profits from financial property income.

• Marginal tax rate of the corporate sector (GKS)

This is the measure of the marginal tax rate proposed by Gordon et al. (chapter 4 of this volume). For comparison with the other measures, we exclude taxes levied at the personal level. This measure is based on the difference between actual tax revenue and the tax revenue that would be generated by an R-based cash flow tax levied in the corporate sector. To compute the latter, we make four adjustments to actual taxable income: (1) add back net interest payments, (2) add back capital allowances, (3) deduct new investment expenditures, and (4) deduct changes in inventories. The precise definitions used are set out in the Data Appendix at the end of this chapter.

As might be expected, the measures listed above give very different accounts of the development of taxes on capital income in the UK corporate sector over the last three decades. At the extreme, for example, in 1981 (in the depth of a recession), the EMTR was around 4 percent, while the Mendoza et al. (1994) approach—ITR—generated a rate of slightly under 75 percent. Of course, these two approaches are not attempting to measure the same thing: the first attempts to measure the impact of taxes on the cost of capital, while the second is based on tax revenues. It has long been known that marginal and average tax rates can be very different from each other. But these difference do imply that, for example, it could be seriously misleading to use the ITR as a measure of the impact of tax on investment at the margin.

Even measures that might be thought to be comparable are very different from each other. Compare, for example, the ITR and the accounting measure ATR. Both are measures of tax revenue—or liabilities—in a year, expressed as a proportion of before-tax income in the same year. Yet the values of ATR are much lower than those of ITR. Further they tend to move in opposite direction: the former tends to fall in recessions, while the latter tends to rise. In fact the correlation between these two series is negative: −0.24.

Both measures generate different values and patterns compared to the measure of the effective average tax rate (EATR). By contrast, the

EATR is more stable over the period analyzed. This reflects the fact that it is based on legal tax provisions rather than tax revenues. In particular, it tends to be reasonably close to the statutory tax rate. But this helps to pinpoint why the other two measures differ so much. Tax liabilities are equal to the statutory tax rate multiplied by the tax base. The evidence from figure 3.1 therefore suggests that the denominator of the ATR measure—accounting before-tax profits—tends to be higher than taxable income, while the denominator of the ITR measure tends to be smaller than taxable income.

Of course, this is not the whole explanation; the ITR measure relates to a wide range of taxes, and not just to corporation tax. For this reason we have used the aggregate data to develop an average tax rate measure for the corporate sector only (ITR-COR). This is more comparable to the other average tax rate measures, generally lying between the EATR and the ATR (we discuss it further in section 3.5).

There is some similarity in the two measures that are aimed at investigating marginal tax rates: the EMTR and GKS. They both rose during the 1980s to a peak around 1989 before falling back. However, the decline in GKS in the 1990s was more dramatic: from about 44 percent in 1989 to just below 19 percent in 1993. In the second half of the 1990s there was a partial recovery. The EMTR fell from around 31 percent but much more slowly. In general, this follows the pattern that the measures based on observed tax liabilities or revenues tend to be more volatile than the measures based on legal tax provisions.

One of the important policy issues relating to this analysis is whether increasing globalization is driving increasing tax competition among countries, and hence lower taxes on capital income. The European Commission (1997) has presented evidence (from the 1980s and first half of the 1990s) in favor of this view, based on a version of the ITR. As can be seen from figure 3.1, the ITR in the United Kingdom does indeed fall over that time period. There was also a fall in the EATR in the first half of the 1980s—when the statutory tax rate was cut from 52 to 35 percent—and a smaller fall thereafter (the statutory tax rate has subsequently been gradually cut to 30 percent).

However, the other measures in figure 3.1 do not support this view. The accounting measure ATR has remained reasonably stable since 1980, and if anything, has increased. The EMTR increased as a result of the 1984 reforms but has subsequently fallen a little. As noted above, the GKS measure has been quite volatile.

However, our aim here is not to evaluate whether taxes on capital income have fallen or not.[7] It is rather to compare alternative measures, try to identify the reasons for differences between them, and discuss how they might be best measured in practice. In order to address this, we now turn to a closer look at some of the main measures.

## 3.3  Effective Tax Rates

Much of the discussion in chapter 2 concerns the assumptions required to generate measures of effective marginal and average tax rates. In particular, chapter 2 raises issues concerning the role of personal taxes, alternative sources of finance, international taxes, and risk. In this chapter we will briefly summarize the impacts of different assumptions for the first two of these: personal taxes and alternative sources of finance.

To begin, though, we investigate the role played by alternative assumptions about the real interest rate and the inflation rate, and by assumptions about the weights corresponding to different assets and sources of finance used in the investment. In figure 3.1 we used actual rates in the United Kingdom to generate measures of both the effective marginal and average tax rates. This gives some indication of the actual effective rate in any particular year. However, it gives a less clear picture of the degree to which effective tax rates have changed as a result of deliberate tax reform, as opposed to changes in underlying economic circumstances.

To investigate this, in figure 3.2 we present series for the EATR and EMTR based on a constant real interest rate (10 percent) and constant inflation rate (3.5 percent). We also hold the weights reflecting the different forms of investment and finance constant over time. Variation in the resulting series therefore reflects only the impact of tax reforms. As can be seen from the figure, these two series correspond closely to those in figure 3.1 (which are reproduced here). The broad conclusions stated above are unchanged. Using constant values of these parameters removes much of the year-to-year volatility in the series, but the longer term movement is not affected.

In figure 3.3 we compute the same tax rates under the assumption that the relevant shareholder is a UK taxpayer who faces the highest rate of personal income tax and capital gains tax. Introducing personal taxes has several effects. Centrally, the required after-tax rate of return

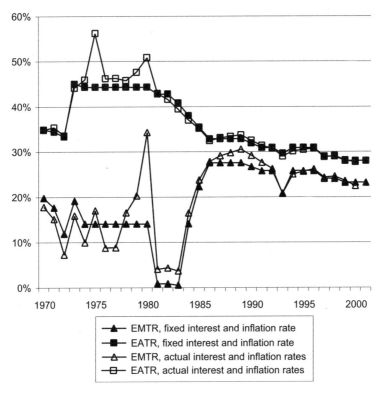

**Figure 3.2**
Effective tax rates, assuming fixed or actual inflation and interest. *EATR·* Effective average tax (economic profit rate 20%; assets: weighted average of plant & machinery and land & buildings; source of finance: weighted average of equity and debt; interest and inflation rates: as specified). *EMTR*: Effective marginal tax rate (assets: weighted average of plant & machinery and land & buildings; source of finance: weighted average of equity and debt; interest and inflation rates: as specified).

from an investment in equity falls, since the after-tax return from the alternative—assumed to be an interest-bearing deposit—also falls as (nominal) interest received is now taxed. The dividend stream is also taxed, but for much of the period analyzed, this tax was reduced by the tax credit available under the UK imputation system; in any case, dividend taxation is only relevant for investment financed by new equity. It should be noted that the top personal income tax rate was very high in the 1970s; in fact, including an investment income surcharge, the rate reached 98 percent between 1974 and 1978. It has since fallen considerably, and has been at 40 percent since the late 1980s.

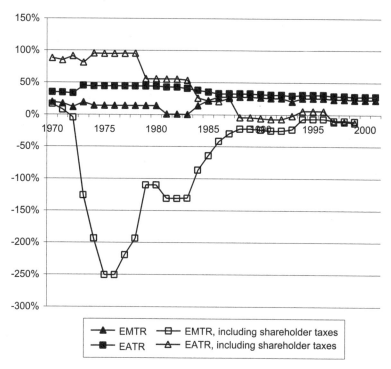

**Figure 3.3**
Effective tax rates, effect of including shareholder level taxes. *EATR*: Effective average tax (economic profit rate 20%; assets: weighted average of plant & machinery and land & buildings; source of finance: weighted average of equity and debt; interest and inflation rates: fixed). *EMTR*: Effective marginal tax rate (assets: weighted average of plant & machinery and land & buildings; source of finance: weighted average of equity and debt; interest and inflation rates: fixed).

Figure 3.3 is based on the case introduced in figure 3.2: the real interest rate, inflation rate, and weights are all fixed over time.

Introducing personal taxes has a dramatic effect on both the EATR and the EMTR.[8] The very high personal tax rates in the 1970s have a striking effect on the EMTR: because nominal interest income was taxed at very high rates, the real after-tax income from lending was negative.[9] As a result the required before-tax return from investment in equity is large and negative. As personal tax rates fell, so the EMTR rose. By the end of the period it is close to zero.

For the EATR, there are offsetting effects. As with the EMTR, the high taxation of interest implies a lower discount rate, which raises the net present value of an investment with a given before-tax return. This

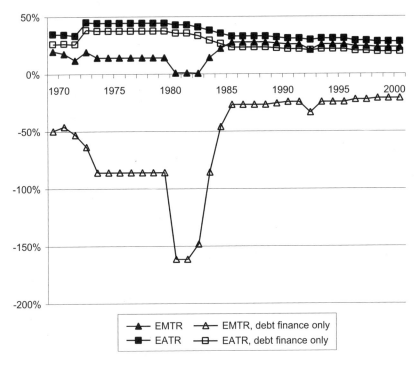

**Figure 3.4**
Effective tax rates, effect of debt finance. *EATR*: Effective average tax (economic profit
rate 20%; assets: weighted average of plant & machinery and land & buildings; source of
finance: weighted average of equity and debt unless specified otherwise; interest and
inflation rates: fixed). *EMTR*: Effective marginal tax rate (assets: weighted average of
plant & machinery and land & buildings; source of finance: weighted average of equity
and debt unless specified otherwise; interest and inflation rates: fixed).

tends to reduce the EATR, as it reduced the EMTR. However, offsetting
this, the return from the investment is also taxed at a higher level, reflecting the personal tax as well as the corporate tax; this second factor
plays a more significant role for an investment that is profitable than
for one that is marginal. Consequently the EATR could move in either
direction. In practice, in the presence of personal taxes, the EATR was
higher in the 1970s but fell at intervals through the period. By the 1990s
the EATR was lower than in the absence of personal taxes.

Figure 3.4 again reproduces the series based on fixed interest and inflation rates from figure 3.2. This time, however, we add a series calculated for investment financed only by debt. As might be expected, both
the EATR and the EMTR are lower in this case, since the impact of in-

terest deductibility is greater. However, the impact is noticeably different between the EMTR and the EATR. Since the latter is defined for a profitable investment, the impact of being allowed to deduct interest payments is fairly small, relative to the income generated from the investment. Hence, although there is some benefit, the EATR does not change very significantly. However, in the case of a marginal investment financed by debt, the effect of the deductibility of the interest payment is much more striking. In cases where depreciation allowances are close to 100 percent (in the early 1980s, this was true for buildings as well as for plant and machinery), the EMTR had large negative values.

In sum, these results confirm the results of other studies that the EMTR depends crucially on assumptions about personal taxes and about the source of finance for the hypothetical investment. The EATR also depends on these factors, although the effects are not as dramatic.

## 3.4 Accounting Data

A common approach in empirical work is to estimate measures of the taxation of income from capital using company accounting data. Such data are now fairly readily available in many countries. We make use of the data for all listed UK companies provided by Thomson Financial Datastream. These data are available from around 1969 onward. The dataset contains just under 3,000 firms. The number of observations per firm ranges from 1 to 32. In total, the dataset contains around 38,000 observations.

The typical approach is to take the ratio of tax liabilities to before-tax profit as specified in the profit and loss account. Chapter 2 analyzed such an approach, and compared it to the effective average tax rate described above. Clearly, there is a distinction, in principle, between the two approaches. The accounting ratio represents the impact of tax at a moment in time, and not over the life of a particular investment. Also it reflects the past history of the company and the tax regime, since many items are carried forward from one year to the next. Nevertheless, it is instructive to compare the two approaches, in practice, to identify whether they produce similar estimates of an average tax rate.

In using such data, however, many accounting issues need to be considered. First, profit is generally computed on an historic cost basis, which typically overstates true profit in periods of reasonably high inflation. But the tax system too is sensitive to inflation. Thus the average tax rate may reflect this distortion to measuring both accounting profit and taxable profit.

Second, most readily available datasets containing accounting records refer to consolidated accounts—and, in particular, include the consolidated accounts of multinational companies which reflect profits earned around the world and taxes paid around the world. It may be possible—and often is in the Datastream data—to identify separately home and foreign tax liabilities.[10] But it is more difficult to identify separately profit generated at home and abroad. Depending on the relative size of the foreign activities of the company, this may pose considerable problems. If, for example, we want to find a measure relating to the UK corporation tax, then we would want to include only UK tax and only UK profit. Including all profit would understate the UK tax rate. Including all taxes paid by the company would result in a measure that is contaminated by taxes paid elsewhere.

A third problem arises in that the published tax charge may not represent the company's current tax liability. Suppose, for example, that the tax regime is more generous than implied by accounting standards, since depreciation allowances are higher than accounting depreciation charges. Then in a period of investment, the recorded tax charge may exceed the actual tax liability, as accountants include a provision for additional tax to be paid in the future. At the extreme, the recorded tax provision may simply be the statutory rate multiplied by before-tax profit. Any difference between this and the actual tax liability could be regarded as deferred tax. Of course, in this case the tax rate generated using the recorded tax charge as a ratio of before-tax profit would therefore simply be the statutory tax rate.

We can largely avoid the third of these problems, since our data identify deferred tax. In the series shown in figure 3.1, we instead make use of an item that is closest to the full UK corporation tax charge.[11] This is divided by before-tax profit (after depreciation and interest payments) to generate the average tax rate measure.

For comparison, figure 3.5 shows this together with three other definitions of taxation:

*i.* UK corporation tax plus the overseas tax charge.

*ii.* Total tax charge as recorded in accounts (including deferred tax).

*iii.* UK corporation tax, less advance corporation tax (ACT) but adding back irrecoverable ACT.[12] This can be thought of as a measure of "mainstream" corporation tax before any income tax due on dividends.

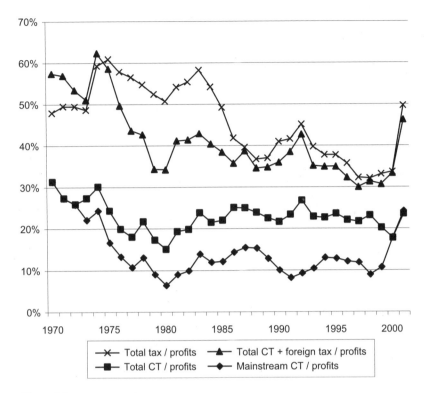

**Figure 3.5**
Accounting data average tax rates. The presented series are all variants of the *ATR*, the average tax rate based on accounting data. *CT* stands for corporation tax. The series presented in figure 3.1 corresponds to the series labeled "total *CT*/profits."

In each case, an average tax rate is formed by taking the ratio of the tax liability to before-tax profits. Because the four measures of the average tax rate in figure 3.5 are all calculated with reference to the same measure of before-tax profit, the differences between them reflect only differences in the measure of taxation. The differences are striking. First, in the early part of this period, the overseas tax charge was very high, at times even greater than the UK tax charge. Measure *i* therefore results in average tax rates of around 60 percent in the early 1970s. However, over time this measure declines substantially. Broadly, by the second half of the 1990s, the base case UK average tax rate was just over 20 percent, and including the overseas tax charge raised this to around 30 percent. Measure *ii*, including overseas tax and deferred tax, results in a similar pattern: very high tax rates in the early 1970s but dropping substantially over the period.

Although measure $i$ does not relate only to UK taxation, arguably it gives a clearer picture of the impact of worldwide taxes, since both the numerator and denominator relate to worldwide activities. Based on this measure, then, there appears to have been a striking decline in the average tax rate. By far the biggest part of this occurred in the 1970s.[13]

Measure $iii$ in the figure is close to mainstream corporation tax—before any income tax is charged to UK shareholders. As might be expected, this is much lower. It too fell in the 1970s, before partly recovering in the first half of the 1980s. In the 1990s it was fairly stable at around 10 percent of before-tax profit.

### 3.5 Measures Based on Macroeconomic Data

The main outlier in figure 3.1 is the overall average tax rate on capital income (ITR). This is based on a measure proposed by Mendoza et al. (1994). A similar series was calculated by Eurostat (1998)[14] and is presented alongside the Mendoza measure in figure 3.7. In 1970 this measure was at a very high rate of 77 percent. It moved considerably with the economic cycle in the 1970s, falling to 51 percent in 1977, but rising to 73 percent again in the recession of 1981. However, since 1981, it has fallen steadily to 32 percent in 1994, before rising again slightly. By the mid 1990s it was at a rate comparable to the statutory tax rate on retained earnings. It is this dramatic fall in the 1980s and early 1990s that drew the attention of the European Commission (1997). It is therefore worth examining this measure in some detail.

The basic approach of this measure is first to classify all taxes—including personal taxes on corporate source income—as being on labor, consumption, or capital.[15] The last of these categories is, in effect, a sweep-up category; it includes taxes on capital income, such as corporation tax, and taxes on property income, but it also includes inheritance taxes and gift taxes. To turn this into a tax rate, these tax revenues are divided by a measure of capital income, taken as the aggregate operating surplus of the economy.

Within the group of taxes on "capital," there are two large categories: corporate income taxes and taxes on ownership of land and property. There are a number of other smaller taxes grouped together. Figure 3.6a shows the overall development of these taxes over time, and figure 3.6b shows the development of each group of taxes, expressed as a proportion of GDP. Each of these groups has generated broadly similar revenue over the period, although all are fairly volatile.

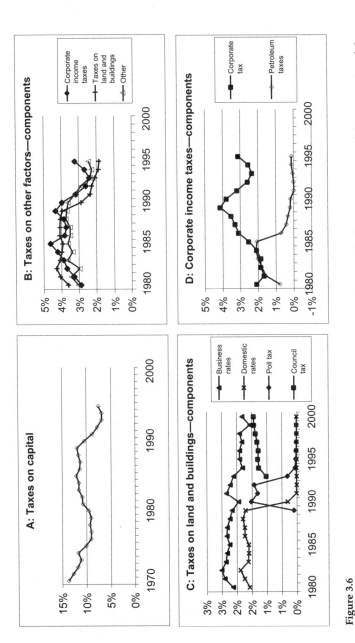

**Figure 3.6**
Analysis of the numerator of the Eurostat implicit capital tax rate. These panels show components of the numerator of the Eurostat (1998) implicit capital tax rate divided by GDP. Panel A shows the total numerator, and panel B splits this up into three components. Panel C splits taxes on land and buildings into subcomponents, and panel D splits corporate income taxes into subcomponents.

Noticeably revenue from all three groups has declined as a proportion of GDP since the end of the 1980s.

To understand these patterns further, we examine in the other parts of figure 3.6 the development of taxes on land and buildings and corporate income taxes. Figure 3.6c investigates the development of taxes on land and buildings in terms of individual components and two other forms of property tax, which are not included. The relatively constant factor in these taxes is a property tax on businesses, known as business rates.

However, the end of the 1980s and early 1990s witnessed changes in the system of domestic property taxes. In 1989 the domestic property tax (domestic rates) was replaced by the Community Charge. This was based on the number of individuals resident in a property and is not included by Eurostat (1998) as a tax on land and buildings. In 1993 this was replaced by the Council Tax, which is again levied primarily on the property.[16] However, this is also not included by Eurostat (1998) as a tax on land and buildings.[17]

The effect is that the aggregate revenue from taxes on land and buildings (expressed again as a share of GDP) appears to fall sharply in 1990 when domestic rates were abolished. Yet the overall level of these local domestic taxes remained fairly constant over the entire period.

Figure 3.6d investigates the development of taxes on corporate income over the same period. Here we distinguish between corporation tax and special taxes on the profits from North Sea oil and gas production (notably Petroleum Revenue Tax). These special taxes raised considerable amounts of revenue in the first half of the 1980s, but these revenues dropped away sharply after that period due to lower oil prices and more costly production. By contrast, revenue from corporation tax[18] rose sharply over the 1980s before falling back in the first half of the 1990s. Abstracting from the oil sector, then, it is true that corporation tax revenues fell in the first half of the 1990s; however, the pattern over a longer period shows that this was merely bringing revenue (as a proportion of GDP) back down to its earlier levels. The pattern shown in figure 3.6a is therefore rather misleading.

The lesson of the analysis of figure 3.6 is that the interpretation of an aggregate average tax rate on capital can be problematic. In this case the fall in the tax rate is caused by a move from a purely property-based tax to a tax that is less directly related to property, together with a fall in the oil price and hence the profitability of the off-shore oil extraction business. Clearly, neither change has more than an indirect effect on the taxation of on-shore capital in the United Kingdom.

For comparison with the other measures in this chapter, where we analyze taxes on capital income generated in the corporate sector, it would be useful to have an average tax rate applying to income generated in the corporate sector. We therefore develop such a measure here.[19] The numerator of this measure is, in principle, straightforward: total UK corporation tax receipts (before deducting ACT). However, the appropriate denominator is trickier. Broadly, we generate a measure of income generated by the corporate sector, net of interest payments to the personal sector, or abroad. Because of the deductibility of interest for tax purposes, interest payments from the corporate sector to the personal sector are taxed by the personal income tax system. As we do not include personal income taxes on interest in the numerator, our measure would be biased downward if we did not make this adjustment.[20] Figure 3.7 presents this series (labeled "ITR-COR, revenue

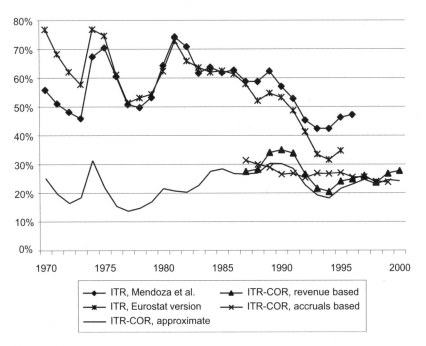

**Figure 3.7**
Implicit tax rates. *ITR* are implicit tax rates on capital from different sources. *ITR-COR* are implicit tax rates for the corporate sector calculated under different assumptions.

based") for the United Kingdom. Unfortunately, it is not possible to generate precise estimates of this measure back as far as 1970. We therefore also present an approximation to the measure (labeled "ITR-COR, approximate") in which the denominator is not corrected for net interest payments by the corporate sector. These two series are fairly close during the period in which they are both available.

As can be seen, both are considerably lower than the original tax rate on capital proposed by Mendoza et al. and the version used by Eurostat. The corporate sector average tax rate does drop significantly in the first half the 1990s. However, it recovers in the second half of the 1990s, and the level by the end of the 1990s was around that at the beginning of the 1980s. We can thus conclude that an overall average tax rate on capital can be misleading, especially if it is taken to be an approximate measure of the average tax rate on income generated in the corporate sector.

We also take one further step in developing this measure, to offset volatility in the measure due to timing. As taxes are paid with a lag, the tax rate is countercyclical: in a recession profits fall, but revenues do not (at least initially) since they are largely based on the previous year's profits. The opposite happens in a boom. We abstract from this effect by using a series on corporation tax accruals,[21] rather than revenues. As a result much of the volatility of the ITR measure disappears. It is also interesting to note that after all of those adjustments, the measure has become much more similar to the measure based on accounting data, the ATR.

The remaining measure of the group of measures based on macroeconomic data is the marginal tax rate of the corporate sector based on the approach by Gordon et al. (2003). Just as the ITR-COR (except for the accruals version) is more volatile than the effective average tax rate measures based on tax legislation, so the GKS measure is more volatile than the effective marginal tax rate. For the few years during which both are available, the correlation is however strong, with a coefficient of correlation of 0.72.

## 3.6  Conclusion

In this chapter we explored the properties of alternative measures of the taxation of income from capital, by applying them to data for the United Kingdom over the last thirty years. We considered several types of measures, reflecting both average and marginal rates.

The main comparison between the broad measures is shown in figure 3.1. It is clear that there is a significant difference among the measures, both in their level and in how they move over time. Our results do not justify the implicit assumption in some empirical work that these measures are broadly comparable to each other. Rather, we found that it can make a substantial difference whether the measure is based on a hypothetical investment or observed tax liabilities or revenues, whether it is average or marginal, and whether data are derived from company accounts or aggregate revenue series.

The remaining analysis considered the derivation of the measures in more detail, and documented how different values can be derived by making different assumptions, or using alternative forms of data. Section 3.3 demonstrated that effective tax rate measures based on hypothetical investments depend crucially on assumptions regarding personal taxes; the source of finance used; and whether underlying economic parameters are allowed to vary over time. Section 3.4 demonstrated that alternative definitions of taxation from company accounts can give a markedly different picture of the development of taxes over time. Section 3.5 explored measures based on aggregate revenue data. It showed that very broad measures of taxes on "capital" depend crucially on what taxes are included in the measure.

Our general conclusion is that appropriate choice of methodology and careful use of data are both vital in the construction and use of tax rates that are intended to summarize the taxation of income from capital. In using such measures, researchers should take care both about the general approach taken, and also about detailed choices made in the construction of tax rates.

**Data Appendix**

Effective Tax Rates

These are calculated as defined in Devereux and Griffith (2003). Further details, including those of the corporate tax regime, are also available in Devereux, Griffith, and Klemm (2002).

Weights for the use of alternative assets and sources of finance are based on the mean of the Datastream sample set out below, where

Weight for plant and machinery $= w_{pm} = \dfrac{328}{327 + 328},$

Weight for debt $= w_D = \dfrac{321}{392}$.

The codes refer to the following Datastream variables:

321   Total loan capital

327   Gross value of land and buildings

328   Gross value of plant and machinery

392   Total capital employed

These weights are applied within each hypothetical investment. Thus, instead of computing the effective tax rate for a single hypothetical investment (e.g., in plant and machinery financed by debt), we consider an investment that consists partly of plant and machinery and partly of buildings, financed by debt and equity. We then compute one effective tax for the combined investment.

   The real interest rate and inflation rate are either assumed to be fixed at 10 and 3.5 percent respectively, or in cases where they are allowed to vary, National Statistics data are used. The real interest rate then is the twenty-year government bond rate (AJLX) plus an 8 percent premium and inflation is the GDP deflator calculated using GDP in nominal (YBHA) and 1995 (ABMI) prices.

Accounting Data Tax Measures

The measure in figure 3.1 is ATR $= 160/154$. The other measures in section 3.4 are

(i)   $(160 + 167)/154$

(ii)   $172/154$

(iii)   $(160 - \text{ACT} + 164)/154,$

where ACT is $(181 + 187)s/(1 - s)$ and where $s$ is the net ACT rate.
   The codes refer to the following Datastream variables:

154   Before-tax profit

160   Corporation tax

164   Irrecoverable ACT

167   Overseas tax

172   Total tax charge

181   Preference dividends

187   Ordinary dividends

The dataset was obtained by downloading data on all UK quoted firms (including dead firms) from Thomson Financial Datastream. From an initial dataset of nearly 4,000 firms, we dropped all observations with accounting periods that differed by more than thirty days from a year. We also dropped observations lacking core data such as sales (104) and cash flow (182 + 136). Finally we dropped all firms for which we had fewer than four consecutive observations. This left us with a sample of nearly 3,000 firms and 38,000 observations

Gordon-Kalambokidis-Slemrod (2003) Measure

This measure is defined as

GKS = (Tax revenue current system − Tax revenue R-base tax)/
         (Tax revenue current system − Tax revenue under R-
         base + $(1 − \tau)r$ capital stock$_{t-1}$)

where

Tax revenue current system − Tax revenue R-base tax

$$= \tau(EABC + NHCK − (NHCM + EABG)$$

$$− CAPALL + NHCJ + DBGP + DBGM + NHCI),$$

Capital stock$_{t-1}$ = (CIXH + CIXJ + CIXI)$_{t-1}$,

$\tau$ is the statutory corporation tax rate, and $r$ is the real interest rate as defined above.

   The four letter codes represent the following National Statistics data series:

EABC    Interest received (nonfinancial corporations)

NHCK    Interest received (financial corporations)

EABG    Interest paid (nonfinancial corporations)

NHCM    Interest paid (financial corporations)

DBGP    Gross fixed capital formation (nonfinancial corporations)

NHCJ     Gross fixed capital formation (financial corporations)

DBGM     Changes in inventories (nonfinancial corporations)

NHCI     Changes in inventories (financial corporations)

CIXH     Net capital stock (private nonfinancial corporations)

CIXJ     Net capital stock (public nonfinancial corporations)

CIXI     Net capital stock (financial corporations)

Data on capital allowances were taken from Inland Revenue Statistics:

CAPALL   Capital allowances of corporations in financial year.

Measures Based on Aggregate Tax Revenues

The Mendoza et al. measure was taken from E. Mendoza's personal Web page (*http://www.econ.duke.edu/~mendozae/*). The Eurostat measure was constructed as described in Eurostat (1998) using Eurostat data.

Our average tax rate for the corporate sector, based on tax revenue, is defined as

$$\frac{\text{ACCD} + \text{ACCJ}}{\text{Gross operating surplus} - \text{Depreciation} + \text{Net taxable property income}},$$

where

$$\text{Gross operating surplus} - \text{NQBE} + \text{NQNV} - \text{NSRV} - \text{EAXB},$$

Depreciation

$$= \left(1 - \frac{\text{EAXB}}{\text{NQBE} + \text{EABC} + \text{FAOG} - \text{EABG} - \text{FBXO}}\right)\text{DBGF} + \text{NHCE},$$

$$\text{Net taxable property income} = \text{EABC} + \text{NHCK} + \text{FAOG} + \text{NHDH}$$
$$- \text{EABG} - \text{NHCM} - \text{FBXO} - \text{NHDK}.$$

The four letter codes represent the following National Statistics data series:

NQBE     Gross operating surplus, nonfinancial corporations

NQNV     Gross operating surplus, financial corporations

NSRV     Adjustment to property income (FISIM), financial corporations

EAXB     Gross trading profit of quasi-corporations

EABC    Interest received, nonfinancial corporations

NHCK    Interest received, financial corporations

FAOG    Rent received, nonfinancial corporations

NHDH    Rent received, financial corporations

EABG    Interest paid, nonfinancial corporations

NHCM    Interest paid, financial corporations

FBXO    Rent paid, nonfinancial corporations

NHDK    Rent paid, financial corporations

ACCD    Corporation tax revenues

ACCJ    Petroleum revenue tax revenues

DBGF    Capital consumption, nonfinancial corporations

NHCE    Capital consumption, financial corporations

The approximate measure is defined in a similar way, with the difference that net taxable property income is not added to the denominator:

$$\frac{\text{ACCD} + \text{ACCJ}}{\text{Gross operating surplus} - \text{Depreciation}}.$$

The accruals-based tax rate is defined as

$$\frac{\text{Tax liability} + \text{ACT setoff}}{\text{Gross operating surplus} - \text{Depreciation} + \text{Net taxable property income}},$$

where the tax liability and ACT setoff are taken from Inland Revenue Statistics, table 11.4, various years.

## Notes

We thank participants at the CESifo conference on measuring the tax burden on labor and capital, two anonymous referees, and Peter Birch Sørensen for helpful comments and advice. The chapter draws on joint work with Rachel Griffith, Michela Redoano, and Julian McCrae. We are grateful for their help and advice.

1. Volkerink et al. (2002) do so, at least for two different definitions of such tax rates: the one suggested by Mendoza et al. (1994) and a version suggested in their paper. They replicate some recent empirical studies and find that results of Mendoza et al. (1997) and Daveri and Tabellini (2000) are not substantially changed by using their measure.

2. Because of different sample sizes due to limited data availability, care needs to be taken when comparing coefficients. For example, the correlation between ITR and ITR-COR suggests that the movements in these measures are significantly positively correlated. However, if calculated over a longer time period of 27 observations using an

approximate version of the ITR-COR (see section 3.5), the coefficient drops to 0.39 and becomes insignificant.

3. That is, we consider only one investment, which is a weighted average of different assets and sources of finance. We do not compute effective tax rates for each type of asset and then find a weighted average of these.

4. This choice is somewhat arbitrary. The EATR as measured here lies between the EMTR and the statutory tax rate. An economic profit rate of around 20 percent generates an EATR that can differ from each of these extreme points.

5. These are based on data from company accounting records, taken from Thomson Financial Datastream. Further details are given in the Data Appendix. On average, these weights are 57 percent plant and machinery, 43 percent buildings, 90 percent equity, and 10 percent debt.

6. The rate for plant and machinery is 12.25 percent, and the rate of buildings is 3.61 percent. These rates are taken from OECD (1991).

7. See Devereux, Griffith, and Klemm (2002) for an analysis of this issue.

8. Without personal taxes it makes no difference whether equity finance represents new equity or retained earnings. With personal taxes the two differ. In figure 3.3 we assume that all equity finance is new equity.

9. We implicitly assume here that the tax system is symmetric; that is, loss-making firms receive a tax rebate. In practice, this is not generally true. Losses can be carried back to offset against earlier profit, but only in a very limited way. Beyond that they can be carried forward indefinitely to set against future profit. But in doing so, the loss-making firms bear a cost of delay in receiving the tax credit.

10. This is not always true. In some cases tax liabilities that are clearly labeled as overseas tax in the published accounts are not separately identified in Datastream. This would lead us to overstate the UK tax liability.

11. Datastream account item 160, labeled "Corporation tax."

12. ACT can be thought of as a prepayment of the shareholders' income tax due on dividend payments by the firm, and was paid by firms until 1999. Until 1997 it could be reclaimed by zero-rated shareholders. ACT payments by the firm could be offset against the full tax charge, but only to the extent that gross dividends did not exceed taxable profit. That part of ACT which was unlikely to be offset within a reasonable period was charged against profit and was known as irrecoverable ACT.

13. This may also be a more reliable measure, given the possible problems in underrecording overseas tax in Datastream.

14. OECD (2001) suggests some modifications to the Mendoza et al. measure. For the United Kingdom their changes reduce the estimate of the tax rate on capital income by on average 9 percentage points. However, the pattern over time is hardly affected, so we do not present this measure here. As the proposed changes to the definition do not affect property taxes or petroleum taxes, the following analysis would equally apply to their measure.

15. In Eurostat terminology this is referred to as a tax rate on "factors of production other than employed labor" rather than "capital." It is, however, usually interpreted as the tax rate on capital, so we stick to this simpler label.

16. Council tax is based on the value of residential property, but it also depends on the circumstances of the residents of a property. There are discounts for second homes and properties inhabited by one person only. For some residents it is waived, such as for full-time students.

17. The Mendoza et al. tax rate does include the Community Charge but not the Council Tax.

18. This includes corporation tax on North Sea activities.

19. There have been previous attempts to define such tax rates for the corporate sector, such as those by Bretschger and Hettich (2002), Nicodeme (2001), OECD (2001), and literature cited therein. None have, however, attempted to deal with taxable property income, including interest.

20. See the Data Appendix for details. Note that these adjustments are particularly important when calculating such a tax rate for a subsector of the economy such as the manufacturing sector. The net interest flows from this sector to the financial sector would be substantial.

21. From Inland Revenue Statistics.

## References

Bretschger, L., and F. Hettich. 2002. Globalisation, capital mobility and tax competition: Theory and evidence for OECD countries. *European Journal of Political Economy* 18: 695–716.

Daveri, F., and G. Tabellini. 2000. Unemployment, growth and taxation in industrial countries. *Economic Policy* 30: 49–104.

Devereux, M. P., and R. Griffith. 2003. Evaluating tax policy for location decisions. *International Tax and Public Finance*, 10: 107–26.

Devereux, M. P., R. Griffith, and A. Klemm. 2002. Corporate income tax reforms and international tax competition. *Economic Policy* 35: 451–95.

European Commission. 1997. Towards tax co-ordination in the European Union: A package to tackle harmful tax competition. COM(97) 495 final Brussels: European Commission.

Eurostat. 1998. *Structures of the Taxation Systems in the European Union.* Luxembourg: Office for Official Publications of the European Communities.

Inland Revenue. Various years. *Inland Revenue Statistics.* London: Stationary Office.

Mendoza, E. G., G. M. Milesi-Feretti, and P. Asea. 1997. On the ineffectiveness of tax policy in altering long-run growth: Harberger's superneutrality conjecture. *Journal of Public Economics* 66(1): 99–126.

Mendoza, E. G., A. Razin, and L. L. Tesar. 1994. Effective tax rates in macroeconomics: Cross-country estimates of tax rates on factor incomes and consumption. *Journal of Monetary Economics* 34: 297–323.

National Statistics. Data from "Time Zone" at *www.nationalstatistics.gov.uk.*

Nicodeme, G. 2001. Computing effective corporate tax rates: Comparisons and results. Economic Paper 153. DG Economic and Financial Affairs, European Commission.

OECD. 1991. Taxing profits in a global economy: Domestic and international issues. Paris: OECD.

OECD. 2001. Tax ratios: A critical survey. Tax Policy Studies 5. Paris: OECD.

OECD. "Revenue Statistics Database" from *www.sourceoecd.org*.

Volkerink, B., J.-E. Sturm, and J. de Haan. 2002. Tax ratios in macroeconomics: Do taxes really matter? *Empirica* 29: 209–24.

# 4

# A New Summary Measure of the Effective Tax Rate on Investment

Roger Gordon, Laura Kalambokidis, and Joel Slemrod

## 4.1 Objectives

Because of their presumed negative effects on investment and growth, taxes on investment income have become high-profile candidates for reduction or repeal. As a result economists have put much effort toward learning how tax systems affect the incentive to invest, typically by measuring the effective tax rate on new investment.

The empirical literature that seeks to measure the effective tax rate on new investment offers a striking paradox. On the one hand, summary measures of the effective tax rate on new investment are normally quite high.[1] On the other hand, the amount of revenue collected is apparently very low. For example, Gordon and Slemrod (1988; hereafter GS) estimated that in 1983 the US tax system collected no revenue from taxing capital income, while Gordon, Kalambokidis, and Slemrod (2001; hereafter GKS) estimated that in 1995 the US tax system collected approximately $18 billion in revenue from corporate capital income, or just 4 percent of total corporate profits (equal to $441.5 billion in 1995 according to the 1999 Economic Report of the President).[2] If the taxation of capital income does generate little or no revenue while imposing large distortions to investment incentives, then this tax structure is hard to defend.

On the other hand, the low revenue figures for existing taxes on capital income could be consistent with a view that the US tax system does not discourage investment as severely as has been thought. The low revenue could reflect an effective tax rate on new capital investment that is much lower than has conventionally been reported in the past. This would be the case if the low revenue figures provide more revealing information about the effective tax rate because they reflect complications in the tax law ignored in standard estimates of this effective tax rate. However, revenue figures are also affected by things that do not matter for investment incentives, such as the income generated by inframarginal decisions, so it is not clear a priori how informative revenue collections are for this purpose.

While GS and GKS estimated the revenue collected from US capital income taxes, they did not convert those estimates into an effective tax rate measure. Our first objective in this chapter is to show explicitly how these revenue figures can be used to estimate the effective tax rate on new investment.

We start with the simplest possible setting in section 4.2, with just a corporate tax and only equity finance. In this setting we define an effective tax rate on new investment using the Hall and Jorgenson (1967) approach, as later refined by King and Fullerton (1984; hereafter KF). In this simple setting the resulting effective tax rate also equals one derived using the Feldstein and Summers (1979; hereafter FS) approach that calculates an effective tax rate equal to the ratio of corporate tax payments (plus any personal taxes on corporate dividend and interest payments) to corporate income. Next we show how the estimates of the revenue collected from taxing capital income, using the procedures in GKS, can be used to measure this same effective tax rate.

In section 4.3 we assess all three measures as we move beyond this initial model of investment incentives. Among the complications we consider are resale of assets (churning), risk, pure profits, debt finance, and choice of organizational form. Except in the case of choice of organizational form, where it would overestimate the effective tax rate, the GKS measure is the only one that consistently equals the desired value. An important strength of this approach to measuring the effective tax rate is that it automatically captures the effects of such complications. In the presence of these complications, the FS and KF measures as used in practice consistently overestimate the desired value for the effective tax rate, providing some help in reconciling the past evidence.

In section 4.4 we explore some further complications that are *not* dealt with appropriately by the GKS measure. The first is debt arbitrage, whereby investors in high tax brackets borrow from those in low tax brackets to buy more lightly taxed equity. The data in GS suggest that such debt arbitrage is a dominant reason why the revenue from existing taxes on capital income in the United States has been so low. With this complication introduced, we find that the GKS measure now underestimates the effective tax rate, while the KF and the FS measures (as used in practice) both overestimate it.

We conclude in section 4.5 that the GKS approach provides a very useful but not fail-safe approach for measuring the effective tax rate on new investment. This measure proves to be much more robust than the KF or the FS measures to many commonly omitted complications in the tax law. Like all backward-looking measures of effective tax rates, it has one blind spot. Because it relies on ex post data on tax payments, it cannot be used to assess the effects of proposed changes in the existing law, and will not accurately reflect a recently changed law. Overall, our attempt to reconcile the high conventional measures of effective tax rates with the low revenue collected leads us to conclude that the actual effective tax rate on new investment is much lower than existing measures suggest, and this is due to various omitted complications.

## 4.2  Effective Tax Rate Measures: Base Case

To explore alternative means of measuring the effective tax rate on new investment, we use the simplest possible setting as used in the seminal work by Hall and Jorgenson (1967). This model, based on the neoclassical theory of optimal asset accumulation, assumes perfect information, perfect competition, zero excess profits on the marginal investment, an unchanging tax law, and no risk. It also ignores any personal taxes on corporate-source income, abstracts from the use of debt finance, and assumes that the firm has sufficient profits to use all of the allowed credits and deductions in the earliest possible year.

Hall and Jorgenson argue that a profit-maximizing firm will purchase a new capital asset as long as the present discounted value of the stream of returns generated by the asset exceeds the cost of acquiring the asset. Such a firm will invest until the present discounted value of the returns on a marginal project just equals the acquisition cost. Normalizing the pre-tax price of the capital good to be one, we can write the single-period equivalent maximization problem as

$$\max f(K) - (r + d)K.$$

Here $r$ is the discount rate and $d$ is the rate of depreciation of the capital goods, which is assumed to be exponential at rate $d$. The solution to this problem is characterized by the following condition for the marginal investment:

$$f'(K) - d = r. \tag{4.1}$$

Here $f' - d$ is the annual net return to one unit of capital. In equilibrium it exactly equals the marginal rate of return to savings for the firm's shareholders, $r$.

Now introduce a corporation tax. The revenue generated by the investment is taxed at the corporate tax rate, denoted $u$. In addition purchasing a capital asset entitles the owner to a stream of depreciation deductions (we ignore any investment tax credits). It is useful to think of the present discounted value of the tax savings generated by the depreciation deductions as a reduction in the acquisition cost of the asset. Let $z$ be the present value of depreciation deductions per dollar of acquisition cost, so that $uz$ is the present value of the tax savings resulting from the deductions allowed on one dollar of new investment. As a result only $(1 - uz)$ dollars need to be raised from investors to finance a dollar of new investment. Similarly only $d(1 - uz)$ dollars need to be raised in each future period to cover replacement expenditures. With these adjustments, equation (4.1) becomes

$$f'(K) = \frac{(r + d)(1 - uz)}{1 - u}, \tag{4.1'}$$

which can be rewritten as

$$f' - d = r + \frac{u(r + d)(1 - z)}{1 - u}. \tag{4.2}$$

Here the second term captures the extent of any tax distortion, measuring the difference between the net return to capital and the investors' marginal rate of return to savings. It will be convenient for future purposes to denote the numerator of this term by $\Delta \equiv u(r + d)(1 - z)$. One can think of $\Delta$ as measuring the extra taxes due as a result of using depreciation rather than expensing, measured as a constant figure in each year. To pay these extra taxes while still yielding a return of $r$ to investors, the firm needs to earn an extra $\Delta/(1 - u)$ before corporate taxes.

We define the effective tax rate, $m$, as that tax rate on net corporate income, $f' - d$, that leads to the same equilibrium value of $f'$, given $r$, as arises under the actual tax law. By definition, then, $m$ satisfies the following equation:

$$(f' - d)(1 - m) = r, \tag{4.3}$$

where the equilibrium $f'$ is characterized by equation (4.2). We find, using equations (4.2) and (4.3), that

$$m = \frac{\Delta}{(1-u)r + \Delta}. \tag{4.3'}$$

Two special cases are important. The first is expensing, under which all investment expenditures are deductible from taxable income when incurred. In this case $z$ equals one, so that $m$ equals zero *regardless of the value of $u$ or $d$*. The other case of interest is the pure income tax where depreciation allowances exactly mirror the decline in value of the asset—its "economic" depreciation. Then $z$ equals $d/(r+d)$. If $d/(r+d)$ is substituted for $z$ in expression (4.2), then $m = u$.

### 4.2.1   King-Fullerton Tax Rate

In the rest of the chapter we focus on the updated version of the Hall and Jorgenson (1967) model developed by King and Fullerton (1984). Given our initial assumptions, their approach is equivalent to that of Hall and Jorgenson, yielding the appropriate measure of the effective tax rate on new investment in this context.

In general, King and Fullerton extended Hall and Jorgenson's cost of capital approach by taking into account personal taxes on corporate income and the range of forms of corporate finance. To do so, they estimated a marginal effective tax rate on new investment with respect to one kind of capital asset, and one kind of financing, at a time. This effective tax rate depends on the source of financing, and consequently on the tax characteristics of the recipient of the returns. Their focus was on the resulting variation in the effective tax rate by type of investment, though in addition they take a weighted average of these effective tax rates to provide a measure of the overall effective tax rate on investment.

To obtain this weighted average effective tax rate, KF assumed that new investment is distributed among different asset types, industries, sources of finance, and ownership characteristics in the same proportions as the current capital stock. Further assumptions arise from the inability to trace specific assets through to their ultimate owners. Specifically, the KF study assumes that "all assets in a particular industry are financed in the same way, that all owners hold debt from the different industries in the same proportions, and that all owners hold equity from the different industries in the same proportions."[3]

These aspects become relevant as we add complications below to the analysis.

## 4.2.2 Average Tax Rate

A number of studies have used observed average tax rates as an approximation of the effective marginal tax rate. As an example of this approach, Feldstein and Summers (1979) calculate an average effective tax rate equal to corporate taxes paid, plus personal taxes due on corporate dividend and interest payments, as a proportion of capital income, measured using accounting data. While the average tax rates are relatively easy to calculate, there are numerous reasons why the average rates would be poor proxies for marginal effective rates on new investment (Fullerton 1984 lists eleven of these reasons).[4] For example, the average effective tax rate is backward-looking: it depends on investments made by the firm over many previous periods. If the tax law has changed over time, prospective investments will face a different regime than past investments. In this case the backward-looking measure will incorrectly characterize the impact of taxes on future investments. As another example, a firm may have little tax liability in a year when it earns high income, because earlier tax losses may have been carried forward. The result will be an average tax rate that may understate the impact of taxes on the incentive to undertake a new investment.

In the simple setting used in this section, however, the average tax rate exactly equals $m$ under specific conditions. In particular, the taxes paid in some year $t$ equal

$$T_t = u\left[f_t(K_t) - \int_{s=0}^{\infty} d_{s,t-s}I_{t-s}\,ds\right],$$

where $d_{s,t-s}$ equals the depreciation deductions allowed for $s$-year-old capital originally purchased in year $t-s$, based on the tax law in force in year $t-s$. Capital purchased in year $t-s$ is denoted by $I_{t-s}$. The estimate for the effective average tax rate is then

$$m_{FS} = \frac{T_t}{f_t(K_t) - dK_t},$$

or tax liability divided by corporate income net of true depreciation.

This expression does equal the marginal tax rate $m$ if (1) the tax law remains fixed over time, (2) real investment has been growing at rate $r$, and (3) there are no business cycle effects so that $f_t$ does not vary with $t$. All of these pertain to the history of the tax system and investment. A fourth assumption is that there is constant returns to scale so that $f(K) = Kf'$. From here on, for the most part we will assume that these assumptions do hold, and explore other advantages and disadvantages of using the average tax rate and other measures as an approximation of $m$. We return to the impact of relaxing some of these assumptions later.

### 4.2.3   GKS Tax Rate

In two earlier papers (GS 1988 and GKS 2001), we estimated the impact on US tax revenue of shifting from the current law to an R-base for both the corporate and the personal income tax, a tax base that excludes financial income, disallows interest deductions, and replaces depreciation, amortization, and depletion deductions with expensing for new investment.[5] The difference between how much is raised under the actual tax system and the amount of revenue a hypothetical R-base tax (with the same tax rates) would raise provides an estimate of the net tax revenue collected from capital income under the current regime.

GS found that under a simulated R-base tax in 1983, the tax liability of nonfinancial corporations would increase by $22.6 billion, and individual tax liability would fall by $15.2 billion. On net, therefore, GS estimated that the existing income taxes collected $7.4 billion *less* in tax revenue than an R-base would have, even though an R-base tax imposes no distortion to savings or investment decisions. Since this figure is a small fraction of total tax revenue, the implication of this result is that, in 1983, the US tax system imposed little or no burden on the return to capital. The question we focus on is why these revenue figures can be so low, despite the high standard estimates of the effective tax rate on new investment.

GKS repeated this experiment using data from 1995 and found a somewhat different result. In 1995, switching to an R-base tax would have reduced corporate tax liability by $18.0 billion and individual tax liability by $90.1 billion, for a net revenue loss of $108.1 billion.[6] Two important reasons for the difference in results were the drop in nominal interest rates from 1983 to 1995, reducing the tax savings from arbitrage through the use of debt, and the much higher investment rate in 1995 compared with 1983. If 1995 had been at a more typical point in the business cycle, GKS estimated that the revenue loss from shifting to an R-base tax would have been $94.9 billion.

In neither paper were the revenue results converted into an effective tax rate summary measure. How would we do so, at least in this simple setting?

Let $TC$ be the tax collected under the existing tax rules. Let $TR$ be the tax that would be collected under an R-based tax, holding both the return to capital and the capital stock at the existing levels, rather than at the values they would have in the equilibrium with an R-base tax. GKS focused on measuring the taxes collected under the existing law relative to an R-base tax that does not distort capital investments: $TC$-$TR$. This difference equals the net taxes collected on income/deductions from financial assets (dividends, interest, and capital gains) plus the effects on tax revenue from use of depreciation and amortization rather than expensing for new investment.

In general, and as calculated in GS and GKS, this measure depends on the relative tax treatments of *all* capital, corporate and noncorporate, real and financial, under existing law compared with under an R-base tax. However, for purposes of this discussion, consider the calculation of this measure in an economy consisting of just a corporate sector with no personal taxes. This expression in any given year then equals

$$TC_t - TR_t = u\left(I_t - \int_{s=0}^{\infty} d_{s,t-s}I_{t-s}\,ds\right).$$

Assume as before (1) an unchanging tax law and (2) real investment growing at rate $r$.[7] Then this expression simplifies to $u(r+d)(1-z)K = \Delta K$, where $\Delta$ is defined as earlier.

To measure $m$, we propose the following definition:

$$m_{\text{GKS}} \equiv \frac{(TC_t - TR_t)/K}{(1-u)r + (TC_t - TR_t)/K}. \tag{4.4}$$

In practice, as in GS and GKS, $(TC_t - TR_t)/K$ can be calculated using actual US tax return data, and the estimated counterfactual amount of revenue that would be collected under an R-base tax.

Note a few things about $m_{\text{GKS}}$. First, if the current tax system were equivalent to an R-base tax, so that $z$ is equal to one, $TC$ would equal $TR$, so that $m_{\text{GKS}} = 0$ regardless of the value of $u$ or $r$. Second, if $TC$

were a pure income tax, so that $z = d/(r + d)$, we would have $m = m_{GKS} = u$.

Therefore, under the assumptions above, all three tax rates correctly measure the disincentive to invest due to taxes. All but the King-Fullerton measure require the tax law to have been unchanging in the past and investment to be growing at a rate equal to $r$. For example, GKS recalculated $TR$ as if investment had been at an average, rather than a high-growth, level. That paper did not attempt to correct for changes in the tax law in the past.[8] The FS measure in addition requires no business cycle effects: Feldstein and Summers (1979) did attempt to control for business cycle effects in making use of their measure of the average tax rate.

## 4.3   Omitted Complications

How do these three proposed measures of the effective tax rate compare with the $m$ in more complicated settings? We examine several possible complications.

### 4.3.1   Churning

In principle, the approach taken by Hall and Jorgenson, or later by King and Fullerton, can deal appropriately with any additional complications as long as a careful effort is made to incorporate these additional complications into the theoretical model. Since the tax law is very complicated and since the range of possible responses is also complicated, it is easy for tax economists to overlook issues that in practice turn out to be important. Clearly, any given study cannot feasibly take account of *all* the detailed provisions in the law, and all the ways that firms and individuals may respond to the tax law.

The FS and GKS measures, however, can potentially take these complications into account automatically, since these complications and any behavioral responses to them will affect the amount of revenue collected by existing taxes. Whether the revenue effects actually measure well the implications of any given complication in the law for marginal investment incentives, however, depends in general on the nature of the specific complication at issue.

One example of particular importance in the United States during the early 1980s was "churning." Churning refers to the sale of existing real capital by one firm to another firm. This sale generates taxable capital gains, which by itself discourages such a sale. However, the firm acquiring the capital can set the tax basis for the capital back up to its current market value, generating higher depreciation deductions in the future than the firm selling the asset would have been eligible for. Churning would be profitable, at least based on tax considerations, if the value of the extra depreciation deductions more than offsets the extra capital gains taxes.

This was often the case in the United States prior to the 1986 tax reform. Yet this type of behavioral response was ignored when many economists first tried to assess the effects of the 1981–83 tax reforms. At the time many studies[9] argued that structures faced a particularly high effective tax rate. Yet, due to churning, structures were actually heavily subsidized under the tax law.[10] What would the value of $m$ be, with churning? How are the three alternative measures affected, assuming that churning exists but that economists are not yet aware of its importance?

Start with $m$. Consider the simple case in which all capital is churned every $c$ years. Each time capital is churned there are transactions costs equal to $\kappa$ percent of the current market value of the capital; $c$ is assumed to be the optimal rate of churning given $\kappa$. The present value of depreciation deductions on the initial investment then equals $z_c = \sum_{j=0}^{\infty} e^{-dcj} \int_0^c d_s e^{-r(s+cj)} ds$, while the present value of capital gains tax liabilities, denoted by $g$, equals $g = \tau_g \sum_{j=0}^{\infty} e^{-rcj} (e^{-dc} - e^{-\int_0^c d_s ds}) e^{-dc(j-1)}$, where $\tau_g$ denotes the capital gains tax rate. Let $uz^* = uz_c - g$. In addition let $\kappa^* \equiv (r+d) \sum_{j=1}^{\infty} \kappa e^{-dcj}$ measure the constant rate of expenditure equivalent to the implied transactions costs. The first-order condition for new investment now equals $f' - \kappa^* - d = r + [u(r+d)(1-z^*)]/(1-u)$. Here, as before, the last term measures the difference between the net real return to new investment and the marginal rate of return to savings.

In practice, the King-Fullerton measure ignored churning, assuming, as did Hall and Jorgenson, that firms invest permanently, so it mistakenly used $z$ to calculate $m_{KF}$. To the extent to which $z^* > z$, because of accelerated depreciation allowances, the measure will be in error.

What about the average tax rate measure? Under the above assumptions, if calculated correctly this measure would equal

$$m_{FS} = \frac{u[f - (r+d)z^*K]}{f - (d+\kappa^*)K}.$$

Under the same assumptions as before, it is easy to show that this measure equals $m$. Note, however, that the extra capital-gains taxes being incurred through churning would need to be taken into account when calculating the correct average tax rate. Instead, the standard approach has been to use an effective tax rate equal to $u + e(1 - u)$. Here $e$ represents the effective personal tax rate on dividends and capital gains, for example, $e = v\tau_d + \tau_g(1 - v)$, where $v$ is the dividend payout rate, $\tau_d$ is the effective personal tax rate on dividends, and $\tau_g$ is the effective capital gains tax rate (e.g., $\tau_g = 0.25\tau_d$). When churning becomes profitable, reported depreciation deductions will jump, but the extra capital gains taxes would easily be overlooked.[11] The average tax rate measure will then underestimate $m$.

What about the GKS measure? Under the behavior described above, the observed $\Delta$ would equal $u(I - (r + d)z^*K) = u(r + d)(1 - z^*)K$. We then find that $m_{GKS} = m$. Therefore the GKS measure does automatically capture the effects of churning on investment incentives, even if economists are not aware of its importance. This is an illustration of an advantage of a measure based on actual tax collections.

### 4.3.2 Risk

The derivations above have ignored the presence of risk. Yet corporate investments are risky, and the risk premia can be very large relative to the required return on a risk-free investment. To what degree is the value of $m$, and each of the three methods for measuring $m$, affected by the presence of risk?

We address this question by considering how the previous results change if the marginal return to new investments, $\tilde{f}'$, is now random.[12] Under the tax structure described above, we would now find in equilibrium that

$$(1 - u)\tilde{f}' = (r + d)(1 - uz) + (1 - u)(\rho + \tilde{\varepsilon}),$$

where the first term on the right-hand side equals the required return, net of corporate taxes, from a risk-free investment, $\rho$ represents the risk premium that shareholders would require to hold the lottery $\tilde{f}'$,[13] while $\tilde{\varepsilon}$ is the random return. By definition, the certainty-equivalent value of the lottery $\tilde{f}'$ then equals $\bar{f}' - \rho \equiv f'_{CE}$, implying that

$$f'_{CE} - d = r + \frac{\Delta}{1 - u}.$$

To measure the effective tax rate in this setting, we want to compare the social return on this investment with the social opportunity cost $r$. If risk has been allocated efficiently in the economy, then the risk premium on any random taxes equals the risk premium required by shareholders. The certainty-equivalent value of $\tilde{f}'$, now from a social perspective, equals the same value $f'_{CE}$ derived based on shareholder preferences. The effective tax rate, defined implicitly by the equation $(f'_{CE} - d)(1 - m) = r$ is then the same as we found without risk.

The KF measure for this tax rate is also unaffected, as is the GKS measure. However, the average tax rate now equals

$$m_{FS} = \frac{u[f_{CE} - \int_{s=0}^{\infty} d_{s,t-s} I_{t-s}\, ds + \rho K]}{f_{CE} - dK + \rho K}. \tag{4.5}$$

The average tax rate no longer equals $m$, but instead is biased toward the statutory tax rate $u$. Intuitively, this measure misinterprets the tax revenue collected on the risk premium as a disincentive to invest rather than as a fair premium for the reduction in risk caused by the tax levy. The larger the risk premium, the larger is the bias.

### 4.3.3  Pure Profits

To this point we have assumed that each firm has constant returns to scale. What if, instead, firms have a concave production function, thus earning profits on inframarginal investments in equilibrium? Would this affect the marginal effective tax rate $m$? Here the answer is an easy no: marginal incentives are unaffected by the rate of return earned on inframarginal projects. For the same reason, $m_{KF}$ is unaffected by having a concave production function. Nothing in the expression for $m_{GKS}$ is affected either. Because the revenue collected on pure profits under the existing system would also be collected by an R-base tax with the same rate structure, the presence of pure profits has no effect on the calculation of $TC_t - TR_t$ above. The $m_{GKS}$ measure is based on the revenues collected over and above the R-base tax. This is an essential and critical advantage of the GKS measure of $m$: by construction, it depends only on those revenues that arise from marginal investments, and ignores those revenues that arise from inframarginal investments.

In contrast, the average tax rate is affected by the presence of pure profits. In particular, recall that our earlier derivation made use of the assumption that $f = f'K$, an assumption that is valid only if the production function has constant returns to scale. Assume, instead, that $f = f'K + \pi$, where $\pi$ represents the profits earned on inframarginal investments. Then the expression for the average tax rate equals

$$m_{\text{FS}} = \frac{u[f'K + \pi - \int_{s=0}^{\infty} d_{s,t-s}I_{t-s}\,ds]}{f'K + \pi - dK}. \tag{4.6}$$

As with risk we find that the average tax rate is biased toward the statutory rate $u$, and the bias increases with the extent of the profits on inframarginal investment. As it does in the presence of risk, the $m_{\text{FS}}$ measure misinterprets the revenue collected from profits on inframarginal investment as evidence of a disincentive to marginal investments.

At this point it is worth commenting briefly on another tax rate measure recently proposed by Devereux and Griffith (1998). They expand the effective tax rate concept by introducing the corporate effective average tax rate, which explicitly allows for the presence of economic rents. This tax rate is defined as the difference between the before- and after-tax economic rent scaled by the net present value of the pre-tax income stream. This measure of the tax rate equals $m_{\text{FS}}$ under the same assumptions needed above to reconcile $m_{\text{FS}}$ and $m$ in a setting without pure profits.

While this expression does not provide an appropriate measure of the effective tax rate on *marginal* investments, being biased toward the statutory tax rate $u$, Devereux and Griffith argue that their tax rate measure may be of value in judging the effects of the tax law on a firm's choice between mutually exclusive investment projects that are expected to generate positive economic rents before tax. If true, the $m_{\text{FS}}$ measure would be useful in the same context.

### 4.3.4   Debt Finance

So far we have assumed that corporate investments are entirely financed with equity. King and Fullerton (1984) devote considerable attention to the implications of debt finance for the incentive to invest. In their calculation of the marginal effective tax rate, they assume that (1) there are no real costs resulting from using debt versus equity finance, but that firms can finance at most a fraction $b^*$ of their investments with debt, and (2) interest payments are tax deductible under the corporate tax, but interest income is taxable at some tax rate $\tau_b$ under the personal income tax.

To investigate the effects of debt finance on alternative measures of the effective tax rate, we follow these assumptions used by King and Fullerton. Furthermore we assume, for simplicity, that the law allows tax depreciation allowances that are equal to economic depreciation, at rate $d$, and we ignore personal taxes on equity income as well as risk.

When a firm undertakes an additional dollar of investment, assume that it raises $b$ dollars from debt and $(1 - b)$ dollars from equity. The opportunity cost equity investors face equals the return they could earn on bonds instead, so it equals $r(1 - \tau_b)$, where $\tau_b$ is their personal tax rate on interest income from corporate bonds. Wealth owners are then indifferent between holding equity and debt if

$$(1 - u)[f' - rb - d] = (1 - b)r(1 - \tau_b), \tag{4.7}$$

implying in equilibrium that

$$f' - d = \frac{r(1 - \tau_b)(1 - b) + rb(1 - u)}{1 - u} = r(1 - \tau_b) + \frac{\Delta_b}{1 - u}, \tag{4.8}$$

where $\Delta_b = ur(1 - \tau_b) - br(u - \tau_b)$.[14] As long as $u > \tau_b$, the cost of funds is minimized if $b$ is as large as possible, implying that firms use as much debt finance as possible, so that $b = b^*$.[15] In other words, the use of debt rather than equity finance generates an effective tax rate of $\tau_b$ rather than $u$, or a tax arbitrage gain of $u - \tau_b$. In this case the tax arbitrage arises because of the differential tax treatment of two otherwise identical ways to raise funds. This arbitrage gain is limited to $b^*$ times the amount of capital, so it amounts to an effective marginal subsidy to investment.

In order to summarize these complicated tax incentives in an "effective" tax rate $m$, we continue to use the following modified identity:

$$(1 - m)(f' - d) = r(1 - \tau_b), \tag{4.9}$$

where $r(1 - \tau_b)$ represents the marginal rate of return to saving. From equations (4.8) and (4.9) we find that

$$m = \frac{\Delta_b}{(1 - u)(f' - d)} = \frac{\Delta_b}{(1 - u)r(1 - \tau_b) + \Delta_b}. \tag{4.10}$$

Tax distortions now arise from both personal and corporate taxes. For example, if $b^* = 1$, then no corporate taxes are paid. However, we still find, after a simple derivation, that $m = \tau_b$, due to the taxes still paid under the personal tax on the interest received by investors.

Under the assumptions above, the King-Fullerton approach calculates the correct effective tax rate $m$. How does the average tax rate compare? To answer this question, note that total (corporate plus individual) taxes paid on the return to corporate investment equal $u(f - dK - brK) + \tau_b brK$. If we divide by the before-tax return to corporate capital, $f - dK$, and simplify, we find that

$$m_{FS} = \frac{\Delta_b}{(1 - u)(f' - d)},$$

so $m_{FS} = m$. The average tax rate calculation generates the correct effective tax rate.

Under the GKS approach, we now find that $TC_t - TR_t = u(I - dK - rbK) + \tau_b rbK$. Given this expression, the value for $m_{GKS}$ in equation (4.4) equals $m$ if and only if $I = (r(1 - \tau_b) + d)K$, that is, when the growth rate in real investment equals the investors' discount rate, $r(1 - \tau_b)$.[16]

How do the results change if, instead of a constraint limiting the debt/capital ratio, the firm faces some real agency costs from having more debt that limit the size of the optimal debt–capital ratio? Assume, for example, that these agency costs as a function of the debt-capital ratio equal $a(b)$.[17] Now optimal investment is characterized by

$$(1 - u)[f' - rb - a(b) - d] = (1 - b)r(1 - \tau_b), \tag{4.7a}$$

so that

$$f' - a(b) - d = r(1 - \tau_b) + \frac{\Delta}{1 - u}. \tag{4.8a}$$

The only substantive change from the situation without real costs of debt when measuring the effective tax rate on new investment is that there is an internal optimum for $b$. None of the three measures for the effective tax rate are affected by this modification.

Note, however, that there are additional efficiency costs, $a(b)$, arising from the tax distortion favoring use of debt that are not reflected in any of these effective tax rate measures that focus strictly on investment incentives. A tax structure that generates the same effective tax disincentive, $\Delta$, without distorting the use of debt finance, instead allowing for more generous depreciation allowances, could in principle avoid this extra efficiency cost, $a(b)$.

### 4.3.5   Choice of Organizational Form

Another complication that is normally ignored when calculating effective tax rates is the choice of organizational form. Under US tax rules, when firms have losses, they generally would prefer to face high tax rates in order to generate larger tax savings, while they would prefer low tax rates when they have profits. If some individuals face personal tax rates above the corporate tax rate,[18] then a firm can structure any capital currently generating losses so that it is part of a subchapter S corporation,[19] owned by investors in high tax brackets. When the capital generates profits, the firm can shift to C-corporation status, and then be taxed at the corporate tax rate.

How does this choice affect $m$, and how does it affect each of the three measures of this tax rate? Consider the following simple case. Assume that depreciation deductions are front loaded, so that projects generate tax losses during their first $s$ years, and taxable profits thereafter. The firm then chooses to be a pass-through entity (i.e., noncorporate or an S corporation) owned by individuals facing a tax rate above the corporate rate while it has losses, and to be a traditional C corporation thereafter. The project is just profitable if

$$\int_0^\infty f' e^{-(r+d)t}\, dt - \int_0^\infty u(t)(f' e^{-dt} - d_t) e^{-rt}\, dt = 1, \tag{4.11}$$

where $u(t)$ represents the statutory marginal tax rate the firm faces in year $t$ of the project. For simplicity we assume that $u(t)$ equals the relevant noncorporate tax rate $\tau$ during the first $s$ years of the project and the corporate rate $u$ thereafter. Let $u^* = (r+d)\int_0^\infty u(t) e^{-(r+d)t}\, dt$ represent the weighted average tax rate faced by the firm, and let $z^* = \int_0^\infty d_t u(t) e^{-rt}\, dt / u^*$. Then equation (4.11) implies

$$f' - d = r + \frac{u^*(r+d)(1 - z^*)}{1 - u^*}. \tag{4.12}$$

The expression for $m$ thus remains unchanged, except that $u^*$ and $z^*$ replace $u$ and $z$.

Applications of the King-Fullerton measure of the effective tax rate have not to date taken into account a firm's ability to choose a tax-efficient organizational form. This measure will therefore be in error to the extent that $u^*$ and $z^*$ differ from $u$ and $z$. Because these shifts in organizational form are done to save on taxes, $m_{KF}$ will be biased upward.

Similarly average tax rate measures in past work have always focused on corporate tax payments, and, in some cases, also on the personal taxes due on this income when it is paid out as dividends or realized in the form of capital gains. Personal taxes saved at an earlier noncorporate stage of the business and shifting of income between the personal and corporate bases at a point in time have been ignored. Since the measure thus ignores the firm's tax savings during its years not subject to the corporation income tax, it also overestimates the effective tax rate.

What about the GKS tax measure? First, note that at any point in time, the firms aged $s$ or less are noncorporate (technically they are pass-through entities), and those aged $s$ or more are corporate. Under an R-base tax, investment by noncorporate firms would be expensed at rate $\tau$, investment by corporate firms (of capital purchased *from* noncorporate firms) would be expensed at rate $u$, while the revenue generated from capital sold by a noncorporate firm would be taxed at rate $\tau$. Under the assumptions above, along with those used earlier, $TC_t - TR_t$ equals

$$\tau I + (u - \tau)Ie^{-(r+d)s} - \int_0^\infty u(t)d_t Ie^{-rt}\, dt. \tag{4.13}$$

Here the first term reflects the cost of expensing for current investment by noncorporate firms. The second term reflects the tax implications under an R-base tax of a sale of capital by the original noncorporate firm and its purchase by a corporate firm, while the third term measures the tax cost of depreciation deductions under current law, assuming that investment has been growing at rate $r$ over time. This expression then equals $u^*(r + d)(1 - z^*)K$, following the same derivation as before.

The resulting measure for the tax rate equals

$$\frac{TC_t - TR_t}{TC_t - TR_t + r(1 - u^*)K} = \frac{\Delta^*}{\Delta^* + r(1 - u^*)},$$

where $\Delta^* = u^*(r + d)(1 - z^*)$. In principle, the GKS approach therefore provides the correct measure of the effective tax rate in this setting.

If the researcher were not aware of these changes in organizational form, as we've presumed in describing the other measures, however, then the second term in expression (4.13) would likely be ignored.[20] In addition $u$, rather than $u^*$, would presumably be used in the denominator, resulting in an *overestimate* of $m$.[21]

## 4.4    Other Complications

So far we have compared the three approaches for measuring the effective tax rate with a baseline measure in a variety of settings. In principle, the KF approach can deal appropriately with any complication, assuming that the model is extended to address it. However, in practice, it is infeasible to address more than a small number of issues. In particular, applications to date have ignored churning and the choice of organizational form, in each case resulting in an overestimate of the effective tax rate.

One advantage of the other two measures is that they have the potential to capture the effects of any and all complications without the researcher having specific knowledge of these complications, since the data on tax payments will automatically reflect these complications. This was to some degree true for the FS measure with respect to churning. However, the FS measure does not deal appropriately with risk, pure profits, or the choice of organizational form, in each case resulting in a substantial overestimate of the investment disincentive due to taxes.

The GKS measure does, however, handle all of these complications well. Even without explicit knowledge of the researcher, it would handle appropriately all but the choice of organizational form, where it would overestimate the investment disincentive.

The results so far (summarized in table 4.1) thus suggest that the low tax revenue observed in GS and in GKS implies that the actual effective tax rate is low, and therefore there is little or no resulting distortion to investment incentives. Likely, due to the implications of the choice of organizational form, both the revenue collected and the resulting distortion have been overestimated. The apparent inconsistency between the high effective tax rates reported in the past literature and the low revenue yield is then explained simply by errors in the calculations of the effective tax rate in the previous literature.

However, this conclusion is not robust. In this section we consider other complications that are not dealt with appropriately under the GKS measure, thus leading us to a more ambiguous set of conclusions. To begin with, we consider the effects of portfolio arbitrage by individual investors, in particular, the tendency of investors in high tax brackets to borrow from those in low tax brackets, saving substantially on the deduction of the interest payments and then investing the funds in more lightly taxed assets. GS found that this form of debt arbitrage was

**Table 4.1**
Summary measures under different complications

| | King-Fullerton | Feldstein-Summers | Gordon-Kalambokidis-Slemrod |
|---|---|---|---|
| Algebraic formula (general) | $m_{KF} = \dfrac{u(r+d)(1-z)}{(1-u)(f'-d)}$ | $m_{FS} = \dfrac{u\left[f_t(K_t) - \int_{s=0}^{\infty} d_{s,t-s}I_{t-s}\,ds\right]}{f_t(K_t) - dK_t}$ | $m_{GKS} = \dfrac{TC_t - TR_t}{Kr(1-u) + TC_t - TR_t}$ |
| Tax law allows expensing | $m_{KF} = 0$ | $m_{FS} = 0$ | $m_{GKS} = 0$ |
| Tax law allows economic depreciation | $m_{KF} = u$ | $m_{FS} = u$ | $m_{GKS} = u$ |
| Churning | $m_{KF} > m$ | $m_{FS} < m$ | $m_{GKS} = m$ |
| Risk | Unchanged | $m_{FS} = \dfrac{u\left[f_{CE} - \int_{s=0}^{\infty} d_{s,t-s}I_{t-s}\,ds + \rho K\right]}{f_{CE} - dK + \rho K}$ | Unchanged |
| Pure profits | Unchanged | $m_{FS} = \dfrac{u\left[f'K + \pi - \int_{s=0}^{\infty} d_{s,t-s}I_{t-s}\,ds\right]}{f'K + \pi - dK}$ | Unchanged |
| Debt finance | With economic depreciation: $m_{KF} = 1 - \dfrac{r(1-\tau_b)}{(f'-d)}$ $= m$ | $m_{FS} = m$ | $m_{GKS} = m$ |
| Choice of organizational form | $m_{KF} > m$ | $m_{FS} > m$ | $m_{GKS} > m$ |

Key to notation: $m$ = effective tax rate, $m$ = discount rate, $r$ = discount rate, $d$ = depreciation rate, $u$ = corporate tax rate, $z$ = present value of depreciation deductions, $\tau_b$ = personal income tax rate on interest income, $f_s(K_s)$ = return to capital in year $s$, $K_s$ = stock of capital in place in year $s$, $d_{s,t-s}$ = depreciation deductions allowed for investments made at time $t - s$, $I_{t-s}$ = investment at time $t - s$, $\rho$ = risk premium, $f_{CE}$ = certainty equivalent value of the return to capital, $\pi$ = profits from inframarginal investments, $TC_s$ = tax revenue collected under current law in year $s$, $TR_s$ = tax revenue collected under $R$-base tax in year $s$.

responsible for a substantial loss of tax revenue, and was an important reason why in 1983 existing US taxes on capital income collected little or no revenue.

### 4.4.1  Debt Arbitrage

In section 4.3.4 we considered the implications of corporate borrowing, but in a setting in which all investors faced the same personal tax rate $\tau$. Consider what happens in a more general setting in which investor $i$ faces a personal tax rate of $\tau_i$, with rates varying by investor. Each individual can now invest in either bonds or equity. If we continue with the simplifying assumption used by King and Fullerton that there is no risk, for each individual one or the other asset will offer a higher after-tax rate of return. In the absence of any restrictions on short holdings and negative tax liabilities, each individual would want to have an unlimited short position in the lower-yielding asset and an unlimited long position in the higher-yielding asset. Thus some further consideration must be added to the analysis to explain the existence of equilibrium portfolios. In what follows we assume that individuals can buy positive amounts of either asset without restriction but can borrow[22] only up to some proportion $\beta$ of their personal savings; that is, if individual $i$ has savings of $S_i$, then she can borrow at most $B_i = \beta S_i$.[23] Let $e$ represent the rate of return on equity, net of any corporate taxes. Then individual $i$ will borrow to buy equity only if $e > r(1 - \tau_i)$—if she borrows, she will borrow up to the allowed limit of $\beta S_i$. If $e < r(1 - \tau_i)$, the individual will, instead, put all her wealth in bonds. Only the marginal investor for whom $e = r(1 - \tau_i)$ will be indifferent between debt and equity. Let the tax rate of this marginal investor be denoted by $\tau^*$.

The marginal after-tax rate of return to savings differs by investor, and clienteles for debt and equity form. For those with $e \le r(1 - \tau_i)$, extra savings are simply invested in bonds so that the marginal return equals $r(1 - \tau_i)$. In contrast, for investors facing $e > r(1 - \tau_i)$, each extra dollar of savings enables the individual to borrow an additional $\beta$ dollars as well. The net return to savings for those that borrow, deduct interest payments on their debt, and invest in equity is then $e + \beta(e - r(1 - \tau_i)) = r(1 - \tau^*) + \beta r(\tau_i - \tau^*)$.

Figure 4.1 graphs this rate of return to an additional dollar of savings, as a function of the individual's tax rate, $\tau_i$. Here we see that savings incentives are a V-shaped function of the tax rate, with a minimum rate of return to savings for the marginal investor for whom

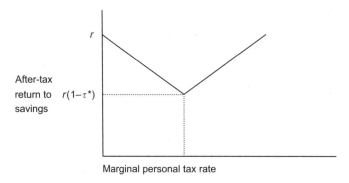

**Figure 4.1**
After-tax rate of return to saving as a function of the marginal personal tax rate.

$e = r(1 - \tau^*)$. Denote the after-tax, or net, return to savings of individual $i$ by $r_i^n$.

What happens to the equilibrium value of $f'$? By definition, the net rate of return to equity is denoted by $e$. Therefore $(f' - d - br)(1 - u) = (1 - b)e$. Since $e = r(1 - \tau^*)$, equation (4.8) continues to hold, now with $\Delta_b = ur(1 - \tau^*) - br(u - \tau^*)$. This focus on the "marginal" investor is the typical strategy used for handling heterogeneous investors under the King-Fullerton approach. Equation (4.8), with $\tau = \tau^*$, then describes $m_{KF}$ in this setting.

In contrast to the setting with a uniform personal tax rate at rate $\tau^*$, however, now virtually all investors earn an after-tax rate of return to savings that is higher than the opportunity cost of funds, $r(1 - \tau^*)$, used in deriving the equilibrium value of $f'$. Therefore, for virtually all investors the $m_{KF}$ measure overestimates the tax distortion between the marginal product of capital and the investor's after-tax marginal rate of return to savings.

More formally, given the equilibrium value of $f'$, we can calculate the effective tax rate faced by any given investor using the equation

$$(f' - d)(1 - m_i) = r_i^n, \tag{4.9a}$$

implying that

$$m_i = \frac{\Delta_b}{(1 - u)(f' - d)} - \frac{r_i^n - r(1 - \tau^*)}{f' - d}. \tag{4.10a}$$

Since $r_i^n \geq r(1 - \tau^*)$, we see that $m_i \leq m_{KF}$, implying that the KF approach overestimates the effective tax rates faced by all investors except those subject to a personal tax rate of $\tau^*$.

Given that effective tax rates vary by investor, what is the right measure of the overall effective tax rate? Or, in other words, what measure best summarizes the distortion caused by the tax system? As tax rates become more heterogeneous, holding the mean tax rate fixed, the excess burden grows, since the excess burden grows approximately with the square of the tax rate. In particular, the excess burden generated by the distorted incentives faced by any individual $i$ equals approximately $0.5m_i dS_i$. If the behavioral response has constant elasticity, then $dS_i/S_i \approx \alpha m_i$ for some $\alpha$, implying an excess burden of $0.5\alpha m_i^2 S_i$ for individual $i$ and an overall excess burden of $\sum_i 0.5\alpha m_i^2 S_i$.

The measure of the effective tax rate that best summarizes the total excess burden should be such that this overall excess burden, $\sum_i 0.5\alpha m_i^2 S_i$, equals $0.5\alpha m^2 \sum_i S_i$. We then infer that

$$m = \left( \frac{\sum_i m_i^2 S_i}{\sum_i S_i} \right)^{0.5},$$

so $m$ equals the weighted root-mean squared average of the $m_i$.

Easier to calculate, but without a clear conceptual underpinning, is the savings-weighted mean tax distortion, $\bar{m} = \sum_i m_i S_i / \sum_i S_i$. As applied to the current US economy, the savings-weighted mean rate is probably quite low, because a large fraction of wealth is held either directly by those in the highest tax brackets or by pension funds and other financial intermediaries that are effectively in a zero tax bracket, giving high weight to the lowest values of $m_i$. However, $\bar{m} < m$: relative to $\bar{m}, m$ gives much more weight to individuals facing high tax rates. It is still the case, however, that $m < m_{KF}$.

In order to understand better the values of the other two tax measures, consider how they compare with $\bar{m}$. Simple algebra reveals that

$$\bar{m} = \frac{\Delta_b}{(1-u)(f'-d)} - \frac{r^n - r(1-\tau^*)}{f'-d}, \tag{4.10b}$$

where $r^n$ is the weighted average return to savings across tax brackets. This becomes our reference point.

Consider, in comparison, an average tax rate measure. Corporate tax payments still equal $u(f' - rb - d)K$. In addition personal taxes are owed on the resulting interest income. Now calculate the average tax rate measure that results if one takes these personal taxes into account but ignores the tax deductions that arise because of borrowing, which is our reading of past practice. The weighted average personal tax rate on interest income, denoted by $\tau^a$, equals $\tau^a = \int_0^{\tau^*} \tau_i S_i \varphi(\tau_i) \, d\tau_i /$

$\int_0^{\tau^*} S_i \varphi(\tau_i) \, d\tau_i$, where $\varphi$ measures the number of investors in each tax bracket.[24] Then taxes on interest income per unit of total capital equal $rb\tau^a$. The average effective tax rate generated using this approach, after some simplifying algebra, equals

$$m_{\text{FS}} = \frac{\Delta_b}{(1-u)(f'-d)} - b\frac{r(1-\tau^a) - r(1-\tau^*)}{f'-d}. \qquad (4.10c)$$

Comparing equations (4.10) and (4.10c), we find that $m_{\text{KF}} > m_{\text{FS}}$, since necessarily $\tau^a < \tau^*$. In equilibrium only those with low marginal tax rates hold debt, so averaging those tax rates will certainly be lower than the tax rate that makes investors indifferent between holding debt and equity.

How does $m_{\text{FS}}$ compare to the measure shown in equation (4.10b)? Answering this question requires a comparison of $r^n$ and $r(1-\tau^a)$. Here $r^n$ is a weighted average of all of the net returns to savings seen in figure 4.1, while $r(1-\tau^a)$ is a weighted average across only those tax rates to the left of the bottom of the V. As the figure is drawn, the two could be quite close. For purposes of discussion, if $r(1-\tau^a) \approx r^n$, then $m_{\text{FS}} > \bar{m}$. How it compares to $m$ is harder to judge.

What about the GKS approach? If, as we do in GS and GKS, one includes in the measure of $TR_s$ the revenue effects of eliminating interest deductions as well as interest income, the resulting estimate for the effective tax rate equals

$$m_{\text{GKS}} = \frac{u(I - dK - rbK) + \int_0^{\tau^*} r\tau_i S_i \varphi \, d\tau_i - \int_{\tau^*}^1 \beta r\tau_i S_i \varphi \, d\tau_i}{(1-u)(f'-d)K}.$$

To see this, recall that in a closed economy all equity and corporate debt is owned by domestic investors. In addition ignore other financial assets, such as noncorporate businesses or government debt. Given these assumptions, net holdings of debt by domestic individuals must equal net corporate borrowing. It follows that

$$m_{\text{GKS}} = \frac{\Delta_b}{(1-u)(f'-d)} - \frac{r^n - r(1-\tau^*)}{(1-u)(f'-d)}. \qquad (4.10d)$$

Comparing equations (4.10b) and (4.10d), we find that $\bar{m} > m_{\text{GKS}}$. Since $m > \bar{m}$, we can conclude that $m_{\text{GKS}} < m < m_{\text{KF}}$. At least in this context, we thus find that the GKS approach underestimates the impact of taxes on the incentive to invest, while the KF approach overestimates it. To learn which approach provides a better approximation will require a close examination of the data.

### 4.4.2   Personal Taxes on Equity Income

So far we have for the most part ignored any personal taxes on dividends or capital gains income from equity holdings. In doing so, we ignored a variety of issues that have been raised in the past literature.

Consider first the size of the distortion generated by the current tax treatment of equity. To make sense of this, the literature has first been forced to come up with a reason why dividends are paid, since dividends are at a clear tax disadvantage relative to share repurchases. One approach, followed, for example, by Auerbach (1979) and Bradford (1981), assumes that shares cannot be repurchased. In their model a tax on dividends lowers the value of existing equity but does not affect investment incentives, at least for investments financed with retained earnings. An alternative explanation for dividends was developed by Bernheim (1991), who argues that dividends and share repurchases are used jointly by firms to signal their profitability. There is some optimal cost for such a signal, inducing firms to use some weighted average of dividends and share repurchase that generate this optimal cost. Any taxes on dividends change the mixture of dividends and share repurchase used, while having no real effect on the firm's investment incentives.[25] While both theories say that taxes on dividends should be ignored, all three methods examined in this chapter view these tax payments as equivalent to other taxes on income from investment, and to that extent overestimate the effective tax rate. In each case an explicit modification in the derivation of the measure would be needed to be consistent with these theories.

Assessing the effects of taxes on realized capital gains raises a different set of complications. As discussed by Stiglitz (1983), under US tax law individuals have an incentive to realize capital losses immediately, and to postpone realizing capital gains at least until they qualify for the lower rate imposed on long-term gains (which they may hold until death when these become tax free). In addition any taxes on capital gains result in risk-sharing with the government, so that the certainty-equivalent tax payment can be much below the expected tax payment. Taking into account both of these effects, Constantinides (1983) found that the existing tax treatment of capital gains likely makes equity investments *more* attractive than in their absence, implying a negative effective tax rate. None of these complications have been taken into account seriously in the public finance literature, and in particular, none of the three measures studied makes any attempt to deal with them, presuming in each case that the expected tax rate is appropriate.[26] As a result each will overestimate the effective tax rate on capital gains.

## 4.5  Conclusions

The past literature investigating taxes on capital income provides a striking contrast between papers that report very high effective tax rates on new investment—with the accompanying distortions—and others that report very low additional tax revenue compared with a tax that does not at all distort savings and investment decisions. If taken at face value, these facts together make a compelling case that the current tax treatment of capital income needs reform.

Alternatively, the low reported revenue from existing taxes may imply that past measures of effective tax rates may be biased upward. The most widely used past measure, developed initially by Hall and Jorgenson (1967) and refined by King and Fullerton (1984), uses a theoretical model to derive an effective tax rate, taking into account what are presumed to be the most important aspects of the tax law and the most important types of behavioral responses. To be feasible, however, many aspects of the law and of behavior have to be ignored in practice. A user must hope that the effects of these omitted issues are of second-order importance. One interpretation of low reported tax revenue is that the omitted issues together are not of second-order importance, and together imply that the actual effective tax rate on new investment is very low.

The other approach, used, for example, by Feldstein and Summers (1979), is to calculate the average tax rate, equal to corporate tax payments plus personal taxes due on corporate income, relative to before-tax corporate income. Any aspect of the tax law and any aspect of behavior will automatically affect observed tax payments. The hope is that the resulting average tax rate provides an appropriate summary of the implications of these many different complications for the incentive to invest, including those omitted in practice from the King-Fullerton type measure of the effective tax rate.

In this chapter we first followed the King-Fullerton framework to define an effective tax rate that correctly measures the impact of taxes on the incentive to invest in any given setting. We then adopted this tax rate as a standard to which we compared the King-Fullerton and Feldstein-Summers measures, *as they have been used in practice*, as well as a third measure developed in this chapter.

The new effective tax rate measure is based on the approach developed initially in Gordon and Slemrod (1988) for estimating the net revenue collected by taxing capital income. Net tax revenue is estimated by calculating how much tax revenue would change if new investment could be expensed, rather than depreciated, and if all financial income were free of tax. As shown in the Meade Committee Report (1978), such an "R-Base" tax leaves savings and investment decisions undistorted. In section 4.2, we proposed a new effective tax rate measure based on this methodology for calculating the net revenue collected from capital income. Ideally this measure automatically captures the effects of any and all complications in the tax law and any and all types of behavioral responses, but it is not biased by the tax revenue that arises from inframarginal investments or risk premia embedded in the average return to capital.

We found that in the simplest setting all three measures are identical, and that they provide a correct estimate of the effective tax rate on new investment. The average tax rate, however, will be strongly biased toward the statutory tax rate once risk and pure profits are taken into account, making it an unreliable approach to measuring the effective tax rate. In several situations, explored in section 4.3, the Gordon-Kalambokidis-Slemrod approach does automatically capture the effects of complications that, in practice, have been omitted from the reported effective tax rates derived using the King-Fullerton approach. In each of these cases, the King-Fullerton measures overestimate the effective tax rate.

Viewed naively, the results of section 4.3 suggest that the difference between the high effective tax rates reported in the past and the low revenue yield may well be due primarily to biases in past measures of the effective tax rate, and that the GKS measure is the best approach of the three for measuring the impact of taxes on investment incentives. However, a notable qualification is that the GKS tax measure relies on ex post data on tax payments under the law, so it cannot be used to assess the effects of proposed changes in the existing law and will not accurately reflect a recently changed law. Even with an unchanging tax law, the GKS approach does not deal appropriately with a set of other complications. In particular, it underestimates the disincentive due to the effects of debt arbitrage, while it overestimates the disincentive due to the current tax treatment of dividends and capital gains.

Because of its superiority on a number of important dimensions, we propose that the GKS measure of the effective tax rate on new investment be added to the pantheon of existing measures. We recognize, though, that any measure of the effective tax rate—including the GKS measure—is imperfect and must therefore be used with caution. At a minimum, any differences in the estimates of the effective tax rates across measures should be investigated further, as these differences may indicate complications ignored by the investigator.

## Notes

1. Feldstein and Summers (1979) found the effective total tax rate on corporate capital income to be about 66 percent in 1977. King and Fullerton (1984) found overall effective total tax rates on capital income to be about 37 percent in 1980.

2. These revenue estimates equal the difference between revenue collected under the current law and revenue collected if income and deductions from financial investments were instead tax exempt and if depreciation deductions on real investments were replaced by expensing.

3. King and Fullerton (1984), p. 235.

4. Among the items on Fullerton's list that are dealt with in this paper are the existence of pure profits, the presence of risk, and the use of debt finance. Fullerton (1984), pp. 28–29.

5. An R-base tax imposes a zero marginal tax rate on new investment and saving; it is described in detail in Meade Committee (1978).

6. This revenue loss figure reflects changes in the tax treatment of all forms of savings and investment, not just investment in corporate capital.

7. In contrast to the FS measure, business cycle effects and possible economies/diseconomies of scale do not affect the estimated revenue figures here.

8. To do so would require recalculating what taxes would have been paid in the current year if the current law had in fact been in effect for the indefinite past. The key correction needed is for depreciation deductions, since investment purchased in the past continues to be depreciated based on the rules existing at the date of the investment rather than under current provisions.

9. See, for example, Fullerton and Henderson (1984) and US Treasury (1984).

10. For further discussion, see Gordon, Hines, and Summers (1987). Note that the firm making use of the structure does not have to change when ownership changes hands. The initial owner may become a renter.

11. Since reported corporate profits fall, presumed capital gains tax payments fall as well.

12. Bulow and Summers (1984) argued that results could differ with random depreciation rather than random return. Gordon and Wilson (1989) explored this issue more carefully, and found that the key factor is the timing of new investment in the future. If new investment tends to be large when the economy is doing well, then individuals pay the resulting taxes on this investment when they can best afford it, so that risk in fact

reduces the effective tax rate. The model discussed in the text has nonstochastic investment rates, so this complication does not arise.

13. For example, in a two-period setting, this risk premium would equal $-\text{cov}(f', U')/EU'$.

14. This expression equals the forgone income each year from not having been allowed to expense the original investment, $ur(1 - \tau_b)$, minus the tax savings arising from the use of debt finance.

15. The difference in the riskiness of equity returns depending on the debt–equity ratio is immaterial in the logic of Miller and Modigliani (1961).

16. Based on the data in the Economic Report of the President, the average annual real growth rate in nonresidential fixed investment between 1959 and 1997 was 4.6 percent, which seems quite close to commonly presumed discount rates.

17. The assumption that $a$ is a function only of $b$ is not an innocuous one. Alternatively, consider the implications if we were to write $a(b, K)$. Then the first-order condition for $K$ would have an additional term that is the partial derivative of $a$ with respect to $K$. In the extreme case in which the non-tax cost of debt was unrelated to $K$—implying that $a(b, K) = a'(b)/K$—the tax benefits of using debt are entirely inframarginal and do not reduce the effective tax rate on new investment. We do not pursue this case because its empirical implication of sharply declining debt–capital ratios with the size of the firm is not observed. Nevertheless, as elaborated by Slemrod (2001), the nature of the non-tax costs of a tax preference, and in particular, whether they are inframarginal or not, is crucial to understanding the relationship between the forgone revenue and the impact on the marginal incentives.

18. This is more likely if the firm has tax losses, since the effective corporate tax rate on losses is close to zero, due to limits on corporate tax loss carry-forwards, but there is immediate deductibility of losses under the personal tax.

19. A subchapter S firm is legally a corporation, but is taxed as a pass-through entity.

20. GS (1988) and GKS (2001) in fact did ignore this term.

21. In particular, relative to $m$, the resulting measure would add $(\tau - u)(r + d)$ to the numerator, and $(\tau - u)(r + d) + r(u^* - u)$ to the denominator. The result is an upward bias as long as the $m$ is below $(m - u)(r + d)/[(m - u)(r + d) + r(u^* - u)] > 0.5$.

22. Borrowing implies negative holdings of debt. We do not allow negative holdings (short sales) of equity.

23. A special case, of course, has no borrowing, in which case $\beta = 0$.

24. Both Feldstein and Summers (1979) and King and Fullerton (1984) used a weighted average of the marginal tax rates on gross interest income calculated with the TAXSIM model of the National Bureau of Economic Research. By this method, the weights are the shares of interest income received by taxpayers facing different tax rates. (See Feldstein and Summers 1979, p. 454, and King and Fullerton 1984, p. 201.)

25. If the tax becomes either too high or too low, however, then the firm's signal will be at a corner solution—either all dividends or all share repurchase—so it will involve costs different from the firm's optimal costs for a signal. With higher costs of a signal, the firm's expenses are higher, and investment can fall.

26. In practice, the KF and FS measures also ignore capital losses, and focus solely on the effective tax rate on capital gains.

# References

Auerbach, A. J. 1979. Wealth maximization and the cost of capital. *Quarterly Journal of Economics* 93: 433–46.

Bernheim, B. D. 1991. Tax policy and the dividend puzzle. *Rand Journal of Economics* 22: 455–76.

Bradford, D. F. 1981. The incidence and allocation effects of a tax on corporate distribution. *Journal of Public Economics* 15: 1–22.

Bulow, J., and L. H. Summers. 1984. The taxation of risky assets. *Journal of Political Economy* 92: 20–39.

Constantinides, G. M. 1983. Capital market equilibrium with personal tax. *Econometrica* 51: 611–36.

Devereux, M. P., and R. Griffith. 1998. The taxation of discrete investment choices. Mimeo. Institute for Fiscal Studies, London.

Feldstein, M., and L. Summers. 1979. Inflation and the taxation of capital income in the corporate sector. *National Tax Journal* 32(4): 445–71.

Fullerton, D. 1984. Which effective tax rate? *National Tax Journal* 37(1): 23–41.

Fullerton, D., and Y. Henderson. 1984. Incentive effects of taxes on income from capital: Alternative policies in the 1980's. In C. R. Hulten and I. V. Sawhill, eds., *The Legacy of Reagonomics: Prospects for Long Term Growth*. Washington: Urban Institute Press.

Gordon, R., and J. R. Hines Jr. 2002. International taxation. National Bureau of Economic Research Working Paper 8854.

Gordon, R., and Y. Lee. 2001. Do taxes affect corporate debt policy? Evidence from US corporate tax return data. *Journal of Public Economics* 82: 195–224.

Gordon, R., J. R. Hines, and L. H. Summers. 1987. Notes on the tax treatment of structures. In M. Feldstein, ed., *The Effects of Taxation on Capital Accumulation*. Chicago: University of Chicago Press, pp. 223–54.

Gordon, R., and J. Slemrod. 1983. A general equilibrium study of subsidies to municipal expenditures. *Journal of Finance* 38(2): 585–94.

Gordon, R., and J. Slemrod. 1988. Do we collect any revenue from taxing capital income? In L. Summers, ed., *Tax Policy and the Economy*, vol. 2. Cambridge: MIT Press, pp. 89–130.

Gordon, R., L. Kalambokidis, and J. Slemrod. 2004. Do we *now* collect any revenue from taxing capital income? *Journal of Public Economics* 88(5): 981–1009.

Gordon, R. H., and J. D. Wilson. 1989. Measuring the efficiency cost of taxing risky capital income. *American Economic Review* 79: 427–39.

Grubert, H., and J. Slemrod. 1998. The effect of taxes on investment and income shifting to Puerto Rico. *Review of Economics and Statistics* 80(3): 365–73.

Hall, R., and D. Jorgenson. 1967. Tax policy and investment behavior. *American Economic Review* 57(3): 391–414.

King, M., and D. Fullerton, eds. 1984. *The Taxation of Income from Capital: A Comparative Study of the United States, the United Kingdom, Sweden, and West Germany.* Chicago: University of Chicago Press.

Meade Committee. 1978. *The Structure and Reform of Direct Taxation.* Boston: Allen and Unwin.

Miller, M. H., and F. Modigliani. 1961. Dividend policy, growth, and the valuation of shares. *Journal of Business* 34: 411–33.

Slemrod, J. 2001. A general model of the behavioral response to taxation. *International Tax and Public Finance* 8(2): 119–28.

Stiglitz, J. 1983. Some aspects of the taxation of capital gains. *Journal of Public Economics* 21: 257–94.

Stiglitz, J. 1985. The general theory of tax avoidance. *National Tax Journal* 38(3): 325–38.

United States Council of Economic Advisers. 1999. *Economic Report of the President, 1999.* Washington: US Government Printing Office.

United States Department of the Treasury. 1984. *Tax Reform for Fairness, Simplicity, and Economic Growth: The Treasury Department Report to the President.* Washington: US Department of the Treasury.

# 5              The Tax Burden on Cross-border Investment: Company Strategies and Country Responses

Harry Grubert

## 5.1   Introduction

Globalization has increased the importance of cross-border direct investment. For example, foreign affiliates of US manufacturing companies accounted for about 25 percent of their worldwide capital expenditures in 1999. Foreign affiliate operations are also important means by which multinational companies exploit the know-how created by their R&D and other investments in intangible assets. An illustration of the importance of these cross-border investments of intangible assets is that in 1999, license fees and royalties from abroad were equal to about 40 percent of total R&D spending in the United States.[1] Because of the importance of cross-border investment, both home and host countries are interested in their competitive position. It is, however, necessary to determine the way in which the international dimension of corporate investment alters conventional domestic measures of effective tax rates.

The relevance of evaluating the tax burdens on these cross-border investments has been recognized in earlier studies, but past attempts to estimate the marginal (and average) effective tax rates on cross-border direct investment have tended to overlook important aspects of both corporate and government behavior. (The 1991 OECD report on taxing profits in the global economy is one example.) First, the earlier estimates do not take into consideration straightforward strategies that companies can use to reduce tax burdens. Putting debt on the books of highly taxed subsidiaries is one simple example. Earlier estimates have also tended to overlook the critical importance of intellectual property, or intangible assets more broadly, in direct investment. Because of the special tax rules that apply to royalties in both the home and host country, a comparison of tax burdens can be reversed when the contribution of intangible income is recognized.

Earlier attempts to measure effective tax rates have also tended to overlook critical features of home and host country systems for taxing cross-border income. For example, in some home country tax systems it is possible to use a finance affiliate in a tax haven into which equity is injected and then loaned to a high-tax subsidiary. The income is therefore taxed neither in the host country nor the home country.

In addition previous analyses of host country provisions have failed to recognize that the host country might vary the burdens they impose on different types of foreign investors depending on their contribution to national welfare. In order to obtain a more complete picture of cross-border tax burdens, it is therefore necessary to distinguish among different types of operations, for example, depending on whether the prospective output is sold in the local market or on world markets.

While it is important to introduce various tax-planning strategies into estimates of tax burdens, it is also necessary to recognize that companies face constraints and costs in engaging in them. If not, they could virtually eliminate their worldwide tax liabilities on cross-border investments using techniques described in this chapter. Evidence on how companies actually behave therefore has to be introduced to make more reliable hypothetical estimates of cross-border tax burdens. For example, the evidence in Altshuler and Grubert (2003) shows that affiliate debt is highly sensitive to the local tax rate, but nevertheless substantial debt remains on the books of low-tax affiliates. This in turn raises a further methodological issue, implicit taxes that reflect the costs of tax avoidance strategies.

Many of the elements that have been overlooked also create new methodological issues, particularly in calculating average effective tax rates relevant for the decision on whether to choose a particular location.[2] One major reason is that many of the company strategies are fundamentally multilateral in nature, involving two or more entities, which complicates the calculation of effective tax rates for each entity separately. For example, if debt can be shifted from a low-tax subsidiary to a high-tax subsidiary, to which one should the tax benefit be attributed in estimating average effective tax rates.

In section 5.2, I begin with a discussion of the methodological issues in estimating cross-border effective tax rates, particularly those presented by the multilateral nature of investment, the role of intangible assets, and companies' tax-minimizing behavior. I proceed to make highly simplified simulations of the effective tax rate on cross-border investment to illustrate the impact of a more complete consideration of both multinational corporation (MNC) strategies and the specific features of systems for taxing cross-border income.[3] I consider two hypothetical operations, one in a high-tax location and the other in a low-tax location. My emphasis is on the tax provisions that apply specifically to cross-border income, namely home country taxes on foreign income and host country taxes on foreign companies. Purely domestic provisions such as accelerated depreciation are not emphasized because they apply to all taxpayers, foreign and domestic. In other words, the main interest is in the costs and benefits of being a multinational company.

In sections 5.3 and 5.4, I introduce new evidence on actual tax burdens and how they depend on the nature of the investments made, the strategies companies use, and government policy choices. In section 5.3, I calculate the actual overall effective tax rate on US manufacturing investment abroad, and then resolve it into its positive and negative components. Rather than relying on hypothetical estimates of the effective tax rate on foreign income, in this section I attempt to determine how US companies' actual average effective tax rate on all foreign investment gets to be what it is. The various possible contributors to lower or higher overall tax burdens on cross-border income discussed are locating a greater share of the investment in low-tax countries, placing more debt on the books of high-tax affiliates, shifting income from high-tax to low-tax locations, and the residual US tax on repatriated income.

In section 5.4, I bring in host governments more explicitly to see how they tax different types of companies. This is difficult to learn simply from tax statutes and regulations, even if we had a fully comprehensive description of the rules in the sixty locations used in this study. Apart from publicly available, transparent rules, such as depreciation schedules for different types of capital, host governments can negotiate special regimes for companies they wish to attract. Relying only on published schedules may give a misleading picture of tax burdens. In the section I therefore use data on effective tax rates at the subsidiary level, derived from company reports to the US Treasury, to discover the kinds companies that pay above average or below average tax rates in a location. (These data are used in more aggregate form in Section 5.3.) The intent of this section is to identify the kinds of investments that host governments value and compete for. In addition to supplementing available information on cross-border tax burdens, the results reveal the extent to which tax competition is evident at the subsidiary level.

In competing for foreign companies, the rational host government will distinguish among them depending on how much they contribute to local welfare and how much the country contributes to the companies' profitability. For example, governments may attempt to extract rents that companies can earn in their country. Similarly they may grant tax concessions to operations that export most of their local production to world markets, and therefore promise gains in national terms of trade and higher real income for local inputs. The question in section 5.4 is whether the tax benefits that host governments grant are consistent with their competing for the operations that contribute the most to national welfare.

## 5.2 How Do the Nature of the Investment and Company Planning Alter Estimates of Effective Tax Rates?

### 5.2.1 Methodological Issues

*What Capital Is Relevant and How Should It Be Modeled?*
A cross-border investment is typically made up of various types of capital, all of which should be accounted for in measures of the tax burden on cross-border investment. These include not only tangible assets like plant, equipment, and inventories but also the return to intangible assets such as patents, trademarks, and other technological or marketing know-how. For investments in the financial sector like banking, tax measures should include the tax on the financial assets that the company has to hold as "capital." Intellectual property, in particular, is a special feature of direct investment because other modes of foreign investment can be used to finance capital in the form of widely available standard plant and equipment or inventories.[4] If a multinational corporation finds that home country taxes on foreign income are burdensome, they could simply lease the plant and equipment from local investors and avoid part of the burden. Indeed, if standard tangible capital that is freely available in world markets is particularly productive in a jurisdiction, purely portfolio inflows could equilibrate worldwide rates of return. (Foreign portfolio investors could be the ones financing the lease above.) In contrast, it is much more difficult to detach intangible assets from the company that developed them,

except perhaps through a merger. As an illustration, only about 30 percent of the royalties received by US companies from abroad are from unrelated parties. If home country rules are restrictive, companies could even expatriate to a tax haven, which is generally much less costly if there are no significant company intangibles being transferred to a foreign tax base. (For example, under the US rules companies would have to pay a "toll charge" that in part depends on the value of intangible assets being expatriated.)

In deciding which types of capital are relevant, it may be helpful to ask why countries want to attract direct investment. Presumably it is because the foreign operation will increase real national income through enhancements in the productivity of local factors, and the like. But the company can offer these benefits for reasons apart from any tangible capital such as plant and equipment it may invest. Why do Frankfurt and London compete for banks, brokers, and insurance companies even though their investment in purely tangible capital is insignificant? Because their capabilities can attract worldwide customers, which increases the demand for local inputs and, furthermore, raises national income through potential improvements in the terms of trade. The effective tax rate relevant for the financial company's location decision is the tax on the return from these enterprise capabilities and from the purely financial assets it uses as capital. (These can of course be located anywhere, which is the source of most of the problems in taxing cross-border financial services.)

Recognizing the contribution of intangible assets is important because the income they produce may be taxed much differently from the return to plant and equipment. If the intangible, such as a patent, was developed at home, the parent should, under normal arm's-length principles, receive royalties for its contribution. These are generally a deductible expense in the host country and subject to tax by the home country. But, as we will see, the actual tax burden on the royalties in the home country can vary.[5]

### Tax-Planning Responses and the Multi-country Nature of Cross-border Investment

Effective tax rates cannot be estimated under the assumption that MNCs will stand still and fail to take advantage of tax-planning opportunities. The tax-planning techniques and behavioral responses we will consider include (1) the locating of debt in high-tax jurisdictions, (2) the shifting of income to low-tax countries through transfer prices for commodities and intangibles, (3) the use of tax haven finance subsidiaries into which equity is injected and then loaned to high-tax affiliates, and (4) the avoidance of home country repatriation taxes. There are also exotic but increasingly important techniques such as the use of hybrid securities and hybrid entities, as we explain below.

Tax-planning behavior creates several methodological issues. One relates to implicit taxes. For example, when MNCs avoid home country repatriation taxes using various planning techniques, they have to bear costs such as accounting, legal, and investment banking fees. Therefore it would be incorrect simply to take actual tax payments on dividends as the only burden of repatriation taxes. Grubert and Mutti (2001) and Altshuler and Grubert (2001) address this issue by adding the "deadweight" loss attributable to restricted dividends; it is derived from an estimated repatriation equation. (This is, of course, only relevant for a low-tax affiliate where there would be a positive home country tax on dividends.) The costs of tax planning are also included in the optimal investment decisions of multinational companies in the Sorensen (2002) simulation model.

Many of the behavioral responses we will consider, such as the shifting of income or debt, generally require the existence of subsidiaries in two or more countries. The large MNCs that account for most of cross-border direct investment have subsidiaries in many locations. But the multi-country nature of tax strategies raises the issue as to which subsidiary the tax saving in a multilateral strategy should be attributed, particularly if we are interested in the average effective tax rate for purposes of a location decision. This is an issue to which we now turn.

### Average versus Marginal Effective Tax Rates and Multi-country Strategies

The discrete all-or-nothing location decision, which motivates the interest in average effective tax rates, is of major interest in addition to the marginal investment decision. Focusing on the average effective tax rate is attractive because it clarifies the importance of intangibles and infra-marginal returns. But consider the case where income is shifted from a high-tax country (e.g., Germany) to a low-tax country (e.g., Ireland). Even for marginal investment decisions in each country after both subsidiaries have been established, it is necessary to know, in addition to the standard cost of capital information, the extent to which an extra dollar of investment in each location adds to total shifted income. This depends in part on the relative size of the two locations because the marginal shifting benefit of additional capital in any location will be greater if it is initially small compared to the other location. (See the simple model in Grubert 2003 as an illustration.) In general, the introduction of income shifting would lower the marginal cost of capital in both locations.

But calculating average effective tax rates can become difficult, or impossible, when the multi-country nature of business strategies is recognized. The average rate becomes more sensitive to what is assumed about the initial starting point. For example, if we assume that neither of the two operations has been established and investing in one is considered, any income shifting benefits are impossible. If one has already been established, all of the shifting benefits will be attributed to the second. But what if neither operation is profitable without income shifting, or both are? In these cases it is not apparent how the average effective tax rate relevant for location decisions is defined for each country separately.

That is not to say that we cannot find what the MNC's optimal decisions are if we had all the profit functions and tax provisions in front of us. It is just that average effective tax rates may not be a useful (or feasible) way of summarizing investment options because they can only be calculated after a series of optimizing decisions, including the choice of location, have been made.

But rather than being deflected by this methodological conundrum, we will make several highly artificial assumptions that permit us to approximate the logic of the marginal calculation. The main goal is finding the potential quantitative significance of various multilateral strategies. As described below, the MNC is considering whether to establish new production lines, with their associated intangible and tangible assets, in two locations. The prospective investments are independent of each other in terms of production costs and markets, and they are of equal size. The company already has large existing operations in each country involving other production lines. These could be used as part of a multi-country strategy by a new operation in one country even if a new operation is not established in the other.

### Mobile versus Locational Rents—What Is the Relevant Effective Tax Measure?

Governments are presumably interested in improving their competitive position in attracting companies. But what it means to be competitive will vary. Consider the comparison of mobile and locational rents. In the former, a valuable product has a worldwide market and low transportation costs, and can therefore be produced in many alternative locations. In the latter, the rents can only be earned if production is in that location. An example would be a branded consumer product that is expensive to transport from one prospective location to another.

In the case of mobile rents, a government is interested in how its effective tax rate, including the taxation of intangible income, compares with other locations. In the case of locational rents, the tax rate on intangible income is relevant only to the extent that any after-tax rents can help finance the tangible investment. The company will enter as long as it can meet its cost of capital on its tangible assets.

It therefore appears that the effective tax rate measure relevant for the discrete location decision differs in the two cases. In the mobile rent case, the choice depends on the net return in this location compared to that in others. In other words, the relevant measure is the effective tax rate on the entire return including the mobile rent. In the case of locational rents, the answer depends on whether the net return from the investment after paying all taxes is enough to earn the required after-tax return on the tangible assets. The company may choose to invest in a very high tax country if the pre-tax locational rents are large enough. (To construct an effective tax rate comparable to an all-tangible investment in terms of location decisions, the cost of capital, i.e., the required pre-tax return, is the required return on the tangible assets less any after-tax return obtained on the rents.) In the case of mobile rents, the company may choose not to invest in a very low tax country if there is an alternative location that is even lower.

### Interest Rates, the Return to Equity, and Constraints on Debt Financing

The benefits of debt-shifting strategies depend in part on the interest rate relative to the required return on equity and on the limits to debt financing by the firm. One assumption in the literature is corporate level arbitrage, as in Sinn (1993) and Weichenrieder (1996). Companies equate the cost of finance, so that $i(1 - t) = r$, where $t$ is the statutory tax rate, $r$ is the required after-corporate-tax return on equity, and $i$ is the interest rate. (We ignore inflation.) Presumably, $t$ is the home country tax rate, but that ambiguity is the problem. The Weichenrieder-Sinn arbitrage condition is difficult to apply consistently in a multi-country framework. It would imply different country interest rates even under a common currency. Why would a Dutch pension fund accept a lower interest rate on Irish bonds than on German bonds? Because of the international mobility of portfolio debt, the assumption of shareholder level arbitrage (i.e., equal worldwide real interest rates) would seem to be more appropriate. Extending shareholder arbitrage to the choice between debt and equity might tend to equalize interest rates and the return to equity, $i = r$.

The ideal solution is, of course, to have a complete capital market model in which the relationship between interest rates and equity returns can vary depending on behavioral responses by investors and companies to changes in tax costs and the risks of bankruptcy. Examples are the comprehensive OECDTAX model used in Sørensen (2002) and the more stripped down computational model in Grubert and Mutti (1994). But this would go beyond the more limited objectives of this chapter.

Whatever the reason, companies do seem to believe that debt is a cheap source of finance, at least when the debt–asset ratio is low. But a company obviously cannot take full advantage of a market equilibrium with $i < r/(1 - t)$ and finance all of its capital with debt. Potential bankruptcy costs would intrude and drive up its borrowing costs. In the simulations we will therefore make the convenient assumption that the company's worldwide debt cannot exceed a fixed percentage of its worldwide assets. If debt is a cheap source of capital but the company is constrained on how much it can borrow in relation to its worldwide assets, the company will have an incentive to put debt in its high-tax subsidiaries. For outside or unrelated party debt, the main question in the simulations is therefore how a given amount of worldwide debt is distributed among the MNC's locations.

The borrowing constraint implicitly assumes that potential bankruptcy costs depend on the company's worldwide debt–asset position. When potential lenders are evaluating a parent's creditworthiness, they will take the subsidiary assets into consideration because they can always be claimed if the parent is in financial distress. To be sure, a subsidiary can go bankrupt without threatening the parent's survival. But if there is a tax advantage to putting a great deal of debt on a highly taxed subsidiary's books, the parent can always provide explicit or implicit guarantees to reassure lenders and lower overall financing costs. In contrast to the worldwide debt constraint assumption, Sørensen (2002) assumes independent debt–asset decisions by each subsidiary. The practical difference for the effective tax rate estimates is that we attribute some of the benefits of the high-tax entity's excess debt to the low-tax entity because the investment in the latter accommodates greater worldwide borrowing.

Other strategies are available for "inside" or intercompany debt. One simple strategy is to capitalize a high-tax subsidiary with loans from the parent instead of equity. A more aggressive strategy is the use of a tax haven finance affiliate if the home country rules allow it. In order to finance a high-tax foreign subsidiary, the MNC injects equity into the tax haven subsidiary, which then lends to the high-tax affiliate. The potentially highly taxed income can therefore be stripped out to the tax haven subsidiary through deductible interest payments, where it is deferred under a worldwide system or repatriated tax free under an exemption system. Because it is inside or intercompany debt, it is not subject to outside creditors' limitations. The return on the company's investment is therefore taxed neither in the home country nor in the host country, though both are nominally high tax. If the initial equity injection can in part be financed with parent debt, the marginal effective tax rate at the corporate level can easily be negative.

### Repatriation Taxes, Trapped Retained Earnings, and Underinvestment —Old View versus New View

If there are home country taxes on repatriations (or host country withholding taxes on dividends), the question arises as to the cost of retained earnings and whether a subsidiary will underinvest initially, as in Sinn (1993), to obtain the benefits of deferral. But this turns out not to be an empirically very important question. As shown in Altshuler and Grubert (2003), MNCs can use a variety of tax planning devices to free trapped retained earnings while avoiding repatriation taxes. Furthermore the evidence in Grubert and Mutti (2001) and Grubert (2001) indicates that the tax burden on repatriations from low-tax countries is very modest even if one adds the tax on actual repatriations and the efficiency loss from having to limit dividends.

### The Interaction of Tax-Shifting Devices

An aggressive tax-planning company has a variety of techniques available. It can, for example, shift third-party debt, alter the prices in intercompany transactions, and establish tax haven finance subsidiaries or hybrid entities. There are two issues here. One relates to the constraints imposed by governments. Will the success of a new vehicle depend on whether the company has already used other shifting techniques because governments are more likely to react to a further reduction in taxable income? The other issue relates to the incentives from the company's point of view. For example, if the company can always use a finance affiliate to strip a given percentage of the subsidiary's income with little risk of penalties, the marginal benefits of other types of income-shifting techniques decline; the statutory tax rate relevant for changes in income on the margin has effectively been reduced.

### 5.2.2   Important Features of Systems for Taxing Cross-border Income

One objective of this chapter is to find whether different rules for taxing cross-border income result in significantly different tax burdens. In addition, to what extent is the comparison altered by the introduction of a wide variety of asset types and of tax-planning responses by companies? As we will see, it is not the most obvious features, such as whether dividends are taxed or exempt, that turn out to be most important.

The questions in characterizing home country rules include:

1. Are direct dividends taxed (with a credit for foreign taxes), or are they exempt?

2. How are royalties taxed, and what foreign tax credits can be used to reduce home country tax liability?

3. Does any allocation of parent overhead expenses such as interest have to be made to foreign income? This can offset the tax benefits of borrowing at home to finance an injection of equity into a low-tax subsidiary. Under a worldwide system with credits for foreign tax, any allocation reduces net foreign income for purposes of calculating the foreign tax credit limitation. Under an exemption (territorial) system, the allocation reduces deductions against domestic taxable income. The United States seems to be the only country that applies serious interest allocation rules.[6]

4. Can a tax haven finance subsidiary that has received an equity injection from the parent be used to lend the funds to a high-tax affiliate, or is any interest it receives subject to current home country tax? Japan, among other countries, apparently allows tax haven finance affiliates. The German rules governing finance subsidiaries were recently tightened.

5. Can a foreign subsidiary be capitalized with hybrid securities, namely securities that are regarded as debt in the host country and equity at home? Under an exemption system, for example, interest on the hybrid security would be deductible in the host country while it is regarded as an exempt dividend by the home country. (MNCs can get equity treatment at home by taking advantage of the usual restrictions on what can be identified as deductible debt. They can exploit rules intended for a purely domestic context.) The Canadian system, which exempts dividends by treaty, has been vulnerable to this device.

6. Can MNCs use a hybrid entity, which is regarded as an offshore, incorporated operation by the host country and as an unincorporated branch, and therefore transparent, by the home country? These can be used instead of tax haven finance affiliates if the latter are barred by the home country rules. The finance hybrid, organized in a tax haven, is invisible to the home country because it is regarded as a branch of the high-tax subsidiary. But the host country permits a deduction for the interest paid to the hybrid.

7. There are other anti-abuse rules that may have an important impact on particular operations. For example, the Unites States has "foreign base sales" rules that tax trading income in low-tax countries currently if no manufacturing has taken place.

Host country rules for outgoing payments can, of course, also be important, although they receive less emphasis in this chapter. Withholding taxes on dividends and royalties increase effective tax rates if they cannot be credited against home country tax liability. In addition host governments frequently implement "thin capitalization" or "earnings-stripping" provisions that attempt to limit the extent to which a subsidiary can rely on debt financing, particularly when some of the debt is extended by the parent or another related party.

### 5.2.3  Effective Tax Rate Simulations—What Is Important?

The purpose of the simulations in this section is to identify the factors that are important in determining the tax burden on cross-border investments. For example, does the composition of assets make a significant difference? Do income shifting and other kinds of tax planning have a notable impact? Are worldwide and territorial systems really very different?

In order to capture the multi-country nature of MNC decision making, we will assume that a parent MNC based in an industrialized high-tax country like the United States is considering locating new production lines of equal size in two locations. One of the locations is low tax with a statutory tax rate of 10 percent and the other is high tax with a statutory tax rate of 40 percent. The home country has a 35 percent tax rate. To concentrate on international tax rules, we assume that there are no investment incentives such as accelerated depreciation or investment credits, so that the marginal and average effective tax rates, for purely domestic investors, are equal to the statutory tax rate.

The MNC already has many production lines in each location and the existing operations are of equal size. Accordingly, any benefits that one of the prospective operations could obtain with triangular strategies like debt shifting does not depend on the decision to establish the other because the existing operations are already available as vehicles. The new potential production lines are small compared to the existing operations so that marginal calculations are a good approximation. The shifting function $s(K_1, K_2)$, which indicates the amount of income that can be shifted from one location to another, is linear homogeneous and symmetric in the $K_i$'s. If both expansions take place, there is a proportionate increase in total shifting. Accordingly, if only one expands, it receives half the total shifting benefit that would accrue if both expanded.

A fixed amount of tangible assets has to be invested in the new production line, and for simplicity, we assume that the scale is not affected by the tax rate. The products in the prospective lines have special features that allow the company to earn above-normal profits on the tangible assets it has to invest. (We ignore the R&D process and how the intangible is created.) The return on the intangible assets is paid to the parent in the form of royalties. The intangibles are implicitly assumed to be mobile because the estimated effective tax rate is based on the taxes paid in relation to the entire return including rents.

The tangible assets are financed with a mix of debt and equity. We will assume that the company can only finance a given percentage of its assets with debt. But the debt that finances assets in one country can be put on the books of any one of the two foreign affiliates or on the books of the parent. The interest rate the company pays is the same in real terms wherever it chooses to borrow. Furthermore, we assume for simplicity that the real interest rate is equal to the pre-tax return on equity.

One of the purposes of the simulations is to compare exemption and worldwide systems for taxing cross-border business income, so it is necessary to briefly summarize the basic features of each that are assumed in our base case.[7] In the worldwide system only repatriated business income is taxed currently by the home country, namely dividends, royalties and interest. A credit is granted for foreign taxes paid including the underlying corporate tax associated with a dividend. But the foreign tax credit is limited to what the home country tax would be on the net foreign income after deductions. Parents with excess foreign tax credits (i.e., with more than they can use) are referred to as being in *excess credit*. If they have credits available less than their allowable limit, they are referred to as being in *excess limit*. We assume that the foreign tax limitation is on an overall basis, so that all repatriated active income is in the same pool for purposes of the calculation. This means that excess credits originating with dividends or other highly taxed income can shield royalties and other lightly taxed income.

In the exemption system, dividends from an active business are exempt from home country tax. But royalties and interest received by the parent, which are deductible in the host country, are generally taxed at the normal corporate rate by the home country with a credit for foreign withholding taxes. (France, an exemption country, taxes royalties at a rate somewhat lower than the basic corporate rate.)

The question of allocated deductions arises in both systems. For example, in the exemption system, do parent overhead expenses such as interest have to be allocated or attributed to exempt income? This means that they would be lost as deductions against domestic taxable income. If no allocation is required, the parent could borrow, get a deduction for the interest at home, and then inject equity into a low-tax subsidiary that would eventually yield exempt dividends. That is, it could receive an interest deduction without any inclusion of income. The simulations will be performed both ways, with and without required allocations, so that we can evaluate the sensitivity of effective tax rates to this provision.

In the worldwide system, the cost of capital in a location may depend critically on whether the parent company is in an excess credit or an excess limit position. Therefore there have to be separate calculations for these two cases. (We assume that the parent's overall position is not affected by the investment decisions being considered.) Accordingly there are effectively three cases, two for the worldwide system and one for the dividend exemption system. Under US rules the parent's excess credit position depends on its repatriated business income from all locations. As stated above, that is assumed here.[8]

The various alternative features of tax systems and possible company responses will be summed up in a series of parameters used in constructing effective tax rates in the alternative scenarios. Appendix B at the end of the chapter presents a complete list of these parameters and the equations used in each scenario. Some of the more important parameters are as follows:

$R$, the share of before-tax income accounted for by royalties.

$l$, the share of the multinational company's worldwide tangible assets that can be financed with debt.

$d_1$, the share of the low-tax affiliate's debt shifted to the high-tax affiliate's books, and $d_2$ the share carried on the parent's books. In these shifts of debt we assume that the interest costs per dollar of debt are unchanged.

$s$, the share of the high-tax subsidiary's marginal equity income that is shifted to the low-tax country over and above the shift of debt. Grubert (2003) finds that almost all of the difference in profitability between high-tax and low-tax countries is attributable to the location of debt and to the shifting of intangible income.

$H_d$, the share of high-tax subsidiary capital that is financed with hybrid securities under a dividend exemption system.

$H_f$, the share of the tangible capital of each subsidiary that is financed with loans from a tax haven finance affiliate or hybrid entity into which equity had been injected by the parent.

$IA$, the portion of $d_2$, the debt shifted to the parent's books, that has to be allocated to foreign income under the home country rules. The allocation can reduce foreign tax credits under a worldwide system or domestic deductions under an exemption system.

As we noted earlier, our calculations are based on highly simplifying assumptions to make it easier to identify the effect of the strategies and provisions we are interested in. Rather than assuming a required after-tax rate of return to construct a cost of capital, or before-tax required return, we assume a given before-tax return on tangible and intangible assets and simply calculate the effective tax rate by accounting for all the tax payments and deductions. (This is what King and Fullerton 1984 call the "fixed $p$" case.)[9] It is only necessary to account for all of the tax payments on the tangible and intangible income to both the host and home governments. The only complication is assigning the benefits of a multi-country strategy. As suggested above, we assume that the benefit of a shift of net taxable income from the high-tax to the low-tax subsidiary when one expands is equal to half of the total shifting benefit when both expand. That is, each hypothetical expansion benefits equally from the existing operations in the other location. When taxable income is shifted from the home country to the low-tax location, we attribute the entire benefit to the low-tax subsidiary.

As we indicated above, residual US taxes on dividends are very modest. Even mature subsidiaries in low-tax countries have low dividend repatriation rates. Altshuler and Grubert (2003) find no evidence that low-tax subsidiaries underinvest in their early years to increase their benefits from deferral, presumably because they have many ways of avoiding home country taxes. Whether one chooses the "old view" or the "new view" on the burden of repatriation taxes would not seem to have an important effect on the estimates of effective tax rates because the tax burden on repatriations is so modest. We choose the old view, in part for simplicity because the issue is not the main subject of this chapter, but also because the evidence does not seem to be consistent with the new view at least as it is usually characterized. Furthermore, for the de novo investment being assumed, it is appropriate to include potential repatriation costs because they would enter into the parent's decision on whether to choose a particular location. Implicitly we assume that in each period the low-tax subsidiary repatriates a given (small) percentage of its net income and, if there is a residual home country tax, it bears both the actual tax paid and the implicit tax reflecting the planning costs of avoiding repatriations. The retained earnings are presumably invested in passive assets or other affiliates, as described in Altshuler and Grubert (2003). The implicit tax includes any sacrifice compared to its normal return that the company has to accept on deferred income. Abstracting from any potential underinvestment period makes it unnecessary to use a multi-period model, even though it is admittedly inconsistent with the Sinn (1993) model of a subsidiary that would, in principle, apply even if repatriation taxes are low.

## 5.2.4   The Table 5.1 Scenarios

The first scenario in table 5.1 is the simplest base case. All of the capital is in the form of tangible capital like plant and equipment, and equity

**Table 5.1**
Effective tax rates for new production lines in high-tax and low-tax locations: Corporate level tax

| High-tax country $t = 0.40$ | | | Low-tax country $t = 0.1$ | | | |
|---|---|---|---|---|---|---|
| Excess credit | Excess limit | Dividend exemption | Excess credit | Excess limit | Dividend exemption | Scenario |
| 0.40 | 0.35 | 0.40 | 0.1 | 0.14 | 0.1 | 1. Tangible capital only; all equity–no income shifting |
| 0.20 | 0.175 | 0.20 | 0.05 | 0.07 | 0.05 | 2. Tangible assets financed with 50% debt–no debt shift |
| 0.15 | 0.21875 | 0.2375 | 0.0375 | 0.14 | 0.125 | 3. Royalties = 25% of income |
| 0.1359 | 0.2089 | 0.2234 | 0 | 0.1105 | 0.0875 | 4. 25% of low-tax debt shifted to high-tax and 25% to home country |
| 0.1359 | 0.2089 | 0.2234 | 0 | 0.0895 | 0.0625 | 5. Royalties respond-reduced by 40% if fully taxed at home and from LT sub |
| 0.1254 | 0.2015 | 0.2129 | −0.0105 | 0.0821 | 0.0520 | 6. 25% of high-tax equity income shifted to low-tax subsidiary; benefit split between them |
| 0.1254 | 0.2015 | 0.2129 | 0.0129 | 0.0821 | 0.0754 | 7. Home country requires that debt shifted to parent be allocated to foreign income |
| 0.1254 | 0.2015 | 0.1502 | 0.0129 | 0.0821 | 0.0947 | 8. Hybrid securities are 50% of high-tax sub-tangible capital under exemption |
| 0.0504 | 0.1359 | 0.1379 | −0.0059 | 0.0559 | 0.0565 | 9. Finance affiliates or hybrid entities are used to finance 25% of tangible capital |

is the only source of finance ($R = 0$ and $l = 0$). As was just noted above, the equity for the investment in this new production line is in the form of an equity injection from the parent. Only a few items require comment. We assume a home country tax of 35 percent. The 35 percent high-tax country effective tax rate in the second column, for excess limit parents, reflects the fact that 5 percentage points of the foreign tax can be credited against other foreign income. In the case of the low-tax subsidiary with excess limit parents, the additional 4 percentage points of tax reflects the burden of the home country repatriation tax under our old view assumption. It is adapted from Grubert and Mutti (2001) and includes both the tax paid on actual distributions and the implicit deadweight loss attributable to repatriation planning.

In the second row, all entities, including the parent, are financed 50 percent with debt ($l = 0.5$). We assume for simplicity that the real interest rate is equal to the before-tax return on tangible assets. The corporate-level effective tax rates in table 5.1 therefore fall by 50 percent.

In the third scenario, 25 percent of affiliate before-tax income is paid to the parent in the form of royalties in return for the intangible assets it has received ($R = 0.25$). (No attempt is made to shift income at this stage.) That is, tangible assets make up the remaining 75 percent of total assets. (We ignore any return to the intangible assets that is not paid out in royalties.) Debt only finances tangible assets so it now accounts for 37.5 percent of total capital. The royalties are deductible against subsidiary net income abroad. (Host country withholding taxes, which are generally low, are also ignored.) Reading across the third row, we see that the effective tax rate declines for excess credit companies because the excess credits can be used to shield the new royalties and effectively exempt them from tax. The effective tax rates for subsidiaries with excess limit parents go up because the home country rate at which they are taxed, 35 percent, is higher than the comparable effective tax rate in the previous row. The effective tax rate also goes up for subsidiaries in an exemption system because royalties are not exempt but fully taxable. Companies in a worldwide system with excess credits gain while those lacking credits or in an exemption system can lose substantially. Note, for example, the effective tax rate in the low-tax affiliate rises from 5 to 12.5 percent in an exemption system, while it falls to 3.75 percent in subsidiaries of parents with excess credits in a worldwide system. This simple example confirms the importance of including the tax on intangible income in assessments of cross-border effective tax rates.

The next three scenarios successively add tax planning in the form of the reallocation of debt in the worldwide enterprise, the reduction of royalty payments where this is advantageous, and other types of income shifting. These responses to tax incentives assumed are approximately in accord with observed behavior.[10] In scenario 4, 25 percent of low-tax debt is shifted to the high-tax subsidiary and a further 25 percent is shifted to the parent ($d_1 = 0.25$ and $d_2 = 0.25$). The shift to the high-tax location is roughly equal to the shifting of debt reported by Altshuler and Grubert (2003). The increased debt on the parent's books is consistent with the higher parent leverage reported in the *1994 Benchmark Survey on US Direct Investment Abroad*. (When we refer to a shift of debt, it just means that the initial capitalization is altered.) The tax benefits from the shift to the high-tax country are attributed equally to each of the subsidiaries and the benefit of the shift of debt to the parent is all attributed to the low-tax affiliate. Comparing this with scenario 3, we see that the reallocation of debt lowers the low-tax subsidiary's effective tax rate by an average of more than 3 percentage points.

In scenario 5, the company lowers royalty payments to the parents by 40 percent if they are fully taxable at home, namely in the exemption and excess limit cases, and if they also originate in a low-tax country. (If they originate in a high-tax location, the extra home country tax is less than the loss in host country deductions when the royalties are switched to taxable equity income.) Net equity income, which is exempt from home country tax or can be deferred, increases by an amount corresponding to the fall in royalties. These responses are consistent with the finding in Grubert (2001) that royalties paid are strongly influenced by the excess credit position of the parent and the local tax rate. The fall in royalties lowers the low-tax country's effective tax rate by about another 2 percentage points.

In scenario 6, 25 percent of the remaining net equity income in the high-tax subsidiary, after all of its extra interest deductions in scenario 4, is shifted to the low-tax subsidiary ($s = 0.25$). Companies can exploit the range of uncertainty in transfer prices for commodities. As indicated in Grubert (2003), this ability to shift income is linked to company intangible assets, particularly those derived from R&D. Effective tax rates drop by about an average of one percentage point.

Scenario 7 shows how home governments can respond to the domestic interest deductions for debt that is used to finance foreign investment. The government mandates that some domestic interest expense be allocated to foreign income depending on the share of total assets that are abroad. A straightforward method would be to implement worldwide fungibility, that is, equal debt–asset ratios at home and abroad. Interest is then allocated to foreign income to the extent that foreign subsidiaries are less leveraged than the parent. If we assume equal debt–asset ratios to start with before the shift of debt in scenario 4, this means that the low-tax debt that has been shifted to the parent now has to be allocated to foreign income. In the worldwide systems this lowers net foreign income and reduces the maximum of foreign taxes that can be credited. In exemption systems, the allocation reduces the interest deductions that can be taken against domestic taxable income. We assume that where required allocations bite, in the excess credit and exemption cases, the debt is moved back to the low-tax country where it can at least get a tax deduction, albeit at a low tax rate.[11]

This home government allocation rule reverses some of the benefits of debt shifting. But note that the required allocation has no effect in the excess limit case. If the parent MNC in a worldwide system continues to be able to credit all of its foreign taxes, it can borrow and inject equity into a low-tax subsidiary without the tax benefit being eroded by the allocation rules.

Scenarios 8 and 9 introduce the use of aggressive devices, hybrid securities and hybrid entities, which appear to be becoming more widespread. One issue, discussed above, is how the use of these schemes affects the incentive to shift income on the margin considered in the earlier scenarios. That is, do they alter the subsidiary's effective statutory tax rate because their use is expanded or contracted proportionately as the subsidiary earns more or less taxable income? Or it may be that both of these devices involve subsidiary debt, at least from the host country's point of view, and are therefore limited mainly by the subsidiary's assets irrespective of how much income it earns. On this point, scenario 8 makes assumptions different from scenario 9.

In scenario 8 hybrid securities are used to capitalize 50 percent of the high-tax subsidiary's tangible assets when the parent is in a dividend exemption country ($H_d = 0.5$). We assume here that all the other income components shrink proportionately, consistent with a change in effective statutory tax rates that scales down the income shifting in the earlier scenarios. The use of the hybrid security, of course, has a dramatic effect on the high-tax affiliate's effective tax rate because its payments on the hybrid security are deductible in the host country but are exempt dividends when received by the parent. Note that the low-tax affiliate's effective tax rate rises in this exemption scenario because its value as a destination for shifted income has declined. This illustrates the difficulty in estimating effective tax rates because it is necessary to specify all of the alternative planning vehicles the MNC has available.

In scenario 9 tax haven hybrid entities, or finance subsidiaries if allowed under home country rules, are used to finance 25 percent of each subsidiary's tangible assets and the interest payments to the tax haven entity are completely free from tax ($H_f = 0.25$). Equity is injected into the tax haven finance subsidiary or hybrid entity and then loaned to the operating companies where the interest payments are deductible from local taxable income. (We ignore host country thin capitalization rules mentioned above, which are another complication.) The interest received by the tax haven entity is either retained there under a worldwide system or repatriated tax free in an exemption system. This scenario assumes that the incentives to shift income on the margin introduced in scenarios 4 to 6 remain unchanged so that the benefit of the hybrid is additive to the other shifting benefits. As expected, effective tax rates drop substantially, particularly in high-tax subsidiaries where hybrid entities seem to be most frequently used.[12]

These elementary calculations sum up as follows:

1. The composition of assets is clearly important. The increasing importance of royalties can have a substantial effect on cross-border effective tax rates, but in differing directions depending on whether the home country has an exemption or worldwide system, and if worldwide, whether the parent has excess credits.

2. Tax planning, such as the shifting of debt, can potentially have a very significant effect. But it is necessary to introduce evidence on actual corporate behavior to avoid overstating its role.

3. As shown in Grubert and Mutti (2001) and Altshuler and Grubert (2001), effective tax rates on foreign income can be higher in an exemption system than in a worldwide system. This reflects the importance of royalties and of parent interest deductions that may be disallowed.

4. Some newer more exotic techniques, like hybrid entities, which are becoming widespread, have the potential for large reductions in tax burdens.

5. Governments can respond to offset some of the impact of MNC tax planning. The high-tax host country can impose "thin capitalization"

rules, which we have not explicitly introduced in table 5.1, to prevent the disappearance of local taxable income. Home governments can implement expense allocation rules, although this may encourage MNCs to expatriate to a more favorable tax environment.

6. The prospect for estimating definitive effective tax rates relevant for a location decision is not encouraging. In the highly simplified calculations in table 5.1, there is a wide range in possible outcomes even though they ignore issues such as those raised by implicit taxes, mobile versus locational intangibles, host country thin capitalization rules, and the availability of more than two potential locations.

### 5.3 The Positive and Negative Components of the Actual Tax Burden on Foreign Income

The objective of this section is to identify the components that are significant in determining the overall tax burden on the foreign manufacturing income earned by US companies. It supplements the hypothetical calculations in the previous section and evaluates the importance of each positive and negative component of the tax burden. Admittedly, looking at foreign manufacturing income in the aggregate abstracts from some of the problems discussed above that arise from the multilateral nature of tax planning.[13] In addition there are, of course, many alternatives in the order in which the decomposition can be presented, and because we are dealing with large discrete changes, the amount attributed to any given component may depend on the particular sequence. (Where the order might appear to affect a conclusion, we will refer to the results of the alternative order.) We start with the tax burden on net equity income abroad and then introduce the roles of royalties, income shifting, and debt. The order is similar but not identical to the illustrative simulations in the previous section.

In determining the actual overall effective tax rate on all the manufacturing income earned abroad by US companies in 1996, we attempt to account for all of the return on the tangible and intangible assets and the corporate level tax paid on this income. This includes the net equity income of the manufacturing affiliates, the royalties paid to the parent, the interest paid on the debt, and the host and home country taxes paid. Some of this information can be taken directly from tax return data, for example, the net income and taxes paid by foreign subsidiaries. (These data are described in appendix A.) Other segments

**Table 5.2**
Decomposing the overall effective tax rate on US manufacturing income abroad (1996): Corporate level

| Steps | Effective tax rate |
| --- | --- |
| 1. Base case. Real capital in each location is proportionate to local GDP. Net income per unit of real assets is same in all locations. No debt financing. No income from intangibles. | 28.6 |
| 2. Capital in its actual location. The shift reflects the response of investment to effective tax rates. All other assumptions in step 1 are retained. | 24.1 |
| 3. Actual net income in each location. This change in the effective tax rate reflects the benefits of income shifting. | 22.3 |
| 4. Royalties paid to the parent included in the total investment return. The royalties are deducted abroad and included in US taxable income. But they may be shielded by available excess credits. | 19.8 |
| 5. Residual US tax on repatriated dividends added. Dividends are taxed but receive a credit for foreign tax including underlying corporate tax. | 20.8 |
| 6. Debt on the books of foreign subsidiaries included as a source of finance for tangible assets. We assume that the interest rate equals the before-tax return to equity. | 11.6 |
| 7. Portion of parent's debt attributed to foreign subsidiaries to reflect greater parent leverage. Interest is deducted at US tax rate. | 8.1 |
| 8. Mandated allocation of parent interest to foreign income for the purpose of calculating the limitation on foreign tax credits. Companies in excess credit can take fewer credits. | 9.3 |

Note: Estimates are based on tax return and survey data described in appendix A, and on author's calculations.

require some assumptions and imputations, such as the amount of US parent debt that finances foreign investment. Because interest payments are included in the income base for purposes of calculating an effective tax rate, the final estimate should not be confused with an effective tax rate on equity alone. It is more comparable to effective tax rates in the literature that are a weighted average of the tax on equity and debt.

Accordingly, the steps given in table 5.2 are as follows:

1. The average overall tax rate on subsidiary income is computed by assuming that real assets in each location are proportional to local GDP and that net equity income per dollar of real assets is the same in all foreign locations. That is, there is no income shifting from high-tax to low-tax locations. Average effective tax rates in each country are

calculated from data for the earnings and foreign taxes paid by manu-facturing subsidiaries in each foreign location. (There is information on 60 countries.) Only equity income is considered. This base effective tax rate turns out to be 28.6 percent.

2. The tax rate is recomputed keeping the equal profitability and all equity assumptions in step 1, but now letting capital be in its actual location, bearing the local average effective tax rate. This lowers the average effective tax rate on equity income to 24.1 percent, or by more than 4 percentage points, which is consistent with the highly sensitive response of investment to local tax rates reported in Altshuler, Grubert, and Newlon (2001) and Grubert and Mutti (2001).

3. Then we compute the tax rate with actual net equity income per unit of assets in each location. This reshuffling of foreign equity income reflects income shifting in response to tax rate differences, either through the reallocation of debt financing among foreign subsidiaries or by other means. The average effective tax rate falls by almost 2 per-centage points to 22.3 percent. *Note that the movement of real capital has a much larger impact than the movement of tax bases, holding real capital constant.* Furthermore this conclusion that real assets are more mobile than tax bases does not depend on which component is calculated first. If the change in the effective tax rate attributable to profit shifting is cal-culated first, before the change attributable to the movement of capital, the profit-shifting component is still only about two-thirds of the capi-tal location component.[14]

4. Royalties are now included as an income component. These are de-ductible against foreign tax and there is only a (generally low) with-holding tax abroad. Royalties payments by US subsidiaries are now substantial, about 20 percent of net before-tax foreign manufacturing income before deducting royalties. The royalties are subject to US tax, but they can be shielded by any excess credits flowing over from highly taxed dividends. Thus 72 percent of total royalties are ef-fectively exempt from US tax because of available excess foreign tax credits.[15] The remaining royalties are taxed at the US rate of 35 percent. The effective tax rate therefore falls by 2.5 percentage points to 19.8 percent.

5. The residual US tax on repatriated dividends is added. As indicated in Grubert (2001), this tends to be small, about 1 percent of income, raising the average effective tax rate to 20.8 percent. Dividends bear a residual US tax only if the host country tax rate is less than the US rate

and the parent company does not have excess foreign tax credits available. The evidence in Grubert and Mutti (2001) shows that repatriations from low-tax countries are very modest.

6. At this point the impact of the *average* level of *foreign* affiliate debt financing, and the associated interest deductions, are introduced. (The shifting of equity income in step 3 in part reflected the reallocation of the average level of foreign debt from low-tax to high-tax subsidiaries, but the estimated tax rate only applied to equity income.) That is, we start with debt on the books of foreign subsidiaries, which is on average 50 percent of tangible assets. As in the simulations we assume, for simplicity, that the real interest rate is equal to the before-tax return on equity. This gives us the weights for debt and equity in affiliates' weighted effective tax rate. The combined corporate level effective tax rate, reflecting both royalties and debt, falls to 11.6 percent.

7. Data in the 1994 Benchmark Survey of US Direct Investment Abroad published by the US Commerce Department indicate that nonfinancial MNCs have a worldwide debt–asset ratio of approximately 60 percent. Parents are therefore more heavily leveraged than their subsidiaries with a debt–asset ratio of only 50 percent. In assessing the significance of this excess parent debt, the neutral assumption is worldwide fungibility, that is, equal debt–asset ratios in each location in the absence of tax distortions. This is based on the assumption that the amount MNCs can borrow depends on their total worldwide assets independently of where the assets are located.

The implication of worldwide fungibility is that 10 percent of foreign tangible assets are in effect financed with parent debt, although it is injected as equity. In contrast to normal debt financing, where the interest deduction is matched by the increased income from the debt-financed assets, this deduction of excess interest against US taxable income is not matched by any inclusion of income we have not accounted for. That is, the foreign tax on the parents' equity injection has already been included as well as any residual US tax on dividends attributable to this equity. Further the tax saving from income shifting in step 3 reflects only the shifting of equity income from low-tax foreign countries to high-tax foreign countries, which may in part reflect a reallocation of foreign debt and not increased debt on the parent's books that finances foreign investment. Step 4 accounts only for the average level of foreign debt in constructing a weighted effective tax rate. These deductions of interest on excess parent debt have a very substantial impact, lowering the effective tax rate to 8.1 percent, or by more than 3 percentage points.

8. But this benefit of US parent debt is overstated because of required expense allocations under US rules. Parent interest has to be allocated to foreign source income for the purpose of calculating the limitation on foreign tax credits, which is based on net foreign income after deductions. The allocation of interest therefore causes a loss of potential foreign tax credits if the parent is in an excess credit position. The adjustment for the overstatement of the benefits of parent debt, derived from tax return data on how much interest companies actually allocate to foreign income, increases the overall effective tax rate on foreign manufacturing income to 9.3 percent.[16] As emphasized earlier, very few, if any, countries other than the United States have effective interest allocation rules. This provides companies based outside the United States even greater opportunities for putting debt in the most "tax-efficient" location.

These calculations show what is important in determining multinational corporations' worldwide tax on cross-border income. They are generally consistent with the simulations in the previous section. Steps 3 and 4 show that income shifting and the tax treatment of royalties together lower the overall effective tax rate by more than 4 percentage points. The ability to deduct interest at home while injecting equity abroad also has a very significant effect, although the required interest allocations under the US rules are a partial offset to this benefit.[17]

The estimates on table 5.2 suggest that there are substantial benefits to being a multinational corporation. The overall average effective tax rate for US manufacturing MNCs can be compared to the tax burden on the average local foreign company that has the same debt-to-asset ratio as the average US company abroad and pays the full local tax rate on any income from intangible assets. These assumptions result in an effective tax burden for the local company of approximately 16 percent, or more than 5 percentage points greater than the burden on US manufacturing income abroad.[18] These benefits derive from the ability of MNCs to choose low-tax locations, rearrange the debt held throughout the worldwide enterprise, shield some of their royalty income with excess credits, and use other strategies to shift income.

After this look at the overall tax rate on cross-border manufacturing income, the next section goes to the other extreme of aggregation and uses subsidiary level data to determine which type of company pays lower than average tax rates in any location.

## 5.4   Which Companies Receive Tax Breaks and Which Receive Penalties?—Tax Competition at the Subsidiary Level

This section has two related objectives. One is to supplement the information in the first two sections by examining actual tax burdens at the subsidiary level. These data are used to identify how effective tax rates vary in a location depending on the subsidiary's characteristics. As stressed at the beginning, these differences would frequently be difficult to identify, even from detailed publicly available host country tax rules.

The second purpose of the section is to explain why governments discriminate among different types of companies. Specifically, it attempts to evaluate tax competition at the company level. Past studies of international tax competition have relied on various types of country level data. Some have used hypothetical Hall-Jorgenson–King–Fullerton effective tax rates estimated from the basic few features of a tax system, that is, the statutory tax rate, depreciation schedules and investment credits (e.g., see Devereux, Lockwood, and Redoano 2002). Some have been based on data for aggregate corporate revenues in relation to GDP (e.g., Slemrod 2001). They try to see whether countries have lowered their tax rates in response to increased capital mobility. Some also estimate how a country reacts to tax reductions by its neighbors. Presumably a tax reduction by a competitor increases the elasticity of the supply of foreign capital that a country faces. However, because of the limited number of observations and the severe methodological difficulties, these studies have not tended to be very conclusive.

But, if governments are engaged in tax competition, this should be observable at the subsidiary level as well, as they would compete for mobile companies that are particularly valuable to the local economy. Governments can be expected to distinguish among different types of potential foreign investors when setting tax burdens. They would consider companies' sensitivity to tax rates in choosing locations and the benefits their prospective operations offer to the host country. (As we will see, it is often difficult to distinguish between these two factors.) For example, some companies will earn locational rents that can be extracted by the host jurisdiction while others control mobile intangibles that can be exploited in a large number of alternative locations. Companies also differ in the benefits they provide to local labor and capital. An important consideration is the extent to which the company sells its output offshore and the extent to which it imports components.

In a model of the world economy with homogeneous capital and a single good, as in Gordon (1986) but with a less than perfectly elastic supply of foreign capital, the host government's optimal tax on inbound capital would depend only on the sensitivity of foreign investment to local tax rates. The government would equate the marginal productivity of capital with its marginal cost, and the latter depends on the elasticity of the supply of capital. The optimal tax rate is given by the difference between the marginal and average supply price of capital.

But in a world with differentiated products and intangible capital, the elasticity of investment is an incomplete guide to policy because different types of investments can have different effects on the price of local production in world markets. To see this, compare two hypothetical companies whose investments are equally responsive to a cut in local tax rates. One invests in a purely domestic sector and the extra capital has the normal effect of increasing the productivity of local labor. Any increase in exports simply represents the investment return eventually going abroad. The other investor produces a differentiated product that will be sold abroad. The increase in export demand leads to a greater improvement in national real income because it causes a greater expansion in the worldwide demand for local factors such as labor. In other words, increased capital in the exporting company both increases the local productivity of labor and increases the value of this productivity relative to imports.

If a new company offers a worldwide market for its local production, local labor is, in effect, bid away from traditional export industries, and its output is sold at higher prices in world markets. Similarly, if the company imports a great deal of its components, the local economy may suffer a terms of trade loss. This conclusion on which type of company should be favored parallels a similar result in trade theory, in which the export facing the highest elasticity of demand should receive a subsidy even in a no-tax world. In the limit, as the elasticity of demand for the export increases, it is like getting a greater demand for your exports and resulting higher terms of trade at no cost.[19]

The potential trade benefits of an investment may be closely linked to the mobility of its intangible assets. If a subsidiary sells most of its output offshore, this may indicate that the company could exploit its know-how in another location. Granting concessions to the company may be due to the mobile intangibles, which increase the company's sensitivity to tax rates, and not any prospective terms of trade benefit. In principle, however, it is possible, at least conceptually, to distinguish between the mobility of the intangibles and the terms of trade improvement. The lower tax to the mobile intangible would increase the demand for the country's exports, but the extent of the terms of trade benefit would depend on the nature of the local economy, such as the elasticity of the supply of labor to the new activity and the elasticity of demand for its other exports. Moreover, as noted in the discussion of the results, a subsidiary using mobile intangibles may also import a great deal of its components, which would offset the terms of trade gain. If the host government nevertheless penalizes imports, this would help identify the significance of the terms of trade objective.

The data used in this section, described in more detail in appendix A, are derived from the basic corporate tax return, the Form 1120, and the Form 5471 that is filed by US multinational companies for each of their controlled foreign corporations (CFCs). (A CFC is a foreign company more than 50 percent of which is owned by US shareholders.) The Form 1120 is used for information on parent profitability, R&D and advertising, and capital and labor intensity. The Form 5471 provides information on the foreign income taxes paid by the CFC and on its Earnings and Profits, a measure of book net income specified in the tax code. These are used to construct the subsidiary's effective tax rate. The Form 5471 also has data on the CFC's date of incorporation, its industry, and its transactions with related parties. The sample is based on the manufacturing CFCs among the largest 7,500 CFCs, for which more complete data are available. The sample is reduced further because, in order to calculate an effective tax rate, the CFC of course has to report positive net profits. Altogether there are 1,751 observations in the sample.

The ratio of parent R&D and advertising to sales are used as measures of company industrial and marketing intangible assets. These might be sources of either mobile or locational rents in the host country. The measure of parent profitability, the ratio of domestic profits to sales, is another potential indicator of rents that might be extracted. Parent labor intensity, measured by the ratio of labor costs to sales, and capital intensity, measured by the ratio of plant and equipment to sales, are other company variables that might indicate the mobility of operations. They are also company characteristics that the host government may use as predictors of benefits to the local economy. Finally we use a measure of parent size, the log of sales, to see if larger parents are able to obtain relatively favorable tax treatment, perhaps because they have many alternative opportunities for expanding investment.

The subsidiary's date of incorporation is used to construct age dummies. We would expect that newer operations have lower effective tax rates because of the greater importance of investment incentives such as accelerated depreciation. The CFC's imports and exports are derived from the data on intercompany sales and purchases of goods, or "stock in trade" as it is referred in the tax return. These are each expressed in relation to CFC sales. Transactions with other foreign affiliates and transactions with the US parent can be distinguished. The CFC's industry category is used to construct a dummy variable for subsidiaries in electronics and computers, which would be expected to have particularly mobile intangibles.

In the regressions in table 5.3, the dependent variable is the controlled foreign corporation's (CFC's) effective tax rate, the ratio of foreign income taxes paid to CFC Earnings and Profits. Because we are interested in how the tax burden on a particular subsidiary compares with other CFCs in the same location, either the country's average effective rate or its statutory tax rate are used as independent variables. (Table 5.3 indicates that the results are not very sensitive to which is used.[20]) The statutory rate is the independent variable in the first 2 regressions. Not surprisingly, the local statutory tax rate has highly significant coefficients. The coefficient of the dummy variable for CFCs incorporated within the last five years shows the expected benefits of recent incorporation, presumably reflecting incentives such as accelerated depreciation and tax holidays.

The highly significant positive coefficient for purchases from related parties and the similar (in absolute terms) highly significant negative coefficient for sales confirm the importance of overseas markets and potential terms of trade benefits to host governments. The coefficient for sales indicates that a subsidiary that sells all of its output offshore achieves an effective tax rate 5 percentage points lower than one that serves the local market exclusively. This is a large effect in view of the mean effective tax rate of 23 percent in the sample. The second column distinguishes between transactions with the parent US company and transactions with other foreign affiliates. Sales to the parent and sales to other offshore locations have a comparable effect in gaining a more

**Table 5.3**
Companies receiving concessions and companies being penalized: Manufacturing subsidiaries in 1996

| Independent variable | (1) | (2) | (3) | (4) |
|---|---|---|---|---|
| Country statutory rate | 0.471 | 0.474 | | |
| | (12.42) | (12.44) | | |
| Country effective rate | | | 0.731 | 0.732 |
| | | | (16.46) | (16.44) |
| Age < 5 years | −0.057 | −0.056 | −0.055 | −0.056 |
| | (3.95) | (3.93) | (3.95) | (3.96) |
| Age 5–15 | −0.008 | −0.008 | −0.107 | −0.107 |
| | (0.83) | (0.79) | (1.12) | (1.13) |
| Parent R&D/sales | 1.022 | 1.03 | 0.997 | 0.982 |
| | (3.34) | (3.36) | (3.35) | (3.30) |
| Parent advertising/sales | −0.131 | −0.118 | −0.102 | −0.113 |
| | (0.97) | (0.86) | (0.77) | (0.86) |
| Sales to all affiliates/ total sales | −0.052 | | −0.034 | |
| | (3.71) | | (2.48) | |
| Purchases from all affiliates/total sales | 0.060 | | 0.071 | |
| | (3.00) | | (2.62) | |
| Electronics and computers | −0.028 | −0.029 | −0.025 | −0.025 |
| | (2.44) | (2.54) | (2.26) | (2.21) |
| Parent size-log of total sales | −0.0053 | −0.0052 | −0.0047 | −0.0046 |
| | (1.70) | (1.69) | (1.58) | (1.54) |
| Parent domestic profits | 0.035 | 0.026 | 0.028 | 0.0244 |
| | (0.52) | (0.39) | (0.43) | (0.37) |
| Parent labor intensity | −0.083 | −0.082 | −0.087 | −0.086 |
| | (2.08) | (2.05) | (2.24) | (2.20) |
| Parent capital intensity | −0.037 | −0.039 | −0.044 | −0.045 |
| | (1.51) | (1.58) | (1.84) | (1.87) |
| Sales to foreign affiliates | | −0.049 | | −0.025 |
| | | (2.97) | | (1.55) |
| Sales to US affiliates | | −0.058 | | −0.053 |
| | | (2.32) | | (2.21) |
| Purchases from foreign affiliates | | 0.029 | | 0.039 |
| | | (1.06) | | (1.49) |
| Purchases from US affiliates | | 0.094 | | 0.077 |
| | | (3.30) | | (2.77) |

Notes: Dependent variable is subsidiary effective tax rate. $t$ values are in parentheses. $N = 1,751$.

favorable tax rate. On the purchases side, imports of components from the United States seem to have a particularly unfavorable effect.

These results on the effect of foreign transactions may, as noted, reflect mobile intangibles and higher sensitivity to taxes rather than potential terms of trade effects. This interpretation might well hold for sales, which indicate the company's ability to sell its products in world markets. The host government would give concessions to this operation that is more responsive to tax rates. But the mobile intangibles interpretation does not explain why greater purchases from related parties result in a tax penalty. A mobile operation might be expected to buy more components from related parties in other countries. Grubert (2003) finds that, if anything, subsidiaries in low effective tax countries, companies that are presumably the ones most responsive to tax rates, import more from related parties abroad, although the effect is statistically significant at only the 10 percent level. The potential terms of trade gain or loss seems to be the most consistent explanation of the transactions results.

Returning to the first regression and the other variables, we can see that parent R&D intensity increases the local tax burden, suggesting rent extraction by the host government. On the average, the rents that companies earn from their R&D investments appear to be locational rather than mobile. There may be several sources of these locational rents. They may derive from the opportunity to produce and sell a company-developed product in the local market. Another possibility is that local skilled labor is necessary for the company to be able to exploit a new technology.

To be sure, some of the R&D linked rents are mobile. The dummy variable for industries with mobile operations, electronics and computers, has a significant negative coefficient. (In regressions not shown, the extraction of rents associated with R&D is evident even when the transactions and other mobility indicators are not used as explanatory variables.) The significance of the electronics and computer dummy variable confirms the expectation that mobility brings more favorable tax treatment. This mobility could reflect either mobile intangible assets or the fact that production is physically easier to move. We also use parent labor and capital intensity to indicate more or less mobile operations, and we see that both tend to lower the host government's tax rate. This might suggest that host governments expect that real activity using local labor and plant and equipment offer greater potential benefits to local inputs compared to more intangible based production.

Finally larger parents, as indicated by their US sales, tend to obtain more favorable tax treatment, although the coefficient is significant only at the 10 percent level. Larger parents are likely to have operations in a greater number of locations and therefore more options in moving capital from one place to another. (There may, for example, be fixed costs of establishing a subsidiary in a new location.) In other words, the larger MNCs have greater bargaining power. An alternative explanation is that larger companies are also likely to have large subsidiaries, which the host government may find less costly to attract in relation to the benefits they can bring. But other regressions, not displayed on the tables, show that larger subsidiaries in fact pay significantly more, and that the parent size variable becomes more significant when subsidiary size is included. Perhaps, the fact that the subsidiary is large indicates that the company values the location and is committed to it, increasing the government's ability to extract rents.

One possible objection to the table 5.3 regressions is that the independent variables are actually endogenous and may be determined by the tax rate. This is conceivable for R&D, but it is not likely to be an important source of bias. The R&D measure used reflects the parent's US R&D, which is unlikely to be strongly influenced by the tax rate in a single location.

A more serious source of possible endogeneity is that CFC tax rates may influence the volume of transactions with related parties. Indeed, Grubert and Mutti (1991), using data aggregated by country, showed that locations with low average effective tax rates attract production for sale offshore. This effect might also operate at the CFC level, and subsidiaries that happen to have below average tax rates in a location might sell a greater share of their production to related parties abroad. But, again, the positive sign on the purchases coefficient tends to reject this direction of causation. Grubert and Mutti (1991) also found that locations with low effective tax rates attract a great deal of US exports to the local US subsidiaries. The evidence in Grubert (2003) cited above showed that this seemed to be observable at the CFC level as well, with CFCs in low-tax countries importing more components from related parties. If the direction of causation goes from CFC tax rates to the level of offshore transactions, one should therefore expect a negative relationship between a CFC's tax rate and its purchases from abroad. In fact the positive and significant coefficient for purchases in the table 5.3 regressions indicates the reverse. Large purchases of goods from related parties are associated with significantly higher than average tax rates. The direction of causation seems to run from the CFC's purchases and sales to the effective tax rate that it is offered, consistent with the terms of trade and national welfare interpretation.

## 5.5   Conclusions

The first two sections demonstrate that it is not the most obvious features of a tax system, such as whether foreign dividends are taxed or exempt, that are important in determining the tax burden on cross-border investment. More significant are how royalties are taxed and whether companies can use tax haven finance subsidiaries or other aggressive tax-planning schemes. Requiring allocations of parent interest expense to foreign income can also be important. Even normal tax planning, such as shifting debt to high-tax foreign locations or the home country, can have a notable effect on tax burdens.

While some general conclusions such as the importance of intangible income can be drawn, the highly simplified simulations in section 5.2 reveal that it is very difficult to make definitive statements about average effective tax rates in a particular country. The complexity of multi-country strategies, and the knowledge required about the company's planning opportunities throughout the worldwide corporation, are the sources of much of this problem.

The second section shows that there appear to be substantial benefits to being a multinational company compared to the average local company that cannot shift debt and has to pay the full tax on any income from intangible assets that it owns. Under the assumption that the average local company has the average amount of debt of US subsidiaries, the differential seems to be close to 5 percentage points. The section also indicates, incidentally, that real assets are more responsive to tax differences than are tax bases, that is, than net income in a location per dollar of real assets.

The third section indicates that host governments impose tax burdens on different types of companies depending on their contribution to national welfare. They seem to distinguish between mobile and locational rents. They grant lower tax rates to mobile high-technology companies, such as those in electronics, while extracting rents from the average R&D intensive company. Improving national terms of trade also seems to be an important policy goal. Governments grant tax concessions to companies that sell a greater share of their output in other markets, and they impose higher tax rates on companies that import more of their components.

**Appendix A: Data Sources**

The principal data sources used in sections 5.3 and 5.4 are the linked US Treasury files for the Forms 1120, 5471, and 1118. The Form 1120 is the basic corporate tax return, giving the parent company's revenues and deductions. Multinational corporations file a Form 5471 for each of their controlled foreign corporations. It gives the CFC's sales and net income, foreign taxes paid, balance sheet, transactions with related parties, and date of incorporation. Net income refers to "Earnings and Profits," which is defined in the tax code and is intended to approximate book income, not local taxable income. The parent claims foreign tax credits on the Form 1118, which has total repatriated foreign income, including dividends, interest, and royalties, as well as deductions against foreign income. (The total allowable credit depends on net income after deductions.)

Information on the parent's R&D is based on the "qualified research and experimentation" reported on the tax return for purposes of the research credit. Only R&E performed in the United States qualifies. In the minority of cases (less than 20 percent) in which a company does not claim a research credit but is reported as performing R&D in its financial statements as compiled in COMPUSTAT, the latter is used to impute qualified research. Parent advertising is taken directly from the Form 1120.

Country statutory tax rates are obtained from Price Waterhouse (1996). Average effective tax rates by country are computed from the taxes and net profits reported on the Form 5471.

**Appendix B: Technical Description of the Table 5.1 Scenarios**

This appendix gives a more specific description of the table 5.1 scenarios in terms of the following parameters:

$t_l$ = low-tax country tax rate.

$t_h$ = high-tax country tax rate.

$t_u$ = home country tax rate.

$t_d$ = tax and non-tax burden of repatriations from the low-tax country if they are taxable on the margin (i.e., excess credits are not available).

$R$ = share of before-tax income accounted for by intangible income paid to the parent as royalties in the absence of income shifting.

$d_R$ = percentage reduction of royalties by low-tax subsidiaries if they are taxable on the margin in the home country.

$l$ = share of the MNC's worldwide tangible assets that can be financed with debt. In the absence of debt shifting, each of the subsidiaries is assumed to borrow this share of its assets.

$d_1$ = share of low-tax debt shifted to the high tax subsidiary. $a_1$ is the share of the tax saving attributed to investment in the low-tax country. The remainder is attributed to investment in the high-tax country.

$d_2$ = the share of low-tax debt shifted back to the parent.

$XC$ = 1 if parent in a worldwide system has excess foreign tax credits.

$XL$ = 1 if parent does not have excess credits.

$DE$ = 1 if home country has a dividend exemption system.

$s$ = share of net equity income remaining in the high-tax subsidiary (after the debt shift) that is shifted to the low-tax subsidiary. $a_2$ is the share of $s$ that is attributed to investment in the low-tax country.

$H_d$ = share of high-tax tangible capital that is financed with hybrid securities if the home country has a dividend exemption system.

$H_f$ = share of the tangible capital of each subsidary that is financed by loans from tax haven finance affiliates or hybrid entities.

$I_A$ = share of $d_2$ that has to be allocated to the low-tax subsidiary under the home country rules.

In each scenario, ETL and ETH, the effective tax rate on a new product line in the low- and high-tax subsidiary respectively are calculated for the three possible cases: excess credit, excess limit, and dividend exemption. They are identified by the three dummy or state variables, $XC, XL$, and $DE$, where relevant. Income is normalized so that all components pre-tax add up to one. As stated in the text, the interest rate is assumed to be equal to the before-tax return to equity. An alternative interpretation of $l$, the company debt–asset constraint, is that it is the share of gross income accounted for by interest deductions.

## Scenario 1

In the first scenario $R = 0$ and $l = 0$. There is only equity investment and no income derives from intangible assets. As described in the text, in calculating the effective tax rate for a new discrete investment, we implicitly adopt the "old view." In the case where the home country repatriation tax can potentially bite, for low-tax affiliates with a parent with no excess credits, we assume that the low-tax affiliate repatriates a fixed amount of its income each period and it bears both the residual tax actually paid and the implicit tax cost of retaining income.

Accordingly, $ETL_1 = t_l + XL * t_d$, where $XL = 1$ if the parent is in excess limit.

$ETH_1 = t_h - XL * (t_h - t_u)$.

We assume that $t_l < t_u < t_h$. The second term in $ETH_1$ reflects the fact that the high-tax subsidiary will repatriate all of its income and some of the tax that it has paid can flow over to shield other foreign income if the parent is in excess limit.

## Scenario 2

Debt is positive. Each operation has the same debt–asset ratio $= l$.
$ETL_2 = (1 - l) * ETL_1$.
$ETH_2 = (1 - l) * ETH_1$.

## Scenario 3

Royalties paid to the parent are $R$ of total before-tax income.
$ETL_3 = (1 - R) * ETL_2 + R * t_u * (XL + DE)$.
$ETH_3 = (1 - R) * ETH_2 + R * t_u * (XL + DE)$.
Royalties are deductible in the host country but do not incur a home country tax if the parent has excess credits in a worldwide system, namely when $XL$ and $DE$ are both zero.

## Scenario 4

Debt shifting.
$SD_1 = d_1 * l * (1 - R)$ of low-tax debt, expressed as a share of total capital, is shifted to the high-tax subsidiary. The total tax reduction

per unit of gross before-tax income is $TD_1 = SD_1 * (ETH_1 - ETL_1)$. The scenario 1 all-equity effective tax rates apply instead of the statutory rates because they include any positive and negative repatriation taxes when taxable income is increased. Depending on whether $XC, XL$, or $DE$ is equal to 1, the appropriate scenario 1 effective tax rates should be used; $a_1$ of the tax saving is attributed to the low-tax investment.

$SD_2 = d_2 * l * (1 - R)$ of low-tax debt is shifted to the parent. The tax saving $= TD_2 = SD_2 * (t_u - ETL_1)$. This is all attributed to the low-tax investment.

$ETL_4 = ETL_3 - a_1 * TD_1 - TD_2$.

$ETH_4 = ETH_3 - (1 - a_1) * TD_1$.

Scenario 5

Royalties decline by $d_R$ if they are paid by a low-tax subsidiary and they are taxable in the home country. The tax saving is $d_R * R * (t_u - ETL_1)$.

$ETL_5 = ETL_4 - d_R * R * (t_u - ETL_1) * (XL + DE)$.

$ETH_5 = ETH_4$.

Scenario 6

A portion, $s$, of the net equity income remaining in the high-tax subsidiary, after the debt shifts in scenario 4, is shifted to the low-tax subsidiary.

The remaining high-tax net equity income, as a share of total pre-tax income before deductions for interest or royalties, is equal to $(1 - R) * (1 - l) - SD_1$, where $SD_1$ was defined in scenario 4; $a_2$ of the tax saving is attributed to the low-tax affiliate.

$ETL_6 = ETL_5 - a_2 * s * ((1 - R) * (1 - l) - SD_1) * (ETH_1 - ETL_1)$.

$ETH_6 = ETL_5 - (1 - a_2) * s * ((1 - R) * (1 - l) - SD_1) * (ETH_1 - ETL_1)$.

Scenario 7

A portion, $IA$, of the debt that was shifted from the low-tax subsidiary to the parent now has to be allocated abroad under the home country rules. We assume that this applies in the dividend exemption regime. In the worldwide system it only affects companies in excess credit because the allocation only enters into the calculation of maximum allowable credits. We assume that if the allocation reduces home country interest deductions, the debt is shifted back to the low-tax subsidiary where it will be deductible.

$ETL_7 = ETL_6 + IA * TD_2 * (XC + DE)$, where $TD_2$ was defined in scenario 4.

$ETH_7 = ETH_6$.

## Scenario 8

$H_d$ of the tangible capital of the high-tax subsidiary under a dividend exemption system is financed with a hybrid security that is classified as debt in the host country and equity in the home country. We assume that the remaining income components are distributed in the same way as in scenario 7. In particular, the income shifting in the earlier scenarios shrink proportionately. Note that the effective tax rate in the low-tax country in the dividend exemption case goes up because it has less value as a shifting vehicle. It receives less income shifted from the high-tax country.

$ETL_8 = ETL_7 + H_d * a_1 * TD_1 + H_d * (ETL_6 - ETL_5)$. $TD_1$ was defined in scenario 4, and the last term reflects the partial loss of the attributed shifting benefit in scenario 6.

$ETH_8 = (1 - H_d) * (ETL_7 - R * t_u) + R * t_u$.

These only apply to the dividend exemption case. The other effective tax rates are the same as in scenario 7.

## Scenario 9

The tax planning in scenario 9 is an alternative to scenario 8. Companies use tax haven finance subsidiaries or hybrid entities to finance $H_f$ of the tangible capital in each subsidiary. This (inside) debt is in addition to the third-party debt already on the subsidiary's books. We assume that in this scenario, in contrast to scenario 8, the incentives to shift income on the margin reflected in the earlier scenarios remain as before.

$ETL_9 = ETL_7 - H_f * (1 - R) * ETL_1$.

$ETH_9 = ETL_7 - H_f * (1 - R) * ETH_1$.

## Notes

Nothing in this paper should be construed as reflecting the views or policy of the US Treasury Department. I am grateful for very helpful comments by Ronald Davies, Peter Merrill, Peter Birch Sørensen, and the participants in the CESifo conference on measuring the tax burden on labor and capital.

1. These data appear in the October 2002 *Survey of Current Business*, which provide details on both US international transaction and preliminary results from the 1999 benchmark survey of US direct investment abroad. More than two-thirds of the license fees and royalties referred to come from affiliates.

2. The importance of average effective tax rates for discrete location decisions is emphasized by Devereux and Griffith (1999).

3. This extends recent papers by Grubert and Mutti (2001) and Altshuler and Grubert (2001) that have started to address some of these issues. They show, for example, that tax burdens on cross-border income can be higher under a territorial (dividend exemption) system than under the alternative worldwide system with deferral and foreign tax credits.

4. Looking at cross-border income flows, one sees that in 1996 royalties accounted for 26.6 percent of the net foreign income received by US manufacturing companies.

5. In addition the subsidiary may keep a significant portion of the return, perhaps as an incentive for exploiting the technology efficiently. The evidence in Grubert (1998) suggested that whatever the reason, the return to R&D is split about equally between parent and affiliate.

6. Many countries use a "tracing" system in which an allocation has to be made only if a foreign investment can be traced directly to contemporaneous borrowing. This is, of course, easy to manipulate. Allocations under the US rules are based on the ratio of foreign assets to worldwide assets.

7. The comparison of worldwide and exemption systems extends the simulations in Grubert and Mutti (2001) and Altshuler and Grubert (2001).

8. Some home countries have a nominal per-country system for credit limitations, but frequently MNCs can get around this by using a "mixer" holding company in a country, such as the Netherlands, with favorable treatment of holding companies.

9. The fixed $p$ assumption makes it more convenient to specify the importance of income from an existing intangible. Otherwise, the return attributable to an intangible asset would vary depending on the grossed-up payments that have to be made to the tangible capital.

10. In contrast to the implicit cost of avoiding repatriation taxes, planning costs are not included in these scenarios. If we make the frequently used assumption that planning or avoidance costs are a quadratic function of the discrepancy between actual income in a location and true income undistorted by tax considerations, then the benefits of planning are just reduced in half.

11. It is possible that more debt could be stuffed in the high-tax foreign country. The estimate assumes that this is infeasible because of host country thin capitalization rules.

12. We assume that the effective tax rate on this investment can be negative because of positive taxable income from other investments.

13. It also ignores implicit planning costs that were included in some of the simulations.

14. One qualification however is that all of the income may not have been accounted for. Some may have been shifted to nonmanufacturing subsidiaries. This possibility becomes more real as hybrid entities become more prevalent.

15. Expenses that have to be allocated to foreign income also contribute to excess credits that can be absorbed by royalties. This is taken into account when the effect of the allocations is estimated.

16. The costs imputed here to the interest allocation rules are greater than would conventionally be estimated as a stand-alone provision. First royalties are taken out of foreign source income, increasing the likelihood that a company has excess credits, and then the effect of the allocations on available tax credits is computed. The reason is that some of the benefit of excess credits attributed to royalties in step 4 may have resulted from interest allocations, but nevertheless the parent ended up in excess limit because of the large volume of royalties. In a stand-alone estimate the benefit to royalties would not be offset by the required allocations because, with the parent in excess limit, the allocations would appear not to impose a cost.

17. The required allocations appear more significant here than in the simulations in table 5.1, which assumed worldwide fungibility as the standard. Current US law mandates allocations to foreign income significantly larger than under the equal worldwide debt–asset ratio standard.

18. The assumption of equal leverage in all foreign countries may be too extreme. Leverage would be expected to be higher in high-tax countries. In addition it is possible that governments grant favors to locally owned companies that they don't extend to foreign-owned companies, although that is not what the tax competition literature would deem to suggest.

19. This result is apparently due originally to de V. Graff (1949–50) who presents a general tariff structure framework and notes that some cases call for subsidies.

20. The statutory tax rate is probably more valid because, unlike the average effective rate, it is not influenced by the particular mix of companies in a location.

## References

Altshuler, R., and H. Grubert. 2003. Repatriation taxes, repatriation strategies and multinational financial policy. *Journal of Public Economics* 87 (1): 73–107.

Altshuler, R., and H. Grubert. 2001. Where will they go if we go territorial? Dividend exemption and the location decisions of U.S. multinational corporations. *National Tax Journal* 54 (4): 787–810.

Altshuler, R., H. Grubert, and T. Scott Newlon. 2001. Has U.S. investment abroad become more sensitive to tax rates? In J. Hines, Jr., ed., *International Taxation and Multinational Taxation.* Chicago: University of Chicago Press, pp. 9–32.

Devereux, M., B. Lockwood, and M. Redoano. 2002. Do countries compete over corporate tax rates? CEPR Discussion Paper 3400. Centre for Economic Policy Research.

Devereux, M., and R. Griffith. 1999. The taxation of discrete investment choices. Institute for Fiscal Studies Working Paper.

de V. Graff, J. 1949–50. On optimal tariff structures. *Review of Economic Studies* 17 (1): 47–59.

Grubert, H. 1998. Taxes and the division of foreign operating income among royalties, interest, dividends and retained earnings. *Journal of Public Economics* 68 (2): 269–90.

Grubert, H. 2001. Enacting dividend exemption and tax revenues. *National Tax Journal* 54 (4): 811–28.

Grubert, H. 2003. Intangible income, intercompany transactions, income shifting, and the choice of location. *National Tax Journal*, part 2, 56 (1): 221–42.

Grubert, H., and J. Mutti. 1991. Taxes, tariffs and transfer pricing in multinational corporation decision making. *Review of Economics and Statistics* 33 (2): 285–93.

Grubert, H., and J. Mutti. 2000. Do taxes influence where U.S. companies invest? *National Tax Journal* 53 (4): 825–39.

Grubert, H., and J. Mutti. 2001. *Taxing International Business Income: Dividend Exemption versus the Current System*. Washington: American Enterprise Institute.

King, M., and D. Fullerton. 1984. *The Taxation of Income from Capital: A Comparative Study of the U.S., U.K., Sweden and West Germany*. Chicago: University of Chicago Press.

OECD. 1991. *Taxing Profits in the Global Economy*. Paris.

Price Waterhouse. 1996. *Corporate Taxes—A Worldwide Summary*. New York.

Sinn, H.-W. 1993. Taxation and the Birth of Foreign Subsidiaries. In H. Herberg and N. V. Long, eds., *Trade, Welfare and Economic Policies: Essays in Honor of Murray Kemp*. Ann Arbor: University of Michigan Press, pp. 325–52.

Slemrod, J. 2001. Are tax rates or countries converging? Mimeo. Presented before World Tax Competition conference, London. Office of Tax Policy Research and the Institute for Fiscal Studies.

Sørensen, P. B. 2002. The German tax reform of 2000: A general equilibrium analysis. *German Economic Review* 3 (4): 347–78.

Weichenrieder, A. 1996. Anti tax-avoidance provisions and the size of foreign direct investment. *International Tax and Public Finance* 3: 67–81.

# 6         Measuring Effective Tax Rates on Human Capital: Methodology and an Application to Canada

Kirk A. Collins and James B. Davies

## 6.1   Introduction

Over the last two decades there has been considerable research on effective tax rates on physical capital. It has been found that these are generally high, and that they vary across types of firms, industries, and types of capital (See Boadway et al. 1984; King and Fullerton 1984; and McKenzie et al. 1998). While the *size* of the impact on investment and its composition is an important question that cannot be addressed simply by estimating tax wedges, these findings have helped to create concern about such impacts. This has added impetus to the movement to reduce capital taxation and to make it more uniform.

While there has also been considerable interest in recent years in the tax treatment of education and training,[1] we do not have estimates of the effective tax rates on human capital. This is a problem since some features of the tax system (e.g., progressivity) tend to discourage human capital formation, while others (e.g., deductions or credits to support education) have the opposite effect. We do not know the net impact, and therefore do not know whether the tax system encourages or discourages human capital, how it treats human capital compared with physical capital, or how effective tax rates on human capital vary across the population.

This chapter provides a conceptual framework for measuring effective tax rates (*ETRs*) on human capital, analyzing how the progressivity of personal income taxes interacts with other PIT features, other taxes, and student loan plans. It then provides estimates for the *ETRs* on human capital formed in first degree university studies in Canada.[2] We find that these are sizable although not as large as effective tax rates on physical capital, and that they vary considerably across individuals. *ETRs* on human capital in Canada are, on average, greater for males than for females, and increase as we go up the income scale. *ETRs* are lower for individuals who take out student loans, and for those who take advantage of Registered Education Savings Plans (RESPs). There are also differences in *ETRs* created by a number of other tax features. The conclusion is thus that Canada has far from uniform tax treatment of human capital.

In assessing fiscal incentives or disincentives for human capital investment, it is essential to take into account the encouragement that governments provide for such investment, on their expenditure side. For a more complete treatment one therefore needs to consider the effective subsidy rate, *ESR*, as well as the *ETR*.[3] The bottom line is given by the *net* effective tax rate, *ETR − ESR*. As we show, this net tax rate is on average negative.

Care must be taken in interpreting the results of our study. This is especially so if one wishes to draw normative implications. First there are some standard considerations from the economics of education. A negative net tax on human capital can, in principle, be justified by positive externalities of education or by capital market imperfections that make it hard for students to borrow. However, while earlier literature claimed to find evidence of large externalities, recent work tends to dispute this (e.g., see Heckman and Klenow 1997; Acemoglu and Angrist 2000; the survey by Davies 2002). Doubt has also recently been cast on the importance of borrowing problems (e.g., see Shea 2000; Cameron and Taber 2000). Merit good arguments are sometimes also used. On the other side, to the extent that education represents private consumption rather than an investment the strength of subsidy arguments declines. Going further, if education pays off for individuals due to screening for ability, or because of the status it confers, it is wasteful from a social viewpoint, and should be discouraged. The bottom line that should be taken from economics of education considerations is thus unclear.

Turning to the public finance literature, there are several strands. A variety of studies have endogenized human capital in dynamic models, either in a neoclassical framework (e.g., see Davies and Whalley 1991; Trostel 1993; Perroni 1995; Jones et al. 1997) or with endogenous growth (e.g., see Pecorino 1993; Jones et al. 1993; Davies et al. 2002). It is well-known that the optimal tax rate on physical capital goes to zero in the long-run in perfect foresight infinite horizon dynamic models (Judd 1985; Chamley 1986). A similar result extends to human capital when it is endogenized (Jones et al. 1997). However, results of recent studies suggest that this need not imply zero labor income taxes. Bovenberg and Jacobs (2002) and Davies et al. (2002) both show that education subsidies can be used to counter the disincentive effect of labor income taxes on human capital formation. An important element in our study is to see how complete this offset is in practice. Another interesting recent insight is provided by Nielsen and Sorensen (1997) who show that if the imposition of capital income taxes cannot be avoided, there may be excess investment in human capital, which can be combatted by levying progressive labor income taxes. In other words, if the effective tax rate on physical capital is unavoidably positive, then the optimal tax rate on human capital may be positive as well.

The remainder of the chapter is organized as follows: In section 6.2 we provide a description of the conceptual framework adopted. In section 6.3 we examine the treatment of human capital under the Canadian tax system. In section 6.4 we present our numerical results, and in section 6.5 offer some concluding remarks.

## 6.2   Conceptual Framework

A common approach in evaluating the impact of factor taxes is to juxtapose effective tax rates on physical capital with tax rates on labor. In this context, if labor income were taxed at a proportional rate of 30 percent, for example, and the EMTR for physical capital were, say, 20 percent, it would appear that the tax system discriminates in favor of physical capital. However, as is now well known (e.g., see Davies and Whalley 1991), if the only private cost of education is forgone earnings, a proportional labor income tax is neutral with respect to human capital investment. (It implicitly subsidizes the costs at the same rate it taxes the benefits of education.) In the example given, the tax system would in fact heavily discriminate in favor of human capital. Thus it is as important to include impacts on investment costs on the labor side as it is on the physical capital side. There is an increasing trend to do this (e.g., see Mintz 2001 for Canada). Our purpose here is to highlight the impact of taking these investment aspects into account.[4]

How can one tell whether a tax system provides a net incentive or disincentive for investment? This problem has been analyzed by previous authors for the case of physical capital. Structures, equipment, and inventories are taxed in different ways, and there are also differences across industries and according to how investment is financed.

In order to summarize these effects and see how they net out, it has proved fruitful to calculate hypothetical effective marginal tax rates (EMTRs) by type of capital, industry, and method of finance (e.g., see Boadway et al. 1984; King and Fullerton 1984; McKenzie et al. 1998).

EMTRs on physical capital are high and nonuniform. Looking only at nonpersonal taxes, McKenzie et al. (1998), for example, find that EMTRs in Canada in 1997 averaged 29.0 percent on inventories, 19.0 percent on machinery, 18.9 percent on structures, and 15.6 percent on land. The overall average EMTR was 21.8 percent. Rates within industries ranged from 8.5 percent in agriculture, fishing, and trapping to 29.5 percent for public utilities. Largely due to their lower rate of corporate income tax, small firms on average faced an EMTR of only 13.3 percent while large firms paid 27.0 percent.

Personal taxation of capital income is also significant and highly nonuniform. Poddar and English (1999) estimate that about 75 percent of investment income is tax free at the personal level in Canada—due to various tax shelters (e.g., retirement savings plans) and other factors such as the nontaxation of imputed rent on owner-occupied housing. On the other hand, tax rates on the interest, dividends, and capital gains that are not sheltered can be quite high. There are no estimates of personal level EMTRs on capital income for Canada. However, most investors would have paid tax on taxable elements of investment income at top marginal rates, which averaged about 46 percent in Canada in 1997, including provincial taxes. Applying the Poddar and English result, the average personal EMTR on investment income may then have been about 10 percent. Added to the McKenzie et al. figure, this suggests an average total (personal plus nonpersonal) EMTR on physical capital of at least 30 percent.

While the problem of measuring effective tax rates on human capital is formally the same as that for physical capital, there are measurement issues that make a different approach necessary in practice.[5] In the case of physical capital one can make plausible assumptions about the rate of return to a hypothetical marginal investment based on observed asset returns in capital markets. For human capital, rates of return are not directly observable. For physical capital, the fact that real-world investments are typically lumpy does not affect the results. Corporate taxes are levied at a flat rate, so the estimated effective tax rate does not depend on the size of the investment. The most important tax for human capital is the personal income tax, whose graduated rate structure makes the effective tax rate depend on the scale of the investment.

For human capital rates of return can be estimated using microdata on education and earnings over the lifetime. Tax treatment depends on individual circumstances and requires a comparison of the taxes that would be paid in the counterfactual, that is, without additional education compared to those paid if extra schooling is obtained. The most meaningful calculation compares the before- and after-tax rates of return to participation in a complete education program, whether it be, for example, community college, undergraduate university study, MA or PhD work.[6] These tax rates are similar to the EMTRs on physical capital in that they measure carefully the effective tax rate on the last unit of education, but since these units are not small, we speak in terms of effective tax rates ($ETRs$) on human capital rather than EMTRs below.

The $ETR$ for human capital is defined as the gap between gross- and net-of-tax rates of return to a whole program of study, $r_g$ and $r_n$, respectively:

$$ETR = \frac{r_g - r_n}{r_g} = 1 - \frac{r_n}{r_g}. \tag{6.1}$$

This definition, which is built on the use of internal rates of return, follows the methodology applied in computing $ETRs$ on personal financial assets by Davies and Glenday (1990).[7]

Suppose that an individual aged $t$ is planning to engage in a program of education that will take $m$ years of study. We will assume that after this program is completed the individual will stay in the labor force until age $T$. Students may continue to earn while going to school. Their wage rates can vary over time, perhaps increasing while they are still in school, and likely rising in real terms over much of the lifetime after graduation. Actual earnings before-tax are given by $E_t$, which is the product of the wage rate and hours worked. Earnings before-tax in the absence of the educational program would have been $E_t^*$, where we assume that $E_t^* < E_t$ in the $T - m$ years after graduation. Forgone earnings costs of education, $FE_t$, are thus $E_t^* - E_t$ in the first $m$ years. In addition to these costs, there are private direct costs of education, $C_t$. After-tax variables will be denoted $E_t^a, E_t^{a*}, FE_t^a$, and $C_t^a$. Initially we will assume that human capital investments are self-financed, that is that student loans are absent.

Rates of return on the investment described are calculated as internal rates of return. For example, we can compute the gross private rate of return, $r_g$, from

$$\sum_{t=1}^{T} \frac{E_t - C_t}{(1+r_g)^{t-1}} = \sum_{t=1}^{T} \frac{E_t^*}{(1+r_g)^{t-1}}. \tag{6.2}$$

By replacing $E_t, E_t^*$, and $C_t$ with the after-tax variables $E_t^a, E_t^{a*}$, and $C_t^a$, we could compute the net after-tax rate of return, $r_n$, using this same equation. Note that in the case of a flat tax with tuition and other direct costs of education deductible $r_n = r_g$, and $ETR = 0$. This is because with such a tax levied at the rate $\tau$ we have $E_t^a = (1 - \tau)E_t$, $E_t^{a*} = (1 - \tau)E_t^*$, and $C_t^a = (1 - \tau)C_t$. That is, the three variables have the same relative values after-tax as before-tax. We will refer to this type of tax system as *neutral* with respect to human capital.[8] It imposes a zero $ETR$ because the forgone earnings and direct costs of education are implicitly subsidized at the same rate $\tau$ at which the gains from education are taxed.

Note that "neutrality" is used here in a special, and very limited, sense. It is simply a benchmark. There is no implication that a zero $ETR$ on human capital is the optimal rate. Externalities of human capital, or capital market imperfections that make it difficult for students to finance their studies, could call for a negative $ETR$. Absent such factors, a nonzero $ETR$ could be needed in the second-best solution if there were a positive $EMTR$ on physical capital. In that case, while a low ETR would avoid depressing investment, it would also tilt the playing field away from physical capital investment, causing a distortion in the composition of investment. Clearly, optimal design of the tax treatment of human capital is contingent on any constraints (political or otherwise) on the tax treatment of physical capital.

By replacing private costs with public costs, $C_t^p$, we can use (6.2) to compute the public rate of return, $r_p$. Given $r_p$ we can define the effective subsidy rate $(ESR)$ on human capital:

$$ESR = \frac{r_g - r_p}{r_g}. \tag{6.3}$$

Whether the tax and expenditure systems combined have an incentive or disincentive effect on human capital investment can be investigated by computing the *net* effective tax rate on human capital, $ETR - ESR$. We proceed here by first analyzing the behavior of $ETRs$, and returning to $ESRs$ at the end of the section.

The behavior of $ETRs$ can best be illuminated if we assume, for the sake of illustration, that the length of the schooling program, $m$, is just one year. Rearrange (6.2) so all the $t = 1$ terms are on one side and the remaining terms on the other:

$$E_1^* - E_1 + C_1 = \sum_{t=2}^{T} \frac{E_t - E_t^*}{(1 + r_g)^{t-1}}.$$

(6.4)

The left-hand side of (6.4) represents the private costs of the education program, made up of forgone earnings, $E_1^* - E_1$, and direct costs, $C_1$. The right-hand side is the present value of future earning increments due to education, $E_t - E_t^*$.

Again for the sake of illustration, suppose that the yearly benefits of additional education, $E_t - E_t^* - C_t$, are constant. Then because $T$ is typically large we have

$$E_s^* - E_s + C \approx \frac{E_w - E_w^*}{r_g},$$

where we use subscripts $s$ and $w$ to denote the schooling and working periods. We now have a simple expression for the before-tax rate of return $r_g$ and a parallel expression for the after-tax rate of return, $r_n$:

$$r_g \approx \frac{E_w - E_w^*}{E_s^* - E_s + C} = \frac{EI}{FE + C},$$

(6.5a)

$$r_n \approx \frac{E_w^a - E_w^{a*}}{E_s^{a*} - E_s^a + C^a} = \frac{(1 - \tau_w)EI}{(1 - \tau_s)FE + C^a},$$

(6.5b)

where $FE$ is forgone earnings and $EI$ is the earnings increment achieved due to the extra education. Both $FE$ and $EI$ are before-tax. The tax rates $\tau_s$ and $\tau_w$ represent the fraction of $FE$ that *would* have been paid in tax, and the fraction of $EI$ that *is* paid, respectively.

If we ignore direct costs for the time being and let $T \to \infty$ for simplicity, we have

$$r_g|_{C=0} = \frac{EI}{FE},$$

(6.6a)

$$r_n|_{C=0} = \frac{(1 - \tau_w)EI}{(1 - \tau_s)FE}.$$

(6.6b)

Applying (6.1), we have the effective tax rate on human capital in this case as

$$ETR|_{C=0} = \frac{r_g - r_n}{r_g} = \frac{\tau_w - \tau_s}{1 - \tau_s}.$$

(6.7)

This simple expression has some interesting implications. It indicates that in the absence of direct costs, the effective tax rate on human capital is directly related to the gap between $\tau_s$ and $\tau_w$. The most obvious possibility is that the graduated rates under personal income tax will make $\tau_s < \tau_w$, resulting in a positive $ETR$. The gap between $\tau_s$ and $\tau_w$ will tend to be largest for those education programs that have the biggest impact on earnings. This is one reason that first-degree university education is of particular interest. Not only is it an important element in our education system, but it is known to increase earnings substantially. In contrast, incomplete university education, or graduate education, have smaller effects on earnings, which will result in a smaller gap between $\tau_s$ and $\tau_w$. Equation (6.7) gives reason to expect smaller $ETR$s in these cases.

Of course other taxes also affect the $ETR$. Since social security and unemployment insurance contributions are capped at maximum insurable earnings, their schedules are regressive. To the extent that contributions represent pure taxes (i.e., not offset by expected benefits), these schemes work towards $\tau_s > \tau_w$ for workers whose $EI$s fall entirely or partly above maximum insurable earnings. It should also be borne in mind that sales taxes reduce real earnings. In the absence of any other taxes, proportional sales taxes on a comprehensive base would give $\tau_s = \tau_w$, that is, neutrality. However, some necessities are widely exempt from sales tax in North America and elsewhere (food, children's clothing, etc.) or taxed at a lower rate, which reinforces the tendency for $\tau_s < \tau_w$, and a positive $ETR$.

Expressions (6.6) and (6.7) also make possible a number of other insights. We note that:

***Result 1*** If $\tau_s < \tau_w$, equal absolute or equal proportional increases in $\tau_s$ and $\tau_w$ will reduce $r_n|_{C=0}$ and increase $ETR|_{C=0}$.

This result hinges on the fact that with $\tau_s < \tau_w$, we have $(1 - \tau_s) > (1 - \tau_w)$. Equal absolute or proportional changes in $\tau_s$ and $\tau_w$ have a greater proportional impact on $(1 - \tau_w)$ than on $(1 - \tau_s)$. The effect is of course stronger in the case of equal proportional changes in the tax rates.

Result 1 is of interest when more than one tax is levied. It points out, for example, that even if a tax is neutral on its own, when added to an existing system that imposes a positive tax rate on human capital, it will increase the size of the tax wedge. If we regard the federal personal income tax as the basic element in the system, then adding even uniform sales taxes or flat-rate provincial income taxes raises the $ETR$.

Moving to the more general case, we need to take into account tuition and other direct costs; the student loan amount, $L$; student loan repayments $iL$, where $i$ is the interest rate; the rate of tax relief on student loan payments, $d$; and credits for tuition and other expenses, $A$.[9] Making the appropriate adjustments to the costs and returns, we have

$$ETR = 1 - \frac{r_n}{r_g} = 1 - \left[ \frac{(1 - \tau_w)EI - i(1 - d)L}{(1 - \tau_s)FE + (C - L - A)} \right] \left[ \frac{FE + C - L}{EI - iL} \right]. \tag{6.8}$$

From (6.8) we have immediately:

**Result 2**  Increases in tuition credits, $A$, or in interest deductibility, $d$, unambiguously reduce the *ETR*.

Note also from (6.8) that the *ETR* is affected by several *non-tax* policy variables, such as tuition fees, student loan amounts, and interest rates on student loans. These interaction effects are perhaps unexpected, and therefore particularly interesting. It should be emphasized that they are independent of the impact of these non-tax variables on the effective subsidy rate on education. We summarize these effects in results 3 and 4. (Proofs are available in an appendix that may be obtained from the authors.)

**Result 3**  A rise in tuition and other direct costs, $C$, raises the *ETR*.

The intuition for this result is that if $C$ rises, with education credits $A$ constant, the implicit rate of subsidy to direct costs of education in the tax system has fallen. The result is of topical interest in Canada and other countries, such as the United States, where tuition fees have been rising rapidly in recent years. In the absence of offsetting action in the tax system, such increases raise the tax distortion affecting human capital. Rising tuition fees may also reflect a reduced rate of public subsidy to colleges and universities, meaning that the *ESR* has been falling. Thus the net effective tax rate on human capital, $ETR - ESR$ tends to rise a fortiori.

In the next section we set out the many steps that have been taken at the federal level in Canada in recent years to ease the tax treatment of human capital. These initiatives will have acted to offset the rise in *ETRs* caused by increasing tuition fees and other direct costs.

The following result reflects the effect of student loans:

**Result 4**  If $d \geq \tau_w$ the *ETR* is strictly decreasing in $L$. If $d < \tau_w$ the sign of the effect of $L$ on the *ETR* is ambiguous.

Thus a sufficient condition for an increase in student loans to reduce the effective tax rate on human capital is that the fraction of student loan interest that is creditable should exceed the tax rate on the earnings increment due to education. In the calculations reported in section 6.4 we find that this is the direction of the effect in most cases we consider.

We should say a few words about the effective subsidy rate, $ESR$, which was defined in (6.3). Note that the $ESR$ depends only on $r_g$ and $r_p$. It is thus independent of any aspects of the tax system (in a partial equilibrium framework). It can, however, be affected by the presence of student loans, since as we saw in (6.8) these affect $r_g$. (Student loans have no effect on $r_p$, however.)[10]

Let $\sigma = 1 - C/C^p$ be the rate of subsidy on the direct costs of education. Then, in the absence of student loans, the wedge between $r_g$ and $r_p$, and therefore the $ESR$, will be greater the larger $\sigma$ or $C^p$, as we can see from

$$ESR|_{L=0} = \sigma\left(\frac{C^p}{FE + C^p}\right) \tag{6.9}$$

which is derived from (6.3) and (6.5a), noting that (6.5a) yields $r_p$ if $C$ is replaced by $C^p$. Introducing student loans will tend to raise $r_g$ if the student loan interest rate is less than $r_g$ (which is plausible). This is likely to raise $r_g$ relative to $r_p$ and increase the $ESR$.

## 6.3 Treatment of Human Capital under Canadian Tax and Student Loan Systems

The calculations in the next section incorporate the effects of both the personal income tax system (federal and provincial) and payroll taxes, as they applied after the federal budget of 1998, which made a number of important changes in the tax treatment of education.[11] Here we describe the relevant features of the PIT and payroll tax systems, noting the reforms introduced in 1998 (as well as changes leading up to those reforms) and developments since. We also describe the student loan system as it existed in 1998, and note more recent changes.

### 6.3.1 Personal Income Tax

A useful benchmark for describing how PIT impinges on human capital is a flat tax system under which direct costs of education or training are fully deductible. Interest on student loans would not be deductible. Under such a neutral system, $ETR = 0$. Canadian PIT departs from neutrality by levying graduated marginal tax rates, in its treatment of direct costs, and (since 1998) by allowing a credit for interest on student loans.

Both federal and provincial PIT are levied on individuals, unlike in the United States where most married couples are taxed jointly. In 1998 basic federal marginal rates of 17, 26, and 29 percent were levied on taxable income in the ranges 0–$29,590, $29,591–$59,180, and $59,181+. (These rates and brackets were in force from 1993 to 1999.) Adding in surtaxes and provincial income tax, the full marginal rates in the three brackets came to about 26, 40, and 46 percent in 1998 (Canadian Tax Foundation 1999, table 3.5). Important deductions made in arriving at taxable income included those for Registered Retirement Savings Plan (RRSP) and Registered Pension Plan (RPP) contributions and child care expenses. Rather than providing personal allowances or exemptions as in most other countries, a system of personal credits was applied. These credits were designed to give all taxpayers the same relief as if they had received personal deductions but were in the 17 percent marginal tax bracket. On this basis the credits given were equivalent to deductions of $6,456 for the taxpayer and $5,380 for a dependent spouse or child over 18.

Refundable tax credits for children under 18 were provided via the Canada Child Tax Benefit (CCTB) and the National Child Benefit Supplement (NCBS). The latter were phased out on family net incomes above $25,921 and $20,921 respectively. These programs have little impact on costs of education, since relatively few students have children, but they increase marginal tax rates for many graduates, and will therefore drive up the $ETR$ on human capital somewhat.[12]

The tax relief on tuition and other direct expenses provided by the PIT comes in the form of various credits, not as a deduction. In 1998 a credit was given for 17 percent of tuition and additional mandatory fees paid to approved postsecondary institutions. A further credit equal to 17 percent of an "education amount" was provided. The education amount was $80 per month prior to 1996, but was raised in steps to $200 per month by 1998. Since most students have low incomes, these credits would in many cases not be very valuable if they were only available to reduce the student's own tax liability. Their value is enhanced by the fact that any unused portion can be transferred to a spouse, parent, or grandparent.[13] Also, in 1997 a carryforward provision for unused education credits was introduced that would allow students to obtain tax relief themselves in later years. These measures ensure that the effective implicit federal subsidy on direct costs of education via PIT is close to being uniform at a 17 percent rate. Adding in provincial tax, the average rate of relief is about 26 percent.

The "education amount" credits are not related to actual expenditures but are simply paid as a lump sum. They are thus similar to a system of student grants. This form of assistance would not have a tax-side rationale under a flat tax, but with progressivity might be advocated as a rough offset to the effect of graduated marginal tax rates on human capital *ETRs*.

The PIT system also provides assistance for education and training via registered savings plans. First, Canadians are able to withdraw funds from their RRSPs without penalty two years after contributions are made. This means that assuming contribution limits are not binding, parents could save for their children's postsecondary education via their RRSPs. While this avenue is sometimes chosen, it is not as attractive as it might seem, since RRSP contribution limits have been held at relatively low levels.[14] Also withdrawals are taxed. Parents will typically be in their peak earning years when their kids go to college, and will therefore face high tax rates on withdrawals. This will also make the RRSP saving route less attractive.

Parents are encouraged to save for their kids' education via Registered Education Saving Plans (RESPs). In contrast to an RRSP, contributions to an RESP are not tax deductible. However, income earned within the plan is tax free, and if the proceeds are spent on the child's education, withdrawals of accrued income enter the child's income for tax purposes. Given that postsecondary students are generally in low tax brackets, the result is that the net of tax rate of return on RESP saving generally exceeds that on nonsheltered saving.[15] While RESPs provide a higher rate of return than on nonsheltered saving, in the pre-1998 regime they were not sufficiently attractive to induce much use. This may have been due to the opportunities for fully sheltered saving (e.g., via RRSPs) or because a higher rate of return could be achieved by paying down mortgages and consumer debt.[16]

The 1996, 1997, and (especially) 1998 federal budgets introduced a number of changes intended to reduce burdens on postsecondary students and to stimulate education and training in Canada. The following were the principal changes:

1. The 1996 and 1997 budgets announced that the education amount would be raised from its original $80 per month to $150 per month in 1997 and $200 per month in 1998.

2. The education amount was extended to part-time postsecondary students in the 1998 budget, at $60 per month. Part-time students also became eligible to claim child care expense deduction (CCED) for the first time, up to $2,200 per year.

3. Canada Study Grants (CSGs) of up to $3,000 per year were created in the 1998 budget for both full- and part-time students in financial need who had children or other dependants.

4. Interest on student loans became eligible for a tax credit at the 17 percent rate in the 1998 budget.

5. Tax-free withdrawals of up to $10,000 per year ($20,000 in total) from RRSPs were introduced in the 1998 budget to finance full-time training or education (or part-time for disabled people). These withdrawals must be repaid within ten years.

6. The 1996 and 1997 budgets raised the annual contribution limits on RESPs from $1,500 to $4,000 per student, and also increased the lifetime limit on contributions from $31,500 to $42,000. The 1998 budget introduced Canada Education Saving Grants (CESGs) equal to 20 percent of RESP contributions up to a limit of a $400 annual grant per student. CESG amounts become part of the RESP. The 1998 budget also made it possible to transfer an RESP balance to an RRSP if the student did not go on to qualifying study after leaving high school.

All of these provisions act to increase the net-of-tax expected return to planned or actual human capital investment for some taxpayers.[17] However, the incidence of the increased returns varies greatly. Increased education amounts raise $r_n$ for almost all students. On the other hand, interest credits only benefit those with student loans, and the RESP/RRSP provisions have similarly limited incidence. Also the value of the RESP/RRSP measures will vary substantially even among those who make use of these savings plans. CESGs are proportional to RESP contributions; the benefit of RESP saving depends on how attractive is the after-tax rate of return on the next-best saving vehicle, the value of the option to rollover unused RESP funds into an RRSP depends on how likely it is that education plans will fall through, and the benefit of being able to take money out of an RRSP temporarily to finance education depends on the size of the tax rate thereby avoided.

Since 1998 the most important PIT changes affecting human capital have been (1) a doubling of the education amounts in the 2001 tax year (to $400 and $120 per month for full-time and part-time students respectively), (2) reductions in federal tax rates and changes in the rate structure, and (3) the freeing-up of provincial PIT rate structures.[18] By the 2001 tax year the federal government had moved from its sharply graduated three-bracket rate structure to more gradual progressivity. Federal rates were applied at the rates of 16, 22, 26, and 29 percent on taxable income in the ranges 0–$30,754, $30,755–$61,509, $61,510–$100,000, and $100,000+. All federal surtaxes had been removed. Including provincial taxes, full marginal rates in the four brackets were 24, 33, 40, and 44 percent. The reduced progressivity should reduce human capital ETRs somewhat.

Prior to the 2001 tax year all nine provinces that were signatories to the federal-provincial tax collection agreements were bound to levy their basic PIT as a flat percentage of the basic federal tax. Quebec levied and collected its own separate PIT. Under this arrangement, federal surtaxes did not affect provincial PIT, and the provinces were free to enact their own surtaxes and credits additional to those provided by Ottawa. While in the 1970s and 1980s provincial PIT payments could broadly be thought of as proportional to federal, by 1998 this approximation was becoming strained. Some provinces, notably Ontario, levied surtaxes, and a wide range of provincial credits were provided, such as for provincial political contributions, qualifying investments, property and sales taxes, and dependent children. Finally the Quebec rate structure was somewhat less progressive than the federal structure, featuring marginal rates of 17, 21.25, and 24.5 percent on taxable incomes of 0–$26,000, $26,001–$52,000, and $52,000+ in 2001, for example.

Beginning in 2001 provinces covered by the tax collection agreements are free to levy tax as a function of federal taxable income rather than basic federal tax. This has already led to significant differences in rate structure across the provinces, and divergence from the federal structure. While six provinces kept the three-bracket structure for 2001, New Brunswick followed the federal lead to create a new $100,000+ bracket. Alberta introduced a flat tax at a 10 percent rate. British Columbia introduced five brackets, with the top one beginning at $85,000.

### 6.3.2 Payroll Taxes

In 1998 employees and employers each paid Canada Pension Plan (CPP) contributions at a rate of 3.2 percent on earnings, with a cap reached at maximum pensionable earnings of $36,900. Employment insurance (EI) contributions were paid at a rate of 2.7 percent by the employee and 3.78 percent by the employer, on earnings up to $39,000. For workers whose earnings did not exceed $36,900 the payroll rate structure was mildly progressive, since the first $3,500 of earnings were not subject to CPP contributions. However, for middle and high earners, the system was clearly regressive. This regressivity should offset the positive effect of PIT progressivity on human capital *ETRs* to some extent.

### 6.3.3 Student Loan Plans

Both the provinces and the federal government help students to finance their education by providing guaranteed student loans. The provinces are responsible for administration. Attempting to take into account variations in provincial plans is beyond the scope of this study. Here we have modelled the effects of the Canada and Ontario Student Loan Plans (CSLP and OSLP). The results should be reasonably representative for the country as whole since the federal and provincial governments instituted reforms in 1995–96 to achieve a fairly high degree of standardization (e.g., see Finnie and Schwartz 1996).

The CSLP/OSLP system allows students to take out loans up to a limit, equal to allowable education expenses minus the student's expected contribution. The latter is calculated taking family resources and dependants (e.g., children of a single parent) into account. Maximum loan amounts are $165 per week from the federal government and about $110 per week from provincial governments, for a total of $9,350 over a 34-week school year. Importantly, interest is paid by the government sponsors of the plan until six months after graduation. Beyond that point the loans must normally be paid back within a period of 9.5 years. Finnie (2001) finds that graduates, on average, pay the loans back quite quickly. Statistics Canada's National Graduate Survey (NGS) found that for 1995 first-degree university graduates (the latest cohort for which figures are available) about 40 percent of debt is repaid after two years (Finnie 2001, fig. 4).

In recent years student loans have become controversial, for two reasons. First, the default rate has been growing, and there have been concerns that defaulters are treated too leniently. Second, there has been some alarm at reports of substantial accumulated debts. A wide range of average amounts of debt has been reported in the media, with differences depending on which students are included, whether the average is taken for just those students in debt or for all students, and so on. According to the Department of Finance (1998), for a typical graduate with student loans, debt loads following a four-year post-secondary program averaged $13,000 in 1990–91, and could be expected to rise to $25,000 in 1998–99. On the other hand, the NGS results show average debt of only about $10,000 for 1990 grads with loans and $13,600 for 1995 grads. The incidence of debt in the NGS was about 46 percent for both the 1990 and 1995 graduates (see Finnie 2001, fig. 1).

To prevent students from defaulting on their loans, prior to 1997 those who could demonstrate financial hardship received up to 18 months of interest relief. In 1997 relief was extended to 30 months. The February 1998 budget extended the maximum period of interest relief to 54 months. In order to qualify for full interest relief, gross earnings had to be less than $22,300 as of April 1998.[19] (Prior to this the cutoff had been $20,460.) In order to go from 30 to 54 months' relief individuals had to qualify as still being in financial hardship after their loans had been rescheduled to cover a 15-year period. Finally, for those individuals who still remain in financial difficulties, the government will reduce the loan principal if annual payments exceed, on average, 15 percent of income. Maximum assistance is limited to the lesser of $10,000 or 50 percent of the loan. To qualify, five years must have passed since the completion of study and normal interest relief must have been exhausted.[20]

Together with the tax provisions discussed earlier, the CSLP changes in the 1998 budget substantially increased support for postsecondary students. The modified CSLP can be viewed as a crude income contingent student loan plan. The expectation is that the majority of students will pay off their loans in full, but very sizable reductions in the effective burden of student loans will be provided to a significant group with low incomes.

## 6.4   Effective Tax Rates on Undergraduate University Education in Canada

### 6.4.1   Data and Assumptions

To gauge the typical size of *ETRs* in Canada, we computed representative values of the net- and gross-of-tax rates of return, $r_n$ and $r_g$. We used Statistics Canada's *1995 Survey of Consumer Finance* (SCF) to model actual and potential earnings, $E_t$ and $E_t^*$, before- and after-tax. We performed our calculations as if the 1995 cross section were a snapshot of an economy in steady state.[21] From this dataset we took median earnings (and other quantiles) of full-time male and female workers holding high school diplomas and bachelor's degrees as the basis for $E_t^*$ and $E_t$ respectively.[22] We used median rather than mean earnings because we wanted to investigate rates of return and *ETRs* for the average student. Since earnings are positively skewed, the mean is above the median and is not representative for the typical student.

The estimation of $E_t, E_t^*$, and their differential required specification of a counterfactual scenario. How much would the university graduate have earned if he or she had stopped formal education after high school? Our counterfactual says that they would have received the median amount earned by high school graduates of the same age and gender. Some authors have argued that university graduates have greater ability and that an ability differential (typically 10 or 15 percent) therefore needs to be applied to the earnings of high school graduates when forming the counterfactual (e.g., see Stager 1994). We take a comparative advantage view, in which it is not necessarily clear that the median university graduate would have earned more than the median high school graduate if his/her education had been terminated after high school.[23]

An alternative to our approach would be to estimate human capital earnings equations, and to form the counterfactual by reducing the value of the years of schooling variable for university graduates. This approach allows more variables that affect earnings to be held constant than are controlled in our approach. We hold constant age, gender, and hours of work. The additional variables that are controlled for in a regression approach could include occupation, industry, region, union membership, marital status, and fertility. While the results of such an exercise would be interesting, we decided that the additional variables would be inappropriately restrictive. High school and university graduates differ in occupation, industry, region, and so on, in part because of their different levels of education. The reason for obtaining a university degree is often to enter an occupation that would otherwise be inaccessible, and reaping the advantage of one's degree often means moving to a different industry or region. Thus we do not see holding constant the additional characteristics in comparing high school and university graduate earnings to be an advantage. We are interested in the total rather than the partial impact of education.

We have specified costs and tax features, as far as possible, to be those prevailing in the academic year 1997 to 1998.[24] In 1997–98 undergraduate tuition for core university programs (and likely for median graduates) averaged $3,253, and additional fees $342 (e.g., for activities), according to Statistics Canada. Other direct expenses (books, supplies, and return transportation to the educational institution) were assumed to be $1,000 a year. Thus we estimated total direct expenses to be $4,595.

In addition to distinguishing between men and women, the calculations we report below consider part-time and full-time students separately. Full-time students are assumed to work the equivalent of four months a year, during which they would earn the same amount as a high school graduate. As in previous studies we reduce these earnings somewhat (by 20 percent) to allow for unemployment and job search.[25] Part-time students are assumed to earn their degrees in six years, as opposed to four for full-time students. We assume that they work year-round—part-time during the winter months and full-time during the summer. They are assumed to earn half as much as if they were employed full-time year round.

In modeling the taxes paid by workers after graduation, we assumed that they do not claim a credit for a dependant spouse, and in the main results ignore the tax consequences of children. The incidence of dependant spouses has been declining rapidly in recent years, and we expect it will be very low over the lifetimes of recent graduates. Ignoring the tax consequences of children leads to an overstatement of tax burdens over the working lifetime, but only a small error in the calculation of the taxes paid on the incremental earnings due to education, as we argued in the last section. We, however, took the tax treatment of children into account when considering the situation of single parents.

We made no allowance in our main results for deductions from income after graduation. (Personal credits and credits for interest on student loans, where appropriate, were taken into account.) The principal deduction that could potentially be modeled is that for Registered Retirement Savings Plan (RRSP) or Registered Pension Plan (RPP) contributions. However, we determined that this would be misleading since our calculations only consider earnings over the working lifetime. If we took the tax relief on RRSP/RPP contributions into account we would have to also model the tax paid on withdrawals. Ignoring both contributions and withdrawals should be approximately offsetting. The deductions for Registered Education Savings Plan (RESP) contributions were taken into account in our modeling of the impact of CESGs.

### 6.4.2   Results

Results from our base case are shown in table 6.1. This case uses the 1998 tax system (i.e., as modified by the 1998 federal budget) and assumes a single student with no dependants who finances his or her education without the help of a student loan or an RESP. The estimated rates of return are lower than those found by Vaillancourt (1997) and Stager (1994) using 1991 census data. Whereas we find that the net-of-tax private rate of return was 7.9 percent for male full-time university students, and 12.6 percent for female, Vaillancourt found figures of 12.3 and 16.1 percent. Stager obtained private rates of return of 13.8 percent for men and 17.6 percent for women. Aside from using

**Table 6.1**
Rates of return and effective tax rates for first university degree graduates: 1998 tax system, no student loans, no dependants (base case)

|  | IRR (%) net of tax (1) | IRR (%) gross of tax (2) | ETR $[(2) - (1)]/(2)$ |
|---|---|---|---|
| *Males* |  |  |  |
| Full-time | 7.94 | 9.84 | 0.193 |
| Part-time | 7.06 | 9.00 | 0.215 |
| *Females* |  |  |  |
| Full-time | 12.63 | 14.34 | 0.119 |
| Part-time | 11.52 | 13.29 | 0.133 |

Source: Authors' calculations using 1995 *Statistics Canada Survey of Consumer Finance* data.
Note: IRR = internal rate of return; ETR = effective tax rate.

more recent earnings data, and incorporating the effects of higher tuition fees, our study differs from the two earlier studies by using median rather than mean earnings, and by assuming retirement after age
60 rather than 64 (in order to reflect the move to earlier retirement).
These differences act to produce lower estimated rates of return.[26]

A notable feature of these results is that as in previous studies, the
rate of return is considerably higher for females than for males. The
reason is that the earnings of women with a university degree are
much closer to those of their male counterparts than is the case for
workers with only high school. We also find somewhat lower rates
of return to part-time than to full-time study. This difference is due
mainly to the delay by two years of the earnings benefits of study for
the part-timers (since they remain in school that much longer).

Table 6.1 shows a relatively small difference between gross and net
private rates of return for university graduates. The proportional difference is, of course, the effective tax rate. At 19.3 and 11.9 percent for
full-time male and female students respectively, the $ETRs$ indicate that
in the no-loan no-RESP case, human capital investment is not taxed as
heavily as physical capital. (Recall our earlier discussion of the Mc-
Kenzie et al. 1998 results.) The difference in $ETRs$ for men and women
reflects the impact of progressivity. Male university graduates still earn
more than women, and on their earnings increments due to education
are therefore taxed more heavily on average. $ETRs$ for those who attend part-time are lower because they spend more time working while
going to school, leading to a higher marginal tax rate (i.e., a higher implicit subsidy) on their forgone earnings.

Turning to table 6.2, we see the effects not only of taxes but also of
subsidies to universities. The second column shows, again, the gross-
of-tax private rate of return, which does not take subsidies into account. The first column figures are direct costs of university education
funded by government that do not enter the private calculation.[27] An
effective subsidy rate ($ESR$) can be calculated as the proportional difference between these rates of return. We find that the subsidy rates
obtained are greater than the effective tax rates shown in table 6.1 for
all cases.[28] We thus find a negative net effective tax rate, $ETR - ESR$,
as shown in the last column of the table. This would imply that overall the public sector *encourages* human capital investment—a conclusion that is in line with the results of earlier studies and that will be
strengthened by taking into account student loans and other forms of
special assistance to postsecondary students analyzed below.

**Table 6.2**
Base case rates of return, effective subsidy rates, and tax minus subsidy rate

|  | IRR (%) public (1) | IRR (%) gross-of-tax private (2) | ESR $[(2) - (1)]/(2)$ | ETR − ESR |
|---|---|---|---|---|
| *Males* |  |  |  |  |
| Full-time | 7.37 | 9.84 | 0.251 | −0.058 |
| Part-time | 6.86 | 9.00 | 0.238 | −0.023 |
| *Females* |  |  |  |  |
| Full-time | 10.39 | 14.34 | 0.276 | −0.157 |
| Part-time | 9.85 | 13.29 | 0.259 | −0.126 |

Source: See table 6.1.
Notes: Definition of base case is as in table 6.1. ESR = effective subsidy rate; for ETR, IRR, see table 6.1.

Next we take into account the impacts of student loan financing on private rates of return and *ETRs*. As table 6.3 shows, both gross and net private rates of return increase with the student loan amount. The reason for this increase lies mainly in the fact that interest is not paid until graduation, providing a subsidy that of course increases with the size of the loan.[29] The net rate of return is more strongly affected because the implicit subsidy is larger relative to after-tax than before-tax earnings. The result is that even without interest deductibility, student loans reduce the effective tax rate significantly. This aspect is reinforced by the provision of interest deductibility on student loans. Both effects are present in table 6.3. For males, the tax rate declines from 19.3 percent in the no-loan case to just 17.2 percent with $15,000 in loans. For females, the drop is even larger: from 11.9 to 8.3 percent.

Table 6.3 illustrates another interesting point. With loan increases up to $15,000, there is a roughly linear decrease in the *ETR*. But, as the loan is raised to $30,000, there is a larger decline in the *ETR*. For females, for example, the *ETR* is even negative, falling to −3.4 percent. The reason is that in Ontario a student with a $30,000 loan would qualify for loan forgiveness on $2,000 of the principal. Once again, the effect on the estimated rates of return is higher for the net- than for the gross-of-tax return. Indeed, the difference in impact is so large that we obtain a negative effective *ETR*.

The single female parent case reported in table 6.3 shows that family status may significantly affect tax impacts on education in Canada. The gross rates of return for a single woman parent are taken to be the same as those for a single woman without children, but the net rates of

Table 6.3
Rates of return and effective tax rates for full-time students: 1998 tax system with student loans

| Sex and dependants | Value of loan ($) | IRR (%) net-of-tax (1) | IRR (%) gross-of-tax (2) | ETR [(2) − (1)]/(2) | ESR* | ETR − ESR |
|---|---|---|---|---|---|---|
| *Male* | | | | | | |
| No dependants | 0 (base case) | 7.94 | 9.84 | 0.193 | 0.251 | −0.058 |
| | 5,000 | 8.15 | 10.03 | 0.187 | 0.265 | −0.078 |
| | 10,000 | 8.39 | 10.24 | 0.180 | 0.280 | −0.100 |
| | 15,000 | 8.66 | 10.46 | 0.172 | 0.296 | −0.124 |
| | 30,000 | 10.31 | 11.77 | 0.124 | 0.374 | −0.250 |
| *Female* | | | | | | |
| No dependants | 0 | 12.63 | 14.34 | 0.119 | 0.276 | −0.157 |
| | 5,000 | 13.20 | 14.83 | 0.110 | 0.299 | −0.189 |
| | 10,000 | 13.88 | 15.38 | 0.098 | 0.324 | −0.226 |
| | 15,000 | 14.70 | 16.03 | 0.083 | 0.352 | −0.269 |
| | 30,000 | 20.49 | 19.81 | −0.034 | 0.475 | −0.509 |
| *Female* | | | | | | |
| Single parent with one child | 0 | 11.59 | 14.34 | 0.192 | 0.276 | −0.084 |
| | 5,000 | 12.04 | 14.83 | 0.188 | 0.299 | −0.111 |
| | 10,000 | 12.56 | 15.38 | 0.184 | 0.324 | −0.140 |
| | 15,000 | 13.16 | 16.03 | 0.179 | 0.352 | −0.173 |
| | 30,000 | 16.99 | 19.81 | 0.142 | 0.475 | −0.333 |

Source: See table 6.1.
Notes: (1) The zero loan case without dependants is the same as the base case considered in tables 6.1 and 6.2. (2) The female single parent is assumed to have had a child at age 18. This child will generate a child care expense deduction until the parent is aged 25. Canada Study Grants, which were offered starting in 1999, are not included. (3) For the $30,000 loan, $2,000 of the principal qualifies for loan forgiveness; see appendix B. (4) ESR* = [(2) − (appropriate entry from column 1 of table 6.2)]/(2).

return are lower since after-tax forgone earnings are enlarged by the child care expense deduction. The result is that the *ETR* is higher for a single parent. Also note that the *ETR* falls less rapidly as the student loan amount is increased than in the case without dependants. This is because before- and after-tax forgone earnings are closer for the single parent, and as a result loan benefits do not differ greatly in relative importance between gross and net-of-tax calculations.

The second to the last column of table 6.3 shows the impact of student loans on the expenditure side. The *ESR* rises quite strongly with the loan amount, increasing from 25.1 percent without loans to 29.6 percent with a $15,000 loan for males, and from 27.6 to 35.2 percent for females. Putting the impacts on the *ETRs* and *ESRs* together, a $15,000 student loan decreases the net effective tax rate, *ETR* − *ESR*, from −5.8 to −12.3 percent for males and from −15.6 to −26.9 percent for females. Roughly, these numbers show that the median *ETR* − *ESR* for all students was about −9 percent for males and −21 percent for females in 1998.[30] For males and females together, the median *ETR* − *ESR* would have been around −15 percent. This represents fairly significant encouragement of human capital investment, especially in light of our earlier conclusion that the average *EMTR* for physical capital in Canada was about 30 percent.

Table 6.4 shows part-time results corresponding to the full-time case shown in table 6.3. In the part-time case we find that the size of loan has little impact on the *ETR*. This is because part-timers pay interest from the time their student loans are received; they do not benefit from the zero interest payments until six months after graduation allowed for full-time students.

Table 6.5 shows results for full-time university students with interest relief. For the individuals in our calculations to qualify for 18 or 30 months of interest relief, it is sufficient that their earnings should be two-thirds of median after graduation. Rates of return are accordingly lower for this group than for the median achievers studied in tables 6.1 through 6.3. We see that providing interest relief has relatively little impact on the calculated effective tax rates. A similar outcome is found for part-time students (see Collins and Davies 2002).

Next we study the effects of Canada Education Savings Grants (CESGs).[31] As of January 1, 1998, Canada Education Saving Grants (CESGs) add 20 percent to RESP contributions annually, up to a grant limit of $400 per child. Net-of-tax rates of return rise and effective tax rates decline. In the case of full-time male university students, for

**Table 6.4**
Rates of return and effective tax rates for part-time students: 1998 tax system with student loans

| Sex and dependants | Value of loan ($) | IRR (%) net-of-tax (1) | IRR (%) gross-of-tax (2) | ETR [(2) − (1)]/(2) | ESR* | ETR − ESR |
|---|---|---|---|---|---|---|
| *Male* | | | | | | |
| No dependants | 0 | 7.06 | 9.00 | 0.215 | 0.238 | −0.023 |
| | 5,000 | 7.02 | 8.98 | 0.218 | 0.236 | −0.018 |
| | 10,000 | 6.97 | 8.95 | 0.221 | 0.233 | −0.012 |
| | 15,000 | 6.92 | 8.92 | 0.224 | 0.231 | −0.007 |
| *Female* | | | | | | |
| No dependants | 0 | 11.52 | 13.29 | 0.133 | 0.259 | −0.126 |
| | 5,000 | 11.58 | 13.35 | 0.133 | 0.262 | −0.129 |
| | 10,000 | 11.63 | 13.42 | 0.133 | 0.266 | −0.133 |
| | 15,000 | 11.70 | 13.49 | 0.133 | 0.270 | −0.137 |
| *Female* | | | | | | |
| Single parent with one child | 0 | 11.17 | 13.29 | 0.159 | 0.259 | −0.100 |
| | 5,000 | 11.21 | 13.35 | 0.160 | 0.262 | −0.102 |
| | 10,000 | 11.25 | 13.42 | 0.161 | 0.266 | −0.105 |
| | 15,000 | 11.30 | 13.49 | 0.162 | 0.270 | −0.108 |

Source: See table 6.1.
Notes: (1) The zero loan case without dependants is the same as the base case considered in tables 6.1 and 6.2. (2) The female single parent is assumed to have had a child at age 18. This child will generate a child care expense deduction until the parent is aged 25. The amount claimed during study is subject to the restrictions imposed in the 1998 federal budget. (See appendix B.) Canada Study Grants, which will be offered starting in 1999, are not included. (3) ESR* = [(2) − appropriate entry from column 1 of table 6.2]/(2).

**Table 6.5**
Rates of return and effective tax rates for full-time students: 1998 tax system with $10,000 student loans and interest relief

| Sex and dependants | Interest relief (months) | IRR (%) net of tax (1) | IRR (%) gross of tax (2) | ETR $[(2) - (1)]/(2)$ |
|---|---|---|---|---|
| *Male* | 0 | 6.54 | 7.45 | 0.122 |
| No dependants | 18 | 6.66 | 7.55 | 0.118 |
| | 30 | 6.72 | 7.60 | 0.116 |
| *Female* | 0 | 10.86 | 11.37 | 0.045 |
| No dependants | 18 | 11.04 | 11.51 | 0.041 |
| | 30 | 11.14 | 11.59 | 0.039 |
| *Female* | 0 | 10.06 | 11.37 | 0.115 |
| Single parent with | 18 | 10.18 | 11.51 | 0.116 |
| one child | 30 | 10.24 | 11.59 | 0.116 |

Source: See table 6.1.
Notes: (1) Assumptions on the female single parent are as in table 6.3. (2) Earnings equal 2/3 of median.

example, table 6.6 indicates that the *ETR* drops from 19.3 to 15.9 percent when parents make $650 annual contributions over a 15-year period. If maximum contributions ($2,000) are made, the *ETR*s fall much further—to just 7.9 percent for full-time males and −2.3 percent for full-time females. Effects for part-time students are also large. These results show that CESGs may have a very powerful effect as they accrue over the years.

Table 6.7 replicates the table 6.1 case (no student loans and no RESPs), assuming alternatively that the graduate earns at the 25th or the 75th percentile of the earnings distribution, rather than at the median.[32] We see that for males there is a drop in rates of return and the *ETR* of going to the 25th percentile case from the median, and there is an increase in going to the 75th percentile. The net-of-tax rate of return varies from 5.4 percent for the 25th percentile earner to 9.9 percent at the 75th percentile, compared with 7.9 percent for the median male in table 6.1. The *ETR* ranges from 10.9 to 24.1 percent, compared to 19.3 percent for the median.

For women, rates of return are also lower at the 25th percentile than at the median. The net-of-tax rate of return for full-time students is 8.5 percent, for example, compared with 12.6 percent at the median. The *ETR* is also lower, at 7.0 percent compared with 11.9 percent in the base case. However, when we move to the 75th percentile the rates of return rise less, proportionally, than for males, reflecting a less skewed

**Table 6.6**
Rates of return and effective tax rates with CESGs: 1998 tax system, no student loans, no dependants

| Sex | Yearly contribu- tion ($) | IRR (%) net of tax (1) | IRR (%) gross of tax (2) | ETR [(2) − (1)]/(2) | ESR* | ETR − ESR |
|---|---|---|---|---|---|---|
| *Male* | | | | | | |
| Full-time | 650 | 8.27 | 9.84 | 0.159 | 0.251 | −0.092 |
| Part-time | 650 | 7.34 | 9.00 | 0.184 | 0.238 | −0.054 |
| *Female* | | | | | | |
| Full-time | 650 | 13.22 | 14.34 | 0.078 | 0.276 | −0.198 |
| Part-time | 650 | 12.01 | 13.29 | 0.096 | 0.259 | −0.163 |
| *Male* | | | | | | |
| Full-time | 2,000 | 9.06 | 9.84 | 0.079 | 0.251 | −0.172 |
| Part-time | 2,000 | 7.98 | 9.00 | 0.114 | 0.238 | −0.124 |
| *Female* | | | | | | |
| Full-time | 2,000 | 14.67 | 14.34 | −0.023 | 0.276 | −0.299 |
| Part-time | 2,000 | 13.18 | 13.29 | 0.008 | 0.259 | −0.251 |

Source: See table 6.1.
Notes: (1) CESG = Canada educational study grant. CESG benefits incorporated here are based on an example provided by Department of Finance (1998, p. 35). Contributions are made over a 15-year period and earn a 5 percent rate of return. (2) ESR* = [(2) − appropriate entry from column 1 of table 6.2]/(2).

**Table 6.7**
Rates of return and effective tax rates for 25th and 75th quantiles: 1998 tax system, no student loans, no dependants

| Sex | Quantile | IRR (%) net of tax (1) | IRR (%) gross of tax (2) | ETR [(2) − (1)]/(2) |
|---|---|---|---|---|
| *Male* | | | | |
| Full-time | 25th | 5.35 | 6.00 | 0.109 |
| Part-time | 25th | 4.29 | 4.92 | 0.129 |
| *Female* | | | | |
| Full-time | 25th | 8.46 | 9.09 | 0.070 |
| Part-time | 25th | 8.69 | 9.49 | 0.081 |
| *Male* | | | | |
| Full-time | 75th | 9.88 | 13.02 | 0.241 |
| Part-time | 75th | 9.16 | 12.19 | 0.248 |
| *Female* | | | | |
| Full-time | 75th | 12.42 | 15.25 | 0.186 |
| Part-time | 75th | 12.95 | 16.22 | 0.202 |

Source: See table 6.1.

distribution of earnings (and therefore lower peak tax rates on earning gains) among female graduates. The *ETR* rises only to 18.6 percent at the 75th percentile, compared to 24.1 percent for males.

The results in table 6.7 indicate the impact of the graduated rates in the tax system. Effective tax rates on human capital investment rise with the lifetime earnings of graduates. Another way of putting this is that the net-of-tax rates of return on human capital investment are depressed more for high earners.

To get a complete assessment of the incentive effect on human capital formation, we deducted the *ESR* from the *ETR*. Looking back at table 6.2, we could see that if the graduates at the 75th percentile had the same *ESRs* as median workers, the *ETR − ESR* figures for males would be −1.0 and 1.0 percent for full-time and part-time students respectively. Those for females would be −9.0 and −5.7 percent for full-time and part-time. However, the assumption that the *ESRs* at higher percentiles are the same as at the median may be incorrect. The highest paid graduates are those in professional programs like engineering and medicine, which in 1997–98 were still more heavily subsidized than general arts and science programs. Vaillancourt (1997) finds that the difference is sufficient that the net subsidy rates (i.e., *ESR − ETR*) in 1990 were highest in science, engineering, and medicine and lowest in the humanities and social science.[33]

Finally, we have generated results (not shown) corresponding to tables 6.1, 6.3, and 6.4 for the tax system as it existed in 1997, that is, prior to the major changes of the February 1998 federal budget. We found that the difference between 1997 and 1998 results for full-time students without student loans or RESPs was small. The difference came from the fact that the education expenses were just $150 a month in 1997 for full-timers compared with $200 a month in 1998. The after-tax rates of return were slightly lower, and *ETRs* slightly higher, in 1997 for part-timers, however, since they received no tax credit for spending on education. A monthly credit of $60 was introduced for part-timers in the 1998 budget.

We also found that the effect of interest credit on student loans introduced in 1998 was quite small. For loans of up to $10,000, net-of-tax rates of return were 0.1 percentage points lower under the 1997 system, with the difference in *ETRs* correspondingly small. Compared to the impacts of CESGs, the credit for interest on student loans had a relatively weak effect.

## 6.5   Conclusion

We argued in this chapter that the effective tax rate is a useful device for summing up the effects of taxes on the incentive to invest in human capital. We illustrated the approach for undergraduate university level education in Canada. Our analysis concentrated on two broad features of effective tax rates: how high they are for human capital at the median level, and how they range across levels.

We found that a notable difference exists between the effective tax rate on human capital coming from the tax system *per se* (the *ETR*) and the net effective tax rate, which subtracts the effective subsidy rate (the *ESR*) on the expenditure side. For the median level earners, the *ETR*s on human capital are sizable but below the effective marginal tax rates for physical capital in Canada. This is true even in the wake of the federal budgets of 1996, 1997, and 1998, which introduced a wide variety of measures that reduced *ETR*s. On the other hand, *ETR* − *ESR* at the median turned out to be about −9 percent for males and −21 percent for females. Thus we learned that government provided more incentive on the expenditure side for investment in university education than disincentive on the tax side.

Whether a net effective tax rate on human capital that averages about −15 percent across the sexes is appropriate remains an interesting issue. For this to be supported on efficiency grounds, it is likely that one would have to appeal to externality arguments. Students' liquidity constraints could further help justify the negative *ETR* − *ESR*, although the potential importance of this factor is eroded by Canada's generous system of student loans. In view of the substantial positive effective tax rates on physical capital, there is a possibility that in the late 1990s Canadian governments provided too much encouragement for university study. However, since then (for the last five years) tuition fees have risen quite significantly, so a correction to the problem may already have occurred.

We also found that the taxation of human capital is far from uniform in Canada. Our results raise the possibility of distortions in the supply of human capital, with too much investment taking place in programs, or by individuals, with low *ETR*s and too little occurring where *ETR*s are high. We found that *ETR*s differ depending on income after graduation, full-time or part-time study, receipt of student loans, gender, presence of dependants, and use of RESPs. For example, we found that *ETR*s for full-time students who go on to earn at the 75th percentile of the earnings distribution throughout their lifetimes are higher than for those earning at the 25th percentile. The strong association between earnings and area of university studies should have some implications for the composition of human capital investment. Other things equal, the highest *ETRs* will be felt by graduates in areas such as business, engineering, and medicine. At the opposite extreme are graduates in the humanities. We learned that in some of the high tax areas there has been in the past an offsetting effect in the form of heavy direct subsidies. However, the tendency to allow tuition fees to rise in recent years, especially in more specialized programs, may be eroding that offset.

It is possible that the provisions of the 1998 federal budget, and the doubling of the tax credit for education in 2001, not only reduced the tax-side disincentive for human capital investment but also reduced the nonuniformity in *ETRs*. Increases in the education credit have a broadly based impact that has lowered *ETRs* for the majority of students. The special provisions for part-time students and those with dependants should reduce *ETRs* for people whose human capital investments were less-favored by the tax system. In the future, as higher income taxpayers increasingly take advantage of Canada Education Savings Grants (CESGs), there should appear some reduction in their *ETRs*.

While the analytical framework we introduced can be applied to human capital investment at any level, our numerical results have confined them to first-degree university graduates. The computations might be extended to include *ETRs* on completed high school, community college, incomplete college and university studies, postgraduate work, and on-the-job training (OJT). Likely the effective tax rates will prove lower for high school completion, community college, and incomplete postsecondary studies than for undergraduate university degrees. This is because of the importance of income level in determining *ETRs*. Results for postgraduates are harder to anticipate as rates of return to graduate studies are usually lower than for undergraduate programs, and *ETRs* can be very sensitive to small absolute differences in gross and net rates of return.

Attention to the *ETR* on OJT should be particularly enlightening, since a large element of human capital is due to training on the job. Nevertheless, there is good reason to expect much lower *ETRs* for OJT than for formal schooling. In general, because firms and workers must share the costs of such training, the workers do so by receiving lower wages or salaries during training. The progressivity effects are therefore likely to be much lower than for formal schooling. The explanation is that only a portion of earnings is being forgone while the tax rate on lost earnings is not much lower than that on the earnings' increment due to training. On the employer's part, at least for corporations, the tax rate is constant, so there is no progressivity effect at all. Hence ETRs for OJT, like effective subsidy rates, may be quite small.

## Appendix A

This appendix provides the general form of the problem presented in section 6.2. Recall that we illustrated the calculation of the ETR for the case where the length of the schooling period $m$ is just one year and the length of life $T$ goes to infinity. If we did not make those assumptions, analytic solutions for the gross and net-of-tax rates of return $r_g$ and $r_n$, and thus for the ETR, would not exist. The purpose of this appendix is to take the analysis to the point where numerical solutions must be sought.

The starting point is equation (6.2) in section 6.2, which can be used to compute $r_g$ in the case where the tax system takes no account of education and there are no student loans:

$$\sum_{t=1}^{T} \frac{E_t - C_t}{(1 + r_g)^{t-1}} = \sum_{t=1}^{T} \frac{E_t^*}{(1 + r_g)^{t-1}}. \tag{6.2}$$

As we explained in section 6.2, this equation can be used to compute the public rate of return $r_p$ if $C_t$ is replaced by the full direct costs of education $C_t^p$. It can further be used to compute $r_n$ if $E_t$ and $E_t^*$ are replaced by the after-tax earnings $E_t^a$ and $E_t^{a*}$.

To bring in the tax treatment of education and student loans, we need to modify (6.2) to take account of (1) amounts $L_t$ borrowed in the form of student loans in the schooling period, (2) repayment of those loans at the interest rate $i$, with tax relief via a credit for a fraction $d$ of interest payments, and (3) tax credits for tuition and education expenses $A_t$. Introducing these elements will modify both $r_g$ and $r_n$ but make no difference to the public rate of return, $r_p$.

As explained in section 6.3, the scheduling of student loan repayments is flexible in Canada, but they must normally be repaid within ten years of graduation. Here we let annual payments during this period of $l$ years equal $i\theta(L_t, t)$, where $\theta(L_t, t)$ gives the amount on which interest must be paid each year. This amount is less than the principal in the first year of loan repayment for all student borrowers in Canada, since loans are interest free for the first 6 months after graduation. Also, as explained in appendix B, in some cases there is interest relief for low-income graduates, which also reduces the effective amount on which interest is paid below principal. In the calculations reported in our tables we assume that principal is paid off on a straight-line basis, but other assumptions can clearly be made.

Finding the internal rates of return $r_g$ and $r_n$ requires solving the general form of (6.2) numerically, which can be done with a variety of computer packages, including standard spreadsheets. Note that the RHS is not altered by taking tax relief for education or student loans into account, since it shows the present value of the earnings stream without the education in question. Thus we focus on the LHS of (6.2), which we denote $PV$ in the before-tax case. Taking student loans, but not tax relief on education, into account we have

$$PV = \sum_{t=1}^{m} \frac{E_t - C_t + L_t}{(1 + r_g)^{t-1}} + \sum_{t=m+1}^{m+l} \frac{E_t - i\theta(L_t, t) - R_t}{(1 + r_g)^{t-1}} + \sum_{t=m+l+1}^{T} \frac{E_t}{(1 + r_g)^{t-1}},$$

$$(6A.1)$$

where $R_t$ is the repayment of student loan principal in year $t$. Turning to after-tax values, we have

$$PV^a = \sum_{t=1}^{m} \frac{E_t^a - C_t + A_t + L_t}{(1 + r_n)^{t-1}} + \sum_{t=m+1}^{m+l} \frac{E_t^a - i(1-d)\theta(L_t, t) - R_t}{(1 + r_n)^{t-1}}$$

$$+ \sum_{t=m+l+1}^{T} \frac{E_t^a}{(1 + r_n)^{t-1}}.$$

$$(6A.2)$$

Again, $r_n$ is found numerically, by setting $PV^a$ equal to the RHS of (6.2) where $E_t^*$ is replaced by the after-tax value $E_t^{a*}$.

Appendix B details the tuition and "education amount" credits that compose $A_t$ in the Canadian case, as well as the rules on student loans.

## Appendix B

Basic Data

1. Our estimates of tuition and additional fees are based on Statistics Canada data for 1997–98. See *http://www.statcan.ca/Daily/English/*

*970825/d970825.htm#art2.* An average was taken over Arts degrees across the country.

2. Data on "other expenses" were taken from a variety of sources: Statistics Canada databases, university Web sites, and university calendars. "Other expenses" refers to items that are only required for schooling (e.g., books and supplies for schooling).

3. The earnings data come from Statistics Canada's *1995 Survey of Consumer Finance* microdata tape.

Assumptions on Earnings

1. Part-time earnings for full-time students are assumed to be summer earnings and therefore comprise a maximum of four months of earnings potential. To account for unemployment and job search, the value is reduced by 20 percent.

2. We assume that part-time students work part-time during the regular school year and full-time in the summer. This motivates the further assumption that their annual earnings are half of full-time earnings. A part-time student is assumed to take, on average, 3.3 courses a year. This assumption allows for a part-time student to get a four-year degree in approximately six years. Taking more than three courses in a normal school year would qualify a person as full-time. Therefore it is assumed that a part-time individual works, as mentioned, year round and goes to school year round. He or she takes 2.5 courses during the school year and 1 during the summer, accordingly, to finish his/her degree (requiring 20 credits in a 5 credit/year school).

Public Rates of Return

1. Data on government spending and enrollment for male and female, full-time and part-time students were obtained from the Statistics Canada Web site. The most recent data available at this site were expenditure values on education and enrollment figures for 1995–96. It is these figures that are used to calculate the public rate of return.

2. Current and capital expenditures on undergraduate instruction are assumed to to equal one-half of operating expenditures. The justification for this assumption is given in the text.

3. Public expenditures per student are calculated as in Vaillancourt (1995). Operating expenditure on universities is divided by full-time

equivalent (FTE) enrollment, where a part-time student counts as one third of a full-time student.

4. Public expenditures per part-time student are assumed to be one-third of those for full-time students, in line with point 3.

Tax Features

### Tax Credits

In addition to basic personal amounts, students are eligible for non-refundable credits on tuition and certain additional fees. They may also be eligible for nonrefundable credits in the form of the education amount, and on interest paid on student loans. As outlined in the chapter, the education amount was $150 a month in 1997 and $200 a month in 1998 for full-time students. Part-time students did not receive the education amount in 1997 but could claim $60 per month in 1998. The taxpayer earns a net credit applicable to federal tax equal to 17 percent of the amount claimed, and there is a further credit against provincial tax. We assume that the sum of the two equals 25 percent, as it did in Ontario in 1998.

### Child Care Expense Deduction (CCED)

1. In 1998, the government allowed taxpayers to deduct from taxable income child care expenses of up to $7,000 for each eligible child under seven years of age. A deduction of up to $4,000 was allowed for children aged 7 to 16.

2. For full-time students we assume that child care expenses equal $4,200 ($350 * 12 months), and that these expenses only last until the child is seven years old. We assume that the child is one year old when the parent is 19. Therefore child care expenses are only deducted up until the age of 25.

3. Most part-time students were not eligible to claim CCED prior to the 1998 budget. The latter allowed part-time students to deduct up to $2,200. We assume that a part-time student with a dependant would be at this maximum.

### Registered Education Savings Plans (RESPs) and Canada Education Savings Grants (CESGs)

1. In both 1997 and 1998 the federal government allowed taxpayers to contribute up to $4,000 per child to an RESP.

2. Since January 1, 1998, the federal government has been providing a CESG, equal to 20 percent of the first $2,000 of RESP contributions per child. We assume alternative RESP contribution values of $650/year and $2,000+/year in calculating the amount of CESG awarded.

3. The calculation for the CESG amount is based on an example in the 1998 Budget documents, which assumed a 5 percent rate of return and a contribution rate of $650/year. For a contribution rate of $2,000/year the CESG amount increases proportionally.

Canada Student Loan Plan

*Basic CSLP Repayment Features*

1. Students have a choice upon consolidating their Canada student loans. They can either choose a maximum fixed interest rate equal to the bank's prevailing unsecured consumer loan rate, which cannot exceed prime plus 5 percent, or a maximum floating interest rate of prime plus 2.5 percent. For Ontario Student Assistance Program (OSAP) loans students pay an interest rate of prime plus 1 percent.

2. Data on interest rates were taken from the *Globe and Mail* Web site (*http://www.globeandmail.ca*) on Tuesday, June 30, 1998. The Canadian prime interest rate on this date was equal to 6.50 percent. Depending on the loan held, the interest rate that a student actually faces may vary significantly. For example, using a prime interest rate 6.5 percent would result in an interest rate of anywhere between 7.5 and 11.5 percent, which would have a dramatic effect on the type of repayment plan chosen. For the purposes of this study a middle rate of 9 percent is used.

3. Information on CSL and OSAP loans was taken from the following Web sites: for CSL, *http://www.hrdc-drhc.gc.ca/student_loans/*; for OSAP, *http://osap.gov.on.ca*.

4. The regulations on loan forgiveness under OSAP were taken from the above-noted government of Ontario address. As of 1997–98 loan forgiveness was only available on loans that exceeded $7,000 for two terms of study; two terms being defined as 21 to 40 weeks of schooling (i.e., any amount of loan exceeding $7,000 for one eight-month school year was forgiven). For our purposes loan forgiveness only figures into the $30,000 loan case, as it is assumed that the loan is broken into four equal parts to coincide with the four years of full-time study. Thus, of the $7,500/year being borrowed, $500 is forgiven each year. It should

also be noted that part of the loan is forgiven only after the loan(s) is (are) consolidated (meaning that a payment schedule has been agreed upon and signed at a bank). For example, upon graduation $2,000 of the $30,000 loan will be forgiven and interest payments will be calculated therefore on the remaining $28,000, and not the entire $30,000. Part-time students receive no loan forgiveness, as they do not qualify for OSAP loans; one must have at least a 60 percent course load (i.e., 3 out of a maximum of 5 courses) to be eligible for such loans.

5. Net-of-tax and gross-of-tax private benefits/costs are calculated taking into account that accruing interest is paid for by government during full-time studies. If individuals are studying part-time, they do not benefit from having the interest that accrues on their loan paid off by the government. Part-time individuals must pay the interest from the moment their loan is acquired.

6. A part-time student is assumed to be working (approx. 20 hours/ week). Therefore it is assumed that he or she will not accumulate as much debt as someone who is not working. Thus a part-time person only faces loan amounts that range from $2,500 to $15,000 in our calculations.

### Interest Relief under CSLP

1. For individuals to qualify for interest relief, a reduction in median earnings is necessary. For the purposes of this study we use two-thirds of median earnings to ensure that individuals fit the specified criteria set forth in the 1998 Budget. As of April 1998 full-time students were able to benefit from full interest relief provided their gross earnings are less than $22,300 (prior to this change the value was $20,460).

2. As recently as 1996, interest relief was only available for up to 18 months, but this was changed in 1997 with an extension of the period to 30 months. Once again in 1998 this period was extended; it was then a maximum of 54 months, although the extension only included those who were in dire straits financially. To qualify for the extended 54-month period, an individual must have exhausted the 30 months of interest relief and still be in financial hardship once the repayment period is extended to 15 years. All of this must take place during the first five years upon leaving school.

3. For those in the most difficulty, the federal government introduced debt reduction in 1998. Upon exhausting all relief and having five years pass since the completion of schooling, if an individual was still

in financial hardship he or she could have the loan principal reduced if annual payments exceeded, on average, 15 percent of his or her income.

## Notes

We gratefully acknowledge the support of the Institute for Research on Public Policy. We would also like to thank John Burbidge for helpful comments and for assistance with the earnings data. Responsibility for any errors or omissions is our own.

1. See, for example, Boskin (1975), Dupor et al. (1996), Kaplow (1996), and Heckman et al. (1999).

2. It would of course be interesting to study ETRs on other levels of education, as discussed briefly in the conclusion. These would include the ETR on incomplete university education. Estimation of these other ETRs is beyond the scope of the present study.

3. Note that tax and expenditure systems may have effects on human capital investment apart from those via tax and subsidy rates. For example, if students are liquidity constrained, taxes that are incurred more after graduation—such as income and payroll taxes—will encourage human capital investment compared with consumption taxes. Future research may allow us to take these other aspects into account, and also to investigate the quantitative impact of ETRs, such as on students' propensity to obtain university education.

4. In the investment context tax burdens may be evaluated on a stock or flow basis. We do our analysis on a stock basis because this facilitates comparisons with the effective tax rate on physical capital. An alternative is to annualize the impacts and express them as a fraction of unit labor costs, that is, to put the analysis on a flow basis. Mintz (2001) partially implements this latter approach.

5. The problems faced when dealing with human capital are quite different than in the study of physical capital. For example, in calculating EMTRs for physical capital, one must specify a scenario concerning the determination of market rates of return. It might be assumed, for example, that Canada is a small player in a perfectly competitive world capital market. In order to pay the world interest rate, a corporation would have to earn a gross rate of return on a debt-financed project sufficient to pay both tax and interest at the world rate. By observing market rates and tax parameters, one can infer the before-tax rate of return on a marginal investment. The after-tax return is then found by deducting all taxes. As we will see, the procedure for human capital is quite different.

6. The situation for on-the-job training is different. (This is one of the reasons that we do not deal with OJT in this chapter. It would require a separate study.) One can imagine OJT being provided in quite small units, and the sensitivity of results to the size of the investment becomes less of a problem. This is because the relevant tax on the employer's side, namely the corporate tax, is levied at a flat rate, and provided investments are not too large, individuals' marginal tax rates will also not be strongly affected by OJT.

7. An alternative is to define the ETR as the ratio of the present value of net taxes on labor income over the lifetime to the present value of lifetime earnings (see Mintz 2001). While the two approaches will often produce similar results, this is not always the case. We prefer the approach followed here, in part because it does not require any assumption to be made about individuals' discount rates.

8. Note that "neutral" is used here in a special sense. We do not imply, for instance, that a tax system that is neutral with respect to human capital is nondistortionary in its treatment of human versus physical capital. That depends on the effective tax rate on physical capital, and also on whether there are any relevant non-tax distortions (e.g., capital market imperfections).

9. How tax relief for education and student loan aspects can be incorporated in the finite lifetime, multi-year schooling case is set out in appendix A. Analytic results are not available for $r_g$, $r_n$, or the $ETR$ in that case. The rates of return must be computed from more general versions of equation (6.2).

10. The public rate of return is similar to the social rate of return. (The only difference is that the public rate of return omits external costs or benefits of education.) From a social viewpoint, whether or not students take out loans has no effect on the costs of, or returns to, education.

11. In a more comprehensive investigation some other taxes would also be taken into account. In the previous section we remarked on the impact of sales taxes. In addition corporate income taxes have impacts on human capital formed via on-the-job training. See Collins and Davies (2002).

12. The NCBS was clawed back at rates ranging from 12.1 percent for one-child families to 26.8 percent for a family with three or more children. This means that the credit was already clawed back completely for most families at net income of $25,921, where the CCTB clawback kicked in at rates from 2.5 to 5.0 percent. The latter relatively low rates mean that the CCTB clawback range is very wide. The clawback affects families with incomes up to between $67,000 and $75,000. However, since the CCTB clawback rates are relatively low, their impact on human capital $ETRs$ would be fairly small.

13. That is, up to a limit of $5,000 minus the part of the credit used by the student to reduce his or her tax liability to zero.

14. The current contribution limit for RRSPs plus Registered Pension Plans is the lesser of $13,500 or 18 percent of earnings per year. The dollar limit is slated to rise to $14,500 in 2004 and to $15,500 in 2005; after that it will be indexed to the average industrial wage. These levels represent a significant retreat, however, from those promised by earlier federal budgets. The 1984 and 1985 budgets promised a limit of $15,500 by 1990, with subsequent indexation.

15. Since withdrawals are generally taxed at a low rate, RESPs approximate Roth IRA plans in the United States, which have nondeductible contributions and tax-free withdrawals. Greater use of this type of sheltered saving has been urged for Canada by, for example, Kesselman and Poschmann (2001).

16. In Canada interest on mortgages and consumer debt is not tax deductible. This makes paying down these forms of debt a popular form of saving for those in the age range of about 25 to 45.

17. The RESP and RRSP provisions might be seen as raising the rate of return to financial assets. However, the benefits in question are only realized as a result of planned or actual human capital investment. They are therefore regarded here as increasing the net expected return on *human* capital.

18. A further change that could have a significant effect on human capital $ETRs$ in the long-run was the re-indexation of federal brackets, credits and deductions announced in the February 2000 budget. Lack of indexation erodes the progressivity of the tax system

over time, as more and more taxpayers' rising nominal incomes push them into the top tax brackets. This may create a tendency for human capital ETRs to fall over time in a non-indexed system.

19. The budget also introduced partial interest relief on a sliding scale for those whose incomes exceeded the threshold for full relief by a small amount.

20. The February 1998 budget also announced a billion dollar Millenium Scholarship Fund, which may reduce the need for student loans somewhat. Finally, in view of the provisions to assist repayment, it was ruled that student loans would survive bankruptcy for ten years after the completion of studies.

21. While this assumption is not completely innocuous, the Canadian earnings distribution was very stable in the 1990s. There was little per capita earnings growth, and relative dispersion trended upward only mildly. Under these circumstances students' forecasts of the earnings gains from education at later ages might not have been markedly different from current differentials.

22. We also examined individuals with some postsecondary education. This group includes those obtaining a community college diploma, but also students who attend university for some time without graduating. Because of the difficulty in estimating costs and the fact that this group is not representative of community college graduates, we do not show results for this group.

23. Studies have shown that skill levels among university graduates are not equivalent and that many end up taking jobs that were predominantly held by high school graduates previously (e.g., see Pryor and Schaffer 1997). Therefore it would be somewhat misleading to assume a positive ability differential.

24. Using 1997–98 for this purpose allows us to capture the large increases in tuition fees, and the major tax changes that occurred over the period 1996 to 1998. When we performed this research, the most recent SCF data we could obtain on earnings were for 1995. We do not regard the slight mismatch in dates as a significant problem as male earnings in Canada changed very slowly in the mid-1990s. Our detailed assumptions, as well as references to data sources, are set out in appendix B.

25. Morisette (1998) reports that the unemployment rate for all men aged 17 to 24 in 1996 was 14.8 percent. In addition 5.3 percent had involuntary part-time employment, for a total of 20.1 percent who did not have full-time employment.

26. The use of medians tends to give lower estimated rates of return because the gap between median and mean earnings rises, both absolutely and proportionally, over the lifetime. Thus our estimates of forgone earnings are closer to those of Vaillancourt and Stager than our estimates of the earnings gain accruing over the working lifetime.

27. In estimating direct costs, one must keep in mind that part of universities' costs are incurred for graduate education, research, and other noninstructional purposes. No estimates are available that separate these functions from undergraduate education. Tenure-track university professors are typically expected to devote 40 to 50 percent of their time to teaching, including graduate teaching. We think a reasonable guess is that about 30 percent of operating costs are incurred for undergraduate education. Estimates are also not available for capital costs (interest, depreciation, etc.) on a national basis, but Stager (1994) estimates that capital costs are about 60 percent of operating costs. On this basis we have a figure of 50 percent ($\cong 1.6 \times 30$ percent) of operating costs as an estimate of total direct costs of undergraduate university education.

28. The significance of the small variations in the subsidy rate across cases in table 6.2 should not be exaggerated. We assume the same tuition fees for male and female students, and are simply pro-rating in our treatment of part-time students. There are no doubt differences in programs of study across these different groups that imply further differences in subsidy rates. Capturing these effects is beyond the scope of our study.

29. We assume a student loan interest rate of 9 percent, which is at the center of the range of rates paid in June 1998 (see appendix B). Since this rate is of similar magnitude to our estimated rates of return to a university degree, the benefit of student loans does not come principally via a low interest rate after graduation.

30. The discussion in the last section indicated that by 1998 it would be reasonable to expect about half of graduates to have had student loans and the average amount to have been about $15,000. We take an average of the *ETRs* for zero and $15,000 debt.

31. We do not attempt to estimate the impact of RESPs per se on the *ETRs* since the effects vary greatly across taxpayers depending on their use of RESPs over other saving vehicles. Also, prior to the introduction of CESGs, RESPs were not very popular. Thus we believe the most important effect to study is that of CESGs.

32. Our counterfactual remains that the university graduates would have earned the median amount if they had finished their formal education after high school. It is possible that this somewhat exaggerates both rates of return and *ETRs* for those at the 75th percentile and has the opposite effect at the 25th percentile. For this reason the results by income level may be less reliable than those at the median.

33. The net subsidy rates implied by Vaillancourt's (1990) results for males are 17.6 percent in medicine, 10.6 percent in engineering, 6.0 percent in natural science, 2.2 percent in social science, and 0.6 percent in humanities. These figures represent the difference between private and public rates of return in panel B of Vaillancourt's table 6.3 (p. 6).

# References

Acemoglu, D. J., and J. Angrist. 2000. How large are the social returns to education? Evidence from compulsory schooling laws. *NBER Macroeconomics Annual* 15: 9–58.

Boadway, R., N. Bruce, and J. Mintz. 1984. Taxation, inflation and the effective marginal tax rate on Capital in Canada. *Canadian Journal of Economics* 17: 62–79.

Boskin, M. J. 1975. Notes on the tax treatment of human capital. In *Conference on Tax Research*. Office of Tax Analysis, Department of the Treasury, Washington, DC.

Bovenberg, A. L., and B. Jacobs. 2001. Redistribution and education subsidies are siamese twins. CentER Discussion Paper 2001-82. Tilburg University.

Cameron, S., and C. Taber. 2000. Borrowing constraints and the returns to schooling. NBER Working Paper 7761.

Canadian Tax Foundation. 1999. *Finances of the Nation 1998*. Toronto.

Chamley, C. 1986. Optimal taxation of capital income in general equilibrium with infinite lives. *Econometrica* 54 (3): 607–22.

Collins, K. A., and J. B. Davies. 2002. Taxing investments in higher education. Mimeo. University of Western Ontario.

Davies, J. B. 2002. Empirical evidence on human capital externalities. Mimeo. University of Western Ontario.

Davies, J. B., and G. Glenday. 1990. Accrual equivalent marginal tax rates for personal financial assets. *Canadian Journal of Economics* 23: 189–209.

Davies, J. B., and J. Whalley. 1991. Taxes and capital formation: How important is human capital? In D. Bernheim and J. Shoven, eds., *National Saving and Economic Performance*. Chicago: University of Chicago Press, pp. 169–97.

Davies, J. B., J. Zhang, and J. Zeng. 2002. Optimal fiscal policy in a two-sector growth model with transitional dynamics. Mimeo. University of Western Ontario.

Department of Finance. 1998. *The Canadian Opportunities Strategy*. Budget paper. Ottawa. February.

Dupor, B., L. Lochner, C. Taber, and M. B. Wittekind. 1996. Some effects of taxes on schooling and training. *American Economic Review* 86: 340–46.

Finnie, R., and S. Schwartz. 1996. *Student Loans in Canada*. Toronto: C.D. Howe Institute.

Finnie, R. 2001. Measuring the load, easing the burden: Canada's student loan programs and the revitalization of Canadian postsecondary education. C.D. Howe Institute Commentary 155. Toronto.

Heckman, J. J., and P. J. Klenow. 1997. Human capital policy. Mimeo. University of Chicago.

Heckman, J. J., L. Lochner, and C. Taber. 1999. General equilibrium cost-benefit analysis of education and tax policies. In G. Ranis and L. K. Raut, eds., *Trade, Growth and Development: Essays in Honor of Prof. T. N. Srinivasan*. New York: Elsevier Science, North-Holland, pp. 291–349.

Jones, L. E., R. E. Manuelli, and P. E. Rossi. 1993. Optimal taxation in models of endogenous technological change. *Journal of Political Economy* 101 (3): 485–517.

Jones, L. E., R. E. Manuelli, and P. E. Rossi. 1997. On the optimal taxation of capital income. *Journal of Economic Theory* 73: 93–117.

Judd, K. L. 1985. Redistributive taxation in a simple perfect foresight model. *Journal of Public Economics* 28: 59–83.

Kaplow, L. 1996. On the divergence between "ideal" and conventional income-tax treatment of human capital. *American Economic Review* 86: 347–52.

Kesselman, J., and F. Poschmann. 2001. A new option for retirement saving—Tax-prepaid savings plans. C.D. Howe Institute Commentary 149. Toronto.

King, M. A., and D. Fullerton. 1984. *The Taxation of Income from Capital: A Comparative Study of the United States, United Kingdom, Sweden, and West Germany*. Chicago: University of Chicago Press.

McKenzie, K. J., M. Mansour, and A. Brule. 1998. The calculation of marginal effective tax rates. Working Paper 97-15. Technical Committee on Business Taxation, Department of Finance. Ottawa.

Mintz, J. M. 2001. *Most Favored Nation: Building a Framework for Smart Economic Policy*. C.D. Howe Institute Policy Study 36. Toronto.

Morisette, R. 1998. The declining labour market status of young men. In Statistics Canada, *Labour Markets, Social Institutions, and the Future of Canada's Children*. Publication 89-553-XPB. Ottawa, pp. 31–50.

Nielsen, S. B., and P. B. Sorensen. 1997. On the optimality of the Nordic system of dual income taxation. *Journal of Public Economics* 63: 311–29.

Pecorino, P. 1993. Tax structure and growth in a model with human capital. *Journal of Public Economics* 52: 251–71.

Perroni, C. 1995. Assessing the dynamic efficiency gains of tax reform when human capital is endogenous. *International Economic Review* 36: 907–25.

Poddar, S., and M. D. English. 1999. Canadian taxation of personal investment income. *Canadian Tax Journal* 47 (5): 1270–1304.

Pryor, F. L., and D. Schaffer. 1997. Wages and the university educated: A paradox resolved. *Monthly Labor Review* 120 (7): 3–14.

Shea, J. 2000. Does parents' money matter? *Journal of Public Economics* 77: 155–84.

Stager, A. A. D. 1994. Returns to investment in Ontario university education, 1960–1990, and implications for tuition fee policy. *Council of Ontario Universities*. December.

Vaillancourt, F. 1995. The private and total returns to education in Canada, 1985. *Canadian Journal of Economics* 28 (3): 532–54.

Vaillancourt, F. 1997. The private and total returns to education in Canada, 1990: A note. Mimeo. Centre de Recherche et Developpement en Economique. Universite de Montreal. September.

# 7

# Tax Ratios on Labor and Capital Income and on Consumption

David Carey and Josette Rabesona

## 7.1 Introduction

In order to assess the effects of taxation on labor markets, investment, savings, and redistribution, it is necessary to construct measures that take account of statutory tax rates, rules that determine the tax base and credits. One approach is to calculate effective tax rates for particular household types or investment/source of finance combinations based on information about these tax factors. This approach, which is used in OECD *Taxing Wages* to calculate average effective tax rates on labor and in Devereux and Griffith (1998) to calculate average effective tax rates on capital, requires a great deal of detailed information and the combination of many individual cases to obtain representative aggregate estimates. Another approach, pioneered by Mendoza et al. (1994), is to calculate tax ratios[1] that relate realized tax revenues directly to the relevant macroeconomic variables in the national accounts. This approach is relatively simple, captures the overall effects of deductions, credits, and taxpayer behavior. However, it relies on a number of limiting assumptions, most of which are needed to allow the available data to be used to form estimates of the value of revenue streams and the relevant macroeconomic variables. Moreover the estimates are backward looking and, in the case of capital tax ratios, may not be well adapted to assessing the effects of taxation on both investment and saving in the presence of cross-border capital flows. Despite these limitations tax ratios may provide a useful starting point for assessing tax burdens on labor and capital—notably to respond to claims that globalization has resulted in a shift in the tax burden from capital to labor—and for analyzing the effects of taxation on labor markets. However, this should be complimented by a broader approach when examining the economic effects of taxation that also considers average

and marginal effective tax rates and, if possible, the effects of tax shifting on final tax incidence.

Tax ratio estimates could be improved by relaxing some of the unrealistic assumptions made by Mendoza et al. (1994). This chapter pro-
poses a number of changes to make the underlying assumptions more
realistic. These changes reduce the increase in labor income tax ratios
and raise the increase in capital income tax ratios compared with the
Mendoza estimates, overturning the conclusion that there has been a
relative shift in the tax burden from capital to labor in recent decades.
The two data sets are, however, highly correlated in most countries.
Even these revised tax ratio estimates are based on a number of unrealistic assumptions that could not be systematically relaxed owing to
a lack of data for certain countries and/or periods. Relaxing these assumptions where possible sometimes results in large changes in tax
ratios, especially when assumptions concerning the treatment of self-
employed income and personal capital income are modified. These results reinforce the view that caution is required when using tax ratios
to support a given policy stance or to advocate a particular direction
for reform.[2] They should be used in conjunction with more broadly
based analyses and with other tax indicators and information that can
corroborate the story they tell.

In section 7.2 the methodology and underlying assumptions used to
calculate tax ratios are outlined, along with some of the data problems
that are encountered. Revised tax ratios are presented in section 7.3,
together with the main differences from tax ratios calculated using the
Mendoza equations and simple regressions relating the revised ratios
to the major macroeconomic variables of interest. In section 7.4, the results of the sensitivity analysis to relaxation of some of the remaining
assumptions that appear to be unrealistic are presented.

## 7.2 Methodology

### 7.2.1 General Approach, Underlying Assumptions and Data Problems

The Mendoza et al. (1994) methodology involves relating realized tax
revenues to estimates of the associated tax bases. Tax shifting is not
taken into account: the initial impact of taxes is assumed to be the final
incidence. Hence the tax burdens calculated using this methodology

will not correspond to the burdens impacting on economic incentives if, as is likely, there is tax shifting. The tax treatment of losses, cross-border flows, and tax planning can distort some tax ratios, notably for capital income. Thus caution is required when using the ratios for analyses of the effects of taxes on relevant macroeconomic variables. Tax revenue data come from OECD *Revenue Statistics*. This database contains time series on revenue streams from various types of tax—on personal incomes, corporate profits, sales, property, and so on—as reported by member countries. Estimates of the value of the associated tax bases come from national accounts. As such data do not readily fit with the tax revenue data, a number of assumptions—some of them very restrictive—are required to align the two data sets. One particular problem of fit concerns data on household taxes. These data do not distinguish between taxes paid on labor and capital income. Mendoza et al. (1994) deal with this problem by assuming that households pay the same effective tax rates on capital and labor incomes (i.e., that the labor component of the household income tax is proportional to labor's share in household income). OECD data on statutory tax arrangements show that this assumption is unlikely to be a good one for many OECD countries (OECD 1994). Some countries have dual income systems that treat capital income differently from labor income and/or provide relief from double taxation of dividends. There are also special arrangements for pensions, owner-occupied housing, and individual share ownership.

Another problem is that no distinction is made in national accounts between the labor and capital components of self-employed income. As noted above, Mendoza et al. (1994) assign all self-employed income to capital. Alternative approaches, presented in section 7.4, are to assign part of this income flow to labor and part to capital or to exclude taxes paid on this income from estimates of the tax ratios on labor and capital. The former entails making an estimate of labor income of the self-employed, which is an inherently difficult task that could be approached in a variety of ways, and the latter approach gets around the problem by setting it aside. Other problems that arise from using national accounts data are as follows:

• Definitions of national accounts data categories (e.g., the definition of the corporate and quasi-corporate sector) may not be fully comparable to analogous tax revenue data categories (e.g., corporate income taxes paid).

• Procedures for estimating the consumption of fixed capital, which is used in calculating net operating surplus, are not comparable across countries (and this has an important influence on the estimates).

• National accounts data may reflect avoidance and evasion incentives created by national tax systems. For example, if a country's tax policies favor capital income over labor income, then there is an incentive to disguise labor income as capital income.[3] The potential for switching reduces the reliability and comparability of estimates of the tax bases associated with capital and labor.

• Differences exist between the concepts of a comprehensive tax base in national accounts and in tax codes, especially for capital income. For instance, capital gains would be included in comprehensive income in a tax code but not in the national accounts (because there is no value added). Similarly the payment of dividends increases the tax base in countries with a classical system for taxing corporate earnings (i.e., there is double taxation of dividends) but does not increase capital income in the national accounts (paying dividends does not create value added).

• *Revenue Statistics* are on a cash basis[4] whereas national accounts are on an accrual basis. This means that the timing of the two data sets does not correspond.

### 7.2.2 Household Income Tax Ratio, $\tau_h$

*Mendoza Method*
To calculate the labor ($\tau_l$) or capital ($\tau_k$) income tax ratios, it is necessary to obtain the household income tax ratio ($\tau_h$). This ratio is used to allocate personal income tax to capital and labor, on the assumption that the average tax rate paid by each factor of production is the same (i.e., $\tau_h$). (The results of sensitivity analysis exploring the importance of this assumption for the estimated labor and capital tax ratios are reported in section 7.4.) The household income tax ratio is equal to personal income tax receipts divided by household income (table 7.1). In the table note that in some countries[5] enterprise taxes are included in personal income tax (1100); symbols and mnemonics are described in appendix A at the end of the chapter. Household income comprises operating surplus of the private unincorporated sector (OSPUE),[6] property and entrepreneurial income (PEI),[7] and dependent wage income ($W$). Note that imputed rentals on owner-occupied housing are

**Table 7.1**
Mendoza and revised tax ratios

| Mendoza method | Revised method | |
| --- | --- | --- |
| | Social security contributions not deductible | Social security contributions deductible |
| *Tax ratio for total household income, $\tau_h$* | | |
| $\tau_h = 1100/(\text{OSPUE} + \text{PEI} + W)$ | Same as Mendoza | $\tau_h = 1100/(\text{OSPUE} + \text{PEI} + W - 2100 - 2300 - 2400)$ |
| *Tax ratio on labor income, $\tau_l$* | | |
| $\tau_l = (\tau_h * W + 2000 + 3000)/(W + 2200)$ | $\tau_l = (\tau_h * W + 2100 + 2200 + \alpha * 2400 + 3000)/(\text{WSSS} + 3000)$ | $\tau_l = (\tau_h * (W - 2100 - \alpha * 2400) + 2100 + 2200 + \alpha * 2400 + 3000)/(\text{WSSS} + 3000)$ |
| | $\alpha = W/(\text{OSPUE} + \text{PEI} + W)$ = share of labor income in household income | $\alpha = (W - 2100)/(\text{OSPUE} + \text{PEI} + W - 2100 - 2300)$ |
| | $\beta = 1 - \alpha$ = share of capital income in household income | Same as not deductible |
| *Tax ratio on consumption, $\tau_c$* | | |
| $\tau_c = (5110 + 5121)/(\text{CP} + \text{CG} - \text{CGW} - 5110 - 5121)$ | $\tau_c = (5110 + 5121 + 5122 + 5123 + 5126 + 5128 + 5200 - 5212)/(\text{CP} + \text{CG} - \text{CGW})$ | Same as not deductible |
| *Tax ratio on labor income and consumption combined, $\tau_{LC}$* | | |
| | $\tau_{LC} = \tau_l + (1 - \tau_l) * \tau_c$ | Same as not deductible |
| *Tax ratio on capital income, $\tau_k$* | | |
| $\tau_k = [\tau_h * (\text{OSPUE} + \text{PEI}) + 1200 + 4100 + 4400]/\text{OS}$ | $\tau_k = [\tau_h * (\text{OSPUE} + \text{PEI}) + 2300 + \beta * 2400 + 1200 + 4000 + 5125 + 5212 + 6100]/(\text{OS} - 3000)$ | $\tau_k = [\tau_h * (\text{OSPUE} + \text{PEI} - 2300 - \beta * 2400) + 2300 + \beta * 2400 + 1200 + 4000 + 5125 + 5212 + 6100]/(\text{OS} - 3000)$ |

included in OSPUE and that pension fund and life insurance earnings, which are imputed to households in the national accounts, are included in PEI.

### Revisions to Mendoza Method

Mendoza et al. (1994) assume that households are not able to deduct social security contributions from their taxable income. While this is true in the United States, it is not so in most other countries.[8] The household tax ratio equations should allow for this possibility, as they do in the third column of table 7.1.

Some reallocation of tax data is also needed to make the estimates more realistic. In particular, business taxes, which are levied on unincorporated enterprises, should be removed from household tax and allocated directly to capital.[9] This treatment would be in line with that accorded to corporate taxes. (Business tax revenues in the countries concerned—Japan, Germany, and Austria—are shown in appendix B, table 7B.1.) Moreover taxes on income, profits, and capital gains that had not been allocated to households or companies (1300) should be allocated to one or the other on the basis of what seems most appropriate; Mendoza et al. (1994) ignored these taxes. The allocations of 1300 made for the revised calculations are as follows:

· Canada, nonresident withholding tax is added to 1200.

· Austria, tax on interest is added to 1100.[10]

· Denmark, almost all of this category represents a tax on pension fund earnings and, as a tax on capital income, is added to 1200.

· Greece, this category (*impôts extraordinaires*) is allocated to households (1100) and companies (1200) according to the relative weights of each in taxes on income, profits, and capital gains (1000).

· Hungary, withholding taxes on dividends and interest are added to 1100.

· New Zealand, taxes on interest and dividends are added to 1100 while the remainder of 1300 is added to 1200.

· Portugal, professional tax (*impôt professionnel*), supplementary personal tax (*impôt complémentaire personnes singulières et collectives*), and capital gains tax (*impôt sur plus-values*) are allocated to 1100, and industrial tax (*impôt industriel*), land tax (*impôt foncier rural et urbain*), agriculture tax (*impôt industrie agricole*), local direct taxes (*impôts directs perçus par les administrations locales*), and interest on late payments (*intérêts payés en retard*) are added to 1200.

### 7.2.3 Labor Income Tax Ratio, $\tau_l$

*Mendoza Method*
The labor tax ratio relates labor's share of household income taxes ($\tau_h * W$) and taxes levied directly on labor income to labor income (see table 7.1). The term for allocating household income taxes to labor ($\tau_h * W$) does this in line with labor's share in household income. All social security charges (2000) and payroll taxes (3000) are also allocated to labor, through the other terms in the numerator. Labor income, which appears in the denominator of the labor tax ratio equation, consists of compensation from dependent employment, including employers' social security contributions (2200) (but excluding employers' contributions to private pension funds).

*Revisions to Mendoza Method*
Private employers' contributions to pension funds and payroll taxes should be added to the labor income base, as they are elements of wage compensation.[11] These items can be included in the labor income base by replacing the denominator of the labor income tax ratio with "compensation of employees" (WSSS) plus "taxes on payroll and workforce" (3000),[12] as in columns 2 and 3 of table 7.1.

Social security contributions of the self-employed (2300) should be allocated to capital, not labor, as self-employed income is treated as capital income in the Mendoza methodology. On the other hand, unallocated social security contributions (2400)[13] should be allocated to capital and labor, not just labor, as they are paid out of both labor and capital incomes. Incorporating these changes entails disaggregating total social security contributions so that employees' (2100) and employers' (2200) contributions can be allocated to labor along with its share ($\alpha$) of unallocated contributions (2400) and allocating self-employed contributions and the remaining unallocated contributions to capital.

### 7.2.4 Consumption Tax Ratio, $\tau_c$

*Mendoza Method*
The consumption tax ratio ($\tau_c$) is calculated as the sum of general consumption taxes on goods and services (5110) and excise taxes (5121)

divided by the sum of private consumption (CP) and government nonwage consumption (CG-CGW) net of these indirect taxes (see table 7.1). Value-added tax, which is by far the largest indirect tax in most countries, is included in the 5110 category. The denominator is considerably wider than the tax base normally subject to indirect taxation, as government nonwage consumption expenditure and many goods and services (e.g., basic food in some countries, financial services, and medical services) in final private consumption expenditure generally are not subject to indirect taxes. This wider tax base is retained on the ground that indirect tax (notably VAT) is generally paid on inputs to produce such goods and services. Hence, contrary to the assumption made for calculating the other tax ratios, it is implicitly assumed that the tax burden on the inputs for such goods and services is passed through into higher output prices. Government wages (CGW) are excluded from the tax base because no indirect tax is levied on purchases of labor. Indirect taxes are deducted in the denominator to reflect the tradition of expressing indirect tax rates as a percentage of the price excluding the tax. For example, a 20 percent VAT adds 20 percent to the before-tax price but represents 16.7 percent of the total price including VAT. This adjustment ensures that the theoretical $\tau_c$ for this tax is 20 percent, not 16.7 percent.

### Revisions to Mendoza Method[14]
A number of other indirect taxes should also be taken into account in the consumption tax ratio. These are taxes on profits of fiscal monopolies (5122), customs and import duties[15] (5123), taxes on specific services (5126), other taxes on specific goods and services (5128),[16] and taxes on the use of goods and performance activities (5200) except motor vehicle charges paid by others (5212).[17] It would also be preferable to express the consumption tax base in gross terms (i.e., including indirect taxes) to improve comparability with the tax ratios on labor and capital income and to facilitate calculating a combined tax ratio on labor income and consumption.

### 7.2.5   Labor and Consumption Tax Ratio Combined, $\tau_{lc}$

The labor and consumption tax ratio combined is of interest because this measures the relevant tax burden for choices between supplying labor or enjoying leisure. Assuming that all net labor income is consumed (now or in the future), it can easily be calculated by adding to the labor tax ratio the consumption tax ratio adjusted for the share of net labor income in gross labor income: workers cannot spend income that has been taxed away. Mendoza et al. (1994) did not calculate a combined labor and consumption tax ratio.

### 7.2.6   Capital Income Tax Ratio, $\tau_k$

*Mendoza Method*
The capital income tax ratio relates the share of household income tax pertaining to capital income ($\tau_h * [\text{OSPUE} + \text{PEI}]$) and taxes paid directly out of capital income or wealth to capital income (see table 7.1). Once again, household income taxes are allocated in line with the productive factor's share in household income, where household capital income comprises unincorporated business net income (OSPUE, which includes self-employed income and imputed rentals on owner-occupied housing) and interest, dividends, and investment receipts (PEI). The taxes paid directly out of capital income are corporate income taxes (1200),[18] recurrent taxes on immovable property (4100) and taxes on financial and capital transactions (4400). While 4100 and 4400 are taxes on stocks of capital and capital transactions, respectively, they nevertheless represent a tax cost levied on capital investment that can be expressed as a percentage of income from capital.

*Revisions to Mendoza Method*
All property taxes (4000) should be included in the capital tax ratio as they can be considered as surcharges on capital income.[19] There is also a number of other taxes paid by business that should be included, including taxes on investment goods (5125),[20] motor vehicle charges paid by others[21] (5212), and other taxes paid solely by businesses (6100).

## 7.3   Results

### 7.3.1   Revised Approach

The tax ratio on capital income (based on net operating surplus) increased by 6.4 percentage points between 1975–80 and 1990–2000 for OECD countries with complete data sets,[22] to 46.3 percent (table 7.2, figure 7.1; see appendix table 7B.2 for tax ratios for individual countries). This increase was greater than that in the labor tax ratio, which

**Table 7.2**
Tax ratios (%)

| | Capital based on net operating surplus | | | | Capital based on gross operating surplus | | | |
|---|---|---|---|---|---|---|---|---|
| | 1975–80 | 1980–90 | 1990–2000 | Change between 1975–80 and 1990–2000 | 1975–80 | 1980–90 | 1990–2000 | Change between 1975–80 and 1990–2000 |
| *Revised approach* | | | | | | | | |
| United States | 42.2 | 37.9 | 39.5 | −2.7 | 29.2 | 25.8 | 27.3 | −1.9 |
| Japan | 35.4 | 47.6 | 50.0 | 14.6 | 24.4 | 31.1 | 27.9 | 3.5 |
| EU-15[a] | | | | | | | | |
| Average | 42.4 | 46.0 | 47.5 | 5.2 | 24.6 | 27.0 | 28.7 | 4.1 |
| Standard deviation | 19.7 | 17.4 | 13.0 | −6.7 | 9.4 | 8.4 | 6.2 | −3.2 |
| OECD[b] | | | | | | | | |
| Average | 39.9 | 43.9 | 46.3 | 6.4 | 24.4 | 26.6 | 28.1 | 3.7 |
| Standard deviation | 15.9 | 15.0 | 12.7 | −3.3 | 8.0 | 7.4 | 5.8 | −2.2 |
| *Mendoza approach* | | | | | | | | |
| United States | 39.3 | 35.3 | 36.4 | −2.8 | 27.2 | 24.1 | 25.2 | −2.0 |
| Japan | 31.4 | 41.9 | 42.5 | 11.1 | 21.7 | 27.4 | 23.8 | 2.2 |
| EU-15[a] | | | | | | | | |
| Average | 33.0 | 36.6 | 37.4 | 4.4 | 20.1 | 22.1 | 23.1 | 3.1 |
| Standard deviation | 15.6 | 15.6 | 11.7 | −3.9 | 8.4 | 8.4 | 6.5 | −1.8 |
| OECD[b] | | | | | | | | |
| Average | 31.9 | 35.7 | 37.2 | 5.3 | 19.5 | 21.1 | 22.1 | 2.6 |
| Standard deviation | 12.8 | 12.6 | 10.6 | −2.2 | 6.7 | 6.7 | 5.6 | −1.0 |

Source: OECD, *Revenue Statistics* and *National Accounts*.
a. Simple averages of the countries with data in 1975. These countries are Austria, Belgium, Finland, France, Germany, Italy, Spain, Sweden, and the United Kingdom.
b. Simple averages of the countries with data in 1975. In addition to the EU countries listed above, these countries are Australia, Canada, Japan, Korea, Norway, Switzerland, and the United States.

rose by 5.3 percentage points to 32.3 percent, and in the consumption tax ratio, which increased by 1.1 percentage point to 15.7 percent. Hence there was a relative shift in the tax burden from labor to capital income, including when the labor tax burden is assessed using the combined labor and consumption tax ratio.[23] The relative shift in the tax burden toward capital was particularly marked in Japan, where the percentage point increase in the capital income tax ratio was twice that in the labor income tax ratio. By contrast, the tax burden shifted from capital to labor in the United States in absolute terms and in EU

**Table 7.2**
(continued)

| Labor | | | | Consumption | | | | Combined labor and consumption | | | |
|---|---|---|---|---|---|---|---|---|---|---|---|
| 1975–80 | 1980–90 | 1990–2000 | Change between 1975–80 and 1990–2000 | 1975–80 | 1980–90 | 1990–2000 | Change between 1975–80 and 1990–2000 | 1975–80 | 1980–90 | 1990–2000 | Change between 1975–80 and 1990–2000 |
| 20.4 | 22.1 | 23.4 | 3.1 | 6.7 | 6.6 | 6.4 | −0.4 | 25.7 | 27.3 | 28.3 | 2.6 |
| 17.3 | 21.7 | 24.1 | 6.8 | 6.0 | 5.8 | 6.4 | 0.4 | 22.9 | 26.8 | 29.4 | 6.5 |
| 32.0 | 35.1 | 38.0 | 6.0 | 15.9 | 17.3 | 17.8 | 1.9 | 42.6 | 46.3 | 48.9 | 6.3 |
| 6.6 | 7.0 | 8.0 | 1.4 | 4.3 | 3.3 | 2.0 | −2.4 | 8.1 | 7.4 | 7.6 | −0.5 |
| 27.0 | 29.6 | 32.3 | 5.3 | 14.6 | 15.6 | 15.7 | 1.1 | 37.3 | 40.4 | 42.6 | 5.3 |
| 9.7 | 10.0 | 10.3 | 0.6 | 5.2 | 5.5 | 5.3 | 0.1 | 10.8 | 10.4 | 10.8 | 0.0 |
| 23.2 | 25.6 | 27.1 | 3.9 | 5.4 | 5.3 | 5.2 | −0.2 | 27.3 | 29.5 | 30.9 | 3.6 |
| 19.7 | 25.1 | 27.6 | 7.9 | 4.6 | 4.9 | 6.1 | 1.6 | 23.4 | 28.7 | 32.0 | 8.7 |
| 35.5 | 39.2 | 42.5 | 7.0 | 16.4 | 18.1 | 18.8 | 2.4 | 45.7 | 49.9 | 53.1 | 7.4 |
| 8.6 | 8.1 | 8.7 | 5.1 | 5.5 | 4.6 | 3.0 | −2.5 | 11.4 | 10.0 | 9.7 | −1.7 |
| 29.7 | 32.8 | 35.6 | 5.9 | 14.0 | 15.5 | 16.0 | 2.0 | 39.0 | 42.7 | 45.4 | 6.4 |
| 11.4 | 11.5 | 11.9 | 0.5 | 7.3 | 7.9 | 7.5 | 0.2 | 14.0 | 13.3 | 13.1 | −0.9 |

countries in relative terms, with the shift in the United States being particularly marked.

A problem with using capital income tax ratios based on net operating surplus to make cross-country comparisons is that charges for depreciation of fixed assets in countries' national accounts vary a great deal from one country to another. This variation is mainly attributable to assumed differences in service lives, which are often based on very old studies of tax lives[24] and are implausibly large. One way of circumventing this problem is to focus on capital income tax ratios based on gross operating surplus for such purposes. On this basis the increase in the capital income tax ratio in OECD countries was 3.7 percentage points, similar to the increases in the European Union and

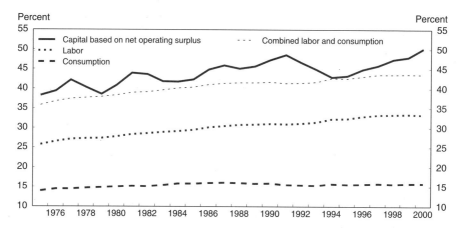

**Figure 7.1**
Tax ratios on labor and capital income and on consumption. Shown are simple averages of Austria, Australia, Belgium, Canada, Finland, France, Germany, Italy, Japan, Korea, Norway, Spain, Sweden, Switzerland, the United Kingdom, and the United States. (Source: OECD, *Revenue Statistics* and *National Accounts*)

Japan but much higher than in the United States, where the capital income tax ratio fell. These movements brought the capital income tax ratios (based on gross operating surplus) more or less into line in the United States, Japan, and the European Union at 27 to 29 percent. The distribution of capital income tax ratios also narrowed for the group of OECD countries for which full data sets are available.

Labor income and consumption tax ratios are well below the OECD average in the United States and Japan and higher in the European Union. The distribution of labor income and consumption tax ratios in OECD countries for which full data sets are available has remained broadly unchanged over the past quarter century. In EU countries, by contrast, the distribution of labor income tax ratios has widened and that of consumption tax ratios has narrowed.

There are a number of caveats to bear in mind when comparing tax ratios across countries. One is that estimates of labor income tax ratios are influenced by the extent to which countries rely on private rather than public arrangements for the provision of retirement income. This is because contributions to private schemes, even if they are compulsory, are (rightly) not considered to be taxes, whereas contributions to public schemes are considered to be taxes. Similarly, predominantly private health insurance arrangements (as in the United States) tend to reduce the labor income tax ratio compared with countries with predominantly social health insurance arrangements. As for the retirement income financing arrangements, this does not mean, however, that cross-country comparisons are false. It just means that readers should be aware that differences in labor income tax ratios may reflect to a considerable extent differences in social insurance coverage. By contrast, cross-country comparisons of capital income tax ratios will be distorted if public enterprises are subject to corporate tax in some countries but not in others (the government taking its share of earnings in the form of higher dividends).[25] It should also be noted that tax ratios on both labor and capital income are somewhat overstated in countries that levy taxes and/or social security contributions on most social security benefits. Such levies are particularly high in Denmark, Finland, the Netherlands, and Sweden (Adema 2001, pp. 27–28); this increases the numerator of the household income tax ratio without affecting the denominator. The effect on the estimates of adjusting for this factor in 1997 (the only year for which data are available) are examined below.

### 7.3.2  Differences from the Mendoza Approach

Capital income tax ratios are higher in the revised approach than in the Mendoza approach. This is especially so in the European Union, where this difference (based on net operating surplus) reaches 10 percentage points in 1990 to 2000. The difference reflects the wider range of taxes taken into account in the revised estimates, including social security contributions of the self-employed (which are larger in EU countries), and, in EU countries, the deduction of payroll taxes from operating surplus in the denominator.[26] These differences are considerably smaller when the tax base is gross operating surplus—as the tax base is bigger, differences in tax revenues are less amplified. The distribution of capital income tax ratios (based on both gross and net operating surplus) has narrowed more using the revised approach than the Mendoza approach, especially for EU countries.

Labor income tax ratios based on the revised approach are somewhat lower than in the Mendoza approach. This reflects the facts that part of social security contributions (2300 and part of 2400) is no longer allocated to labor and that the tax base is wider, including employer contributions to private pension schemes and payroll taxes. These changes do not, however, affect the ranking of labor income tax ratios —they remain much higher in EU countries than in the United States or Japan. While there is no change in the distribution of labor tax ratios for OECD countries in both sets of estimates, there is a widening in the distribution for EU countries in the revised estimates that is not present in the estimates based on the Mendoza approach.

Consumption tax ratios are lower in the revised method, despite a wider range of indirect taxes being included. This is because the base is expressed in gross terms (i.e., including indirect taxes). Consumption taxes continue to be much higher in the European Union than in the United States or Japan, although the difference is somewhat less marked than in the Mendoza approach.

Whereas there is a relative shift in the tax burden in OECD countries from labor to capital (based on net operating surplus) in the revised approach, the opposite occurs in the Mendoza approach. The relative shift in the tax burden from labour to capital in Japan is much stronger in the revised approach than in the Mendoza approach but somewhat weaker in EU countries. In the United States the absolute shift in the tax burden from capital to labor is somewhat weaker in the revised approach than in the Mendoza approach.

Despite these differences, tax ratios in the revised approach are highly correlated with those based on the Mendoza approach in the majority of cases, suggesting that many empirical results would not be affected by the choice of approach (table 7.3). There are, however, a number of exceptions to this rule: approximately 10 percent of the correlation coefficients are less than 0.8.

### 7.3.3   Relations with Variables of Interest

The revised labor tax ratios are inversely correlated across countries with hours worked per member of the working age population (figure 7.2). Results are similar when the tax burden on labor is measured using the combined tax ratio on labor income and consumption expenditures.[27] Denmark, Finland, and Sweden, which have the highest labor income tax ratios, stand out for having higher hours worked per member of the working-age population than would be predicted on the basis of this relationship. This may reflect favorable child care arrangements, which would help to compensate for the effects of high labor taxation by facilitating female labor force participation. By contrast, neither labor income nor combined labor and consumption tax ratios are significantly related to structural unemployment.[28] This is what would be expected if real wage rates are flexible in the long run.

**Table 7.3**
Correlation between Mendoza and revised approaches, 1975–2000

| | Capital based on net operating surplus | Capital based on gross operating surplus | Labor | Consumption | Combined labor and consumption |
|---|---|---|---|---|---|
| United States | 0.99 | 0.99 | 0.98 | 0.94 | 0.98 |
| Japan | 0.98 | 0.99 | 1.00 | 0.82 | 1.00 |
| Germany[a] | 0.96 | 0.96 | 0.98 | 0.97 | 0.99 |
| France | 0.92 | 0.92 | 1.00 | 0.95 | 1.00 |
| Italy | 0.98 | 0.98 | 0.99 | 0.99 | 0.99 |
| United Kingdom | 0.97 | 0.98 | 0.98 | 0.98 | 0.98 |
| Canada | 0.99 | 0.99 | 1.00 | **0.09** | 0.98 |
| Australia | 0.98 | 0.99 | 1.00 | 0.94 | 0.98 |
| Austria | **0.77** | 0.87 | 0.99 | 0.95 | 0.98 |
| Belgium | 0.99 | 0.98 | 1.00 | 0.88 | 0.99 |
| Czech Republic[b] | 0.99 | 0.99 | **0.49** | 0.81 | **0.69** |
| Denmark | 0.98 | 0.97 | 1.00 | 1.00 | 0.99 |
| Finland | 1.00 | 0.99 | 1.00 | 1.00 | 0.99 |
| Greece | 1.00 | 1.00 | 0.99 | 0.86 | 1.00 |
| Hungary | — | 0.93 | — | **−0.78** | — |
| Ireland | 0.97 | — | 1.00 | 0.97 | 0.99 |
| Korea | 1.00 | 1.00 | 1.00 | **0.31** | 0.96 |
| Netherlands | **0.79** | **0.70** | 0.97 | 0.98 | 0.96 |
| New Zealand | 0.96 | — | 0.98 | 0.93 | 0.99 |
| Norway | 0.90 | 0.95 | 0.91 | 0.98 | 0.96 |
| Poland | — | 0.93 | — | 0.80 | — |
| Portugal[c] | 0.98 | 0.96 | **0.42** | 0.92 | 0.95 |
| Spain | 0.98 | 0.98 | 0.94 | 0.98 | 0.98 |
| Sweden | 0.92 | 0.91 | 0.97 | 0.96 | 0.98 |
| Switzerland | 0.97 | 0.90 | **−0.18** | 0.96 | **0.17** |

Source: OECD, *Revenue Statistics* and *National Accounts*.
Notes: Correlation coefficients less than 0.8 are in boldface. Czech Republic: 1993–2000; Denmark: 1998–2000; Ireland: 1977–2000; Greece: 1990–2000; Hungary: 1995–2000; Poland: 1991–2000; Netherlands: 1990–2000; New Zealand and Portugal: 1990–2000.
a. West Germany before 1991.
b. It is assumed that the tax ratio on capital in 2000 is the same as in 1999.
c. It is assumed that the tax ratios on capital in 1999 and 2000 are the same as in 1998.

Hours worked

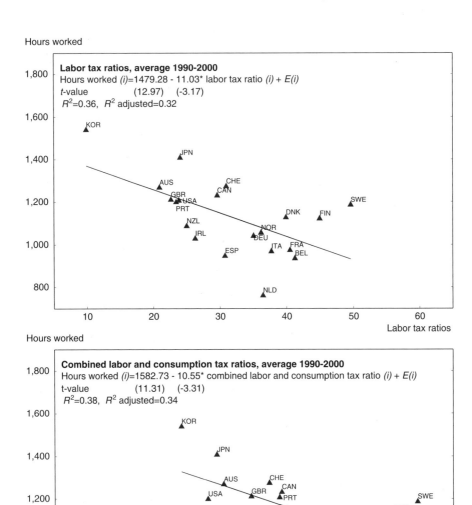

Figure 7.2
Labor tax ratios and hours worked per person in the working age population. (Source: OECD, *Revenue Statistics* and *National Accounts*)

Similarly capital income tax ratios are not significantly related to either investment rates (business sector investment/GDP) or private saving rates (private saving/GDP).[29] This could reflect high international capital mobility in OECD countries, which weakens the link between domestic saving and investment. In these circumstances, taxes that discourage household saving may not have much effect on investment because the decline in household saving would tend to raise gross investment returns, attracting foreign capital and so driving rates of return back toward the level in world capital markets. Similarly taxes that discourage domestic investment need not reduce domestic saving if gross rates of return are determined in world capital markets. Capital income tax ratios that distinguish between taxes on returns from domestic savings and taxes on returns from domestic investment would be more suited to assessing the effects of taxation on investment and savings decisions.

## 7.4 Effects of Modifying Certain Assumptions

There are a number of other adjustments to the tax ratio equations that could be made to obtain more realistic estimates. These relate to accounting for self-employed income (it is not all capital income, as assumed above), taxes on government transfer payments, and preferential tax treatment for household capital income. Unfortunately, such changes cannot be made systematically owing to a lack of data for certain countries and/or periods. We need to assess the extent to which the inability to make these adjustments in most cases matters. We do this by estimating the impact on the revised estimates, henceforth referred to as the baseline, of making these adjustments whenever possible.

### 7.4.1 Dividing Self-employed Income into Capital and Labor Components

Self-employed income does not fit neatly into either of the available categories—labor or capital income—in the estimates above. It does not entirely consist of capital income, as assumed above, but rather contains elements of both labor and capital income. Unfortunately, SNA data do not provide a breakdown of self-employed income into these two categories. One approach to making such a breakdown is to assign this income flow to both labor and capital. Making such an

**Table 7.4**
Dividing self-employed income into labor and capital components: Modified tax ratios

| Social security contributions not deductible | Social security contributions deductible |
|---|---|
| $WSE = ES * (W - 2100)/EE$ | $WSE = ES * (W - 2100)/EE$ |
| $\alpha = (W + WSE)/(OSPUE + PEI + W)$ | $\alpha = (W - 2100 + WSE - 2300)/$ $(OSPUE + PEI + W - 2100 - 2300)$ |
| $\tau_l = (\tau_h * (W + WSE) + 2100$ $+ 2200 + 2300 + \alpha * 2400 + 3000)/$ $(WSSS + WSE + 2300 + 3000)$ | $\tau_l = (\tau_h * (W - 2100 + WSE - 2300$ $- \alpha * 2400) + 2100 + 2200$ $+ 2300 + \alpha * 2400 + 3000)/$ $(WSSS + WSE + 2300 + 3000)$ |
| $\tau_k = [\tau_h * (OSPUE + PEI - WSE)$ $+ 1200 + \beta * 2400 + 4000]/$ $(OS - WSE - 2300 - 3000)$ | $\tau_k = [\tau_h * (OSPUE + PEI - WSE - \beta * 2400)$ $+ 1200 + \beta * 2400 + 4000]/$ $(OS - WSE - 2300 - 3000)$ |

assignment is inherently difficult and could be done in a number of ways. The approach adopted here is to assume that the self-employed "pay themselves" the same annual salary net of social security contributions (WSE) as that earned by the average employee: wages and salaries of dependent employment (W) minus employees' social security contributions (2100), all divided by dependent employment (EE); see table 7.4.[30] The product of this imputed wage rate and the number of self-employed (ES) gives the imputed "wage bill" for the self-employed (WSE), excluding social security payments. This estimate of self-employed labor income is then used to calculate a labor income tax ratio that includes self-employed labor income and a capital income tax ratio that excludes such income.

This adjustment substantially raises the capital income tax ratio (the average increase is 15 percentage points in OECD countries) and slightly reduces the labor income tax ratio (the average reduction is 1 percentage point) in most countries (table 7.5). The increase in the capital income tax ratio between 1975–80 and 1990–2000 is smaller than in the baseline in most countries (2 percentage points less, on average) while that in the labor income tax ratio is broadly unchanged. With these changes the conclusions that there was a relative shift in the tax burden from labor to capital on average in OECD countries and in Japan over the past quarter century are reversed. Moreover the relative shift in the tax burden toward labor in EU countries[31] on average and the absolute shift in the United States are stronger than in the baseline estimates. Nevertheless, the adjusted and baseline series are highly correlated in almost all countries for labor income tax ratios and in most countries (the correlation coefficient is 0.8 or more in 77 percent of countries) for capital income tax ratios. There are, however, a number of exceptions to this conclusion: the adjusted and baseline capital income tax ratios are not highly correlated in Japan, France, Australia, Austria, and Ireland, while the labor income tax ratios are not highly correlated in the Czech Republic.

A weakness of this approach is that it may not accurately reflect the split of self-employed income into labor and capital income components. There is a great variety of labor and capital income components for self-employed persons. At one extreme, the capital input can be almost zero (e.g., an opera singer), while at the other, it can be very high (e.g., a farmer) (Directorate-General of the European Commission 1998). It is not obvious that an assumption that self-employed persons pay themselves the average wage accurately reflects the average labor income for the self-employed—it certainly doesn't for the two extreme cases cited.

### 7.4.2    Separating Self-employed Income from Labor and Capital Income

In view of the difficulties in decomposing self-employed income into labor and capital components, the alternative of abstracting from taxes on such income altogether in the labor and capital income tax ratios has been followed in some studies (Directorate-General of the European Commission 1998; Volkerink and de Haan 2001). As no data are available in OECD *Revenue Statistics* on household income taxes paid on self-employed income, they must be estimated. Following the general approach above, this can be done by assuming that taxes are paid on such income in proportion to its share in household income. Putting this adjustment into effect entails only allocating to capital the share of household income taxes relating to interest, dividends, and investment receipts (PEI) (table 7.6). The share of PEI in household income ($\gamma$) must also be calculated so as to allocate unallocated social security contributions (2400) to labor and (pure) capital income.

This adjustment, which can only be made for most countries in the 1990s, does not affect the labor income tax ratio but has a large positive effect (28 percentage points, on average) on the capital income tax ratio in many countries (table 7.7). Differences from the baseline capital income tax ratios tend to be greater than for the previous adjustment. Of the countries for which data are available to make the adjustment

**Table 7.5**
Effect of dividing self-employed income into labor and capital components, 1975–2000

| | Labor income tax ratio | | | Capital income tax ratio[a] | | |
|---|---|---|---|---|---|---|
| | Change in average level[b] | Difference in change between 1975–80 and 1990–2000 | Correlation coefficient[c] | Change in average level[b] | Difference in change between 1975–80 and 1990–2000 | Correlation coefficient[c] |
| United States | -0.19 | 0.16 | 1.00 | 4.82 | -3.39 | 0.94 |
| Japan | -1.36 | 0.58 | 1.00 | 50.30 | -33.03 | -0.48 |
| Germany | -1.01 | 0.76 | 0.99 | 4.46 | -4.98 | 0.93 |
| France | -1.17 | 1.28 | 1.00 | 2.11 | -12.30 | 0.58 |
| Italy | -3.45 | -0.16 | 1.00 | 12.75 | 1.38 | 0.90 |
| United Kingdom | -0.67 | -0.32 | 1.00 | 21.86 | 2.21 | 0.94 |
| Canada | -0.75 | -0.50 | 1.00 | 17.32 | 17.49 | 0.98 |
| Australia | -0.44 | -0.11 | 1.00 | 21.84 | -9.70 | 0.65 |
| Austria | -2.63 | — | 1.00 | 51.76 | — | -0.27 |
| Belgium | -1.28 | -0.51 | 1.00 | 13.29 | -4.19 | 0.88 |
| Czech Republic[d] | -0.87 | — | 0.77 | 2.78 | — | 1.00 |
| Denmark | 0.00 | — | 1.00 | 21.61 | — | 0.97 |
| Finland | -1.00 | -0.07 | 1.00 | 12.07 | 4.55 | 0.93 |
| Greece | -9.09 | — | 0.99 | 4.09 | — | 1.00 |
| Hungary | — | — | — | — | — | — |
| Ireland | -1.65 | — | 1.00 | 8.57 | — | 0.72 |
| Korea | — | — | — | — | — | — |
| Netherlands | 0.96 | — | 1.00 | 2.21 | — | 0.96 |
| New Zealand | 0.18 | — | 1.00 | 9.43 | — | 0.96 |

| | | | | | | |
|---|---|---|---|---|---|---|
| Norway | −1.08 | 0.71 | 0.94 | 0.05 | 1.92 | 0.98 |
| Poland | — | — | — | — | — | — |
| Portugal[e] | −2.39 | — | 0.98 | 21.52 | — | 0.97 |
| Spain | −3.70 | 2.41 | 0.96 | 9.87 | −3.80 | 0.93 |
| Sweden | −0.70 | −0.25 | 1.00 | 16.84 | −21.50 | 0.88 |
| Switzerland | −0.36 | −1.43 | 0.98 | 20.34 | 39.67 | 0.89 |
| Average[f] | −1.48 | 0.18 | | 14.99 | −1.83 | |

Source: OECD, *Revenue Statistics* and *National Accounts*.

a. Based on net operating surplus.

b. Compared with the revised approach baseline, percentage points.

c. Correlation coefficients less than 0.8 are in boldface.

d. It is assumed that the capital income tax ratio in 2000 is the same as in 1999.

e. It is assumed that the capital income tax ratios in 1999 and 2000 are the same as in 1998.

f. Simple average.

**Table 7.6**
Separating self-employed income from labor and capital income: Modified tax ratios

| Social security contributions not deductible | Social security contributions deductible |
|---|---|
| $\gamma = \text{PEI}/(\text{OSPUE} + \text{PEI} + W)$ | $\gamma = \text{PEI}/(\text{OSPUE} + \text{PEI} + W - 2100 - 2300)$ |
| $\delta = 1 - \alpha - \gamma$ | $\delta = 1 - \alpha - \gamma$ |
| $\tau_k = [\tau_h * \text{PEI} + 1200 + \gamma * 2400 + 4000 + 5125 + 5212 + 6100]/ (\text{OS} - 3000 - \text{OSPUE})$ | $\tau_k = [\tau_h * (\text{PEI} - \gamma * 2400) + 1200 + \gamma * 2400 + 4000 + 5125 + 5212 + 6100]/(\text{OS} - 3000 - \text{OSPUE})$ |
| $\tau_s = [\tau_h * \text{OSPUE} + 2300 + \delta * 2400]/ \text{OSPUE}$ | $\tau_s = [\tau_h * (\text{OSPUE} - 2300 - \delta * 2400) + 2300 + \delta * 2400]/\text{OSPUE}$ |

since 1975, it reinforces the shift in the tax burden from capital to labor in the United States and Norway between 1975–80 and 1990–2000 and strengthens the opposite (relative) shift in Finland and Korea. The adjustment also reverses the relative shift in the tax burden (from labor to capital) in Australia. The adjusted and baseline capital income tax ratios are highly correlated in most countries (the correlation coefficient is 0.8 or more in 78 percent of countries); the exceptions are France, Australia, Austria, Ireland, and Switzerland.

### 7.4.3 Excluding Tax on Government Interest (Transfer) Payments

Government interest payments are transfers, not distributions of earnings on the factor of production capital. As such, taxes on government interest payments should be excluded from the calculations.[32] This can be done by deducting an estimate of residents' government interest receipts (YPEPG) from household capital income in the numerator of the capital income tax ratio: this way the part of household income taxes relating to government interest receipts is not allocated (table 7.8). It is also necessary to deduct nonresident withholding taxes on government interest payments from corporate tax receipts (1200) in the numerator of the capital income tax ratio.[33] The nonresident withholding tax rate ($t_{\text{NRW}}$) used in each country to make this calculation is the modal rate.[34] A difficulty in making this adjustment is that there are no data in most countries on nonresidents' share of government interest payments. Based on such evidence for Australia and New Zealand, it is assumed that the nonresident share of government bond holdings is one-third.

**Table 7.7**
Effect of separating self-employment income from labor and capital income, 1975–2000

| | Capital income tax ratio[a] | | |
|---|---|---|---|
| | Change in average level[b] | Difference in change between 1975–80 and 1990–2000 | Correlation coefficient[c] |
| United States | 8.98 | −4.68 | 0.95 |
| Japan | 28.14 | 16.54 | 0.82 |
| Germany | 22.60 | — | 0.90 |
| France | 110.92 | — | **0.21** |
| Italy | 20.98 | — | 0.98 |
| United Kingdom | 29.98 | — | 0.89 |
| Canada | 13.48 | — | 0.99 |
| Australia | 39.55 | −12.83 | **0.58** |
| Austria | 27.41 | — | **0.69** |
| Belgium | 30.48 | — | 0.87 |
| Czech Republic[d] | 14.77 | — | 1.00 |
| Denmark | 44.68 | — | 0.95 |
| Finland | 23.56 | 2.65 | 0.89 |
| Greece | 41.50 | — | 0.99 |
| Hungary | — | — | — |
| Ireland | 8.97 | — | **0.66** |
| Korea | 24.16 | 6.67 | 0.92 |
| Netherlands | 7.13 | — | 0.93 |
| New Zealand | 12.10 | — | 0.96 |
| Norway | 16.83 | −12.23 | 0.92 |
| Poland | — | — | — |
| Portugal[e] | 24.81 | — | 1.00 |
| Spain | 23.93 | — | 0.97 |
| Sweden | 48.64 | — | 0.98 |
| Switzerland | 28.29 | — | **0.62** |
| Average[f] | 28.34 | −0.64 | |

Source: OECD, *Revenue Statistics* and *National Accounts*.
a. Based on net operating surplus.
b. Compared with the revised approach baseline, percentage points.
c. Correlation coefficients less than 0.8 are in boldface.
d. It is assumed that the capital income tax ratio in 2000 is the same as in 1999.
e. It is assumed that the capital income tax ratios in 1999 and 2000 are the same as in 1998.
f. Simple average.

**Table 7.8**
Excluding tax on government interest payments: Modified tax ratios

| Social security contributions not deductible | Social security contributions deductible |
|---|---|
| $\tau_k = [\tau_h * (\text{OSPUE} + \text{PEI} - 0.67 * \text{YPEPG}) + 1200 + 2300 + \beta * 2400 - 0.33 * \text{YPEPG} * t_{\text{NRW}} + 4000 + 5125 + 5212 + 6100]/(\text{OS} - 3000)$ | $\tau_k = [\tau_h * (\text{OSPUE} + \text{PEI} - 2300 - \beta * 2400 - 0.67 * \text{YPEPG}) + 1200 + 2300 + \beta * 2400 - 0.33 * \text{YPEPG} * t_{\text{NRW}} + 4000 + 5125 + 5212 + 6100]/ (\text{OS} - 3000)$ |

This adjustment does not affect the labor income tax ratio and, in general, only reduces capital income tax ratios by a small amount (3 percentage points, on average) (table 7.9). However, the adjustment has quite a large effect on capital income tax ratios in Denmark, Sweden, and Belgium, where government interest payments have been substantial. The adjustment reinforces the relative shift in the tax burden from capital to labor in EU countries[35] between 1975–80 and 1990–2000 but reverses the relative shift (from labor to capital) in OECD countries.[36] Nevertheless, the correlation between this and the baseline series is high for all countries; even in Belgium and Ireland, where there have been large changes in public debt interest payments over the past quarter century, the correlation coefficient is over 0.80.

### 7.4.4   Excluding Direct Taxes and Social Security Contributions on Government Benefit (Transfer) Payments

Government benefit payments are also transfers, not factor incomes. Accordingly direct taxes and social security contributions paid on them should be excluded from the tax ratio calculations. This can be done by deducting direct taxes on social security benefits (DTB) from household income taxes (1100) in the numerator of the household income tax ratio and by deducting social security contributions levied on social security benefits (SSCB) from the numerator of the labour income tax ratio (table 7.10).[37] Estimates of these taxes and social security contributions come from Adema (2001) and are only available for 1997.[38]

Adjusting for direct taxes and social security contributions on government benefit payments reduces both labor and capital income tax ratios, with the decline in the former (3 percentage points, on average) being greater than that in the latter (1 percentage point, on average) (table 7.11). The decline in labor income tax ratios is particularly large in the Netherlands, Denmark, Finland, and Sweden where such tax

**Table 7.9**
Effect of excluding tax on government interest payments, 1975–2000

| | Capital income tax ratio[a] | | |
|---|---|---|---|
| | Change in average level[b] | Difference in change between 1975–80 and 1990–2000 | Correlation coefficient |
| United States | −1.78 | −0.79 | 0.99 |
| Japan | −1.41 | −1.08 | 1.00 |
| Germany | −1.35 | −0.75 | 0.99 |
| France | −0.97 | −1.02 | 1.00 |
| Italy | −3.23 | −3.40 | 1.00 |
| United Kingdom | −2.32 | 1.67 | 1.00 |
| Canada | −6.73 | −5.81 | 0.97 |
| Australia | −2.52 | −0.31 | 0.99 |
| Austria | −2.23 | −1.38 | 0.99 |
| Belgium | −8.18 | −3.52 | 0.87 |
| Czech Republic[c] | −0.43 | — | 1.00 |
| Denmark | −10.67 | — | 0.99 |
| Finland | −2.30 | −3.04 | 0.99 |
| Greece | −0.96 | — | 1.00 |
| Hungary | — | — | — |
| Ireland | −2.51 | — | 0.86 |
| Korea | −0.09 | −0.05 | 1.00 |
| Netherlands | −2.77 | — | 0.91 |
| New Zealand | −3.40 | — | 0.87 |
| Norway | −1.89 | 0.06 | 1.00 |
| Poland | — | — | — |
| Portugal[d] | −2.65 | — | 0.99 |
| Spain | −0.95 | −1.56 | 1.00 |
| Sweden | −9.06 | −3.48 | 0.99 |
| Switzerland | −1.48 | −0.39 | 1.00 |
| Average[e] | −3.04 | −1.55 | |

Source: OECD, *Revenue Statistics* and *National Accounts*.
a. Based on net operating surplus.
b. Compared with the revised approach baseline, percentage points.
c. It is assumed that the capital income tax ratio in 2000 is the same as in 1999.
d. It is assumed that the capital income tax ratios in 1999 and 2000 are the same as in 1998.
e. Simple average.

**Table 7.10**
Excluding direct tax and social security contributions on public social benefits: Modified
tax ratios

| Social security contributions not deductible | Social security contributions deductible |
|---|---|
| $\tau_h = (1100 - DTB)/(OSPUE + PEI + W)$ | $\tau_h = (1100 - DTB)/(OSPUE + PEI + W - 2100 - 2300 - 2400)$ |
| $\tau_l = (\tau_h * W + 2100 + 2200 + \alpha * 2400 + 3000 - SSCB)/(WSSS + 3000)$ | $\tau_l = (\tau_h * (W - 2100 - \alpha * 2400) + 2100 + 2200 + \alpha * 2400 + 3000 - SSCB)/(WSSS + 3000)$ |

**Table 7.11**
Effect of excluding direct tax and social security contributions on public social benefits,
1997

|  | Tax ratios | | Change in level[a] | |
|---|---|---|---|---|
|  | Labor | Capital[b] | Labor | Capital[b] |
| United States | 23.7 | 38.5 | −0.54 | −0.26 |
| Japan | 24.2 | 49.7 | −0.33 | −0.10 |
| Germany | 33.5 | 32.5 | −2.03 | −0.36 |
| Italy | 38.0 | 40.8 | −4.05 | −2.63 |
| United Kingdom | 21.3 | 50.8 | −0.53 | −0.34 |
| Canada | 27.9 | 59.4 | −2.45 | −1.33 |
| Australia | 21.9 | 47.5 | −0.41 | −0.33 |
| Austria | 38.0 | 46.3 | −3.89 | −0.45 |
| Belgium | 39.4 | 52.5 | −2.41 | −1.67 |
| Czech Republic | 41.2 | 34.2 | 0.00 | 0.00 |
| Denmark | 34.6 | 64.8 | −6.79 | −4.44 |
| Finland | 39.8 | 40.1 | −6.20 | −3.48 |
| Ireland | 25.7 | 23.0 | −0.47 | −0.17 |
| Korea | 11.6 | 23.0 | 0.00 | 0.00 |
| Netherlands | 27.7 | 51.0 | −7.44 | −0.63 |
| New Zealand | 21.8 | 40.4 | −2.52 | −2.21 |
| Norway | 32.5 | 38.1 | −4.06 | −1.41 |
| Sweden | 46.1 | 57.1 | −5.46 | −5.12 |
| Average[c] | 30.5 | 43.9 | −2.75 | −1.39 |

Source: OECD, *Revenue Statistics* and *National Accounts* and Adema (2001).
a. Compared with the revised approach baseline, percentage points.
b. Based on net operating surplus.
c. Simple average.

revenues are important. (Indeed, in taking this factor into account, we find that the labor income tax ratio in the Netherlands is actually well below the OECD average, not above it.) The effect of the adjustment on the capital income tax ratio is much smaller than on the labor income tax ratio in countries, such as the Netherlands, where most taxes on social security benefits take the form of social security contributions. Unfortunately, no data are available to calculate the effect of this adjustment over time. There is a risk that such taxes and contributions have increased over time, exaggerating the increase in tax ratios, notably for labor income, in the countries where these taxes had a large impact in 1997.

### 7.4.5    Allowing for Preferential Tax Treatment of Household Capital Income[39]

Households pay lower tax rates on many forms of capital income than on labor income, contrary to the assumption underlying the standard tax ratio methodology that all household income is taxed at the same rate. Earnings on investments of pension funds and life insurance and imputed rentals on owner-occupied dwellings are usually not taxed at all, there is widespread relief from the double taxation of dividends and interest receipts are often taxed at a low rate. Each of these cases is examined in the remainder of this section for 1994 to 2000,[40] along with the effects of allowing for all of them at once.

*Excluding Property Income Attributable to Members of Pension Funds and Life Insurance Policy Holders from Household Income*
Earnings (excluding capital gains, which are not income in the SNA) on the investments of pension funds and life insurance policies (PIAPH) are imputed to their beneficial owners in SNA. They are included in the category of household income entitled "interest, dividends, and investment income" (PEI). However, households do not pay tax on such earnings;[41] in the rare cases[42] where tax is levied on such earnings, it is paid by the pension fund or insurance company and, as such, is included in corporate taxes (1200).[43] Accordingly PIAPH should be deducted from the household income series used to allocate personal income taxes and unallocated social security contributions to labor and capital income (table 7.12).

This adjustment results in a small decline in the capital income tax ratio (2 percentage points, on average) and a small increase (1 percent-

**Table 7.12**
Excluding pension fund and life insurance earnings from household income: Modified tax ratios

| Social security contributions not deductible | Social security contributions deductible |
| --- | --- |
| $\alpha = W/(OSPUE + PEI - PIAPH + W)$ | $\alpha = (W - 2100)/(OSPUE + PEI$ $- PIAPH + W - 2100 - 2300)$ |
| $\tau_h = 1100/(OSPUE + PEI - PIAPH + W)$ | $\tau_h = 1100/(OSPUE + PEI - PIAPH$ $+ W - 2100 - 2300 - 2400)$ |
| $\tau_k = [\tau_h * (OSPUE + PEI - PIAPH)$ $+ 1200 + 2300 + \beta * 2400 + 4000$ $+ 5125 + 5212 + 6100]/(OS - 3000)$ | $\tau_k = [\tau_h * (OSPUE + PEI - PIAPH$ $- 2300 - \beta * 2400) + 1200 + 2300$ $+ \beta * 2400 + 4000 + 5125$ $+ 5212 + 6100]/(OS - 3000)$ |

**Table 7.13**
Effect of excluding pension fund and life insurance earnings from household income, 1994–2000

|  | Labor income tax ratio | | Capital income tax ratio[a] | |
| --- | --- | --- | --- | --- |
|  | Change in average level[b] | Correlation coefficient | Change in average level[b] | Correlation coefficient |
| United States | 0.69 | 1.00 | −1.66 | 1.00 |
| Japan | 0.32 | 1.00 | −0.90 | 1.00 |
| Germany | 0.33 | 1.00 | −0.87 | 1.00 |
| France | 0.33 | 0.87 | −0.93 | 1.00 |
| Italy | 0.15 | 1.00 | −0.19 | 1.00 |
| United Kingdom | 1.16 | 1.00 | −2.96 | 1.00 |
| Austria | 0.27 | 1.00 | −0.85 | 1.00 |
| Belgium | 0.46 | 0.99 | −1.06 | 1.00 |
| Denmark | 1.97 | 1.00 | −6.59 | 1.00 |
| Finland | 0.39 | 1.00 | −0.87 | 1.00 |
| Netherlands | 1.61 | 1.00 | −3.53 | 0.97 |
| Portugal | 0.09 | 1.00 | −0.19 | 1.00 |
| Spain | 0.17 | 1.00 | −0.31 | 1.00 |
| Sweden | 1.23 | 1.00 | −4.73 | 1.00 |
| Average[c] | 0.66 | | −1.83 | |

Source: OECD, *Revenue Statistics* and *National Accounts*.
Note: This adjustment is required for all countries but can only be made for the countries shown owing to data availability.
a. Based on net operating surplus.
b. Compared with the revised approach baseline, percentage points.
c. Simple average.

**Table 7.14**
Nontaxation of imputed rentals on owner-occupied housing

| Deductibility of social security contributions / countries | Modified tax ratios |
| --- | --- |
| *Not deductible*<br>Australia, Canada, Portugal, United Kingdom, United States | $\alpha = W / (\text{OSPUE} + \text{PEI} + W - \text{IROOHN})$<br>$\tau_h = 1100 / (\text{OSPUE} + \text{PEI} + W - \text{IROOHN})$<br>$\tau_k = [\tau_h * (\text{OSPUE} + \text{PEI} - \text{IROOHN})$<br>$\quad + 2300 + \beta * 2400 + 1200 + 4000$<br>$\quad + 5125 + 5212 + 6100] / (\text{OS} - 3000)$ |
| *Deductible*<br>Austria, Finland, France, Germany, Italy (1995–98), Spain (1999–2000) | $\alpha = (W - 2100) / (\text{OSPUE} + \text{PEI} + W$<br>$\quad - 2100 - 2300 - \text{IROOHN})$<br>$\tau_h = 1100 / (\text{OSPUE} + \text{PEI} + W - 2100$<br>$\quad - 2300 - \text{IROOHN})$<br>$\tau_k = [\tau_h * (\text{OSPUE} + \text{PEI} - 2300 - \text{IROOHN})$<br>$\quad + 2300 + \beta * 2400 + 1200 + 4000 + 5125$<br>$\quad + 5212 + 6100] / (\text{OS} - 3000)$ |

age point, on average) in the labor income tax ratio (table 7.13). Although it is not possible to calculate the adjusted series before 1994, owing to a lack of information on tax systems, the impact of the adjustment over 1994 to 2000 generally seems to be too small to have much effect on shifts in the tax burden over the past quarter century. In addition adjusted and baseline labor and capital income tax ratios are highly correlated for all countries. These results suggest that not making this adjustment is unlikely to matter for empirical results in most countries.

### Nontaxation of Imputed Rentals on Owner-Occupied Housing

Another form of household income that is often not taxed is imputed rental income on owner-occupied housing net of expenses (IROOHN). In countries where IROOHN is not taxed,[44] it should be removed from the household income series used to allocate personal income taxes and unallocated social security contributions to labor and capital income (table 7.14).[45]

Adjusting for the nontaxation of imputed rentals on owner-occupied housing reduces the capital income tax ratio (by 4 percentage points, on average) and causes a small increase in the labour income tax ratio (by 1 percentage point, on average) (table 7.15). The effect of this adjustment is quite large on capital income tax ratios in Finland, Canada, and Australia. It could alter conclusions about shifts in the tax burden

**Table 7.15**
Effect of adjusting for nontaxation of imputed rentals on owner-occupied housing, 1994–2000

|  | Labor income tax ratio | | Capital income tax ratio[a] | |
|---|---|---|---|---|
|  | Change in average level[b] | Correlation coefficient[c] | Change in average level[b] | Correlation coefficient[c] |
| United States | 0.29 | 1.00 | −0.70 | 1.00 |
| Germany | 0.86 | 1.00 | −2.28 | 1.00 |
| France | 1.11 | **0.30** | −3.11 | 1.00 |
| Italy | 1.15 | 1.00 | −1.48 | 1.00 |
| United Kingdom | 1.01 | 1.00 | −2.59 | 1.00 |
| Canada | 2.99 | 0.99 | −7.77 | 0.99 |
| Australia | 2.35 | 1.00 | −5.08 | 1.00 |
| Austria | 1.04 | 0.99 | −3.30 | 0.99 |
| Finland | 4.01 | 1.00 | −9.08 | 0.96 |
| Portugal | 0.46 | 0.88 | −0.83 | 1.00 |
| Spain | 0.93 | — | −2.43 | — |
| Average[d] | 1.47 | | −3.51 | |

Source: OECD, *Revenue Statistics* and *National Accounts*.
Note: This adjustment cannot be made in the Czech Republic (1998–2000), Hungary, Iceland (1999–2000), Ireland, Luxembourg (1994–97), Mexico, and New Zealand owing to a lack of data.
a. Based on net operating surplus.
b. Compared with the revised approach baseline, percentage points.
c. Correlation coefficients less than 0.8 are in boldface.
d. Simple average.

in these countries if the effect of the adjustment had been very small in the late 1970s. The correlation coefficient for the adjusted and baseline tax ratios is high in all cases except for the labor income tax ratio in France. These results may be influenced by different methods of assessing imputed rentals in the national accounts in different countries. For example, the methods adopted in Spain, the United Kingdom, and Italy appear to yield lower imputed rentals (adjusted for the proportion of households that are owner-occupiers) than do the methods followed in Canada, France and Germany.

These estimates understate the effect on tax ratios of not taxing imputed rentals in countries where owner-occupiers' housing-related interest expenses are nevertheless deductible.[46] This is because gross (as opposed to net) imputed rentals would need to be deducted from household property income in the equations to allocate household taxes (1100) and unallocated social security contributions (2400) in

**Table 7.16**
Dividend imputation and dividends taxed as ordinary income

| Deductibility of social security contributions/countries | Modified tax ratios |
|---|---|
| *Not deductible* United Kingdom | $\tau_h = (1100 + D * t_{IR})/(\text{OSPUE} + \text{PEI} + W)$ $\tau_k = [\tau_h * (\text{OSPUE} + \text{PEI}) - D * t_{IR} + 2300 + \beta * 2400 + 1200 + 4000 + 5125 + 5212 + 6100]/(\text{OS} - 3000)$ |
| *Deductible* France, Germany, Spain | $\tau_h = (1100 + D * t_{IR})/(\text{OSPUE} + \text{PEI} + W - 2100 - 2300)$ $\tau_k = [\tau_h * (\text{OSPUE} + \text{PEI} - 2300) - D * t_{IR} + 2300 + \beta * 2400 + 1200 + 4000 + 5125 + 5212 + 6100]/(\text{OS} - 3000)$ |

these countries. Such an adjustment would increase labor income tax ratios and reduce capital income tax ratios by more than in the above calculations. Unfortunately, such an adjustment cannot be made owing to a lack of data on owner-occupiers' housing-related interest expenses.

### Relief from Double Taxation of Dividends Received by Resident Individuals

Another form of household income that is often taxed at low rates is dividends (D). Most countries provide relief to residents from double taxation of dividends, either through dividend imputation and/or low flat rate tax systems.[47] In countries with global income tax systems, this can be adjusted for by adding back the tax saving from the imputation-related rate reduction ($t_{IR}$) to household income tax receipts in the household income tax ratio and by deducting this tax saving from capital income taxes in the capital income tax ratio (table 7.16).[48]

The imputation-related rate reduction ($t_{IR}$) is calculated as the difference between the normal household tax ratio ($\tau_{h*}$) and the actual tax rate paid by households on dividends ($t_d$). The latter ($t_d$) is calculated as the difference between the normal household tax ratio and the imputation credit rate ($t_{cr}$), all grossed up (by $1 - t_{cr}$, the rate used to gross up dividends). This gives the following equations:[49]

$$t_d = \frac{\tau_{h*} - t_{cr}}{1 - t_{cr}}, \qquad (7.1)$$

$$t_{IR} = (\tau_{h*} - t_d). \qquad (7.2)$$

**Table 7.17**
Imputation credit rates ($t_{cr}$)

|  | Imputation credit rate ($t_{cr}$) |
|---|---|
| France | 33.3% in 1994–2000 |
| Germany | 25% in 1994–97 |
|  | 48.47% in 1998–2000 |
| Spain | 25% in 1994–97 |
|  | 28.57% in 1998–2000 |
| United Kingdom | 20% in 1994–99 |
|  | 10% in 2000 |

**Table 7.18**
Dividends taxed separately at flat rates

| Deductibility of social security contributions / countries | Modified tax ratios |
|---|---|
| *Not deductible* | |
| Portugal | $\alpha = W/(\text{OSPUE} + \text{PEI} - D + W)$ |
|  | $\tau_h = (1100 - D * t_{hd})/(\text{OSPUE} + \text{PEI} - D + W)$ |
|  | $\tau_k = [\tau_h * (\text{OSPUE} + \text{PEI} - D) + D * t_{hd} + 2300$ $+ \beta * 2400 + 1200 + 4000 + 5125 + 5212$ $+ 6100]/(\text{OS} - 3000)$ |
| *Deductible* | |
| Austria, Belgium, Denmark, Finland, Greece, Italy, Norway, Sweden | $\alpha = (W - 2100)/(\text{OSPUE} + \text{PEI} - D + W$ $- 2100 - 2300)$ |
|  | $\tau_h = (1100 - D * t_{hd})/(\text{OSPUE} + \text{PEI} - D + W$ $- 2100 - 2300)$ |
|  | $\tau_k = [\tau_h * (\text{OSPUE} + \text{PEI} - D - 2300) + D * t_{hd}$ $+ 2300 + \beta * 2400 + 1200 + 4000 + 5125$ $+ 5212 + 6100]/(\text{OS} - 3000)$ |

Countries' imputation credit rates ($t_{cr}$) are shown in table 7.17.

In countries with scheduler tax systems, dividends are taxed at a different (generally lower) rate than other household income. This can be adjusted for by removing dividend income (D) from household income and by deducting household taxes paid on dividends ($D * t_{hd}$, where $t_{hd}$ is the household tax rate on dividends net of imputation credits) from household taxes and adding them directly to taxes on capital (table 7.18). Household tax rates on dividends net of imputation credits $t_{hd}$ are shown in table 7.19.[50]

Adjusting for special tax treatment of household dividend income generally reduces the capital income tax ratio somewhat (by 2 percent-

**Table 7.19**
Household dividend tax rates net of imputation credits

| | |
|---|---|
| Austria | 22% in 1994–96 |
| | 25% in 1997–2000 |
| Belgium | 25% in 1994–95 |
| | 15% in 1996–2000 |
| Denmark | 30% in 1994–95 |
| | 25% in 1996–2000 |
| Finland | 0% in 1994–2000 |
| Greece | 0% in 1994–2000 |
| Italy | 12.5% in 1995–2000 |
| Norway | 0% in 1994–2000 |
| Portugal | 25% in 1994–2000 |
| Sweden | 0% in 1994–97 |
| | 30% in 1998–2000 |

age points, on average) and slightly increases the labour income tax ratio (by 1 percentage point, on average) (table 7.20); the exceptions are Austria and Portugal where the flat tax rates imposed on dividends are higher than the household income tax ratio. These effects are particularly great in Germany, the United Kingdom, and Norway. Indeed, they could alter conclusions about shifts in the tax burden between labor and capital over the last quarter century in Germany and Norway if the effects of this adjustment were small in the late 1970s. The size of the adjustment for Germany has increased greatly since 1998, owing to a jump in the imputation credit rate, while the opposite has occurred in the United Kingdom since 2000 (see table 7.17). The correlation coefficient for the adjusted and baseline tax ratios is high for all countries except Germany and, in the case of labor income tax ratios, France and Spain.

### Interest Taxed at Flat Rates
Many countries offer taxpayers the option of paying a flat tax rate ($t_{int}$) on interest income (INT) that is lower than the taxpayer's marginal rate.[51] This departure from the assumption that all personal income is taxed at the same rate can be taken into account by excluding interest income from household income and by imputing tax on interest income directly to capital (table 7.21).[52] Flat tax rates on personal interest income ($t_{int}$) are shown in table 7.22.

Table 7.20
Effect of adjusting for relief from double taxation of dividends, 1994–2000

|  | Labor income tax ratio | | Capital income tax ratio[a] | |
|---|---|---|---|---|
|  | Change in average level[b] | Correlation coefficient[c] | Change in average level[b] | Correlation coefficient[c] |
| Germany | 4.43 | **−0.39** | −11.54 | **−0.11** |
| France | 0.80 | **0.72** | −2.22 | 1.00 |
| Italy | 0.35 | 1.00 | −0.46 | 0.98 |
| United Kingdom | 2.11 | 0.84 | −5.35 | 0.99 |
| Austria | −0.45 | 0.99 | 1.40 | 1.00 |
| Belgium | 0.24 | 0.90 | −0.56 | 0.98 |
| Denmark | 0.44 | 1.00 | −1.52 | 0.99 |
| Finland | 0.52 | 0.99 | −1.11 | 1.00 |
| Greece | 0.14 | 1.00 | −0.10 | 1.00 |
| Norway | 2.45 | 0.97 | −4.76 | 0.97 |
| Portugal | −0.32 | 0.80 | 0.40 | 1.00 |
| Spain | 1.03 | **0.70** | −1.89 | 1.00 |
| Sweden | 0.63 | 0.99 | −2.12 | 1.00 |
| Average[d] | 0.95 | | −2.29 | |

Source: OECD, *Revenue Statistics* and *National Accounts*.
Note: This adjustment cannot be made in Australia, Canada, the Czech Republic, Hungary, Ireland (1994–98), Korea, New Zealand, and Poland owing to a lack of data.
a. Based on net operating surplus.
b. Compared with the revised approach baseline, percentage points.
c. Correlation coefficients less than 0.8 are in boldface.
d. Simple average.

While these flat tax rates may be considerably lower than top marginal income tax rates, they are often higher than the household income tax ratio. This is so in Austria, France, Italy, Japan, and Portugal—half of the countries for which this adjustment is necessary and with data available to make it. In such cases this adjustment increases the capital income tax ratio and reduces the labour income tax ratio (table 7.23). For the remaining countries the adjustment has the opposite effect. This adjustment has a very small effect on tax ratios in all countries except Belgium and Portugal, where the effect on the capital income tax ratio nevertheless remains modest (2 percentage points). The adjusted and baseline tax ratios are highly correlated in virtually all cases (the only exception is the labour income tax ratio in Portugal).

**Table 7.21**
Interest taxed at flat rates

| Deductibility of social security contributions/countries | Modified tax ratios |
|---|---|
| *Not deductible* Portugal | $\alpha = W/(OSPUE + PEI - INT + W)$ $\tau_h = (1100 - INT * t_{int})/(OSPUE + PEI - INT + W)$ $\tau_k = [\tau_h * (OSPUE + PEI - INT) + INT * t_{int} + 2300$ $\quad + \beta * 2400 + 1200 + 4000 + 5125 + 5212$ $\quad + 6100]/(OS - 3000)$ |
| *Deductible* Austria, Belgium, Finland, France, Italy, Japan, Sweden | $\alpha = (W - 2100)/(OSPUE + PEI - INT + W - 2100$ $\quad - 2300)$ $\tau_h = (1100 - INT * t_{int})/(OSPUE + PEI - INT + W$ $\quad - 2100 - 2300)$ $\tau_k = [\tau_h * (OSPUE + PEI - INT - 2300) + INT * t_{int}$ $\quad + 2300 + \beta * 2400 + 1200 + 4000 + 5125$ $\quad + 5212 + 6100]/(OS - 3000)$ |

**Table 7.22**
Flat tax rates on interest income

| | |
|---|---|
| Austria | 22% in 1994–96 |
| | 25% in 1997–2000 |
| Belgium | 13% in 1994 |
| | 15% in 1995–2000 |
| Finland | 25% in 1994–95 |
| | 28% in 1996–99 |
| | 29% in 2000 |
| France[a] | 39.4% in 1994 |
| | 19.4% in 1995 |
| | 20.9% in 1996 |
| | 25% in 1997–2000 |
| Italy[b] | 30% in 1995–96 |
| | 28% in 1997 |
| | 27% in 1998–2000 |
| Japan | 20% in 1994–2000 |
| Portugal | 20% in 1994–2000 |
| Sweden | 30% in 1994–2000 |

a. These rates comprise a final withholding tax of 35 percent in 1994 and 15 percent thereafter and a variety of surcharge taxes, the most important of which is the general social contribution (CSG). These surcharge taxes were 4.4 percent in 1994–95, 5.9 percent in 1996, and 10 percent thereafter.
b. There are no data for 1994.

**Table 7.23**
Effect of adjusting for flat tax rates on interest income, 1994–2000

|  | Labor income tax ratio | | Capital income tax ratio[a] | |
|---|---|---|---|---|
|  | Change in average level[b] | Correlation coefficient[c] | Change in average level[b] | Correlation coefficient[c] |
| Japan | −0.38 | 0.99 | 1.07 | 1.00 |
| France | −0.45 | 0.94 | 1.26 | 1.00 |
| Italy | −1.28 | 0.98 | 1.63 | 0.98 |
| Austria | −0.17 | 1.00 | 0.55 | 1.00 |
| Belgium | 0.94 | 0.90 | −2.16 | 1.00 |
| Finland | 0.06 | 1.00 | −0.14 | 1.00 |
| Portugal | −1.02 | **0.78** | 2.13 | 1.00 |
| Sweden | 0.06 | 1.00 | −0.23 | 1.00 |
| Average[d] | −0.28 | | 0.51 | |

Source: OECD, *Revenue Statistics* and *National Accounts*.
a. Based on net operating surplus.
b. Compared with the revised approach baseline, percentage points.
c. Correlation coefficients less than 0.8 are in boldface.
d. Simple average.

## The Combined Effect of Preferential Arrangements for Capital Income Taxation

Bringing together the four cases of reduced capital income taxation for households—pension fund and life insurance earnings, imputed rentals on owner occupied housing, relief from double taxation of dividends, and flat tax rates on interest receipts—gives the modifications to the tax ratios shown in table 7.24. Only six countries—France, Germany, the Netherlands, Spain, the United Kingdom, and the United States—have data available to make all the necessary adjustments for preferential tax treatment of personal capital income. Taken together, these adjustments substantially reduce the capital income tax ratio in these countries (by 8 percentage points, on average) and significantly increase the labour income tax ratio (by 3 percentage points, on average) (table 7.25). These effects are especially large in Germany and the United Kingdom. The correlation coefficient between the adjusted and baseline tax ratios is high (more than 0.8) in most cases, the exceptions being the labor income tax ratios in Germany, France, and Spain and the capital income tax ratio in Germany. These results suggest that many empirical results would not be affected by using tax ratios that

**Table 7.24**
Combined effect of preferential tax arrangements for household capital income

| System/countries[a] | Tax ratio equations |
| --- | --- |
| *Global personal income, social security contributions not deductible*<br>United States | $\tau_h = 1100/(\text{OSPUE} + \text{PEI} - \text{PIAPH} + W - \text{IROOHN})$<br>$\tau_k = [\tau_h * (\text{OSPUE} + \text{PEI} - \text{PIAPH} - \text{IROOHN}) + 1200 + 2300 + 4000 + 5125 + 5212 + 6100]/(\text{OS} - 3000)$ |
| *Global personal income, social security contributions deductible*<br>Netherlands | $\tau_h = 1100/(\text{OSPUE} + \text{PEI} - \text{PIAPH} + W - 2100 - 2300)$<br>$\tau_k = [\tau_h * (\text{OSPUE} + \text{PEI} - \text{PIAPH} - 2300) + 1200 + 2300 + 4000 + 5125 + 5212 + 6100]/(\text{OS} - 3000)$ |
| *Dividend imputation, global personal income, social security contributions not deductible*<br>United Kingdom | $\alpha = W/(\text{OSPUE} + \text{PEI} - \text{PIAPH} + W - \text{IROOHN})$<br>$\tau_h = (1100 + D * t_{\text{IR}})/(\text{OSPUE} + \text{PEI} - \text{IROOHN})$<br>$\tau_k = [\tau_h * (\text{OSPUE} + \text{PEI} - \text{PIAPH} - \text{IROOHN}) - D * t_{\text{IR}} + 1200 + 2300 + \beta * 2400 + 4000 + 5125 + 5212 + 6100]/(\text{OS} - 3000)$ |
| *Dividend imputation, global personal income, social security contributions deductible*<br>Germany and Spain[b] | $\tau_h = (1100 + D * t_{\text{IR}})/(\text{OSPUE} + \text{PEI} - \text{PIAPH} + W - \text{IROOHN} - 2100 - 2300)$<br>$\tau_k = [\tau_h * (\text{OSPUE} + \text{PEI} - \text{PIAPH} - \text{IROOHN} - 2300) - D * t_{\text{IR}} + 1200 + 2300 + 4000 + 5125 + 5212 + 6100]/(\text{OS} - 3000)$ |
| *Dividend imputation, dividends taxed as ordinary income, flat rate on interest income, social security contributions deductible*<br>France | $\tau_h = (1100 + D * t_{\text{IR}} - \text{INT} * t_{\text{int}})/(\text{OSPUE} + \text{PEI} - \text{PIAPH} - \text{INT} + W - \text{IROOHN} - 2100 - 2300)$<br>$\tau_k = [\tau_h * (\text{OSPUE} + \text{PEI} - \text{PIAPH} - \text{INT} - \text{IROOHN} - 2300) + \text{INT} * t_{\text{int}} - D * t_{\text{IR}} + 1200 + 2300 + 4000 + 5125 + 5212 + 6100]/(\text{OS} - 3000)$ |

a. Only countries for which all necessary adjustments can be made are shown.
b. IROOHN (net imputed rentals on owner-occupied housing) is set to zero in Spain before 1999, when imputed rentals were taxed.

**Table 7.25**
Combined effect of preferential arrangements for household capital income, 1994–2000

| | Labor income tax ratio | | Capital income tax ratio[a] | |
| --- | --- | --- | --- | --- |
| | Change in average level[b] | Correlation coefficient[c] | Change in average level[b] | Correlation coefficient[c] |
| United States | 1.02 | 1.00 | −2.44 | 0.99 |
| Germany | 6.27 | **−0.40** | −16.39 | **−0.14** |
| France | 2.01 | **−0.45** | −5.63 | 0.88 |
| United Kingdom | 4.90 | 0.86 | −12.51 | 0.97 |
| Netherlands | 4.52 | 0.96 | −5.51 | 0.96 |
| Spain | 2.23 | **0.58** | −4.28 | 0.99 |
| Average[d] | 3.49 | | −7.79 | |

Source: OECD, *Revenue Statistics* and *National Accounts*.
a. Based on net operating surplus.
b. Compared with the revised approach baseline, percentage points.
c. Correlation coefficients less than 0.8 are in boldface.
d. Simple average.

do not make such adjustments for preferential treatment of household capital income.

## 7.5 Conclusion

Tax ratios are widely used in empirical economic analyses to approximate the taxes that distort key economic decisions, notably in the areas of employment, saving, and investment. This chapter proposed some modifications to the well-known methodology developed by Mendoza et al. (1994) for calculating tax ratios. While these modifications do not deal with many of the criticisms that have been addressed to this methodology, they do make the underlying assumptions more realistic. The main changes are that deductibility of social security contributions is taken into account, labor income is enlarged to include employer contributions to pension funds, and the definition of capital taxes is widened to include a number of property taxes. This and the other changes made increase capital income tax ratios relative to the Mendoza approach and reduce somewhat labor income and consumption tax ratios. The revised estimates suggest that OECD countries have focused the increase in the tax burden during the past quarter century slightly more on capital than on labor, whereas the opposite conclusion is reached using the Mendoza approach. Nevertheless, although differences between tax ratios in the revised and Mendoza approaches are sometimes quite large, the two sets of tax ratios are in most cases highly correlated, suggesting that many empirical results are not affected by the choice of approach. In relating the revised tax ratios to macroeconomic variables of interest, we found that labor income (and combined labor income and consumption) tax ratios are inversely related across countries to hours worked per member of the working age population but are not related to structural unemployment. Moreover we learned that the revised capital income tax ratios are not related to either investment or private savings rates.

There are still a number of unrealistic assumptions underlying the revised estimates that could not be systematically relaxed owing to a lack of data for certain countries and/or periods. These are that all unincorporated business net income is capital income, households do not receive government interest (transfer) payments and do not pay tax on social security benefits, and household capital income is taxed at the same rates as other income. Relaxing these assumptions, where possible, sometimes results in tax ratio estimates that differ substantially from the baseline estimates and/or are not highly correlated with the baseline. In the case of adjustments concerning self-employed income (dividing it into labor and capital components or separating it from labor and capital income), capital income tax ratios generally rise substantially. However, these adjustments have little or no effect on labor income tax ratios and yield tax ratio series that are highly correlated with the baseline series in most cases (but not for capital income tax ratios in a significant minority of countries). While the variety of adjustments made to account for preferential tax treatment of household capital income individually have only small effects, taken together they markedly reduce capital income tax ratios and increase labor income tax ratios but mostly yield series that are highly correlated with the baseline. These results reinforce the view that caution is required when using tax ratios to support a given policy stance or to advocate a particular direction for reform. Tax ratio estimates need to be corroborated by a significant volume of other information before conclusions can reasonably be drawn. This applies both to conclusions about a country's tax system and to the relative shifts in the tax burden suggested by the estimates in this chapter.

## Appendix A: Variable Names and Symbols Used

The tax revenue data are identified using the OECD system *(OECD Revenue Statistics)*:

1100   Taxes on income, profits, and capital gains of individuals or households

1200   Taxes on income, profits, and capital gains of corporations

1300   Unallocated taxes on income, profits, and capital gains

2000   Total social security contributions (2100 is paid by employees; 2200 by employers; 2300 by the self-employed and persons outside of the labor force; 2400 is unallocated)

3000   Taxes on payroll and workforce

4000   Taxes on property

4100   Recurrent taxes on immovable property

4400   Taxes on financial and capital transactions

5110   General taxes on goods and services (5111 VAT)

5120   Taxes on specific goods and services (5121 excise taxes; 5122 profits of fiscal monopolies; 5123 customs and import duties; 5125 taxes on investment goods; 5126 taxes on specific services; 5128 other taxes)

5200   Taxes on use of goods and performances (5212 taxes on motor vehicles paid by others—i.e., other than households)

6100   Other taxes paid solely by businesses

The variables from *National Accounts* are as follows:

CP       Private final consumption expenditure

D        Household dividend receipts

EE       Dependent employment

ES       Self-employment

CG       Government final consumption expenditure

CGW      Government final wage consumption expenditure

IG       Investment by general government

INT      Household interest receipts

IP       Investment by private sector

| IROOHN | Imputed rental income on owner-occupied housing net of expenses |
|--------|--------|
| OS | Net operating surplus of the overall economy (normally includes the statistical discrepancy) |
| OSPUE | Unincorporated business net income (including imputed rentals on owner-occupied housing); the mnemonics reflect the definition in SNA68/ESA79, "operating surplus of unincorporated enterprises" |
| PEI | Interest, dividends, and investment receipts; the mnemonics reflect the definition in SNA68/ESA79, "property and entrepreneurial income" |
| PIAPH | Property income attributable to policyholders (life insurance and pension funds, excluding capital gains) |
| W | Wages and salaries of dependent employment |
| WSSS | Compensation of employees (including private employers' contributions to social security and to pension funds) |
| YPEPG | Government interest payments |

## Appendix B: Business and Corporate Taxes and Tax Ratios for Individual Countries

Table 7.B1
Business and corporate taxes in selected countries, percent of GDP

|  | Business taxes in 1100[a] | | | Corporate taxes (1200)[b] | | |
|--|--------|--------|--------|--------|--------|--------|
|  | 1975–89 | 1990–2000 | 1975–2000 | 1975–89 | 1990–2000 | 1975–2000 |
| Japan | 0.04 | 0.05 | 0.04 | 5.62 | 4.50 | 5.14 |
| Germany | 1.20 | 1.21 | 1.20 | 1.98 | 1.50 | 1.78 |
| Austria | 0.89 | 0.52 | 0.74 | 1.37 | 1.74 | 1.52 |

Source: OECD, *Revenue Statistics* and *National Accounts*.
a. These countries have business taxes that are included in the 1100 series of *Revenue Statistics*.
b. The 1200 series of *Revenue Statistics*.

**Table 7.B2**
Tax ratios: Revised approach

| | Capital based on net operating surplus | | | | Capital based on gross operating surplus | | | |
|---|---|---|---|---|---|---|---|---|
| | 1975–80 | 1980–90 | 1990–2000 | Change between 1975–80 and 1990–2000 | 1975–80 | 1980–90 | 1990–2000 | Change between 1975–80 and 1990–2000 |
| United States[a] | 42.2 | 37.9 | 39.5 | −2.7 | 29.2 | 25.8 | 27.3 | −1.9 |
| Japan | 35.4 | 47.6 | 50.0 | 14.6 | 24.4 | 31.1 | 27.9 | 3.5 |
| Germany[b] | 37.5 | 38.7 | 34.9 | −2.6 | 23.6 | 23.1 | 21.2 | −2.4 |
| France | 42.0 | 51.9 | 55.9 | 14.0 | 25.3 | 30.0 | 33.2 | 7.9 |
| Italy | 21.7 | 32.7 | 42.7 | 21.0 | 15.2 | 23.6 | 31.0 | 15.8 |
| United Kingdom[a] | 64.2 | 69.9 | 53.2 | −11.1 | 37.2 | 40.5 | 34.0 | −3.2 |
| Canada[a] | 45.2 | 46.2 | 59.5 | 14.2 | 30.8 | 31.0 | 36.8 | 6.0 |
| Australia[a] | 44.5 | 46.2 | 49.4 | 4.9 | 27.3 | 28.4 | 30.7 | 3.5 |
| Austria | 45.1 | 40.3 | 42.2 | −2.9 | 23.7 | 22.3 | 24.3 | 0.6 |
| Belgium | 49.6 | 50.0 | 51.4 | 1.8 | 31.5 | 31.3 | 32.7 | 1.3 |
| Czech Republic[c] | — | — | 40.7 | — | — | — | 21.6 | — |
| Denmark | — | 87.3 | 71.9 | — | — | 46.1 | 39.5 | — |
| Finland | 36.5 | 40.2 | 48.9 | 12.4 | 21.5 | 22.7 | 26.0 | 4.5 |
| Greece | — | — | 15.1 | — | — | — | 12.9 | — |
| Hungary[a] | — | — | — | — | — | — | 14.7 | — |
| Ireland | — | 25.1 | 24.1 | — | — | — | — | — |
| Korea | 9.7 | 13.2 | 22.5 | 12.8 | 8.3 | 10.5 | 16.7 | 8.4 |
| Netherlands | — | — | 52.8 | — | — | — | 32.7 | — |
| New Zealand | — | — | 43.8 | — | — | — | — | — |
| Norway | 42.4 | 50.3 | 39.4 | −3.0 | 24.6 | 29.3 | 24.7 | 0.1 |
| Poland | — | — | — | — | — | — | 20.9 | — |
| Portugal[a,d] | — | — | 28.1 | — | — | — | 17.6 | — |
| Spain | 12.8 | 20.5 | 28.8 | 15.9 | 9.1 | 14.2 | 20.0 | 11.0 |
| Sweden | 71.8 | 70.3 | 69.9 | −1.9 | 34.1 | 35.3 | 35.7 | 1.6 |
| Switzerland | 38.4 | 47.0 | 53.2 | 14.8 | 24.4 | 26.5 | 27.1 | 2.7 |
| EU-15[e] | | | | | | | | |
| Average | 42.4 | 46.0 | 47.5 | 5.2 | 24.6 | 27.0 | 28.7 | 4.1 |
| Standard deviation | 19.7 | 17.4 | 13.0 | −6.7 | 9.4 | 8.4 | 6.2 | −3.2 |
| OECD[e] | | | | | | | | |
| Average | 39.9 | 43.9 | 46.3 | 6.4 | 24.4 | 26.6 | 28.1 | 3.7 |
| Standard deviation | 15.9 | 15.0 | 12.7 | −3.3 | 8.0 | 7.4 | 5.8 | −2.2 |

Source: OECD, *Revenue Statistics* and *National Accounts*.
a. Social security contributions are not deductible.
b. West Germany before 1991.
c. It is assumed that the capital income tax ratio for the Czech Republic in 2000 is the same as in 1999.
d. It is assumed that the capital income tax ratios for Portugal in 1999 and 2000 are the same as in 1998.
e. Simple averages of the above countries with data in 1975.

| Labor | | | | Consumption | | | | Combined labor and consumption | | | |
|---|---|---|---|---|---|---|---|---|---|---|---|
| 1975–80 | 1980–90 | 1990–2000 | Change between 1975–80 and 1990–2000 | 1975–80 | 1980–90 | 1990–2000 | Change between 1975–80 and 1990–2000 | 1975–80 | 1980–90 | 1990–2000 | Change between 1975–80 and 1990–2000 |
| 20.4 | 22.1 | 23.4 | 3.1 | 6.7 | 6.6 | 6.4 | −0.4 | 25.7 | 27.3 | 28.3 | 2.6 |
| 17.3 | 21.7 | 24.1 | 6.8 | 6.0 | 5.8 | 6.4 | 0.4 | 22.9 | 26.8 | 29.4 | 6.5 |
| 32.8 | 33.2 | 35.0 | 2.3 | 12.5 | 12.6 | 13.4 | 0.9 | 42.5 | 42.8 | 44.9 | 2.4 |
| 32.7 | 37.9 | 40.5 | 7.8 | 15.7 | 15.7 | 15.1 | −0.6 | 45.3 | 49.6 | 51.3 | 6.0 |
| 25.8 | 32.1 | 37.7 | 11.9 | 10.6 | 11.7 | 13.9 | 3.3 | 35.0 | 41.5 | 47.9 | 12.9 |
| 25.5 | 24.4 | 22.6 | −2.8 | 13.4 | 16.0 | 15.7 | 2.3 | 35.4 | 36.5 | 34.8 | −0.7 |
| | | | | | | | | | | | |
| 21.2 | 25.0 | 29.6 | 8.4 | 16.0 | 16.3 | 13.9 | −2.0 | 33.8 | 37.2 | 39.4 | 5.6 |
| 18.8 | 20.6 | 20.9 | 2.1 | 12.8 | 13.9 | 12.1 | −0.7 | 29.2 | 31.6 | 30.5 | 1.3 |
| 33.1 | 36.0 | 39.6 | 6.5 | 16.8 | 17.2 | 16.2 | −0.5 | 46.4 | 49.1 | 51.2 | 4.9 |
| 35.5 | 39.6 | 41.3 | 5.7 | 14.9 | 14.3 | 15.0 | 0.1 | 47.1 | 49.9 | 51.7 | 4.6 |
| — | — | 41.5 | — | — | — | 13.0 | — | — | — | 47.2 | — |
| — | 36.1 | 39.9 | — | 19.4 | 20.9 | 20.6 | 1.2 | — | 53.8 | 56.0 | — |
| 33.4 | 35.2 | 45.0 | 11.6 | 17.2 | 18.7 | 18.7 | 1.5 | 47.4 | 50.3 | 58.0 | 10.5 |
| — | — | 34.9 | — | 13.6 | 14.4 | 15.5 | 1.9 | — | — | 46.5 | — |
| — | — | — | — | — | — | 22.2 | — | — | — | — | — |
| — | 25.0 | 26.3 | — | 17.6 | 21.4 | 21.2 | 3.6 | — | 41.0 | 41.9 | — |
| 3.4 | 4.5 | 9.9 | 6.6 | 13.7 | 16.3 | 15.8 | 0.8 | 17.9 | 20.0 | 24.2 | 6.3 |
| — | — | 36.4 | — | 16.3 | 16.8 | 18.0 | 1.6 | — | — | 47.9 | — |
| — | — | 25.1 | — | 11.7 | 15.0 | 18.5 | 6.8 | — | — | 38.9 | — |
| 35.7 | 35.6 | 36.2 | 0.5 | 23.8 | 25.7 | 25.7 | 1.8 | 51.0 | 52.1 | 52.5 | 1.5 |
| — | — | — | — | — | — | 17.1 | — | — | — | — | — |
| — | — | 23.9 | — | 13.3 | 17.8 | 19.9 | 6.7 | — | — | 39.0 | — |
| 24.7 | 30.0 | 30.7 | 6.0 | 5.2 | 11.5 | 14.5 | 7.6 | 29.9 | 38.0 | 40.8 | 10.8 |
| 44.6 | 47.9 | 49.6 | 5.0 | 18.3 | 20.6 | 19.8 | 1.5 | 54.7 | 58.6 | 59.6 | 4.8 |
| 26.9 | 27.7 | 30.9 | 4.0 | 8.8 | 9.0 | 9.3 | 0.5 | 33.3 | 34.2 | 37.3 | 4.1 |
| | | | | | | | | | | | |
| 32.0 | 35.1 | 38.0 | 6.0 | 15.9 | 17.3 | 17.8 | 1.9 | 42.6 | 46.3 | 48.9 | 6.3 |
| 6.6 | 7.0 | 8.0 | 1.4 | 4.3 | 3.3 | 2.0 | −2.4 | 8.1 | 7.4 | 7.6 | −0.5 |
| | | | | | | | | | | | |
| 27.0 | 29.6 | 32.3 | 5.3 | 14.6 | 15.6 | 15.7 | 1.1 | 37.3 | 40.4 | 42.6 | 5.3 |
| 9.7 | 10.0 | 10.3 | 0.6 | 5.2 | 5.5 | 5.3 | 0.1 | 10.8 | 10.4 | 10.8 | 0.0 |

## Notes

The authors would like to thank Christopher Heady, Willi Leibfritz, Carlos Martinez-Mongay, Steven Clark, Kathryn Gordon, Jeffrey Owens, Paul Atkinson, Chiara Bronchi, Jørgen Elmeskov, Andreas Woergoetter, and members of the Working Party on Tax Policy Analysis and Tax Statistics of the OECD Committee on Fiscal Affairs as well as other OECD colleagues for drafting suggestions and/or comments on an earlier draft of this chapter. The authors would also like to thank Lyn Urmston and Diane Scott for technical support.

1. This is the terminology used in Volkerink and de Haan (2001), which we follow. Tax ratios are also known as effective tax rates, implicit tax rates and average tax ratios.

2. The OECD takes the view that further work relying on micro-data is required to assess the magnitude of potential biases to tax ratio estimates. In a recent OECD study (Volkerink and de Haan 2001), the authors conclude that average tax rates measured using aggregate data can generate misleading indicators of the tax burdens on taxpayers, on factors of production, and on consumption. They recommend that policy makers be made aware that such ratios have substantial shortcomings. In OECD (2000) it is noted that while average tax rates represent a more informative indicator of the burden and impact of tax systems than a simple reliance on nominal (statutory) tax rates or tax revenue as a share of GDP, their calculation raises several potentially significant methodological problems. The Working Party No. 2 on Tax Policy Analysis and Tax Statistics of the OECD Committee on Fiscal Affairs takes the view that average tax rate results relying on aggregate tax and national accounts data are potentially highly misleading indicators of relative tax burdens and tax trends. Work is currently under way by Working Party No. 2 delegates using micro-data to assess the magnitude of potential biases to average tax rate figures derived from aggregate data.

3. The ease with which such a switch could be effected would depend on legal and labor market practices in the country concerned.

4. This can result in tax data in a given year including revenue from a tax that no longer exists, as occurred in Austria following the abolition of the business tax (*Gewerbesteuer*) at the end of 1993.

5. These countries are Japan, Germany, Italy, Austria, and Greece.

6. For ease of comparison with Mendoza et al. (1994) and other studies in this field, we retain the variable names based on the definitions in SNA68/ESA79, though the variables used are from SNA93/ESA95. OSPUE corresponds to "unincorporated business net income" in the new system.

7. PEI corresponds to interest, dividends, and investment receipts in SNA93/ESA95.

8. The other countries in which employees' social security contributions are not deductible are Australia, Canada, Hungary, Mexico, Portugal, and the United Kingdom. Such contributions are low by OECD standards in all of these countries except Hungary and Portugal. In Germany, Ireland, Poland, and Turkey deductions are for a flat amount. Treating employees' social security contributions as not deductible when they are results in too much household tax being allocated to labor (overstating the labor income tax ratio) and not enough household tax being allocated to capital (understating the capital income tax ratio).

9. As data on unincorporated business income including imputed rentals on owner-occupied housing are not available in all of these countries, such income was not deducted from household income for the purposes of allocating the remaining household taxes to labor and capital. This tends to overstate the capital income tax ratio (too much of household taxation is allocated to capital) and understate the labor income tax ratio.

10. Insofar as this tax is paid by households, such a treatment would be consistent with that in countries such as Germany that have resident withholding taxes.

11. With this change, the denominators of the labor and capital income tax ratios sum to GDP, ensuring that taxes are entirely allocated to one or other of the factors of production.

12. The inclusion of 3000 in the denominator of the labor income tax ratio follows the suggestion made in Volkerink and de Haan (2001).

13. There are unallocated social security contributions (2400) in the following countries: Greece (until 1987), Hungary, Mexico, Portugal (1985–87), the Slovak Republic, Switzerland, and the United Kingdom. Note that it is not necessary to include 2400 data for Austria to ensure that the sum of the other components of social security contributions (2100, 2200, and 2300) equals total contributions (2000).

14. A problem with the consumption tax ratio that cannot be resolved owing to data limitations is that it includes indirect taxes on investment goods in the numerator. In the case of VAT, this occurs for VAT-exempt industries that supply inputs to produce investment goods. Neither the purchasers of these inputs nor the tax-exempt suppliers themselves are able to claim back the VAT paid on the VAT-exempt industries' inputs. This problem mainly concerns the finance industry, which is generally VAT-exempt owing to the difficulty of measuring value added; by contrast, the problem does not affect government or the not-for-profit sector, as their outputs are classified as final consumption in the national accounts. For general indirect taxes other than VAT (e.g., sales tax and turnover tax), which are only levied in a few countries—the United States, Canada, Australia (until 2000), Hungary, Iceland, Switzerland (until 1995), and Turkey—the problem is more direct in that such taxes may apply to investment expenditures more generally. Data are not generally available on VAT paid by tax-exempt sectors that supply inputs to produce investment goods or on the proportion of their outputs that are inputs to produce investment goods. With respect to other general indirect taxes, data are not readily available on the proportion of such taxes that relate to consumption goods. Hence the consumption tax ratio will be overstated because indirect taxes on investment are included in the numerator. However, the degree of overstatement is unlikely to be great, especially as countries tend to have either a VAT or other general indirect taxes, but not both; the exceptions are Canada, Hungary, Iceland, and Turkey.

15. Mendoza et al. (1994) excluded customs and import duties on the ground that they were not significant in G7 countries but noted that these duties should be taken into account in extending the study to other countries.

16. In other words, we include all taxes on specific goods and services except taxes on exports (5124), taxes on investment goods (5125), and other taxes on international trade and transactions (5127).

17. This tax has already been allocated to capital.

18. The inclusion of 1200 in the numerator of the equation for the capital income tax ratio presupposes that this item relates entirely to capital. In fact there are many small corporations in some countries that are more comparable to small unincorporated enterprises,

which are considered to pay taxes on both labor and capital income. It would be consistent to treat these corporations in the same way as unincorporated enterprises. However, this cannot be done owing to the lack of aggregate data. In the absence of this adjustment, capital tax ratios tend to be overstated, although the degree of the distortion is unlikely to be great because such companies pay only a small share of total corporate taxes.

19. It is implicitly assumed that all such taxes relate to the income flows appearing in the denominator of the equation for the capital income tax ratio. While this is true for most property taxes (4000), it is not true for taxes on wealth in the form of art, racehorses, or foreign property. Accordingly the revised estimates tend to overstate the capital income tax ratio.

20. Only Norway levies such a tax.

21. These are taxes paid by entities other than households.

22. See the notes to table 7.2 for a list of the countries with full data sets. This includes countries for which other household income (YPE plus OSPUE) was estimated for periods before which SNA93/ESA95 data are available.

23. This does not necessarily mean that international tax competition has not caused a relative shift in the tax burden toward the least mobile factor of production, labor. Capital income tax ratios do not adequately capture the effects of international tax competition because both the numerator and denominator are reduced by it.

24. The methodologies are sometimes based on a variety of sources (lives of capital assets used for tax purposes, lives based on estimates made using company accounts or using survey data). These give rise to very different average lives. For example, estimates of capital consumption allowances are based on an assumed average economic life for equipment of 7 years in Switzerland, 11 years in Japan, and 26 years in the United Kingdom (OECD 1992).

25. Changes in the tax treatment of public enterprises, including through privatization, will also distort trends in capital income tax ratios. For example, when the Austrian central bank was made taxable in 1994, this increased corporate tax revenue by more than 10 percent.

26. There are no payroll taxes (*Revenue Statistics* category 3000) in the United States and Japan.

27. Using a growth accounting model, Prescott (2002) also finds that labor and consumption taxes have a very important negative effect on labor inputs. For example, he finds that the 30 percent shortfall of output per member of the working age population in France relative to the United States is accounted for by lower labor inputs in France, which in turn can be explained by higher labor and consumption taxes.

28. This is based on the following OLS regressions (with *t*-values in brackets) based on average values for each country over 1990 to 2000:

$$\text{NAIRU}_i = 5.43 + 0.05 * \tau_{li} + u_i$$
$$\phantom{\text{NAIRU}_i = }(2.07)\ \ (0.62)$$

$R^2$ adjusted $= -0.04$

$$\text{NAIRU}_i = 4.13 + 0.07 * \tau_{lci} + u_i$$
$$\phantom{\text{NAIRU}_i = }(1.34)\ \ (0.96)$$

$R^2$ adjusted $= 0.0$

where

NAIRU = nonaccelerating inflation rate of unemployment

$\tau_l$ = labor income tax ratio

$\tau_{lc}$ = combined labor income and consumption tax ratio

29. This is based on the following OLS regressions (with $t$-values in brackets) based on average values for each country over 1990 to 2000:

$$\left(\frac{INVB}{GDP}\right)_i = 12.64 - 0.0 * \tau_{ki} + u_i$$
$$\quad\quad\quad (3.84) \quad (-0.02)$$

$R^2$ adjusted = $-0.06$

$$\left(\frac{PSAV}{GDP}\right)_i = 21.95 - 0.05 * \tau_{ki} + u_i$$
$$\quad\quad\quad (5.55) \quad (-0.66)$$

$R^2$ adjusted = $-0.03$

where

INVB = gross business investment expenditures

PSAV = private sector saving

$\tau_k$ = capital income tax ratio

30. Only baseline equations that change when an assumption is modified appear in this and the following sections.

31. EU countries with data available from 1975 are Germany, France, Italy, the United Kingdom, Belgium, Finland, Spain, and Sweden.

32. This also ensures that two otherwise identical countries with the same government interest payments net of tax will have the same tax ratios on labor and capital, even if one does not tax such payments at all while the other imposes a very high tax on them. Without this adjustment, the standard tax ratio methodology wrongly suggests that the burden of taxation (on capital) is higher in the country that taxes government interest payments.

33. No adjustment to corporate income tax receipts (1200) is made in respect of residents because government bonds held directly by residents other than households are mainly in the hands of pension funds and life insurance companies, who generally do not pay tax on earnings. Moreover, insofar as bonds are held by domestic financial intermediaries, the other major holder, tax is effectively shifted back to the household sector as intermediaries borrow from it to finance their bond holdings: interest on such loans is deductible for intermediaries but taxable for households.

34. This rate is 15 percent in Belgium, Canada, and Portugal. It is 10 percent in Australia, Italy, Japan, Korea, New Zealand, Poland, Spain, and Switzerland and 0 in other countries.

35. EU countries with data available from 1975 are Germany, France, Italy, the United Kingdom, Austria, Belgium, Finland, Spain, and Sweden.

36. The average increases in the baseline capital income tax ratio (based on net operating surplus) between 1975–80 and 1990–2000 in EU and OECD countries for which data were available to make the adjustment were 5.2 and 6.3 percentage points, respectively.

37. These modifications also ensure that two otherwise identical countries with the same net government benefit payments will have the same labor and capital tax ratios, even if such payments are not taxed at all, while the other imposes a very high tax on them. Without this adjustment, the standard approach to calculating tax ratios wrongly suggests that the burden of taxation (on capital and especially on labor) is higher in the country that taxes government benefit payments.

38. Adema (2001) contains combined estimates of direct taxes and social security contributions on government benefits (tab. 7, pp. 27–28). These had to be divided into direct tax and social security components to adjust for this factor in the tax ratio estimates. To do this, direct tax and social security contributions for three household types (single, no children, earning 67 percent of average production wages, APW; single, two children, earning 67 percent of APW; and married, two children, household head earns 100 percent of APW, spouse earns nothing) were calculated using the OECD *Taxing Wages* database. The average proportion of each component in total direct tax and social security contributions for the three household types was then used to allocate Adema's series to its direct tax and social security contributions components.

39. Tables in this section listing the necessary adjustments to allow for preferential tax treatment of household income only cover countries for which data are available to make these adjustments.

40. Information on the tax treatment of each of these forms of household capital income comes from the OECD *Tax Database*, which only starts in 1994.

41. The tax on pension benefits that households pay in schemes subject to exempt-exempt-tax (EET) rules is effectively levied on deferred labor income, not the earnings of the pension scheme. The fact that earnings are not taxed when benefits are taxed can be seen by considering the case of a contributor to a scheme subject to tax-exempt-exempt (TEE) rules. If tax rates and gross investment returns are the same, this contributor will get exactly the same net return on pension contributions as the contributor subject to EET rules, despite the fact that pension benefits are not taxed.

42. Such tax is levied only in Australia, Denmark, New Zealand, and Sweden.

43. The distinction between corporate income taxes and individual income taxes in OECD *Revenue Statistics* is that corporate income taxes are levied on the corporation as an entity, not on the individuals who own it, and without regard to the personal circumstances of these individuals. Following this logic, "Taxes paid on ... the income of institutions, such as life insurance or pension funds, are classified as corporate taxes (1200) if they are charged on ... the institution as an entity without regard to the personal circumstances of the owners" OECD *Revenue Statistics* (2001, p. 266).

44. These countries are: Australia, Austria, Canada, Czech Republic (1998–2000), Finland, France, Germany, Hungary (1997–2000), Iceland (1999–2000), Ireland, Italy (1994–98), Japan, Luxembourg (1994–97), Mexico, New Zealand, Portugal, Spain (1999–2000), the United Kingdom, and the United States.

45. This does not mean that there is no preferential treatment of imputed rentals in countries where they are taxed. As imputed rentals tend to be assessed at less than market values, they still receive favorable treatment. In fact taxation of imputed rentals can be more favorable to the owner-occupier than tax exemption if he/she is able to offset tax losses (usually owing to high mortgage interest charges) against other income. This is the case in the Netherlands and Switzerland.

46. These countries are the Czech Republic (1998–2000), Finland, Italy (1994–98), Mexico (1994, 2000), Portugal (1994–98), and the United States. Countries with small capped deductions for interest expenses (so that they are mostly not deductible) are not included in this category.

47. The exceptions operate a classical corporate income tax system and a global personal income tax system, as assumed in the standard tax ratio methodology. They are Ireland in 2000, Japan, Luxembourg, the Netherlands, Switzerland, and the United States.

48. Countries with dividend imputation systems and that tax dividends as ordinary income but are not included in table 7.16, owing to a lack of data, are Australia, Canada, Ireland (1994–99), Korea (1997), Mexico (1996–2000), and New Zealand.

49. As an example of calculating $t_{IR}$, consider an Australian resident in 2000 subject to the top marginal tax rate (48.5 percent). The imputation credit rate is 36 percent (the corporate tax rate) and the dividend must be grossed up to its pre-corporate tax value for inclusion in the individual's global income subject to tax. Hence

$$t_d = \frac{0.485 - 0.36}{1 - 0.36}$$

$$= 0.195.$$

In words, the individual only has to pay a tax rate of 19.5 percent on dividend income. Hence the tax saving from the imputation credit ($t_{IR}$) is 29 percent, the difference between his marginal income tax rate (48.5 percent) and the tax rate actually paid on dividend income (19.5 percent).

50. Countries that tax dividends separately at flat rates but that are not included in table 7.18 owing to a lack of data are Hungary, Mexico (1994–95), the Czech Republic, Iceland, Korea (1998–2000), and Poland.

51. Countries that tax interest receipts separately at flat rates but that are not included in table 7.21 owing to a lack of data are the Czech Republic, Hungary, Iceland, Ireland, Korea, Mexico, and Poland.

52. These adjustments mirror those for dividends in a scheduler household income tax system.

# References

Adema, W. 2001. *Net Social Expenditure*, 2nd ed. OECD Labour Market and Social Policy Occasional Paper 52. Paris.

Devereux, M. P., and R. Griffith. 1998. The taxation of discrete investment choices. Institute for Fiscal Studies Working Paper 98/16.

Directorate-General of the European Commission. 1998. How to measure the burden of taxation: Implicit tax rates according to the (primary) functional incidence approach. Mimeo.

European Commission. 1997. Effective taxation and tax convergence in the EU and the OECD. Background paper.

Mendoza, E. G., A. Razin, and L. L. Tesar. 1994. Effective tax rates in macroeconomics: Cross-country estimates of tax rates on factor incomes and consumption. NBER Working Paper 4864. September.

OECD. 1992. *Methods Used by OECD Countries to Measure Stock of Capital*. December.

OECD. 1994. *The Taxation of Household Savings*. Paris.

OECD. 2000. Tax burdens: Alternative measures. *OECD Tax Policy Studies* 2. Paris.

Prescott, E. C. 2002. Prosperity and depression. *American Economic Review* 92 (2): 1–15.

Volkerink, B., and J. de Haan. 2001. Tax ratios: A critical survey. *OECD Tax Policy Studies* 5.

# 8 The "Taxing Wages" Approach to Measuring the Tax Burden on Labor

Christopher Heady

## 8.1 Introduction

The tax burden on labor has substantial policy relevance, and one that has been growing in recent years, particularly in Europe. On the one hand, the burden on labor as opposed to capital income, and on higher-paid workers as opposed to lower-paid workers, has obvious implications for the distribution on income. On the other hand, the tax burden on labor affects the efficiency of the labor market, influencing both participation rates and unemployment rates. This was highlighted a few years ago by the OECD's *Jobs Study* (OECD 1995) and the heavy tax burden on labor has been recently recognised by the European Union as a factor that is holding back the performance of European economies.

In the light of this policy interest, the purpose of this chapter is to describe the way that the tax burden on labor is calculated in the OECD's *Taxing Wages* publication, to discuss its relationship to other approaches to measuring the tax burden on labor, to identify the policy issues to which it is relevant, and to illustrate its use.

The basic *Taxing Wages* methodology and initial results were first published as an appendix to the 1975 edition of the OECD's *Revenue Statistics* publication. Independent status as a series was achieved in 1979 with the publication of *The 1978 Tax/Benefit Position of a Typical Worker*. In 1984 the series changed name to *The Tax/Benefit Position of Production Workers*, and with the 1996 edition it changed again to *The Tax/Benefit Position of Employees*. It finally became *Taxing Wages* with the 1999 edition. The methodology developed over these years, most notably by increasing the range of incomes and family types considered, but the focus has remained on the 'average production worker' (APW). The purpose of the publication is to complement the *Revenue*

*Statistics'* reporting of economy-wide tax ratios with data on the taxes that are applied directly to "typical" employees.

The basic approach of the OECD is conceptually straightforward. A small number of "typical" families are chosen and the tax rules for each country are applied to them in order to calculate both the average and the marginal effective tax rates. For the purpose of these calculations, universal family benefits paid in cash in respect of dependent children are treated as negative taxes. This is to permit comparisons between those countries that mainly assist families through the tax system and those that mainly assist them with cash benefits. The measures of effective tax rates, their uses, and their limitations are discussed next in section 8.2. There are a number of practical issues, described in detail in the publication, that need to be recognized in order to understand the nature of the results. These are the subject of section 8.3. Following that, section 8.4 discusses the methodology and gives results from the 2001 edition of *Taxing Wages*.

The *Taxing Wages* approach is fundamentally different from the implicit average effective tax rate studies based on macroeconomic data and from micro-simulation models based on household survey data. These differences, and what they imply about the usefulness of these three approaches, are discussed in section 8.5. Section 8.6 provides some concluding remarks.

## 8.2   Measures of Effective Tax Rates

The main measures of average effective tax rates provided in *Taxing Wages* are the personal taxes and the overall 'tax wedge' for each of the typical families. In addition, the corresponding marginal tax rates are provided, taking account of the fact that these rates can be different for the two workers in a two-earner household.

The tax wedge, and the corresponding marginal rates, comes close to the standard definition of an effective tax rate, such as that used in the King-Fullerton approach to taxation of capital, which can be expressed as "the share of the value added generated by an economic decision that is taken in tax." It is the sum of income tax, social security contributions (employer's and employee's), and payroll taxes minus the universal family benefits, expressed as a proportion of total wage cost (wage plus employer's social security contribution and payroll tax). However, it does not include the taxes that workers pay when they spend their income, an issue that is discussed further below.

The personal taxes, in contrast, ignore employer's social security contributions and payroll taxes, and simply report income tax and employee's social security contributions minus universal family benefits as a proportion of the wage. It can therefore be thought of as that part of the taxation of labor that is visible to the employee.

In a competitive labor market, the division of the tax wedge between the amount that legally falls on the employee (the personal taxes) and the amount that legally falls on the employer is irrelevant to any economic outcome in terms of employment, hours of work and after-tax income. This suggests that the personal taxes are a less useful measure than the tax wedge. However, for workers who are paid a legally defined minimum wage, the personal taxes are important in terms of determining their after-tax income, although it will be the employer's social security contributions and payroll tax that affects how many are employed. Personal taxes may also be important for workers whose wages are determined by trade union agreements, at least until the wage agreement is renegotiated.

The tax wedge results from *Taxing Wages* were used in the *Jobs Study* (OECD 1995) and continue to be extensively used by the OECD in their country *Economic Surveys*. The size of the tax wedge is used to analyze the incentives for people to enter the formal labor market, while the marginal tax wedge is used to examine the incentives for workers to increase their hours of work. International comparisons have, in some cases, led to recommendations that countries try to reduce the size of the tax wedge in order to solve labor market problems; for example, see the recent *Economic Survey* of Finland (OECD 2002).

The comparison of tax wedges by different household types can also be used to examine the extent to which personal income tax and social security contributions have a distributional effect among households with different income levels or with different demographic characteristics.

However, users of the *Taxing Wages* results for these purposes need to take account of their limitations. Some of these are due to the nature of the publication being a basic statistical resource, which is something that cannot be easily changed, while others are due to the methodological assumptions, which can be reviewed and possibly revised. However, frequent revisions could compromise the value of *Taxing Wages* as a statistical resource for time-series comparisons.

The two main limitations to its use as a basic statistical resource by researchers who undertake independent studies are as follows: First, there is no attempt to measure the economic incidence of taxes. This is because the estimation of such incidence would involve the estimation of demand and supply elasticities, together with a host of additional assumptions. The resulting measures would be much less firmly based than the tax wedge figures and therefore less likely to be accepted by member countries. It is more appropriate for the OECD to provide the basic tax wedge information, and leave the analysis of incidence to independent researchers. Second, there is no attempt to measure the incidence on labor of taxes that can affect labor demand, such as taxes on capital. While there is no doubt that taxes on capital can be expected to alter labor demand and thus have an incidence on labor, the difficulties of estimating this are even greater than those of measuring the incidence of labor taxes, and again, these effects are more suitable for study by independent researchers.

Probably the most important methodological limitation is the exclusion of taxes on the goods that workers consume. Theoretically a uniform sales tax has the same incentive and distributional effects as a proportional income tax on workers who do not save. Thus the exclusion of sales taxes can be seen as arbitrary. It also has the potential to distort international comparisons, as countries such as Japan and the United States have substantially lower sales taxes than European countries. It would therefore be desirable to include sales taxes if a suitable methodology could be agreed and the necessary data obtained. It is the availability of the data for all OECD countries that is the greatest obstacle. As different goods are subject to different sales tax rates, and the differences vary widely across OECD countries, any serious attempt to incorporate sales taxes requires household budget studies for each country that have enough detail in the classification of goods to match the tax classification reasonably well. This represents a significant challenge, but one that the OECD is keeping under review.

Other methodological assumptions are described in section 8.3. They include the assumption that the typical households have no capital income and do not receive nonstandard tax reliefs. In principle, these limitations could be removed if sufficient information becomes available from household surveys and/or administrative data.

## 8.3 The Methodology

It is assumed that an employee's annual income is equal to a certain fraction of the average gross wage earnings of adult, full-time workers in the manufacturing sector of each OECD economy. Additional assumptions are made about other relevant circumstances of wage earners in order to determine their tax/benefit position. The taxes considered are personal income tax, social security contributions, and more rarely payroll taxes, payable on gross wage earnings. Consequently any income tax that might be due on nonwage income, as well as all other kinds of taxes—such as corporate income tax, net wealth tax, and consumption taxes—are not taken into account.

### 8.3.1 Taxpayer Characteristics

The present methodology identifies eight types of taxpayers:

• The single individual with no children whose income amounts to 67, 100, and 167 percent of APW earnings.

• The single parent with two children whose income is 67 percent of APW earnings.

• The married couple with two children and a single wage earner at the APW level.

• Three cases of dual-income married couples, whose earnings are split at 100–33 percent of APW earnings, both with and without children, plus the couple with children whose earnings are split 100–67 percent of APW earnings.

   In the categories of families with children, the children are assumed to be aged between five and twelve years. The family is assumed to have no income source other than employment and—depending on family size—universal cash benefits.

### *An Example*
Before we take a closer look at the methodology, we need to understand how the calculations are made by way of an example. Tables 8.1 and 8.2 show the layout of the country tables for one of the countries in the 2001 edition of *Taxing Wages*. The columns (4 in each table) correspond to the eight types of taxpayers, while the rows represent the steps in the calculations (several of which are too complicated to show in the tables and are based on tax equations for each country). The main sections are numbered:

**Section 1.** The gross earnings in national currency.

**Section 2.** The standard tax allowances that are subtracted from the central government tax base, separated by type.

**Table 8.1**
Example of country table for single workers

| Denmark | 2000 | | | |
|---|---|---|---|---|
| *The tax/benefit position of single individuals* | | | | |
| Earnings (% of APW) | 67 | 100 | 167 | 67 |
| Number of children | None | None | None | 2 |
| 1. *Gross earnings* | 188,400 | 282,600 | 471,000 | 188,400 |
| 2. *Standard tax allowances* | | | | |
| Basic allowance | | | | |
| Married or head of family | | | | |
| Dependent children | | | | |
| Deduction for social security contributions and income taxes | 17,770 | 26,248 | 43,204 | 17,770 |
| Work-related expenses | 6,840 | 6,840 | 6,840 | 6,840 |
| Other | | | | |
| Total | 24,610 | 33,088 | 50,044 | 24,610 |
| 3. *Tax credits or cash transfers included in taxable income* | 0 | 0 | 0 | 0 |
| 4. *Central government taxable income (1 − 2 + 3)* | 163,790 | 249,512 | 420,956 | 163,790 |
| 5. *Central government income tax liability (exclusive of tax credits)* | 11,845 | 22,989 | 67,544 | 11,845 |
| 6. *Tax credits* | | | | |
| Basic credit | 2,338 | 2,338 | 2,338 | 2,338 |
| Married or head of family | | | | |
| Children | | | | |
| Other | | | | |
| Total | 2,338 | 2,338 | 2,338 | 2,338 |
| 7. *Central government income tax finally paid (5 − 6)* | 9,507 | 20,651 | 65,206 | 9,507 |
| 8. *State and local taxes* | 42,768 | 70,885 | 127,119 | 42,768 |
| 9. *Employees' compulsory social security contributions* | | | | |
| Gross earnings | 24,610 | 33,088 | 50,044 | 24,610 |
| Taxable income | | | | |
| Total | 24,610 | 33,088 | 50,044 | 24,610 |
| 10. *Total payments to general government (7 + 8 + 9)* | 76,885 | 124,623 | 242,368 | 76,885 |
| 11. *Cash transfers from general government* | | | | |
| For head of family | | | | |
| For two children | 0 | 0 | 0 | 48,980 |
| Total | 0 | 0 | 0 | 48,980 |
| 12. *Take-home pay (1 − 10 + 11)* | 111,515 | 157,977 | 228,632 | 160,495 |
| 13. *Employer's compulsory social security contributions* | 1,353 | 1,353 | 1,353 | 1,353 |

**Table 8.1**
(continued)

| 14. *Average rates* | | | | |
|---|---|---|---|---|
| Income tax | 27.7% | 32.4% | 40.8% | 27.7% |
| Employees' social security contributions | 13.1% | 11.7% | 10.6% | 13.1% |
| Total payments less cash transfers | 40.8% | 44.1% | 51.5% | 14.8% |
| Total tax wedge including employer's social security contributions | 41.2% | 44.4% | 51.6% | 15.4% |
| 15. *Marginal rates* | | | | |
| Total payments less cash transfers: principal earner | 50.7% | 50.7% | 63.3% | 50.7% |
| Total payments less cash transfers: spouse | na | na | na | na |
| Total tax wedge: principal earner | 50.7% | 50.7% | 63.3% | 50.7% |
| Total tax wedge: spouse | na | na | na | na |

**Section 3.** Items that are added to the central government tax base.

**Section 4.** The central government's income tax base.

**Section 5.** The result of using the country's tax schedule to calculate the central government income tax.

**Section 6.** The tax credits that are set against the calculated central government tax, separated by type.

**Section 7.** The result of subtracting these credits.

**Section 8.** The result of the same exercise as sections 2 to 7 for state and local taxes.

**Section 9.** Employee social security contributions, separated by whether the contribution base is gross earnings or taxable income.

**Section 10.** Total of the three payments $(7 + 8 + 9)$.

**Section 11.** Cash transfers (benefits) from the government, separated by type.

**Section 12.** Take-home pay, after income taxes, social security contributions and transfers.

**Section 13.** Employer social security contributions.

**Section 14.** Four average tax rates:
1. For income tax only.
2. For employee social security contributions only.
3. For income tax plus employee social security contributions minus cash transfers (the personal taxes).
4. For income tax plus employee and employer social security contributions minus cash transfers (the "tax wedge").

**Table 8.2**
Example of country table for married workers

| Denmark | 2000 | | | |
|---|---|---|---|---|
| *The tax/benefit position of married couples* | | | | |
| Earnings (% of APW) | 100–0 | 100–33 | 100–67 | 100–33 |
| Number of children | 2 | 2 | 2 | None |
| 1. *Gross earnings* | 282,600 | 376,800 | 471,000 | 376,800 |
| 2. *Standard tax allowances* | | | | |
| Basic allowance | | | | |
| Married or head of family | | | | |
| Dependent children | | | | |
| Deduction for social security contributions and income taxes | 26,248 | 35,539 | 44,017 | 35,539 |
| Work-related expenses | 6,840 | 13,680 | 13,680 | 13,680 |
| Other | | | | |
| Total | 33,088 | 49,219 | 57,697 | 49,219 |
| 3. *Tax credits or cash transfers included in taxable income* | 0 | 0 | 0 | 0 |
| 4. *Central government taxable income (1 − 2 + 3)* | 249,512 | 327,581 | 413,303 | 327,581 |
| 5. *Central government income tax liability (exclusive of tax credits)* | 17,466 | 23,690 | 34,834 | 23,690 |
| 6. *Tax credits* | | | | |
| Basic credit | 4,676 | 4,676 | 4,676 | 4,676 |
| Married or head of family | | | | |
| Children | | | | |
| Other | | | | |
| Total | 4,676 | 4,676 | 4,676 | 4,676 |
| 7. *Central government income tax finally paid (5 − 6)* | 12,790 | 19,014 | 30,158 | 19,014 |
| 8. *State and local taxes* | 59,930 | 85,536 | 113,653 | 85,536 |
| 9. *Employees' compulsory social security contributions* | | | | |
| Gross earnings | 33,088 | 49,219 | 57,697 | 49,219 |
| Taxable income | | | | |
| Total | 33,088 | 49,219 | 57,697 | 49,219 |
| 10. *Total payments to general government (7 + 8 + 9)* | 105,807 | 153,770 | 201,508 | 153,770 |
| 11. *Cash transfers from general government* | | | | |
| For head of family | | | | |
| For two children | 19,000 | 19,000 | 19,000 | 0 |
| Total | 19,000 | 19,000 | 19,000 | 0 |
| 12. *Take-home pay (1 − 10 + 11)* | 195,793 | 242,030 | 288,492 | 223,030 |
| 13. *Employer's compulsory social security contributions* | 1,353 | 2,706 | 2,706 | 2,706 |

**Table 8.2**
(continued)

| | | | | |
|---|---|---|---|---|
| 14. *Average rates* | | | | |
| Income tax | 25.7% | 27.7% | 30.5% | 27.7% |
| Employees' social security contributions | 11.7% | 13.1% | 12.2% | 13.1% |
| Total payments less cash transfers | 30.7% | 35.8% | 38.7% | 40.8% |
| Total tax wedge including employer's social security contributions | 31.0% | 36.2% | 39.1% | 41.2% |
| 15. *Marginal rates* | | | | |
| Total payments less cash transfers: principal earner | 45.2% | 50.7% | 50.7% | 50.7% |
| Total payments less cash transfers: spouse | 46.1% | 50.7% | 50.7% | 50.7% |
| Total tax wedge: principal earner | 45.2% | 50.7% | 50.7% | 50.7% |
| Total tax wedge: spouse | 46.8% | 50.7% | 50.7% | 50.7% |

The first three are measured as a percentage of the gross earnings, while the fourth is measured as a percentage of labor costs (gross earnings plus employer social security contributions).

**Section 15.** Four marginal tax rates:

1. The marginal personal taxes on an increase in income of the principal earner.

2. The marginal personal taxes on an increase in the income of the spouse.

3. The marginal "tax wedge" for an increase in the income of the principal earner.

4. The marginal "tax wedge" for an increase in the income of the spouse.

### 8.3.2 Calculation of Gross Wages

The data relate to average earnings (of both men and women) in the manufacturing sector, but a few countries include firms in the mining sector. Such differences do not significantly affect the comparability of the data, as in most countries the mining sector is either very small or has wage levels more or less similar to those in the manufacturing sector. The type of worker is an adult directly engaged in a full-time production activity and is assumed to be fully employed during the year.

Where sickness payments are made by the employer, either on behalf of the government or on behalf of private sickness schemes, these amounts are included in the wage calculations. Average amounts of overtime and regular cash supplements (e.g., Christmas bonuses, thirteenth month) are included in the earnings calculation, as are vacation payments typically paid to production workers. Profit-sharing plans that involve dividend distributions are excluded from the calculations.

Fringe benefits are, where possible, excluded from the calculation of average earnings because these benefits cannot be evaluated in a consistent way. Generally, such benefits rarely account for more than 1 percent of gross wage earnings. Employers' contributions to private pension, family allowance or health, and life insurance plans are also excluded, although the amounts involved can be significant. The issue of comparability between countries with and without substantial private plans is an issue that remains unresolved.

### 8.3.3   Coverage of Taxes and Benefits

The main taxes included are personal income tax and employee and employer social security contributions payable on wage earnings. All central, state, and local government income taxes are included. In addition payroll taxes are included in the calculation of the total wedge between labor costs to the employer and the corresponding net take-home pay of the employee.

Compulsory social security contributions paid to general government are treated as taxes because they are compulsory, unrequited payments to general government. They may, however, differ from other taxes in that the eligibility for social security benefits depends, in most countries, on appropriate contributions having been made, although the size of the benefits is not necessarily related to the amount of the contributions, so they cannot be regarded as requited. Countries finance their compulsory public social security programs to a varying degree from general tax and non-tax revenue and earmarked contributions, respectively. This means that better comparability between countries is obtained by treating social security contributions as taxes, but as a separate category that can be identified in an analysis.

### 8.3.4   Calculation of Personal Income Taxes

The first step in the calculation of personal income taxes involves the determination of the tax allowances applicable to a taxpayer with the relevant characteristics and income level. Next the schedule of tax rates is applied, and the resulting tax liability is reduced by any relevant tax credits. An important issue that arises in the calculation of personal income tax due involves determining which tax allowances should be taken into account. Two broad categories of reliefs may be distinguished:

*Standard tax reliefs.* Reliefs that are unrelated to the actual expenditures incurred by the taxpayer and are automatically available to all taxpayers that satisfy the eligibility rules specified in the legislation. Standard tax reliefs are usually fixed amounts or fixed percentages of gross income and are typically the most important set of reliefs in the determination of the income tax paid by production workers. Standard reliefs are taken into account in calculating the initial tax position of employees and include:

1. The *basic relief* that is fixed and is available to all taxpayers or all wage earners, regardless of their marital or family status.
2. The *standard relief* that is available to taxpayers depending on their *marital status*.
3. The *standard child relief* granted to a family with two children between the ages of five and twelve.
4. The *standard relief* in relation to *work expenses*, which is usually a fixed amount or fixed percentage of (gross) wage earnings.
5. Tax reliefs allowed for *social security contributions* and other (subcentral government) *income taxes* are also considered as standard reliefs, since they apply to all wage earners and relate to compulsory payments to general government.

*Nonstandard tax reliefs.* These are reliefs that are wholly determined by reference to actual expenses incurred. They are neither fixed amounts nor fixed percentages of income. Examples of nonstandard tax reliefs include reliefs for interest on qualifying loans (e.g., for the purchase of a house), private insurance premiums, contributions to private pension schemes, and charitable donations. Nonstandard reliefs are not taken into account in calculating the initial tax position of employees.

### State and Local Income Taxes

Personal income taxes levied by subcentral levels of government—state, provincial, cantonal, or local—are included in the calculations. When tax rates and/or the tax base of subcentral government income taxes vary within a country, it is sometimes assumed that the average production worker lives in a typical manufacturing area. The income taxes (and benefits) applicable in this area are used. In other cases the average rate of subcentral government income taxes for the country as a whole is used.

### Social Security Contributions

Compulsory social security contributions paid by employees and employers to general government or to social security funds under the effective control of government are included in the coverage of this report. Social security contributions outside the general government are not included in the calculations.

### Payroll Taxes

The tax base of payroll taxes is either a proportion of the payroll or a fixed amount per employee. Payroll taxes are distinguished from social security contributions by the fact that they do not generate any entitlement to social benefits.

### Family Cash Benefits from General Government

Tax reliefs and family cash transfers are universally paid in respect of dependent children between five and twelve years of age who are attending school are included. If tax reliefs or cash transfers vary within this age range, the most generous provisions are taken. The case of twins is explicitly disregarded.

### 8.3.5 Limitations of the Income Tax Calculation

The exclusion of nonwage income and the limited number of tax reliefs covered imply that the average rates of income tax will not necessarily reflect the actual rates confronting taxpayers at these levels of earnings. Actual rates may be lower than the calculated rates because the latter does not take into account non-standard expense-related reliefs. On the other hand, actual rates may be higher than calculated rates because the latter do not take into account nonwage income received by employees and the tax on it.

The decision to exclude nonwage income (e.g., dividends, interest) was taken because the main focus of *Taxing Wages* is on the tax treatment of wage income, as this is a major policy interest. For taxpayers at the income level of average production workers (APW), nonwage income is generally not significant. In Australia, Austria, Finland, and Ireland, for example, nonwage income constitutes less than 0.5 percent of the average production worker's total earnings. There are, however, some countries where APW-type taxpayers do typically have nonwage income. In the United States, for example, over 60 percent of production workers have nonwage income that accounts, on average, for about 5 percent of their incomes.

### 8.3.6   Limitations to Time-Series Comparisons

It should be noted that results up to and including the 1995 edition covered just two family-types: the single person with no children and the married one-income couple with two children. The earnings were the same in both categories and equal to those of an average production worker.

There are also a number of limitations that apply to the interpretation of the results over time. Any dynamic analysis of the results has to take into account the following qualifications:

• The earnings data do not necessarily relate to the same taxpayer throughout the period. The average earnings in the manufacturing industry are calculated for each year. Therefore the reported results do not show the change in earnings and tax position of individuals over time but rather refer to the position of workers earning a wage equal to average earnings in the manufacturing industry in each particular year.

• For technical reasons the procedures countries follow to determine the benchmark earnings level of the national average production worker may change over time.

• In exceptional cases the taxes covered in the report for a given country may differ over the years. Starting with the 1998 edition, Korea extended the coverage of its social security contributions. The extended coverage largely explains why the wedge between labor costs and net take-home pay of a single average production worker in Korea doubled, from 6.3 percent (1996) to 12.4 percent (1997).

• Of the twelve countries with state and/or local income taxes, in two countries (Switzerland and the United States) the tax rates applied to the APW refer to a typical manufacturing region. The movements in tax rates in this region may not be representative of changes in income taxes elsewhere in the country. So they could provide a poor indication of how countrywide average rates of taxes are evolving.

### 8.3.7   Limitations to Marginal Rates

In the calculation of marginal tax wedges for the spouse, editions before 1998 considered the income increase due to a spouse entering the labor market as an increase from zero to one currency unit (e.g., one dollar a year) of employment income. This rate was hardly representative as typically a spouse entering the workforce would have experienced a more significant (though discrete) jump in earnings than that of just a single currency unit. Moreover the former approach disregarded discrete jumps in social security contributions and wastable tax credits that occur in certain tax-benefit systems where the spouse's employment income increased from zero to one currency unit. Such payments, or transfers, which are not proportional to income, were not factored into spousal marginal tax rates in the (100–0) case, since their inclusion would result in misleadingly large (positive or negative) tax wedge values (e.g., in excess of 1,000 percent). To avoid the necessity of fudging the numbers in this way, it was decided—starting with the 1998 edition—to reconstruct the calculation of the marginal tax wedge in the (100–0) case to reflect the spouse's entering the workforce as an increase in labor income from zero monetary units to 33 percent of the gross wage earnings of an average production worker.

However, it is important to note that a number of OECD Member countries means-test universal cash benefits: benefits are reduced as income increases. For the new employees the reduction of benefits is equivalent to an additional tax on the couple's combined (explicit and implicit) marginal rate.

### 8.4   Some Results

The information in *Taxing Wages* can be used for a range of purposes: comparisons of average or marginal tax rates, compared across household types or countries or years. It is not practicable to illustrate all such comparisons in this brief chapter. I therefore will concentrate on a current issue that has received considerable attention in Europe: the differing trends in the average tax rate on production workers.

Table 8.3 reports the figures since 1995 for the personal taxes on a single worker with no children (and thus not receiving family cash benefits), earning the APW wage. From 1995 to 2001 increases of more than one percentage point have occurred in six countries: Austria,

**Table 8.3**
Income tax plus employee contributions (% of gross wage), 1995–2001: Single workers without children

|  | 1995 | 1996 | 1997 | 1998 | 1999 | 2000 | 2001 |
|---|---|---|---|---|---|---|---|
| Australia | 24.0 | 24.4 | 24.8 | 25.4 | 25.9 | 22.8 | 23.1 |
| Austria | 27.0 | 27.3 | 28.3 | 28.6 | 28.8 | 27.9 | 28.5 |
| Belgium | 41.1 | 41.3 | 41.5 | 41.8 | 41.9 | 41.9 | 41.7 |
| Canada | 27.1 | 27.6 | 27.7 | 27.1 | 26.5 | 26.6 | 25.3 |
| Czech Republic | 23.2 | 22.5 | 22.9 | 22.8 | 22.7 | 23.2 | 23.1 |
| Denmark | 45.2 | 44.8 | 44.9 | 43.4 | 44.2 | 44.1 | 43.8 |
| Finland | 38.0 | 37.6 | 35.8 | 35.4 | 33.7 | 33.6 | 32.4 |
| France | 27.4 | 27.8 | 28.1 | 27.3 | 27.7 | 26.8 | 27.0 |
| Germany | 40.5 | 41.3 | 42.3 | 42.1 | 41.9 | 42.0 | 40.6 |
| Greece | 17.6 | 17.8 | 17.9 | 18.3 | 17.8 | 18.1 | 18.1 |
| Hungary | 27.9 | 29.6 | 29.3 | 28.9 | 30.1 | 32.4 | 34.3 |
| Iceland | 20.6 | 21.7 | 21.5 | 21.6 | 20.6 | 21.4 | 22.2 |
| Ireland | 29.2 | 28.5 | 26.0 | 24.9 | 24.3 | 20.3 | 16.9 |
| Italy | 27.5 | 28.0 | 29.0 | 29.1 | 29.1 | 28.5 | 27.9 |
| Japan | 13.4 | 13.7 | 15.0 | 13.8 | 16.1 | 16.2 | 16.2 |
| Korea | 4.8 | 4.2 | 5.6 | 6.4 | 8.8 | 9.2 | 9.3 |
| Luxembourg | 25.6 | 25.9 | 26.4 | 24.6 | 25.8 | 26.6 | 24.8 |
| Mexico | 7.7 | 5.3 | 1.4 | 2.6 | 1.6 | 2.9 | 3.1 |
| Netherlands | 40.5 | 39.2 | 39.3 | 34.4 | 35.4 | 36.2 | 33.0 |
| New Zealand | 24.5 | 22.3 | 21.6 | 20.0 | 19.4 | 19.5 | 19.6 |
| Norway | 29.6 | 29.7 | 29.5 | 29.6 | 29.4 | 29.2 | 29.0 |
| Poland | 18.1 | 18.0 | 16.9 | 15.8 | 31.4 | 31.4 | 31.3 |
| Portugal | 18.0 | 18.1 | 18.2 | 18.1 | 17.6 | 17.7 | 16.5 |
| Slovak Republic | — | — | — | — | — | 19.9 | 19.9 |
| Spain | 19.6 | 19.9 | 20.2 | 20.2 | 18.2 | 18.5 | 18.9 |
| Sweden | 32.6 | 33.7 | 34.5 | 34.4 | 34.1 | 32.9 | 31.7 |
| Switzerland | 22.5 | 22.4 | 21.9 | 21.9 | 21.7 | 21.3 | 21.4 |
| Turkey | 30.5 | 31.6 | 32.8 | 33.1 | 22.9 | 28.7 | 30.4 |
| United Kingdom | 26.7 | 25.8 | 25.2 | 25.2 | 26.4 | 23.6 | 23.3 |
| United States | 25.8 | 25.8 | 25.8 | 25.8 | 25.8 | 25.5 | 24.6 |

Hungary, Iceland, Japan, Korea, and Poland. Reductions of more than one percentage point have occurred in eleven countries: Canada, Denmark, Finland, Ireland, Mexico, the Netherlands, New Zealand, Portugal, Switzerland, the United Kingdom and the United States. In addition Sweden cut its personal taxes rapidly in 2000 and 2001. Although the picture is diverse, there is a general tendency to reduction of taxes.

Table 8.4 reports figures for the same worker, but now for the "tax wedge." The pattern here is basically that of table 8.3, but the differences are of some interest for they are produced by the employers' social security contributions. Italy appears to have the most noticeable tax reduction. Mexico's reduction in tax is seen as much larger than before. In contrast, the reduction in the Netherlands is much smaller, and Poland changes from being a country with a substantial tax increase to a country with a modest decrease. Turkey had no discernible trend in its personal taxes, though it has experienced a substantial increase in its tax wedge.

These differences between tables 8.3 and 8.4 show how important it is to define an appropriate measure of taxation for studies of the burden of taxs on labor. As we saw in section 8.2, the standard competitive market theory suggests that only the tax wedge matters. However, this may well not apply if workers are near to the minimum wage or are represented by strong trades unions, and in such cases different measures may be relevant for distributional concerns from those appropriate to judging impacts on unemployment. Also, even in a basically competitive market, wages may take some time to adjust.

Tables 8.5 and 8.6 report corresponding figures for a married worker on the APW wage with a nonworking spouse and two children. A comparison of table 8.5 with table 8.3 reveals a very different tax treatment. Only Mexico and Turkey tax at exactly the same rate, and Greece applies a (very slightly) higher tax rate to the married couple. In all other countries the married couple pays less tax, and in some countries a very much lowered tax, with a few countries even providing net transfers to the one working spouse family.

The comparison also shows that the degree of preference shown to married couples with children has altered over the past six years. Australia, Germany, Italy, and Spain have cut taxes for the family with children despite giving no significant tax cuts to single people. Austria, on the other hand, lowered the taxes of families with children but raised the taxes of single people. Ireland, Luxembourg, Portugal, the

**Table 8.4**
Income tax plus employee and employer contributions (% of labor cost), 1995–2001: Single workers without children

|  | 1995 | 1996 | 1997 | 1998 | 1999 | 2000 | 2001 |
|---|---|---|---|---|---|---|---|
| Australia | 24.0 | 24.4 | 24.8 | 25.4 | 25.9 | 22.8 | 23.1 |
| Austria | 41.2 | 41.5 | 45.6 | 45.8 | 45.9 | 44.9 | 44.7 |
| Belgium | 56.3 | 56.4 | 56.6 | 56.8 | 56.9 | 56.2 | 55.6 |
| Canada | 31.5 | 32.1 | 32.3 | 31.7 | 31.1 | 31.3 | 30.2 |
| Czech Republic | 43.2 | 42.6 | 42.9 | 42.8 | 42.7 | 43.1 | 43.0 |
| Denmark | 45.2 | 44.8 | 45.1 | 43.7 | 44.5 | 44.4 | 44.2 |
| Finland | 51.2 | 50.3 | 48.9 | 48.8 | 47.4 | 47.3 | 45.9 |
| France | 49.1 | 49.7 | 48.7 | 47.6 | 48.1 | 48.2 | 48.3 |
| Germany | 50.2 | 51.2 | 52.3 | 52.2 | 51.9 | 51.8 | 50.7 |
| Greece | 35.6 | 35.8 | 35.8 | 36.1 | 35.7 | 36.0 | 36.0 |
| Hungary | 51.4 | 52.0 | 52.0 | 51.6 | 50.7 | 52.0 | 52.6 |
| Iceland | 23.1 | 24.5 | 24.4 | 24.8 | 24.2 | 25.0 | 25.7 |
| Ireland | 36.9 | 36.1 | 33.9 | 33.0 | 32.4 | 28.9 | 25.8 |
| Italy | 50.3 | 50.8 | 51.5 | 47.5 | 47.2 | 46.7 | 46.2 |
| Japan | 19.5 | 19.4 | 20.7 | 19.6 | 24.0 | 24.1 | 24.2 |
| Korea | 6.9 | 6.3 | 12.4 | 14.7 | 16.1 | 16.5 | 16.6 |
| Luxembourg | 34.3 | 34.5 | 35.2 | 33.8 | 34.6 | 35.5 | 33.9 |
| Mexico | 27.2 | 25.4 | 20.8 | 21.9 | 14.1 | 15.4 | 15.6 |
| Netherlands | 44.8 | 43.8 | 43.6 | 43.5 | 44.3 | 45.1 | 42.3 |
| New Zealand | 24.5 | 22.3 | 21.6 | 20.0 | 19.4 | 19.5 | 19.6 |
| Norway | 37.5 | 37.6 | 37.4 | 37.5 | 37.3 | 37.2 | 37.0 |
| Poland | 44.7 | 44.7 | 43.9 | 43.2 | 43.0 | 43.0 | 42.9 |
| Portugal | 33.7 | 33.8 | 33.9 | 33.8 | 33.4 | 33.5 | 32.5 |
| Slovak Republic | — | — | — | — | — | 41.9 | 42.0 |
| Spain | 38.5 | 38.8 | 39.0 | 39.0 | 37.5 | 37.6 | 37.9 |
| Sweden | 49.3 | 50.2 | 50.7 | 50.7 | 50.5 | 49.5 | 48.6 |
| Switzerland | 30.6 | 30.4 | 30.0 | 30.0 | 29.8 | 29.5 | 29.5 |
| Turkey | 35.3 | 38.3 | 39.6 | 39.8 | 30.3 | 40.4 | 43.2 |
| United Kingdom | 33.4 | 32.6 | 32.0 | 32.0 | 30.8 | 30.1 | 29.7 |
| United States | 31.0 | 31.1 | 31.1 | 31.0 | 31.1 | 30.8 | 30.0 |

**Table 8.5**
Income tax plus employee contributions less cash benefits (% of gross wage), 1995–2001:
One-earner family with two children

|  | 1995 | 1996 | 1997 | 1998 | 1999 | 2000 | 2001 |
|---|---|---|---|---|---|---|---|
| Australia | 16.1 | 15.0 | 14.5 | 15.5 | 16.1 | 13.5 | 13.1 |
| Austria | 9.5 | 10.3 | 10.7 | 11.3 | 10.0 | 7.6 | 8.7 |
| Belgium | 19.5 | 19.8 | 20.2 | 20.5 | 20.7 | 21.1 | 21.5 |
| Canada | 16.6 | 18.2 | 18.2 | 17.7 | 15.9 | 16.0 | 14.9 |
| Czech Republic | 3.3 | 7.1 | 7.1 | −3.4 | −2.1 | −1.0 | 2.5 |
| Denmark | 30.9 | 31.1 | 31.1 | 29.7 | 30.7 | 30.7 | 30.9 |
| Finland | 26.3 | 27.1 | 25.7 | 25.3 | 23.9 | 24.3 | 23.5 |
| France | 13.8 | 15.1 | 15.3 | 14.6 | 15.0 | 15.0 | 14.4 |
| Germany | 25.0 | 21.9 | 22.1 | 22.4 | 20.7 | 19.6 | 18.8 |
| Greece | 16.7 | 17.0 | 18.4 | 18.7 | 17.8 | 18.2 | 18.3 |
| Hungary | 7.3 | 12.6 | 12.9 | 12.3 | 9.1 | 14.7 | 15.4 |
| Iceland | −14.5 | −5.4 | −6.8 | −3.9 | −4.3 | −2.7 | −1.8 |
| Ireland | 17.9 | 14.6 | 14.6 | 13.2 | 10.5 | 5.4 | 2.3 |
| Italy | 19.6 | 17.7 | 17.0 | 15.7 | 15.5 | 14.8 | 13.8 |
| Japan | 8.6 | 9.0 | 9.6 | 7.7 | 11.5 | 12.0 | 12.0 |
| Korea | 3.8 | 4.7 | 4.7 | 5.6 | 8.0 | 8.4 | 8.5 |
| Luxembourg | 1.2 | 1.4 | 1.3 | −0.2 | −1.3 | −0.8 | −0.7 |
| Mexico | 7.7 | 5.3 | 1.4 | 2.6 | 1.6 | 2.9 | 3.1 |
| Netherlands | 29.8 | 28.0 | 27.9 | 22.4 | 23.6 | 25.0 | 21.4 |
| New Zealand | 22.4 | 16.2 | 16.2 | 14.8 | 14.1 | 15.5 | 16.8 |
| Norway | 14.9 | 15.4 | 15.4 | 16.2 | 16.8 | 17.6 | 17.9 |
| Poland | 10.1 | 10.3 | 9.5 | 7.2 | 25.4 | 25.6 | 25.4 |
| Portugal | 9.2 | 9.5 | 9.4 | 9.0 | 8.4 | 8.7 | 6.2 |
| Slovak Republic | — | — | — | — | — | 3.2 | 3.6 |
| Spain | 12.8 | 13.0 | 13.2 | 12.8 | 8.9 | 9.3 | 9.9 |
| Sweden | 23.1 | 26.2 | 27.2 | 26.1 | 26.0 | 24.0 | 22.2 |
| Switzerland | 9.5 | 8.2 | 8.2 | 8.3 | 8.4 | 8.2 | 8.4 |
| Turkey | 30.5 | 31.6 | 32.8 | 33.1 | 22.9 | 28.7 | 30.4 |
| United Kingdom | 18.6 | 17.3 | 17.3 | 17.4 | 16.2 | 14.1 | 10.3 |
| United States | 18.6 | 18.4 | 18.3 | 17.9 | 15.0 | 15.3 | 13.2 |

**Table 8.6**
Income tax plus employee and employer contributions less cash benefits (% of labor costs), 1995–2001: One-earner family with two children

| | 1995 | 1996 | 1997 | 1998 | 1999 | 2000 | 2001 |
|---|---|---|---|---|---|---|---|
| Australia | 16.1 | 15.0 | 14.5 | 15.5 | 16.1 | 13.5 | 13.1 |
| Austria | 27.2 | 28.0 | 32.2 | 32.7 | 31.6 | 29.5 | 29.4 |
| Belgium | 40.3 | 40.4 | 40.8 | 41.1 | 41.2 | 40.5 | 40.2 |
| Canada | 21.7 | 22.7 | 23.4 | 22.9 | 21.2 | 21.4 | 20.5 |
| Czech Republic | 28.5 | 31.4 | 31.2 | 23.4 | 24.4 | 25.2 | 27.8 |
| Denmark | 30.9 | 31.1 | 31.3 | 30.1 | 31.1 | 31.0 | 31.3 |
| Finland | 42.1 | 42.0 | 40.8 | 40.7 | 39.6 | 39.9 | 38.8 |
| France | 39.5 | 40.7 | 39.5 | 38.5 | 38.9 | 39.8 | 39.4 |
| Germany | 37.3 | 35.0 | 35.6 | 35.9 | 34.4 | 33.3 | 32.6 |
| Greece | 34.9 | 35.9 | 36.2 | 36.5 | 35.8 | 36.1 | 36.1 |
| Hungary | 37.4 | 40.4 | 40.8 | 40.3 | 35.9 | 39.5 | 38.9 |
| Iceland | −10.9 | −6.6 | −2.8 | 0.4 | 0.4 | 2.0 | 2.8 |
| Ireland | 26.8 | 25.6 | 23.8 | 22.5 | 20.1 | 15.5 | 12.8 |
| Italy | 44.9 | 43.8 | 43.3 | 37.5 | 37.0 | 36.5 | 35.6 |
| Japan | 15.1 | 15.1 | 15.6 | 14.0 | 19.8 | 20.2 | 20.4 |
| Korea | 6.0 | 5.3 | 11.6 | 13.9 | 15.4 | 15.8 | 16.0 |
| Luxembourg | 12.7 | 12.9 | 13.0 | 12.0 | 10.7 | 11.4 | 11.5 |
| Mexico | 27.2 | 25.4 | 20.8 | 21.9 | 14.1 | 15.4 | 15.6 |
| Netherlands | 34.9 | 33.5 | 33.0 | 33.2 | 34.1 | 35.5 | 32.4 |
| New Zealand | 22.4 | 18.8 | 16.2 | 14.8 | 14.1 | 15.5 | 16.8 |
| Norway | 24.4 | 25.0 | 24.9 | 25.6 | 26.2 | 26.9 | 27.2 |
| Poland | 39.3 | 39.5 | 38.9 | 37.4 | 38.1 | 38.2 | 38.0 |
| Portugal | 26.6 | 26.9 | 26.8 | 26.5 | 26.0 | 26.2 | 24.2 |
| Slovak Republic | — | — | — | — | — | 29.8 | 30.1 |
| Spain | 33.3 | 33.5 | 33.7 | 33.3 | 30.4 | 30.6 | 31.0 |
| Sweden | 42.2 | 44.6 | 45.2 | 44.4 | 44.4 | 42.9 | 41.4 |
| Switzerland | 18.9 | 18.6 | 17.7 | 17.8 | 17.8 | 17.7 | 17.9 |
| Turkey | 35.3 | 38.3 | 39.6 | 39.8 | 30.3 | 40.4 | 43.2 |
| United Kingdom | 26.1 | 25.3 | 24.8 | 24.9 | 23.3 | 21.4 | 17.8 |
| United States | 24.4 | 23.9 | 24.1 | 23.7 | 21.1 | 21.3 | 19.4 |

United Kingdom, and the United States lowered taxes more for the family than for the single person. Denmark lowered taxes for single persons but not for families, whereas Belgium, Greece, Iceland, and Norway noticeably raised taxes for families while holding the taxes of single persons relatively constant. The variations in these results suggest that despite the near consensus on the desirability of taxing families less heavily than single people, the size of this preference differs across countries and over time.

Similar results are seen in comparing table 8.6 with table 8.4. The comparison reveals that employers' social security contributions do not depend on the type of household a worker lives in.

## 8.5   A Comparison with Alternative Approaches

The *Taxing Wages* approach is not the only way in which the taxation of labor income can be assessed. One alternative is to calculate the implicit average effective tax rate, by estimating the total amount of tax paid on labor earnings in a country and dividing that by an estimate of total wages or labor costs. Pioneering work of this sort was undertaken by Mendoza, Razin, and Tesar (1994). This stimulated a substantial literature including OECD (2001) and chapter 7 in this volume by Carey and Rabesona. Another alternative is to use a micro-simulation model (based on publicly available sample survey data) to calculate labor taxes for a representative sample of a country's population. An interesting example of this is the construction of the European tax-benefit model, EUROMOD, described by Sutherland (2001).

These approaches differ from one another in four important ways:

• In the amount of detail they provide. An implicit average effective tax rate calculation for any one country in one year produces just one tax ratio. The *Taxing Wages* methodology uses a clearly structured calculation to generate results for a small number (currently eight) of typical families, whereas the micro-simulation models produce results for each household or stratified group in their databases.

• In the extent to which they are based on actual data. Implicit average effective tax rates have the advantage of being based entirely on observed quantities (although there are disputes over whether these are exactly the appropriate quantities), and thus reflect all the factors that influence the taxes paid. Micro-simulation models are based on real households, and the results are therefore more representative of the population. However, the taxes paid are simulated in a similar way to the *Taxing Wages* calculation. The calculations in *Taxing Wages* take no account of observed data.

• In the tax rate information that they provide. Both micro-simulation models and *Taxing Wages* are able to provide marginal and average effective tax rates, but the implicit effective tax rate calculations yield only an average rate.

• In taking account of cash benefits to families. *Taxing Wages* takes account of cash benefits to families, as can micro-simulation models. This is not done with the currently calculated implicit effective tax rates, and would only be possible if data on aggregate cash benefits to families were available.

Quantitatively these differences can be partly assessed by comparing the results obtained for the implicit average effective tax rate on labor by Carey and Rabesona with the *Taxing Wages* "tax wedge" results for two key household types: the single worker with no children and APW earnings, and the single-earner couple with two children and APW earnings. A cross-country correlation analysis, for the year 2000, shows correlation coefficients of 0.85 for the single worker and 0.83 for the couple.

A more complex picture emerges from time-series correlations for individual countries, shown in table 8.7. For six countries (Australia, Austria, Canada, Finland, Germany, and Korea) the correlation coefficients for the single worker are larger than 0.9, and for three others (Belgium, Greece, and New Zealand) they are larger than 0.8. In contrast, three countries (Czech Republic, Denmark, and the United States) show negative correlation coefficients, while the rest show only weak positive correlations. The cases of Denmark (−0.84) and the United States (−0.47) are particularly interesting because they both show a declining tax wedge in recent years, while the implicit rate was increasing.

The results for the couple's "tax wedge" show a similarly complex picture, but with a generally lower degree of correlation with the implicit rate. Only four countries (Canada, Finland, Korea, and New Zealand) have a correlation coefficient above 0.9 and two extra countries have negative correlations: Italy (−0.12) and Switzerland (−0.68). The weaker correlations for the couples should be expected as the "tax wedge" subtracts family cash benefits, while implicit tax rates do not. However, this cannot be part of the explanation for the mixed results

**Table 8.7**
Correlations between the tax wedge and the implicit average effective tax rate on labor

| Countries | Years covered | Correlation for single worker | Correlation for single-earner couple |
|---|---|---|---|
| Australia | 1979–2000 | 0.92 | 0.65 |
| Austria | 1979–2000 | 0.90 | 0.89 |
| Belgium | 1979–2000 | 0.84 | 0.84 |
| Canada | 1979–2000 | 0.96 | 0.95 |
| Czech Republic | 1993–2000 | −0.01 | −0.51 |
| Denmark | 1989–2000 | −0.84 | −0.77 |
| Finland | 1979–2000 | 0.93 | 0.91 |
| France | 1994–2000 | 0.77 | 0.82 |
| Germany | 1979–2000 | 0.90 | 0.87 |
| Greece | 1991–2000 | 0.82 | 0.87 |
| Ireland | 1979–2000 | 0.34 | 0.46 |
| Italy | 1979–2000 | 0.44 | −0.12 |
| Japan | 1979–2000 | 0.60 | 0.58 |
| Korea | 1995–2000 | 0.99 | 0.99 |
| Netherlands | 1991–2000 | 0.78 | 0.70 |
| New Zealand | 1991–2000 | 0.88 | 0.93 |
| Norway | 1979–2000 | 0.03 | 0.20 |
| Portugal | 1991–2000 | 0.37 | 0.54 |
| Spain | 1979–2000 | 0.03 | 0.11 |
| Sweden | 1979–2000 | 0.37 | 0.60 |
| Switzerland | 1979–2000 | 0.70 | −0.68 |
| United Kingdom | 1979–2000 | 0.55 | 0.27 |
| United States | 1979–2000 | −0.47 | −0.73 |
| Cross-sectional correlation in 2000 | — | 0.85 | 0.83 |

for single workers because they do not receive cash benefits. The true explanation could come from changes in the extent to which the *Taxing Wages* households are representative of all workers and/or the various special assumptions that are required by each methodology to arrive at their results.

Whatever the explanation, these results show that users of effective tax rates on labor need to choose their measure with care. The value of the approach that lies behind each measure depends on what is being studied, so different approaches are likely to be most suitable in attempting to answer different questions. The particular strength of the

*Taxing Wages* approach is comparability between countries: the typical households are the same in each country (with the wage received bearing the same relationship to the APW level) and so differences between effective tax rates are always due to differences in the tax systems and not to differences in the structure of the population. In contrast, differences in implicit average effective tax rates between countries reflect a combination of differences in tax systems (both policy and administration) and differences in population structure (in terms of income distribution, demographics, and other factors that affect tax liability).

This source of strength for some purposes is also a limitation for others. For example, the limited range of incomes considered in *Taxing Wages* makes it impossible to obtain an overall picture of how labor is taxed. In contrast, the implicit average effective tax rate takes account of the taxation of all workers. This is useful in analyzing how the tax base is allocated among labor, capital, and consumption. Nevertheless, neither of these approaches is able to cast light on the taxation of high-income workers, for whom international comparisons may be the most relevant because of their greater mobility.

In principle, it is the micro-simulation model that can produce the combination of comprehensive coverage and individual detail. However, even these models can fail to produce accurate figures for the taxation of high-income individuals, as their databases do not contain enough information to identify all the tax deductions or tax avoidance techniques that are available to such people and rarely contain information on the amount of tax actually paid. The tax authorities, of course, do know how much tax people at different income levels pay and are sometimes prepared to make that information public. This is very useful in establishing the effective progressivity of the tax systems in individual countries, but international comparisons of these data are hard to make, as there is not enough information on the situations of these taxpayers to ensure that they really are similar.

The reason why *Taxing Wages* does not cover a wider range of incomes partly reflects the difficulties that micro-simulation models have in dealing with high-income individuals. As explained in the section 8.3, *Taxing Wages* only takes account of "standard" tax reliefs, in order to focus on the "typical" taxpayer. This is not realistic for high-income individuals because of the significant opportunities to reduce tax liability on wage income that they have in many countries. This means that the mere extrapolation of the tax equations used in producing the publication could seriously overstate the amount of taxes paid. In addition *Taxing Wages* assumes that households have no income from savings, an assumption that is untenable for high-income individuals but that would be very difficult to drop without adding considerable complications.

*Taxing Wages* also does not consider the situation of people on very low incomes, in order to avoid dealing with the complexities of social assistance programs beyond the universal family benefits that it treats as negative taxes, although it is worth noting that the incomes covered are sufficiently low to require a modeling of the nonwastable tax credits that an increasing number of OECD countries are using to increase the incentives for low-skilled people to work. The interaction of the tax and benefit systems and their effects on work incentives are covered in another OECD publication, *Benefit Systems and Work Incentives*, which uses the tax equations from *Taxing Wages* and combines them with information on benefit systems to analyze the incentives for greater work participation that faces households in a variety of situations.

Besides extending the picture from *Taxing Wages* to lower income households, *Benefit Systems and Work Incentives* provides crucial information on out-of-work benefits that are needed to supplement average effective tax rates in any analysis of the incentives for labor force participation. Thus the OECD's regular *Economic Surveys* of its member countries typically use it to analyze labor force participation, while using the marginal tax rates from *Taxing Wages* to analyze hours of work.

### 8.6  Concluding Comments

This chapter provided a view of the contribution that the *Taxing Wages* methodology can make to the measurement of the tax burden on labor. It has shown that the effective tax rate measures obtained can differ significantly from those derived from the implicit tax rate approach. It is therefore necessary for users of effective tax rates to choose their measures with care for the questions that they wish to answer.

The chapter showed that the strength of the *Taxing Wages* methodology lies in its ability to make international comparisons of the tax systems, without the results being affected by differences in the structure of populations. However, the methodology is limited in that it considers particular "typical" workers within a fairly narrow income range and does not capture the entire tax burden on labor nor permit the comparison of tax burdens on the most mobile workers. Also it currently only considers a restricted range of household demographic characteristics, which may need to be extended in order to provide a more comprehensive picture of the taxation of labor. Thus *Taxing Wages* represents a complement to other methodologies, rather than a replacement for them.

It is also important to note that taxes and the cash benefits included in *Taxing Wages* are not always sufficient to analyse the incentive for individuals to participate in the labor market. It is often necessary to take account of the social benefits that such people would receive if they did not work. Such information is provided in a related OECD publication: *Benefit Systems and Work Incentives*. It should also be note that the methodology excludes consideration of non-tax factors that might affect the working of the labor market, including both compulsory and voluntary payments to social security plans administered in the private sector.

Finally the chapter provided a limited selection of data to show the variety of tax systems within the OECD, and the very different directions that they have taken over the last few years.

## Note

The author is grateful to Peter Birch Sørensen and two anonymous referees, as well as Steven Clark, Marcel Gérard, and the other participants in the CESifo Venice Summer Institute workshop on Measuring the Tax Burden on Capital and Labour, July 15–16, 2002, for their comments on an earlier draft. The views expressed here are the author's own and do not necessarily reflect the views of the OECD or its member countries.

## References

Mendoza, E. G., A. Razin, and L. L. Tesar. 1994. Effective tax rates in macroeconomics: Cross-country estimates of tax rates on factor incomes and consumption. NBER Working Paper 4864.

OECD. 1995. *The OECD Jobs Study: Taxation, Employment and Unemployment*. Paris: OECD.

OECD. 2001. *Tax Ratios: A Critical Survey*. OECD Tax Policy Studies No. 5. Paris: OECD.

OECD. 2002. *OECD Economic Surveys: Finland*. Paris: OECD.

Sutherland, H. 2001. EUROMOD: An integrated European benefit-tax model. EUROMOD Working Paper EM9/01.

# 9      How to Measure the Tax Burden on Labor at the Macro Level?

Jakob de Haan, Jan-Egbert Sturm, and Bjørn Volkerink

## 9.1 Introduction

Various recent studies have investigated the impact of the labor tax burden on unemployment, using some kind of macroeconometric model. Generally, it is found that this impact depends on the institutional features of the labor market.[1] For instance, Elmeskov, Martin, and Scarpetta (1998) conclude that different collective bargaining arrangements influence the way in which the tax wedge affects unemployment. The strongest impact is found for countries with intermediate levels of centralization/co-ordination in the labor market.[2] Likewise Daveri and Tabellini (2000) argue that the increase in unemployment and the slowdown in economic growth in continental and non-Nordic Europe stem from higher labor taxes in combination with the institutional characteristics of the labor market. An exogenous and lasting increase in labor costs reduces labor demand. Due to a substitution of capital for labor, the marginal product of capital falls, according to these authors, diminishing the incentive to invest and thus to grow.

Daveri and Tabellini (2000) have used the so-called tax ratios of Mendoza, Milesi-Ferretti, and Asea (1997) as approximations for effective tax rates. To calculate tax ratios, tax revenues are expressed as a ratio of some aggregate tax base (e.g., labor income, capital income, and consumption). In other studies, for example, that by Elmeskov, Martin, and Scarpetta (1998), the tax burden on labor is proxied by the tax wedge, namely the difference between gross labor costs to employers and the consumption wage paid to employees (Scarpetta 1996).

In this chapter we first survey the way in which the tax burden on labor has been proxied for in recent macroeconomic studies that relate to a number of OECD countries. However, we focus on studies at the macro level and do not take microeconometric evidence into account.[3] We also do not deal with country specific studies.[4]

Next we compare the various proxies used. We find that even though the various proxies for the tax burden on labor differ substantially, their correlation is generally quite high. Amazingly many authors examining the relationship between the tax burden on labor and unemployment hardly bother to identify the attributes of a tax burden measure that are important in explaining the possible impact of labor taxes on unemployment. For instance, is a marginal or an average tax rate needed, and should income-tested benefits be included or not?

Finally we examine to what extent the conclusions of some widely cited studies change if some alternative indicator for the tax burden on labor is employed. To be more specific, we re-estimate the unemployment models of Daveri and Tabellini (2000) and Nickell (1997) and the investment model of Mendoza et al. (1997). In general, we conclude that the significance of the impact of the tax burden on unemployment is not very sensitive to the choice of indicator, which is in line with the reported high correlation of most indicators.

The chapter is organized as follows: Section 9.2 summarizes studies that we are aware of and discusses the tax wedge, and section 9.3 discusses labor tax ratios. The tax wedge and the labor tax ratio are widely used in the empirical literature as proxies for the tax burden on labor. Section 9.4 presents our empirical results, and the final section offers some concluding comments.

## 9.2 Tax Burden on Labor: Tax Wedge

Table 9.1 summarizes recent macroeconomic cross-country studies that examine the effect of taxes on labor.[5] Basically two (not mutually exclusive) approaches can be discerned. In one group of studies indicators for the tax wedge are used, while in another group of studies tax ratios (sometimes also called effective or implicit tax rates) are used as proxies for the tax burden on labor. Although they are quite different, both proxies are average tax rates.[6]

Taxes drive a wedge between the price of labor to employers and the return of labor for the employees. Therefore taxation influences decisions of employees about labor force participation and labor supply. Similarly taxation of labor affects the wage offered by employers. Simple economic theory does not provide a clear answer as to how agents will react to taxes (OECD 1995). For instance, an increase in tax rates on labor income may induce workers to work more in order to compensate for the loss of consumption possibilities. Alternatively, they may decide to work less as leisure has become more attractive due to the higher tax rate. Likewise higher taxes on labor will raise the cost of employing someone and will therefore reduce employment to the extent that wages do not fall correspondingly. Under competitive markets, wages will fall by the amount of the tax increase provided that labor is inelastically supplied. However, labor (and product) markets may not be competitive. Unions and employers may take tax changes into account when bargaining for wages. Trade unions may, for instance, try to shift the higher burden of taxation to employers. So it depends on the bargaining structure at the labor market and the bargaining power of the parties involved how taxes will affect the labor market.[7]

Unfortunately, most of the papers summarized in table 9.1 do not provide some explicit theoretical reasoning that leads to a clear identification of the tax burden measure one would want to consider. Most of the studies summarized in table 9.1 examine the impact of the average effective tax rate on a typical worker. Thereby they implicitly refer to the theory of imperfect labor markets that implies that a higher average tax rate on labor income generates a tax push effect on real wages, which is likely to create additional unemployment.

To show this, let us take the bargaining model of Scarpetta (1996) in which imperfectly competitive profit-maximizing firms face exogenously determined product market conditions and predetermined capital and technology (Layard, Nickell, and Jackman 1991). Ignoring labor growth and productivity effects, the model can be summarized by three equations that describe (the logarithm of) labor demand $(L_d)$, the wage-setting schedule, and (the logarithm of) labor supply $(L_s)$.

$$L_d = -\alpha(w - p) - \beta Z_n - w^u, \tag{9.1}$$

where $w$ and $p$ are the logarithms of gross wages (including taxes) and prices, respectively. $Z_n$ is a vector of variables influencing labor demand and $w^u$ is unanticipated wages, which account for expectational errors. Real wages are assumed to be decreasing in actual unemployment $(u)$ and increasing in wage push factors $(Z_w)$, including features of the wage bargaining process and the average tax rate:

$$w - p = \delta_1 Z_w - \gamma_1 u - p^u, \tag{9.2}$$

**Table 9.1**
Summary of recent studies examining the effects of the tax burden on labor

| Study | Countries | Period | Indicator used | Conclusions |
|---|---|---|---|---|
| Scarpetta (1996) | 15–17 OECD countries | 1983–93 | Tax wedge for average production workers (both average and marginal) defined as total personal income tax on wage income, plus employee and employer social security contributions, plus the amount of consumption tax typically paid if all after-tax income is consumed divided by total labor costs (gross wage earnings plus employer social security contributions) | No significant effect of labor taxes on total unemployment; use of marginal instead of average tax wedge does not alter this noticeably, though there is a significant effect on long-term unemployment. |
| Alesina and Perotti (1997) | 14 OECD countries, panel estimates | 1965–90 | Total of direct taxes paid by households, social security taxes paid by employers and employees and payroll taxes, expressed as share of GDP | Degree of shifting of labor taxation is a hump-shaped function of the degree of centralization of labor markets. |
| Nickel (1997) | 20 OECD countries, two cross sections | 1983–88 and 1989–94 | Total tax rate (i.e., sum of average payroll), income, and consumption tax | Payroll taxes have negligible coefficient; overall tax burden may raise unemployment and reduce labor supply. |
| Mendoza et al. (1997) | 18 OECD countries, panel estimates | 1966–90 | Updates of Mendoza et al. (1994) | Factor income tax ratios are negatively and consumption tax ratios significantly positively related to investment, but effects of taxes on growth are "negligible." |

| | | | | |
|---|---|---|---|---|
| Elmeskov et al. (1998) | 18/19 OECD countries, panel estimates | 1983–95 | Tax wedge, defined as total value of employers' and employees' social security contributions and personal income tax, divided by gross earnings plus employers' social security contributions | Tax wedge is significantly related to unemployment but not where high levels of degree of centralization/coordination affect the labor market. |
| Nickell and Layard (1999) | 20 OECD countries, two cross-sections | 1983–88 and 1989–94 | Total tax rate (i.e., sum of average payroll), income, and consumption tax | Total tax wedge affects unemployment, while payroll taxes alone have no additional effect. |
| Blanchard and Wolfers (2000) | 20 OECD countries, panel estimates | 1960–95+ (eight 5-year periods) | Payroll tax variable from Nickell (1997) and total tax ratio: sum of average payroll, income, and consumption tax rates | Higher taxation increases unemployment, but the effect is small. |
| Daveri and Tabellini (2000) | 14 OECD countries, panel estimates | 1965–95 | Tax ratios of Mendoza et al. (1997) | High unemployment and the slowdown in economic growth in Europe stem from high labor taxes in combination with the characteristics of the labor market. |
| Martinez-Mongay (2000) | EU plus Japan and US panel correlations | 1970–97 | ECFIN tax ratios | Labor tax ratios affect private investment and growth negatively. No effects on (un)employment, which is not surprising as the interplay with market institutions is not taken into account. |
| Fiorito and Padrini (2001) | G7 without Japan, estimates for each country | 1970–94 (quarterly) | Variant of tax ratios of Mendoza et al. (1997) | Increasing taxation (especially labor taxation) negatively leads both the labor force and employment, while increasing taxation positively leads unemployment. |

**Table 9.1**
(continued)

| Study | Countries | Period | Indicator used | Conclusions |
| --- | --- | --- | --- | --- |
| Palley (2001) | 20 OECD countries, pooled time series model | 1983–94 | Nickell tax ratios | No robust effect of taxes on unemployment. |
| Nickell et al. (2001) | 20 OECD countries, panel | 1960–94 | Tax wedge defined as direct + indirect + payroll tax rate (total taxes on labor) | Taxes have positive effect on unemployment, which is lower in economies with coordinated wage bargaining. Effect is much lower than in Daveri-Tabellini (10% increase leads to 1% rise in unemployment at average levels of coordination). |
| Nunziata (2001) | 20 OECD countries, panel | 1960–94 | Tax wedge defined as direct + indirect + payroll tax rate | Significant positive effect of taxes on labor costs, with coordination having a negative effect, both in levels and through interaction with taxes. |
| Belot and van Ours (2001) | 18 OECD countries, panel | 1960–94 | Employment tax rate (ratio between employers' contributions to social security and pension schemes and compensation of employees net these contributions) plus direct tax rate (ratio between sum of household contributions to social security and income taxes and households' current receipts) | Without fixed effects, taxes affect unemployment significantly. With country and time effects, there is no direct effect of taxation, but there is a positive and significant interaction between the tax rate and the replacement rate. |
| Volkerink et al. (2002) | 14 OECD countries panel regressions | 1960–95 | Tax ratios of Volkerink and De Haan (1997) and of Mendoza et al. (1997) | Results confirm those of Daveri and Tabellini (2000). |

where $p^u$ denotes unexpected price changes. Labor supply depends on factors affecting participation decisions $(Z_p)$:

$$L_s = \delta_2 Z_p. \tag{9.3}$$

Taxes are also included in $Z_p$. The marginal tax rate seems to be the relevant rate for addressing the issue of whether or not to increase hours worked, while the average tax rate would seem to be the relevant rate for the labor market participation decision. Equilibrium unemployment $(u^*)$ is

$$u^* = \frac{\alpha \delta_1 Z_w}{1 + \alpha \gamma_1} + \frac{\delta_2 Z_p + \beta Z_n}{1 + \alpha \gamma_1}. \tag{9.4}$$

So the equilibrium unemployment rate is determined by various factors, including the average tax rate. Still, the analysis also suggests that the marginal tax rate may be relevant.[8] If the marginal and average tax rates are highly correlated, regressions that only include the average tax rate may lead to a biased estimate of the effect of the average tax rate. Scarpetta (1996) is the only study summarized in table 9.1, which also takes marginal tax rates into account.

The analysis suggests that if one is interested in the possible tax-push effect of the average labor tax on unemployment, it is important that the tax rate used isolates taxes on labor and does not include taxes on transfers. A tax that falls evenly on wages and benefits may not generate a tax-push effect on wage claims, since it does not increase the net replacement ratio. So in evaluating the usefulness of alternative tax ratios for the purpose of estimating the effects on unemployment it becomes important to consider the extent to which measures are "contaminated" by taxes on transfers.[9]

While it is clear from this simple model that some (properly defined) average tax rate can be used in a macroeconometric model explaining unemployment, the model does not provide much guidance on some other important attributes of the tax burden measure. For instance, should other than labor income taxes be included in the tax wedge? In principle, just about every tax can have an effect on the labor market. Still most studies are confined to taxes on labor, although there are differences as to how the tax wedge is measured. The most important difference is whether consumption taxes should be included in the calculation of the tax wedge. Nickell (1997) argues that total taxes (i.e., payroll, income, and consumption taxes) are the tax burden on labor.

The total tax rate is a crude measure of the tax wedge between labor costs and take-home pay.[10] Switching between these taxes will not have an important effect. Nickell (1997, p. 69) argues:

Employees are interested in what their wages can buy. So if their income taxes are cut by 10 percent and the cost of consumption is raised by 10 percent, post-tax real wages are unchanged and so is labour market behaviour. So, broadly speaking, what really counts is the sum of payroll taxes, income taxes and consumption taxes; the total tax burden on labour.

One strategy to estimate the tax wedge is to combine the analysis of statutory tax schedules with data on income distribution of the household and business sectors. McKee, Visser, and Saunders (1986) have calculated the (average and marginal) tax wedge on annual labor income data in nineteen OECD countries using the income level of the average production worker (APW) and information on individual income tax and social security schedules. The basic approach is straightforward: a small number of typical families are chosen and the tax rules for each country are applied to them in order to calculate average and marginal effective tax rates. Nowadays the OECD publishes data for eight types of tax payers in *Taxing Wages* (see Heady 2002 for further details). McKee et al. define the tax wedge as the difference between gross labor costs to employers and the consumption available to employees from increasing labor input by an additional unit. The tax rate is the ratio of the tax wedge to gross labor costs. However, the tax burden for the average production worker may not be representative for the tax burden on all workers.[11] Furthermore estimates from statutory tax rates are complicated because each country has a range of exemptions and allowances that change over time and are difficult to aggregate in each period and even more so in a time-series setting (Fiorito and Padrini 2001). So various empirical studies in which the effects of the tax wedge are examined employ other proxies for the tax wedge.

A good example is the study by Elmeskov, Martin, and Scarpetta (1998), who have estimated various reduced-form models for unemployment. They define the tax wedge as the total value of employers' and employees' social security contributions and personal income tax, divided by gross earnings plus employers' social security contributions. These authors conclude that different collective bargaining arrangements influence the way in which the tax wedge affects unemployment. The effect of the tax wedge on unemployment is absent in countries with a highly centralized/coordinated wage bargaining system, and only marginally significant in countries with a decentralized system, but it is highly significant in countries with intermediate levels of centralization/coordination at the labor market.

These results contrast somewhat with those of Blanchard and Wolfers (2000), who find that their tax variable is significant in their full sample of twenty OECD countries.[12] In sharp contrast, Palley (2001) finds no effect of taxes on unemployment. These diverging conclusions are quite remarkable because many of the studies summarized in table 9.1 consist of simple reduced-form models for unemployment of the form (see also Daveri 2001):

$$U_{i,t} = \text{constant}_i + \beta \text{TAX}_{i,t} + \gamma X_{i,t} + e_{it}, \tag{9.5}$$

where $i$ is the country index, $t$ is the time index (often referring to period averages), $U$ is the unemployment rate, TAX is some proxy for the tax burden on labor, and $X$ is a vector of control variables.

As pointed out before, instead of using some indicator for the tax wedge, many studies have employed so-called tax ratios to examine the relationship between labour taxes and unemployment. Probably the best-known study in this line of research is by Daveri and Tabellini (2000). They have used the tax ratios constructed by Mendoza, Milesi-Ferretti, and Asea (1997) in a panel model like equation (9.5) for fourteen OECD countries over the period 1965 to 1995. These authors conclude that high labor taxes—in combination with the institutional setup of the labor market—strongly contribute to current high unemployment levels in Europe.[13] Their results suggest that over a period of thirty years, the observed rise of about nine percentage points in the labor tax rate corresponds to a rise in unemployment of about four percentage points. These findings are often used to support a reduction in taxes on labor in Europe—preferably in a coordinated fashion—to stimulate employment growth. In the following section we discuss the construction of tax ratios in more detail.

## 9.3   Tax Burden on Labor: Tax Ratios

A number of recent studies have used so-called tax ratios (or effective tax rates). These are based on a methodology inspired by Lucas (1990) and developed by Mendoza, Razin, and Tesar (1994) with a subsequent update by Mendoza, Milesi-Ferretti, and Asea (1997). Tax ratios aim to give an easy to compute indication of the tax burden on, for example, different sources of income or production factors. On the basis of limited information—a few entries from the OECD's *National Accounts* statistics and the *Revenue Statistics*—it is possible to calculate indicators of the tax burden on, for example, labor.[14]

The fundamental methodological problem in constructing labor income tax ratios is that most tax categories as distinguished in the OECD *Revenue Statistics* relate to more than one macroeconomic category (labor and capital income). Consequently the tax ratios cannot be calculated without some way to artificially separate out the amounts to be allocated to various macroeconomic categories. This is most evident for the personal income tax. The category taxes on income, profits, and capital gains on individuals in the OECD *Revenue Statistics* includes taxes on labor, taxes on capital, personal taxes on income paid by the self-employed, and—at least in some countries—taxes on transfers. Other revenue categories as distinguished in the OECD *Revenue Statistics* are plagued by the same problem. Social security contributions (category 2000) are, for example, paid by employees (labor) and—in various countries—also by recipients of social security benefits and by the self-employed, whose income is partly earned by employing capital.

Table 9.2 shows (employed) labor income tax ratios as calculated in the studies that we are aware of. Our starting point, the study of Mendoza, Razin, and Tesar (1994), distinguishes five tax ratios. Two are relevant for this study: the *personal income tax ratio* ($\tau_{per}$) and the *labor income tax ratio* ($\tau_{lab}$).[15]

The personal income tax ratio developed by Mendoza, Razin, and Tesar (1994) is defined as the ratio of revenues from taxes on income, profits, and capital gains of individuals (category 1100 in the OECD *Revenue Statistics*) to the tax base that consists of wages and salaries ($W$), the operating surplus of unincorporated enterprises (OSPUE) and the property and entrepreneurial income of households (PEI).

Directorate General II of the European Commission (1997), OECD (2000), Martinez-Mongay (2000), and Fiorito and Padrini (2001) use the same detour as Mendoza, Razin, and Tesar (1994). They first calculate a personal income tax ratio in order to calculate labor (and capital) income tax ratios. The EC study and Fiorito and Padrini (2001) use the same methodology as Mendoza, Razin, and Tesar (1994), whereas the OECD study includes category 2400 (social security contributions not allocable to any specific group) in the numerator.

**Table 9.2**
Labor income tax ratios: An overview[a]

| Mendoza, Razin, and Tesar (1994) | |
| --- | --- |
| $\tau_{per}$ | $1100/(W + OSPUE + PEI)$ |
| $\tau_{lab}$ | $(\tau_{per} \cdot W + 2000 + 3000)/W + 2200$ |

| Directorate General II of the European Commission (1997) | |
| --- | --- |
| $\tau_{per}$ | Same method as Mendoza et al. (1994) |
| $\tau_{lab}$ | Same method as Mendoza et al. (1994) |

| OECD (2000) | |
| --- | --- |
| $\tau_{per}$ | $1100/(W - 2100 + OSPUE + PEI - 2300 - 2400)$ |
| $\tau_{lab}$ | $(\tau_{per} \cdot (W - 2100 + WSE) + 2100 + 2200 + 2300 + \alpha \cdot 2400 + 3000)/$ $(CoE + WSE + 2300)$, where $WSE = ES \cdot ((W - 2100)/EE)$, and $(W - 2100 + WSE/(OSPUE + PEI - 2300 + W - 2100) = \alpha$ |

| Fiorito and Padrini (2001) | |
| --- | --- |
| $\tau_{per}$ | Same method as Mendoza et al. (1994) |
| $\tau_{lab}$ | $(\tau_{per} \cdot (W + YSEL) + 2000)/(W + 2100 + 2200 + YSEL)$, where $YSEL = (W/EE) \cdot ES$ |

| Volkerink and De Haan (2001)[b] | |
| --- | --- |
| $\tau_{lab}$ | $(\lambda \cdot 1100 + 2100 + 2200 + 3000)/(CoE + 3000)$ |

Source: Adapted and updated from Volkerink and De Haan (2001).
a. Eurostat (1997) and Martinez-Mongay (2000) are not shown here due to incompatibilities with the methodologies displayed here.
b. $\lambda$ is explained in the text.
c. Besides wages and salaries, compensation of employees consists of employers' contributions to social security contributions and employers' contributions to private pension and social welfare plans.
Keys:

| | |
| --- | --- |
| 1000 | Taxes on income, profits, and capital gains |
| 1100 | Taxes on income, profits, and capital gains on individuals |
| 1110 | Taxes on income and profits |
| 1120 | Taxes on capital gains |
| 1200 | Taxes on income, profits, and capital gains on corporations |
| 2000 | Social security contributions |
| 2100 | Social security contributions of employees |
| 2200 | Social security contributions of employers |
| 2300 | Social security contributions of self- and nonemployed |
| 2400 | Social security contributions unallocable between 2100, 2200, and 2300 |
| 3000 | Taxes on payroll and workforce |
| OS | Operating surplus of corporate and quasi-corporate enterprises |
| OSPUE | Operating surplus of private unincorporated enterprises |
| $W$ | Wages and salaries |
| PEI | Property and entrepreneurial income |
| CoE | Compensation of employees[c] |
| EE | Employment (number of dependent employees) |
| ES | Number of self-employed |

Mendoza, Razin, and Tesar (1994) define the labor income tax ratio as the product of the personal income tax ratio ($\tau_{per}$) and wages and salaries ($W$) plus total social security contributions (2000) and taxes on payroll and workforce (3000) over the sum of wages and salaries ($W$) plus employers' social security contributions (2200). The calculation of the tax ratio on labor income by Mendoza, Razin, and Tesar (1994) was copied by the Directorate General II of the European Commission (1997).

The OECD (2000) study has also used this concept, albeit with different components. As shown in table 9.2, the expression for $\tau_{per}$ is different; the factor is not multiplied by $W$, but by $W$ minus employee's social security contributions ($W - 2100$). It is thus assumed that the self-employed "pay" themselves a salary that equals the average employment wage. This income is proxied by multiplying labor income, excluding social security contributions ($W - 2100$), by the share of the self-employed ($SE$) to the number of dependent employees ($EE$). The numerator of the labor income tax ratio furthermore includes both employees' (2100) and employers' (2200) social security contributions as well as part of nonallocable social security contributions ($\alpha \cdot 2400$). The tax base consists of total compensation of employees plus the "income" of the self-employed plus social security contributions by the self- and nonemployed ($CoE + WSE + 2300$). The "compensation of employees" equals the sum of wages and salaries, employer's contributions to social security, and employers' contributions for private pension and welfare plans.

Carey and Rabesona (2002) have presented a modified OECD (2000) methodology for calculating the labor income tax ratio. The major changes with respect to the original methodology are allowing for the deductibility of social security contributions, enlarging the tax base for the labor income tax ratio by including payroll taxes, and a refinement in the separation of security contributions bearing on labor or capital income. Moreover the authors test for the sensitivity of the estimates by relaxing several assumptions about, for example, the split of income taxes paid by the self-employed. The modified estimates that result are, however, highly correlated with the original estimates.

Because of incompatibilities in data, the methodology used by Martinez-Mongay (2000) is not explicitly displayed in table 9.2.[16] All in all, his approach is quite comparable to the Mendoza, Razin, and Tesar (1994) methodology. The main differences with respect to the personal income tax ratio are the inclusion of (part of) the net operating surplus in the denominator, thus implicitly assuming that profits are fully distributed, and assigning more property income to personal income, supplementary to PEI. The major differences compared to the methodology of Mendoza, Razin, and Tesar (1994) are that self-employed income is decomposed into two components, attributed to labor and capital income, respectively. Furthermore the denominator includes the compensation of employees, and not just wages and salaries.

Fiorito and Padrini (2001) use a similar method to separate the income from the self-employed into a component that can be attributed to labor and capital, respectively. This is done by multiplying the average wage sum (total wages over the number of employed, or $W \cdot EE$) by the number of the self-employed ($SE$). The labor income tax ratio is rather similar to the one derived by Mendoza, Razin, and Tesar (1994). However, not only the total wage sum but also the imputed wage of the self-employed (YSEL) is multiplied by the personal income tax ratio to estimate the tax burden on labor income. Item 3000 (taxes on payroll and workforce) is not included in the numerator. Obviously the denominator also includes the imputed labor income of the self-employed (YSEL).

Eurostat (1997) has also constructed a tax ratio on employed labor. The ratio is defined as the fraction of taxes on employed labor and the compensation of employees—which includes gross wages, wage taxes, and social security contributions of both employees and employers. Eurostat uses its own data, however, so that the exact construction of the tax ratios differs significantly from the Mendoza, Razin, and Tesar (1994) approach. National authorities in some cases have indicated the percentage of taxes on income that can be attributed to labor or other income.

What is wrong with labor tax ratios in general? Some studies use the personal income tax ratio as an intermediate step in calculating labor and capital income tax ratios. This is problematic since income from labor, capital income, and transfers is included in the tax base of personal income. Furthermore these studies assume that the same average tax rates apply to all these income categories. This assumption is intuitively implausible, since some income components are largely exempted from taxation, and furthermore most OECD countries apply different statutory tax rates to different sources of income. The OECD (2000) study goes somewhat in the right direction by refining the personal income tax ratio to control for, for example, the (lower) income tax rates on social security, as shown in Adema et al. (1996) and

Adema (1999). This still does not correct for the fundamental problem caused by different tax rates on labour and capital income. Eurostat (1997) has opted for a more piecemeal approach. The initial problem remains unsolved, however, since this approach still assumes that average tax rates on both types of income are more or less the same.

Because of lack of data, the problem identified here is hard to overcome. Based on the OECD *Revenue Statistics* for only three countries, a (global) split in revenues from income taxes by different sources of income can be made. However, sometimes further information can be used (Directorate General XXI of the European Commission 1998). In several cases, withholding taxes on certain kinds of income (e.g., wage taxes) can be identified that may serve to approximate the parts of the income tax attributable to income from labor, capital, and so on. Another possibility is to split the income tax revenues on the basis of data provided by the member states concerned. This is done in the *Structures of the Taxation Systems* in the EU for some countries. Third, a rough split can be obtained by using National Accounts data on main aggregates (e.g., gross salaries divided by gross salaries plus the net operating surplus). However, if this differentiated approach (denoted by $\lambda$ in table 9.2) is followed, a uniform method can no longer be applied to all countries under review. This is the approach followed by Volkerink and De Haan (2001).

As far as the income from self-employment is concerned, this income is typically earned by combining labor and capital. As the Directorate General XXI of the European Commission (1998) points out, the capital input can be almost zero (an opera singer) or very high (farmers) and it is difficult, if not impossible, to split income taxes paid by the self-employed into a labor and capital part. Therefore it seems desirable not to subsume these taxes under labor or capital taxes but to present them as a separate category.

A further difficulty with the labor income tax ratio is the choice of the correct tax base. Mendoza, Razin, and Tesar (1994), the Directorate General II of the European Commission (1997) and Fiorito and Padrini (2001) use the items wages and salaries and employers' social security contributions. Eurostat (1997) and Martinez-Mongay (2000) use the item compensation of employees. This includes employers' contributions for private pension and welfare plans. Since the taxes are assigned to total labor costs of employers, the second approach seems preferable. A significant part of the employer contributions may be voluntary, but they undoubtedly are part of total labor costs. This is also in line with National Accounts conventions. Volkerink and De Haan (2001) redefined the denominator to include the compensation of employees and all taxes on payroll and workforce. These are the total labor costs of employees to employers. Under this approach the following items have to be lumped together: gross wages, employers' social security contributions (2200), category 3000, and employers' contributions for private pension and welfare plans. The numerator should then include employers' and employees' social security contributions (2100 and 2200, excluding social security contributions paid by self- and nonemployed), taxes on payroll and workforce (3000), and all income taxes paid on labor income.

All variables discussed so far, aim to proxy for the tax burden on labor. To what extent do they provide similar information? To answer this question, we will first analyze some simple correlation coefficients. Table 9.3 shows the correlation of the following indicators for the tax burden on labor:

· The indicator of Alesina and Perotti (1997) (AP)
· The tax wedge of Elmeskov et al. (1998) (EMS)
· The tax wedge of Nickell and Layard (1999) (NL)

Table 9.3
Correlation between various indicators for the tax burden on labor

|      | AP        | EMS       | NL        | MMA       | M-M       | OECD       | VdH        |
|------|-----------|-----------|-----------|-----------|-----------|------------|------------|
| AP   | 1         | 0.945     | na        | 0.861     | 0.874     | 0.920      | 0.684      |
|      | (638/43)  | (545)     |           | (351)     | (423)     | (291)      | (164)      |
| EMS  | 0.937     | 1         | na        | 0.917     | 0.928     | 0.914      | 0.894      |
|      | (39)      | (593/41)  |           | (377)     | (391)     | (317)      | (169)      |
| NL   | 0.780     | 0.807     | 1         | na        | na        | na         | na         |
|      | (37)      | (39)      | (40)      |           |           |            |            |
| MMA  | 0.813     | 0.865     | 0.780     | 1         | 0.904     | 0.928      | 0.918      |
|      | (33)      | (35)      | (35)      | (379/35)  | (244)     | (203)      | (127)      |
| M-M  | 0.878     | 0.929     | 0.813     | 0.845     | 1         | 0.861      | 0.859      |
|      | (33)      | (31)      | (30)      | (25)      | (459/34)  | (249)      | (164)      |
| OECD | 0.926     | 0.910     | 0.799     | 0.930     | 0.848     | 1          | 0.804      |
|      | (39)      | (41)      | (39)      | (35)      | (31)      | (328/41)   | (134)      |
| VdH  | 0.644     | 0.854     | 0.524     | 0.888     | 0.826     | 0.810      | 1          |
|      | (17)      | (17)      | (17)      | (15)      | (17)      | (17)       | (169/17)   |

Note: Calculations in the upper-right part of the table are based on annual observations, while in the lower-left part we have used period averages for 1983–88 and 1989–94. Number of observations given in parentheses.

- The labor tax ratio of Mendoza et al. (1997) (MMA)
- The labor tax ratio of Martinez-Mongay (2000) (M-M)
- The labor tax ratio of OECD (2000) (OECD)
- The labor tax ratio of Volkerink and De Haan (2001) (VdH).[17]

Every correlation coefficient has been calculated for the maximum number of observations possible (shown in parentheses). The Nickell-Layard indicator is only available for time-period averages, whereas the other indicators are available on an annual basis. This explains why the correlations on an annual basis (shown in the upper-right part of table 9.3) could not be calculated for the NL indicator. The correlations between the various indicators using the period averages over 1983 to 1988 and 1989 to 1994 are shown in the lower-left part of table 9.3. To calculate these correlations, we first transformed the annual data for the other indicators into period averages.

It is remarkable that the correlations are generally quite high. With the exception of the correlations between the indicators of Alesina and Perotti (1997), Nickell (1997), and the tax ratio of Volkerink and De Haan (2001), all correlation coefficients are higher than 0.75.

To analyze this issue in somewhat more detail, consider the indicators for Austria and Belgium shown in figures 9.1 and 9.2. These countries were selected on the basis of the availability of information on the distribution of components of the personal income tax. For these countries the labor tax ratio as calculated in Volkerink and De Haan (2001) appears to be a reliable proxy for the tax burden on labor in comparison to the tax ratios calculated by the methodology of Mendoza et al. (1994). The various indicators follow a very similar trend, although the estimates of the level of the tax burden differ substantially.

## 9.4  Empirical Results

For illustrative purposes only, we look at the results of some well-known models in which an indicator for the tax burden on labor was used to examine to which extent the choice of a certain proxy drives the outcomes. We start with unemployment using the model and data of Daveri and Tabellini (2000).[18] We take their model specification, sample of countries included, and time period covered. The model estimated is

$$U_{i,t} = \text{constant}_i + \beta TAX_{i,t} + \gamma_1 UB_{i,t} + \gamma_2 EP_{i,t} + e_{i,t}, \tag{9.6}$$

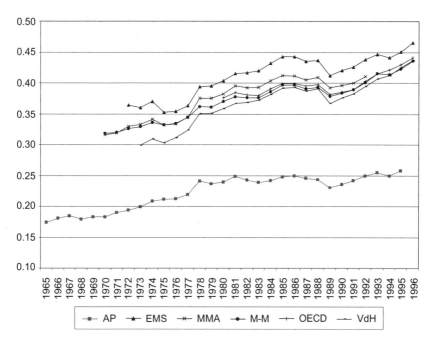

**Figure 9.1**
Various indicators for the tax burden on labor for Austria

where *UB* is unemployment benefit and *EP* is employment protec-
tion.[19] These authors argue that labor taxes will have the strongest
effect on unemployment if wage negotiations are decentralized and
trade unions are powerful but not too large. Therefore they partition
their sample in three groups: continental Europe (Austria, Belgium,
France, Germany, Greece, Ireland, Italy, Luxembourg, Netherlands,
Portugal, Spain, United Kingdom [1965–1980], and Australia and New
Zealand), the Anglo-Saxon countries (Canada, Switzerland, United
Kingdom [1981–1996], United States, and Japan) and the Nordic countries (Denmark, Finland, Iceland, Norway, and Sweden). They report
that no correlation between unemployment and labor taxes can be detected across countries. However, when they differentiate among the
three groups of countries in their panel over the period 1965 to 1995,
they find a very significant effect of labor taxes in continental Europe.

The first column of table 9.4 reports our replication of Daveri and
Tabellini's (2000) model from the first column of their table 9. The
model includes country-specific constants, which is in line with the
outcome of the likelihood ratio test ($\chi^2 = 131.02$ with $p = 0.00$). Our

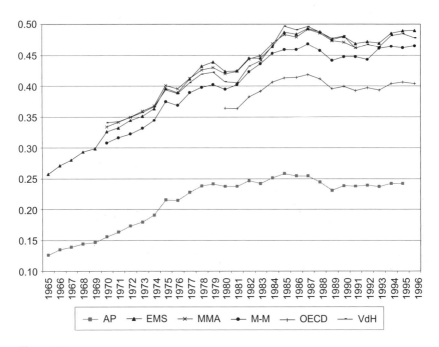

**Figure 9.2**
Various indicators for the tax burden on labor for Belgium

results are exactly the same as those of Daveri and Tabellini (2000). The coefficient of the labor tax ratio in continental Europe is significantly different from the coefficient of the labor tax ratio in the Nordic and Anglo-Saxon countries. The same conclusion is reached if the model is estimated with additional time-fixed effects (not shown).

If the tax ratios of Martinez-Mongay (2000) and Volkerink and De Haan (2001) are used, we have very similar results (see column 4 and 6 of table 9.4).[20] These results do not hold for the OECD labor tax ratio (column 5). This is probably due the limited time period for which the OECD indicator is available (1981–1995/96). Interestingly we found that if alternative proxies for the tax burden on labor are used, again very similar results are attained.[21] The same case holds for the indicators of Alesina-Perotti (column 2) and Elmeskov et al. (column 3). It seems that the general conclusion is not very sensitive to the choice of the indicator for the tax burden on labor; this is in line with the reported high correlation among most indicators.

As we noted earlier, one objection to the use of tax ratios on labor in a model for unemployment is that these tax ratios do not take indirect

**Table 9.4**
Some simple panel regressions using the Daveri-Tabellini model, 14 OECD countries, five-year averages, 1965–95

| Tax proxy | (1) MMA (DT) | (2) AP | (3) EMS | (4) M-M | (5) OECD | (6) VDH | (7) MMA$_{adj}$ (DT) | (8) M-M$_{adj}$ |
|---|---|---|---|---|---|---|---|---|
| $\tau_{labEUR}$ | 0.54 (8.60) | 0.75 (7.62) | 0.30 (5.59) | 0.58 (5.49) | 0.02 (0.06) | 0.55 (4.26) | 0.28 (5.92) | 0.61 (4.71) |
| $\tau_{labANGLO}$ | 0.25 (2.36) | 0.44 (2.05) | 0.22 (1.78) | 0.19 (0.81) | 0.00 (0.01) | 0.82 (1.03) | 0.23 (1.83) | 0.20 (0.75) |
| $\tau_{labNORDIC}$ | 0.11 (0.71) | 0.23 (1.60) | −0.10 (−0.62) | 0.19 (0.93) | 0.54 (1.64) | −0.10 (−0.14) | −0.10 (−0.72) | 0.14 (0.55) |
| UB | 0.14 (2.82) | 0.21 (5.45) | 0.30 (4.61) | 0.29 (3.00) | 0.13 (0.98) | −0.04 (−0.28) | 0.28 (4.00) | 0.27 (2.39) |
| EP | −1.00 (−1.76) | −1.45 (−2.39) | −0.76 (−1.24) | −3.02 (−3.08) | −4.07 (−1.67) | 5.46 (1.80) | −0.30 (−0.50) | −2.45 (−2.37) |
| $R^2$ (adj) | 0.78 | 0.73 | 0.70 | 0.79 | 0.80 | 0.69 | 0.71 | 0.78 |
| F-test that τ's are equal | 6.96 (0.2%) | 5.32 (0.7%) | 3.79 (2.8%) | 2.94 (6.5%) | 1.20 (32.0%) | 0.58 (57.7%) | 4.10 (2.1%) | 3.13 (5.5%) |
| Number of observations | 84 | 84 | 82[a] | 55[b] | 42[c] | 24 | 81 | 55 |

Notes: Dependent variable: unemployment rate, $U$. Countries included are Australia, Belgium, Canada, Finland, France, Germany, Italy, Japan, Netherlands, Norway, Spain, Sweden, United Kingdom, and United States. The periods considered are 1965/66–1970, 1971–1975, 1976–1980, 1981–1985, 1986–1990, and 1991–1995/96. Estimation is with country dummies (no time dummies). $t$-statistics in parentheses.

a. 82 observations due to missing observations for Norway for the periods 1965/66–1970 and 1971–1975.

b. No observations available for Australia, Canada, Norway, and the period 1965/66–1970.

c. Data available only since 1980.

taxes into account. Columns 7 and 8 of table 9.4 present outcomes in which we adjusted the labor tax ratios of Mendoza et al. (1997) and Martinez-Mongay (2000) to include taxes on consumption. Our basic conclusion does not change: in continental European countries taxes exert a negative effect on unemployment.

We also estimated the unemployment model of Nickell (1997), which is very similar to the model of Nickell and Layard (1999). This model is

$$U_{i,t} = \text{constant} + \beta TAX_{i,t} + \gamma_1 EP_{i,t} + \gamma_2 RR_{i,t} + \gamma_3 BD_{i,t} + \gamma_4 \text{ALMP}_{i,t}$$

$$+ \gamma_5 UD_{i,t} + \gamma_6 UCI_{i,t} + \gamma_7 CO_{i,t} + \gamma_8 CPI_{i,t} + \gamma_9 \text{Dummy}_{8994} + e_{i,t},$$

$$(9.7)$$

where $RR$ is the replacement rate, $BD$ benefit duration, ALMP active labor market policies, $UD$ labor union density, $UCI$ union coverage index, $CO$ coordination, and $CPI$ change in inflation. Again, we used the same set of 20 OECD countries and time periods (1983–1988 and 1989–1994) as in the original studies.[22] It follows that Nickell's total tax ratio is significant (column 1 of table 9.5). The same result shows up for AP, EMS, MMA, M-M, and OECD (columns 2–6), although the MMA indicator is only significant at the 10 percent level. This outcome is remarkable as, in contrast to the Nickell ratio, these proxies only take a limited number of taxes into account. Only the coefficient of the VDH indicator is not significantly different from zero. However, if we adjust the labor tax ratios by including taxes paid on consumption, the coefficient of the tax ratio of Volkerink-De Haan also becomes significantly different from zero (not shown).

Next we examine whether tax ratios are related to private investment, following Mendoza et al. (1997). Mendoza et al. use an endogenous growth model to derive the theoretically expected signs of the tax coefficients. In this model, investment and growth are jointly determined by taxes and other exogenous variables. Output is produced with a Cobb-Douglas, CRS technology that uses human capital $H$ and physical capital $K$ as inputs:

$$Y_t = A(v_t K_t)^\alpha (u_t H_t)^{1-\alpha}, \tag{9.8}$$

where $v(u)$ is the share of $K(H)$ devoted to the production of goods. Mendoza et al. (1997) conclude that taxes can affect growth and investment in various ways that may offset each other. This is the case for the tax on capital, as a higher tax rate reduces the after-tax rate of return on physical capital, thereby reducing growth. At the same time a tax

**Table 9.5**
Some simple panel regressions using the Nickell model, 20 OECD countries, 1983–88 and 1989–94

| | (1) | (2) | (3) | (4) | (5) | (6) | (7) |
|---|---|---|---|---|---|---|---|
| Tax proxy | NL | AP | EMS | MMA | M-M | OECD | VDH |
| TAX | 0.03 (4.88) | 0.05 (3.26) | 0.03 (3.58) | 0.02 (1.85) | 0.04 (4.46) | 0.03 (2.48) | 0.00 (0.24) |
| EP | 0.01 (0.74) | 0.02 (1.58) | 0.03 (1.68) | 0.02 (0.87) | 0.00 (0.08) | 0.03 (1.66) | 0.00 (0.08) |
| RR | 0.01 (2.63) | 0.01 (2.63) | 0.01 (2.64) | 0.01 (1.36) | 0.01 (2.93) | 0.01 (1.83) | 0.01 (0.73) |
| BD | 0.11 (2.59) | 0.05 (1.29) | 0.08 (1.81) | 0.09 (1.70) | 0.05 (1.08) | 0.09 (1.80) | −0.04 (−0.38) |
| ALMP | −0.03 (−4.51) | −0.02 (−3.26) | −0.02 (−3.62) | −0.02 (−2.81) | −0.02 (−3.40) | −0.02 (−3.20) | 0.05 (2.14) |
| UD | 0.01 (3.36) | 0.01 (1.38) | 0.01 (2.04) | 0.01 (2.40) | 0.00 (1.05) | 0.01 (2.57) | 0.00 (−1.01) |
| UCI | 0.30 (1.85) | 0.29 (2.01) | 0.28 (1.51) | 0.35 (1.68) | 0.19 (1.10) | 0.22 (1.06) | 0.32 (1.06) |
| CO | −0.45 (−7.34) | −0.42 (−7.76) | −0.45 (−6.52) | −0.43 (−4.88) | −0.47 (−7.21) | −0.44 (−5.89) | −0.38 (−4.99) |
| CPI | 0.04 (2.06) | 0.03 (1.33) | 0.05 (1.77) | 0.05 (1.39) | 0.05 (2.33) | 0.05 (1.69) | 0.00 (0.02) |
| Dummy$_{8994}$ | 0.33 (3.16) | 0.22 (2.32) | 0.29 (2.57) | 0.33 (2.40) | 0.13 (1.38) | 0.31 (2.52) | −0.01 (−0.03) |
| $R^2$ (adj) | 0.72 | 0.69 | 0.67 | 0.54 | 0.73 | 0.61 | 0.51 |
| Number of observations | 40 | 37[a] | 39 | 35[b] | 30[c] | 39 | 17[d] |

Notes: Dependent variable: log unemployment rate, $U$. Countries included are Australia, Austria, Belgium, Canada, Denmark, Finland, France, Germany, Ireland, Italy, Japan, Netherlands, New Zealand, Norway, Portugal, Spain, Sweden, Switzerland, United Kingdom, and United States. The periods considered are 1983–1988 and 1989–1994. Estimation is with time random effects.
a. No observations available for Switzerland.
b. No observations available for Ireland and Portugal.
c. No observations available for Australia, Canada, New Zealand, Norway, and Switzerland.
d. No observations available for Australia, Canada, Denmark, New Zealand, Norway, Portugal, Spain, Sweden, Switzerland, and United States.

on capital reduces $(vK/uH)$, thus increasing the gross-of-tax return on capital, which positively affects growth. In contrast, a tax on human capital raises $(vK/uH)$ reduces the gross-of-tax return on capital, which has a negative effect on growth. A tax on consumption will affect the labor-leisure decision, which in turn affects the capital–labor ratio in production. In the model the effect of a consumption tax on growth is negative. Simulations of the model, using calibrated parameters, suggest that the effect of reducing taxes on capital and labor and increasing consumption taxes hardly impinges on investment, thereby supporting Harberger's claim that the tax mix is not an important determinant of long-run growth and investment rates. In line with these simulations, the empirical results of Mendoza et al. (1997) suggest that the effect of capital and labor taxes on investment is strongly negative, whereas the effect of consumption tax is strongly positive. They also find that tax rates are generally not statistically significant for explaining growth.

We start with replicating the private investment model of Mendoza et al. (1997) using a time-fixed effects model for five-year averages of investment $(I)$. The only explanatory variables considered are the convergence factor (log of GDP per capita in 1965, $Y_0$), and the tax ratios on labor, capital, and consumption ($\tau_{\text{lab}}$, $\tau_{\text{cap}}$, and $\tau_{\text{con}}$, respectively). The estimated panel model is

$$I_{i,t} = \alpha Y_{0i} + \beta_1 \tau_{\text{lab}\,i,t} + \beta_2 \tau_{\text{cap}\,i,t} + \beta_3 \tau_{\text{con}\,i,t} + \text{time}_t, \tag{9.9}$$

where $t$ denotes a five-year period index and $i$ is the country index (data are the same as in Volkerink et al. 2002). Following Mendoza et al. (1997), time dummies ($\text{time}_t$) are also included, although the likelihood ratio test indicates that it is not necessary to include them ($\chi^2 = 4.32$ with $p$-value $= 0.36$), while country dummies are not included.

The results as shown in column 1 of table 9.6 are very similar to those of Mendoza et al. (1997): the consumption tax ratio has a significant positive coefficient, while the impact of the other tax ratios is significantly negative.[23] The same results show up for the M-M indicator (column 2), whereas the results with the OECD tax ratios differ, which is probably due to the limited period for which these data are available (column 3).

So far we have followed Mendoza et al. (1997) and only used time dummies. However, as shown by Islam (1995), neglecting unobserved differences among countries generates an omitted variables problem. The hypothesis that country dummies can be ignored must be rejected.

**Table 9.6**
Some simple panel regressions for private investment

| Estimation by | Time fixed effects (1) | Time fixed effects (2) | Time fixed effects (3) | Time random effects, country dummies (4) | Time random effects, country dummies (5) | Time random effects, country dummies (6) | Time random effects, country dummies (7) | Time random effects, country dummies (8) | Time random effects, country dummies (9) |
|---|---|---|---|---|---|---|---|---|---|
| Explanatory variable | MMA[a] | M-M[b] | OECD[c] | MMA[a] | M-M[b] | OECD[c] | MMA[a] | M-M[b] | OECD[c] |
| $Y_0$ | 1.70 (1.17) | −0.43 (−0.37) | 0.15 (0.10) | 2.66 (17.04) | 2.85 (19.08) | 2.70 (10.84) | 2.99 (15.44) | 2.79 (7.17) | 2.11 (3.90) |
| $\tau_{lab}$ | −0.16 (−4.04) | −0.24 (−3.51) | −0.09 (−1.29) | −0.19 (−2.80) | −0.51 (−11.83) | −0.57 (−5.35) | | | |
| $\tau_{labEUR}$ | | | | | | | −0.37 (−4.13) | −0.49 (−9.79) | −0.51 (−3.32) |
| $\tau_{labANGLO}$ | | | | | | | −0.19 (−2.70) | −0.47 (−2.89) | −0.32 (−1.32) |
| $\tau_{labNORDIC}$ | | | | | | | 0.25 (2.18) | −0.56 (−7.38) | −0.77 (−4.67) |
| $\tau_{cap}$ | −0.28 (−4.16) | −0.15 (−1.90) | 0.04 (1.46) | −0.05 (−0.98) | −0.05 (−0.63) | 0.02 (0.86) | −0.08 (−1.73) | −0.06 (−0.77) | 0.02 (0.81) |
| $\tau_{con}$ | 0.17 (2.61) | 0.19 (2.04) | 0.02 (0.28) | −0.03 (−0.28) | 0.22 (1.82) | 0.67 (3.96) | −0.36 (−2.78) | 0.24 (1.97) | 0.66 (3.87) |
| $R^2$ (adj) | 0.33 | 0.37 | 0.12 | 0.84 | 0.84 | 0.71 | 0.87 | 0.83 | 0.70 |
| $\chi^2(2)$-test that $\tau_{lab}$'s are equal | | | | | | | 21.69 (0.0%) | 0.61 (73.8%) | 3.03 (22.0%) |
| Number of observations | 60 | 80 | 54 | 60 | 80 | 54 | 60 | 80 | 54 |

Note: Dependent variable: gross investment as share of GDP.

a. Countries included are Australia, Austria, Belgium, Canada, Denmark, Finland, France, Italy, Japan, Netherlands, New Zealand, Norway, Spain, Sweden, Switzerland, United Kingdom, and United States. The periods considered are 1965/66–1970, 1971–1975, 1976–1980, 1981–1985, and 1986–1990.

b. Countries included are Austria, Belgium, Denmark, Finland, France, Greece, Ireland, Italy, Japan, Luxembourg, Netherlands, Portugal, Spain, Sweden, United Kingdom, and United States. The periods considered are 1971–1975, 1976–1980, 1981–1985, 1986–1990, and 1991–1995/96.

c. Countries included are Australia, Austria, Belgium, Canada, Denmark, Finland, France, Greece, Ireland, Italy, Japan, Netherlands, New Zealand, Norway, Portugal, Spain, Sweden, Switzerland, United Kingdom, and United States. The periods considered are 1981–1985, 1986–1990, and 1991–1995/96.

The next three columns of table 9.6 show the results where we employ a model with country dummies. Note that the results change drastically: the capital tax ratio is no longer significant, no matter which indicator is used. The labor tax ratio becomes always significant. These results differ substantially from those reported by Mendoza et al. (1997). However, we must stress that this is not so much caused by the choice of the tax ratios but by the specification of the model.

Finally, we tested the argument of Daveri and Tabellini (2000) that high labor taxes in combination with the institutional setup of the labor market affect investment. According to these authors, an exogenous and lasting increase in labor costs reduces labor demand. As capital is substituted for labor, the marginal product of capital falls, diminishing the incentive to invest. Daveri and Tabellini presume that this effect is strongest if wage negotiations are decentralized and trade unions are powerful but not too large. So the labor tax ratio is negatively related to investment, depending on the institutional characteristics of the labor market. In other words, the labor tax ratio should be different among the three groups of countries as distinguished by Daveri and Tabellini (2000). Rows 7 to 9 in table 9.6 present the outcomes. The results are mixed. Only if we use the Mendoza tax ratio as provided by Daveri and Tabellini, we can reject the hypothesis that the coefficients of all labor tax ratios are the same. These results therefore do not yield much support for the Daveri-Tabellini point of view concerning the impact of labor taxes on investment.

## 9.5   Concluding Comments

In this chapter we first surveyed the way in which the tax burden on labor has been proxied for in recent cross-country macroeconomic studies. Most of these studies estimate unemployment models, in which the tax burden on labor is one of the explanatory variables. Basically two (not mutually exclusive) approaches can be discerned. In one group of studies indicators for the tax wedge are used, in another group of studies tax ratios are used as proxies for the tax burden on labor. We find that although the various proxies for the tax burden on labor differ substantially, their correlation is generally quite high.

The most important difference between various proxies for the tax wedge used is whether or not consumption taxes are included in the calculation of the tax wedge. By definition, consumption taxes are not included in the calculation of labor tax ratios. One may therefore wonder whether labor tax ratios are the proper variables to be used in esti-mating cross-country macroeconomic models for unemployment. The fundamental methodological problem in constructing labor income tax ratios is that most tax categories as distinguished in the OECD Reve-nue Statistics relate to more than one macroeconomic category (labor and capital income). Consequently it is impossible to calculate tax ratios without using some technique to artificially separate out the amounts to be allocated to various macroeconomic categories. We argue that the way this is done by Mendoza et al. (1994) and in more recent studies is rather unreliable.

Finally, we examined to what extent the conclusions of some studies change if some alternative indicator for the tax burden on labor is employed. We conclude that the significance of the impact of the tax burden on unemployment is not sensitive to the choice of the indicator. This is in line with the reported high correlation among the various indicators. Essentially the same conclusion holds for our replications of the Nickell model: in almost all variants the coefficient of the tax vari-able is significant. Another finding is that in contrast to the reasoning of Daveri and Tabellini (2000), the significance of the labor tax ratio in the simple investment model of Mendoza et al. (1997) does not depend on the institutional characteristics of the labor market.

## Appendix: Data Sources

Sources for Table 9.3

| AP | EMS | NL | MMA | M-M | OECD | VDH |
|---|---|---|---|---|---|---|
| Own calculations using OECD data | Own calculations using OECD data | Palley (2001) | Data published by authors (MMA) | Data published by authors | Data published by authors | Data published by authors |

Sources for Table 9.4

| AP | EMS | MMA | M-M | OECD | VDH |
|---|---|---|---|---|---|
| Own calculations using OECD data | Own calculations using OECD data | Data published by authors (DT) | Data published by authors | Data published by authors | Data published by authors |

Sources for Table 9.5

All data for the Nickell model taken from Palley (2001). The other indicators for the tax burden on labor are as listed in table 9.3.

**Notes**

We would like to thank the participants in the CESifo Venice Summer Institute 2002 workshop, especially Steven Clark, two referees, and Peter Birch Sørensen for their very helpful comments on a previous version of the chapter.

1. The OECD (1995, p. 93) nevertheless stresses that while tax rates are important for the labor supply and demand decisions of households and firms, there "is no evident simple link between the tax burden and the level of unemployment, which suggests that taxation may not be the principal determinant of unemployment." This conclusion may be due to the labor market characteristics not being properly taken into account. Daveri and Tabellini (2000) report that no correlation between unemployment and labor taxes can be detected across countries. However, when they differentiate among the labor market institutions in the three groups of countries, they find a very significant effect of labor taxes in continental Europe.

2. Similarly Alesina and Perotti (1997) report that the degree of shifting of labor taxation is a hump-shaped function of the degree of centralization of labour markets, peaking in countries with an intermediate degree of centralization.

3. Some may doubt whether analyses at the macro level make sense, as a single rate averaged across taxpayers may be problematic in the sense that it neglects, for example, the distribution of labor income. As will be explained in more detail in section 9.2, a substantial literature has recently addressed the impact of labor taxes on unemployment from a cross-country macroeconomic perspective.

4. Country-specific studies produce a variety of conclusions. For a summary, see OECD (1995).

5. Earlier studies provide evidence on the impact of taxes in reduced-form wage equations (e.g., see Knoester and van der Windt 1987). Hamermesh (1993, tab. 5.1) summarizes studies estimating Phillips curve type equations with a (payroll) tax term appended. According to Daveri (2001), there was no consensus in this earlier literature either about the size of the tax shift or about the likely causes of the estimated differences.

6. Mendoza et al. (1994, p. 302) write that their method "by suggesting the use of data on pre- and post-tax income and prices, produces aggregate effective tax rates that in fact correspond to realized *average* tax rates. These tax rates aggregate the information on statutory taxes, credits, deductions, and exemptions implicit in national accounts and revenue statistics in a manner that captures the overall tax burden from each tax and maintains consistency with the representative agent framework." We discuss in section 9.3 the approach of Mendoza et al. (1994) in more detail.

7. There are alternative approaches to model unemployment and its relationship to taxes, like efficiency wage models, search and matching models and bargaining models. See, for example, Koskela (2001) for further details.

8. We owe this point to Steven Clark.

9. We owe this point to Peter Birch Sørensen.

10. Bean et al. (1986) give some more details about the calculation of this total tax ratio. It consists of the sum of (1) ratio of employers' contributions to social security and pensions to the wage bill, (2) household contributions to social security and direct taxes as proportion of income, and (3) indirect taxes (net of subsidies) as a proportion of consumers' expenditure.

11. The APW income level is the average of earning of production workers in the manufacturing sector. Despite its name, the APW does not represent the income level of an average production worker nor is it otherwise a meaningful average for workers or households (McKee et al. 1986).

12. Apart from the use of different indicators for the tax burden on labor, the studies of Elmeskov et al. (1998) and Blanchard and Wolfers also differ somewhat in terms of country and period coverage and with respect to the other variables taken up in the model. The main difference between both studies, however, is that in contrast with Blanchard and Wolfers, Elmeskov et al. interact their tax variable with proxies for the level of centralization of the labor market.

13. A serious concern with the study of Daveri and Tabellini is the way labour market institutions are taken into account by simply dividing the countries in three groups. On the basis of which criteria this is done remains unclear from the paper. According to Nunziata (2001), the composition of each country group suffers from a certain degree of subjectivity. To what extent the grouping of a certain country affects the results is not examined. There are various aspects of the labor market that may influence unemployment and labor costs and not necessarily in the same direction. In his model for labor costs, Nunziata (2001) divides his countries also in three groups depending on either the degree of bargaining coordination or the degree of bargaining centralisation. In the first case, the tax variable has a positive impact on all groups of countries and not only on the intermediate group. In the second case, the impact of the tax variable is not significant in centralised countries only, while in decentralized and intermediate countries wage costs are significantly affected by employment taxation.

14. Tax ratios are average tax rates rather than marginal tax rates. In general, this might seem more relevant to evaluate the impact of taxation. However, Fiorito and Padrini (2001) argue that this point should not be overstated for two reasons. First, average and marginal tax rates are considerably correlated as shown by Nickell and Layard (1999). Second, marginal tax rates are plagued by larger measurement errors than tax ratios. We doubt, however, whether this second argument is correct (as we explain later). Finally, for some issues (including the effect of taxes on unemployment) average tax rates should be used.

15. The personal income tax ratio is sometimes used as an intermediary step in calculating the labour income tax ratio, and should therefore be considered as well.

16. Martinez-Mongay (2000) uses the so-called AMECO (*Annual Macroeconomic*) database. This database is less detailed than the *Revenue Statistics* and the detailed tables from the *National Accounts* statistics from the OECD. The main advantage compared to the use of OECD data is that these are available more rapidly, and are available for a longer time period.

17. In calculating these correlations we have used, as far as possible, the data as published in the original studies. Only for AP and EMS data of the OECD have been used, given the general definitions of the various tax burdens provided by the authors. See the appendix for our data sources.

18. We thank the authors for kindly providing their data.

19. One may criticize this specification as many potential control variables are not included. However, as our aim is to examine how sensitive the results are for the choice of a certain indicator for the tax burden on labor, we have used the same model as Daveri and Tabellini (2000).

20. However, the F-test that the coefficients of the various tax indicators are the same cannot be rejected (at the 5 percent significance level) for the M-M and VdH indicators.

21. The Nickell indicator is not used here due to data availability.

22. The data have been taken from Palley (2001).

23. See column 1 of table 4 of Mendoza et al. (1997).

# References

Adema, W. 1999. Net public social expenditure. OECD Labour Market and Social Policy Occasional Papers 39.

Adema, W., M. Einerhand, B. Eklind, J. Lotz, and M. Pearson. 1996. Net public social expenditure. OECD Labour Market and Social Policy Occasional Papers 19.

Alesina, A., and R. Perotti. 1997. The welfare state and competitiveness. *American Economic Review* 87 (5): 921–39.

Bean, C. R., R. Layard, and S. Nickell. 1986. The rise in unemployment: A multi-country study. *Economica* 53: 1–22.

Belot, M., and J. C. van Ours. 2001. Unemployment and labor market institutions: An empirical analysis. OSA Working Paper 2001-10.

Blanchard, O., and J. Wolfers. 2000. The role of shocks and institutions in the rise of European unemployment: The aggregate evidence. *Economic Journal* 110: C1–C33.

Carey, D., and J. Rabesona. 2002. Average effective tax rates on capital, labor and consumption. Paper presented at CESifo Venice Summer Institute, 2002.

Daveri, F. 2001. Labor taxes and unemployment: A survey of the aggregate evidence. Mimeo., IGIER at Bocconi University, Milan.

Daveri, F., and G. Tabellini. 2000. Unemployment, growth and taxation in industrial countries. *Economic Policy* 30: 49–104.

Directorate General II of the European Commission. 1997. Effective taxation and tax convergence in the EU and the OECD. Unpublished memo. May.

Directorate General XXI of the European Commission. 1998. How to measure the burden of taxation: Implicit tax rates according to the (primary) functional incidence approach. Mimeo.

Elmeskov, J., J. P. Martin, and S. Scarpetta. 1998. Key lessons for labour market reforms: Evidence from OECD countries' experiences. *Swedish Economic Policy Review* 5(2): 205–52.

Eurostat. 1997. *Structures of the Taxation Systems in the European Union, 1970–1995*. Series 2A. Luxembourg.

Fiorito, R., and F. Padrini. 2001. Distortionary taxation and labour market performance. *Oxford Bulletin of Economics and Statistics* 63(2): 173–96.

Hamermesh, D. S. 1993. *Labour Demand*. Princeton: Princeton University Press.

Heady, C. 2002. The "taxing wages" approach to measuring the tax burden on labour. Paper presented at CESifo Venice Summer Institute. 2002.

Islam, N. 1995. Growth empirics: A panel data approach. *Quarterly Journal of Economics* 110: 1127–70.

Knoester, A., and P. van der Windt. 1987. Real wages and taxation in 10 OECD countries. *Oxford Bulletin of Economics and Statistics* 49: 151–69.

Koskela, E. 2001. Labour taxation and employment in trade union models: A partial survey. Bank of Finland Discussion papers 19.2001.

Layard, R., S. Nickell, and R. Jackman. 1991. *Unemployment: Macroeconomic Performance and the Labor Market*. New York: Oxford University Press.

Lucas, R. E. 1990. Supply-side economics: An analytical review. *Oxford Economic Papers* 42: 293–316.

Martinez-Mongay, C. 2000. ECFIN's effective tax rates: Properties and comparisons with other tax indicators. *European Commission Economic Papers* 146.

McKee, M. J., J. J. C. Visser, and P. G. Saunders. 1986. Marginal tax rates on the use of labour and capital in OECD countries. *OECD Economic Studies* 7: 45–101.

Mendoza, E. G., G. M. Milesi-Ferretti, and P. Asea. 1997. On the ineffectiveness of tax policy in altering long-run growth: Harberger's superneutrality conjecture. *Journal of Public Economics* 66(1): 99–126.

Mendoza, E. G., A. Razin, and L. L. Tesar. 1994. Effective tax rates in macroeconomics. Cross-country estimates of tax rates on factor incomes and consumption. *Journal of Monetary Economics* 34(3): 297–323.

Nickell, S. J. 1997. Unemployment and labour market rigidities: Europe versus North America. *Journal of Economic Perspectives* 11: 55–74.

Nickell, S. J., and R. Layard. 1999. Labor Market Institutions and Economic Performance. In O. Ashelfelter and D. Card, eds., *Handbook of Labor Economics*, vol. 3C. Amsterdam: North Holland.

Nickell, S. J., L. Nunziata, W. Ochel, and G. Quintini. 2001. The Beveridge curve, unemployment and wages in the OECD from the 1960s to the 1990s. Centre for Economic Performance Discussion Paper 502.

Nunziata, L. 2001. Institutions and wage determination: A multi-country approach. Mimeo: Nuffield College.

OECD. 1995. *Taxation, Employment and Unemployment*. Paris: OECD.

OECD. 2000. Effective average tax rates on capital, labour, and consumption goods: Cross-country estimates. Economics Department, Working Paper 258.

Palley, T. I. 2001. The role of institutions and policies in creating high European unemployment: The evidence. Mimeo.

Scarpetta, S. 1996. Assessing the role of labour market policies and institutional settings on unemployment: A cross-country study. *OECD Economic Studies* 26: 43–98.

Volkerink, B., and J. de Haan. 2001. Tax ratios: A critical survey. *OECD Tax Policy Studies* 5.

Volkerink, B., J.-E. Sturm, and J. de Haan. 2002. Tax ratios in macroeconomics: Do taxes really matter? *Empirica* 29: 209–24.

# 10 Using Micro Data to Assess Average Tax Rates

W. Steven Clark

## 10.1 Introduction

This chapter reports work by Delegates of Working Party No. 2 of the OECD Committee on Fiscal Affairs (CFA) on examining the use of tax-payer micro data to assess average tax rates on various income types. The work follows that published in *Tax Burdens—Alternative Measures*, OECD Tax Policy Studies No. 2, on various "backward-looking" and "forward-looking" tax burden measures.[1] The purpose of the exercise was to examine in detail backward-looking measures. In particular, it explored the relative strengths of tax revenue-based approaches that rely on micro data collected from personal and corporate income tax returns as an alternative to measures based on aggregate tax revenue data reported in OECD *Revenue Statistics*.

Interest in the calculation of average tax rates on various categories of income, for example, labor or capital income, measured using tax revenue data, can be traced to at least three considerations. First, other often-cited tax rates, including statutory tax rates, and marginal and average effective tax rates based on models of taxpayer behavior, may provide limited information on tax burdens on labor and capital income. Depending on the modeling approach, forward-looking measures tend to give less than full consideration of certain factors that influence the amount of tax collected, and therefore may provide imprecise indicators of tax burdens on employment, savings and investment activities.

*Statutory tax rates*, while relevant to tax-planning incentives, work effort, and investment decisions, ignore special tax allowances, tax credits, and other provisions important to effective tax rate calculations. *Marginal effective tax rates* (METRs), while taking into account a number of factors thought relevant to work and investment behavior, ignore factors pertaining to infra-marginal activities and tax-planning, which may be important in assessing tax burdens and incentive effects of tax systems. Similarly, forward-looking *average effective tax rates* derived for capital income, while capturing the taxation of inframarginal rents and provisions relevant to the after-tax cost of acquiring capital, take less than full account of tax-minimizing strategies, the influence of business loss carryover provisions, and other factors determining actual tax burdens on income from capital.

Backward-looking *average tax rates*, on the other hand, measured using actual revenue figures, take into account the effects of statutory income tax rates, tax deductions, and tax credits in determining the tax take. They also take into account the effects of tax planning, tax relief provided by lax or discretionary administrative practice, as well as noncompliance. Thus revenue-based average tax rates in principle offer certain advantages in measuring actual tax burdens. However, as backward-looking measures, they may give misleading information on effective taxation of returns on prospective investment. On the other hand, given that they account for tax planning, they may be useful in assessing the likely tax burden on past investment. They could be used, for example, as a check against model-based average effective tax rate (AETR) measures that are properly forward-looking but ignore factors that may be of critical importance in particular cases.

In addition to these possible advantages encouraging the use of actual tax return data, there is a view, perhaps mistaken, that average tax rate analysis based on revenue data is intrinsically a simpler exercise than model-based approaches, for example, AETR analysis. In particular, there is no need to delve into the detailed rules that go into the determination of capital cost allowances, investment tax credits, the cost of financial capital, and so on, that must be encoded into a METR or AETR formula. The net effect of these and other rules on tax burdens is captured in the (numerator) measure of tax revenues collected.

Third, it is recognized that whatever the relative strengths of average tax rates based on aggregate revenue data, such numbers will be generated, quoted, interpreted and used to influence tax policy debate. Given this, an interest emerges in developing a better understanding of what goes into the making of average tax rates based on aggregate data, and what can and cannot be made of them.

With this background, Delegates of Working Party 2 agreed to a project that would consider and implement frameworks relying on *micro-level data* to assess average tax rates on various categories of income. This work would build on earlier work undertaken by the group in this area.[2] The results from the project would be of interest in their own right, while at the same time could shed light on the extent to which average tax rates derived from aggregate (e.g., *Revenue Statistics* and *National Accounts*) data could be used to inform policy debate. A number of Delegates volunteered (or were asked to volunteer!) to assist in this project, relying on confidential data drawn from tax returns. This chapter provides a summary of work undertaken by Delegates from Austria, Belgium, Canada, Denmark, and Norway, reporting on the use of taxpayer-level data to assess average tax rates on labor, capital, and transfer income.

Section 10.2 reviews work by Norway and Denmark, focusing on advantages that micro data offer in isolating tax revenues raised from various types of income. This precision enables a check on results derived from aggregate data, and possibly more accurate estimates of economywide average tax rates on labor, capital, and transfer income. This section also reviews work by Austria that serves to illustrate the strengths of micro data in permitting the computation of average tax rates on labour income at various wage levels, and across different household types.

Section 10.3 reports work by Belgium and Canada, analyzing how micro data can be used to calculate average tax rates at the corporate level on income from capital. This work is important, given widespread policy interest in assessing average corporate tax rates and given the general inability of aggregate data to generate a meaningful annual corporate average tax rate series. The considerations also have implications for implicit capital tax rates derived from aggregate data. A number of examples are provided to illustrate the impact of cyclical effects on corporate tax burden measures, the importance of correcting for business losses in average tax rate calculations, and possible adjustments using micro data. This section also reports variations in tax rates at the industry level and by firm size.

## 10.2  Assessing Average Tax Rates on Personal Income

A key attribute of micro data is the flexibility it provides, enabling the modeler to derive average tax rates at various levels of aggregation ranging from the individual taxpayer to the overall economy level. While a disaggregate view is required to address many policy-related questions, figures reporting levels and trends in the *economywide* average tax rate on different categories of income may also be of interest—for example, to address the sharing of tax burdens between labor and capital, and so the overall fairness of the tax system. Macro modelers may also be interested in single economywide tax rate series for labor and capital income. This section considers advantages of relying on micro data to assess economywide average tax rates on labor income, with reference to the Norwegian tax system. It also reports on economywide average tax rates on transfer income based on micro data, with illustrations by Denmark. These strengths are assessed relative to the implicit tax rate approach that relies on aggregate *Revenue Statistics* and *National Accounts* data.[3]

A main concern with implicit tax rate analysis is the relatively crude manner in which revenues from a given comprehensive or schedular personal income tax are allocated across (attributed to) different categories of income included in the tax base. The implicit tax rate method in effect assumes that a single economywide average tax rate on personal income may be taken as the effective tax rate on all income included in the personal tax base for all taxpayers.[4] This assumption is generally unrealistic, and calls for more detailed work as considered in this chapter. As reviewed below, micro data permit a more targeted assessment of the amount of personal income tax revenue raised from labor income and other types of income. This in turn may enable improved estimates of average tax rates by income type, or more generally, provide results that confirm or lead one to reconsider certain results based on aggregate data.

Obtaining good estimates of the (notional) allocation of personal tax revenues across income types, to calculate economywide average tax rates on labor, capital, and other income, is important, given the importance of this tax. In OECD Europe, taxes on personal income accounted for roughly one-quarter of total tax revenues in 2000. In OECD America, almost 40 percent of revenues were raised from personal income tax, while in OECD Pacific the figure was about 30 percent.

In addition to offering possible refinements to economywide average tax rate measures, micro data enable *disaggregate analysis* to guide policy making. For example, in assessing distribution effects of the tax system, and the impact of taxation on labor markets, attention may be given to effective tax rates on wage income measured separately for various taxpayer groups that differ by income level and household structure. The ability to measure average tax rates for different tax-payer groups is important to the extent that effective tax rates vary across taxpayer groups (i.e., the tax wedge depends on the income level and the household structure). It is also important to the extent that the behavioral response to a given tax wedge differs depending on the taxpayer situation.[5]

To illustrate this point, work by Austria is reviewed that finds significant variability in average tax rates on wage income across wage levels. This raises questions over the use of implicit labor tax rates to assess the tax burden on labor income taxed on a progressive basis, as reliance on aggregate data means that only a single summary labor tax burden measure may be assessed for a given country in a given year. Attempts to use average tax rates to assess fairness in the tax system are therefore severely limited without information on the distribution of the tax burden. The chapter argues that assessments of the possible impact of the tax system on labor market participation are strengthened where one is able to measure average tax rates on labor income at various income levels and for different taxpayer groups.

The analysis by Austria shows that an average tax rate measure, even if derived for a tax that applies to one type of income alone, for example, a wage tax on labor income, may not be particularly informative for policy purposes where the rate is derived from aggregated data. Problems of interpretation are shown to arise where the average tax rate measure is sensitive to the distribution of labor income such as under a progressive tax rate structure. These problems may become pressing where employment concerns are concentrated on blue-collar workers, for example, earning an average production wage.

### 10.2.1 Isolating Revenues from Different Income Categories

Examples by Norway and Denmark illustrate how micro data may permit more direct measurement of the amount of tax revenue raised from different categories or types of income. There may be policy interest, for example, in measuring average tax rates on capital income, or on labor income, or more narrowly on wage and salary income, or transfer income.[6] In such cases two advantages may be identified when relying on micro data: one in relation to the treatment of taxes that include a single category or type of income in the tax base, and another in relation to taxes with two or more types of income in the tax base and where a notional revenue split is required.

### Identification of Taxes Levied on a Single Income Category

Where there is policy interest in measuring the effective tax rate on a specific category of income, and a given tax is levied on that income category alone (as can occur under a schedular tax system), in general, the revenues from that tax should be accounted for in their entirety when measuring an average tax rate for that income. However, the revenues from such a tax are typically factored in only partially when they are based on aggregate personal income tax revenue data. Under the implicit tax rate approach, aggregate personal tax revenues are scaled to approximate a notional labor tax component. In contrast, the use of micro data can permit the identification and separate measurement of the relevant tax revenue amount. This precision holds out certain advantages, as the implications of partial inclusion are generally unknown, leading to uncertainty over the accuracy of implicit tax rate results.

The Norwegian dual income tax example illustrates this advantage. Under this schedular system, tax is imposed at a flat (proportional) rate on ordinary income, which includes labor and capital income.[7] Separately, an income surtax is imposed under a two-step progressive rate schedule on gross labor income alone (alternatively called tax on personal income). Micro data can isolate the amount of tax collected on labor income by this income surtax, which is not possible when working with aggregate individual income tax data—for example, *Revenue Statistics* data that combine tax on ordinary income, tax on personal (labor) income, and tax on capital income and report a single aggregate personal income tax revenue amount in a given year.[8]

To illustrate, consider the following equation set relying on micro data to measure the total amount of tax imposed in Norway in a given year on labor income:

$$\text{IT(labor)} = \sum_j (w^L{}_j \cdot \text{OT}_j) + S + \text{SSC}, \tag{10.1a}$$

$$S = \sum_j S_j, \tag{10.1b}$$

$$\text{SSC} = \sum_j \text{SSC}^{ee}{}_j + \sum_j \text{SSC}^{se}{}_j + \sum_j \text{SSC}^{er}{}_j, \tag{10.1c}$$

where the summation term $\sum_j$ is over all individual taxpayers (or alternatively a representative weighted sample of $n$ taxpayers, with $j = 1, \ldots, n$).

The first term in equation (10.1a) estimates the total amount of tax on ordinary income (OT) derived from the labor income component of the ordinary income tax base, using taxpayer-specific weights $w^L_j$ measuring the fraction of net ordinary income that is labor income.[9] The third term measures aggregate social security contributions collected on labor income, with the components shown in equation (10.1c). The first two, social security contributions of employees ($\sum_j SSC^{ee}_j$) and the self-employed ($\sum_j SSC^{se}_j$), are levied on labor income.[10] The third, employer social security contributions ($\sum_j SSC^{er}_j$), is levied on wage and salaries alone. All three contributions relate to labor income, and may be included in full in estimating the total amount of tax imposed on labor income.

This discussion focuses on the second term S in (10.1a), measuring income surtax revenues.[11] As with social security contributions, the surtax is imposed on labor income alone, and it should be included in full when estimating total tax revenues raised on labor income. This precision is possible with micro data, as reflected in equation (10.1a).

In contrast, the implicit tax rate approach factors in some fraction $f^L$ of total personal income tax revenues—comprised of ordinary income tax plus income surtax revenues—in measuring the total amount of tax imposed on labor income, as follows:[12]

$$IT^{(agg)}(labor) = f^L(OT + S) + SSC, \tag{10.2}$$

where OT denotes total tax revenues on ordinary income, S denotes total income surtax revenues, and SSC denotes total social security contributions.

If equations (10.1a) and (10.2) are compared, two differences are evident. First, the micro data approach allows one to rely on taxpayer-specific weights ($w^L_j$), rather than an overall average weight ($f^L$), when estimating the labor component of the tax on ordinary income. The advantages of relying on taxpayer-specific weights are taken up below.

Second, whereas the income surtax (tax on personal [labor] income) is accounted for in full in equation (10.1a), only some fraction ($f^L$) of S is included in the implicit tax rate model, with the weight ($f^L$) assessed as the percentage of total individual income that is labor income. As noted, since the base of S is labor income alone, the surtax amount should be included in full in measuring total tax imposed on labor income in order to feed into the corresponding calculation of the average tax rate on labor.

When working with aggregate data, the implications of partially rather than fully including the income surtax are generally unclear. The potential for underestimating labor tax revenues (and thus the average tax rate on labor income) increases as the contribution of the surtax to total tax revenues collected on labor income becomes larger. The percentage contribution of the income surtax is uncertain when relying aggregate personal income tax revenue statistics reported in *Revenue Statistics*.

*Analysis by Norway of Average Tax Rates on Labor Income*    Work by Norway investigates the importance of micro data in assessing the average tax rate on labor income by a variant of equation set (10.1):[13]

$$\tau^{L(\text{Norway})} = \frac{w^L \cdot OT + S + SSC}{W + SSC^{er}}, \tag{10.3a}$$

$$w^L = \frac{W}{OY}, \tag{10.3b}$$

where the first term ($w^L \cdot OT$) gives an estimate of the labor portion of total tax revenues raised on ordinary income, S is total income surtax, SSC is total social security contributions, $SSC^{er}$ is total employer social security contributions, and W denotes labor income. The scaling factor used to weight total tax on ordinary income is given by (10.3b), where W includes total wages and salaries of employees plus the total labor portion of remuneration of the self-employed, and OY measures total ordinary income.[14] The average tax rate on labor income (including pension income) is estimated to be 33.1 percent on average over the period 1997 to 1999 based on tax return data.

With the implicit tax rate approach, the income surtax S is factored into the numerator only in part, as follows:

$$\tau^{L(\text{implicit})} = \frac{w^L \cdot (OT + S) + SSC}{W + SSC^{er}}. \tag{10.4}$$

When aggregate data are used, the average effective tax rate on labor is estimated to be 33.0 percent in the same period. Thus the micro data usefully lend support in this instance to the results derived from aggregate data. In particular, if the income surtax is included in part rather than in full, there is no substantial change in the estimates of the average tax rate on labor income in Norway over the years considered. This finding reflects the relatively low percentage contribution of the surtax to the total tax on labor income. Conversely, in systems where a tax levied on a single income category accounts for a larger portion of total tax on that income (with that amount buried in aggregate tax data), the use of micro data can provide for more precise average tax rate measures.

### Treatment of Taxes Levied on Multiple Income Types

Micro data may also enable more precise measurement of taxes on certain categories or income types where a tax includes more than one type of income in its tax base. Depending on what average tax rate is being measured, interest arises in accurately measuring tax collected, for example, on labor income, or wage income, or transfer income. In such cases micro data allows one to link features of a tax system that treat different types of income differently to the distribution of these income flows across taxpayers subject to varying average tax rates.

More precisely, to measure the average tax rate on labor income, in which there must be incorporated an estimate of the (notional) amount of tax revenue raised from a broad-based tax that can be attributed to labor income, the use of taxpayer-level data enables a more close assessment of the influence of special features targeted at labor income.[15] This discussion draws on the preceding discussion of the Norwegian tax system and examines how micro data can be used to measure the amount of total tax on ordinary income that can be tied to labor income, or more narrowly, wage income.[16]

Consider first a simple framework that illustrates how micro data may be used to estimate (notional) tax revenues raised by a certain tax on one income type (e.g., personal income tax on wage income) where that income is one of a number income types in the tax base. The general results obtained can be compared with those under the implicit tax rate methodology. While the analysis focuses on measuring an average tax rate on labor income, the issues raised generally carry over when assessing the tax burden on other income types in a broadly defined (pooled) tax base. We then turn to an application of the general approach by Denmark for an example of a broad-based personal income tax that includes an assessment of personal tax revenues derived from pension and benefit income.

The illustrative framework assumes an economy with two taxpayers and a single tax (personal income tax). Taxable income includes labor income $W_j$ and other income $Y_j$, where $j$ is an index over taxpayers $(j = 1, 2)$.

*Taxpayer 1* We can model taxpayer 1's personal income tax liability in a general fashion as follows:

$$PIT_1 = t(W_1 + Y_1 - \lambda E_1 - A) - C_1, \tag{10.5a}$$

where $t$ denotes the personal income tax rate,[17] $W_1$ measures labor income, $Y_1$ measures other taxable income, $\lambda E_1$ measures deductible expenses in earning other income with the deductible portion $\lambda$ given by the tax code, $A$ measures a basic tax allowance, and $C_1$ denotes a general or targeted tax credit.[18]

The portion of taxpayer 1's personal income tax liability linked to labor income can be estimated as the portion that labor income is to the taxpayer's total economic (or accounting) income:

$$PIT(lab)_1 = PIT_1 \left( \frac{W_1}{W_1 + Y_1 - E_1} \right) = f^L_1 \cdot PIT_1. \tag{10.5b}$$

The amount raised from other income is given by

$$PIT(oth)_1 = PIT_1 \left( \frac{Y_1 - E_1}{W_1 + Y_1 - E_1} \right) = f^O_1 \cdot PIT_1. \tag{10.5c}$$

Consider the income weights for labor (wage) and other income for taxpayer 1:

$$f^L_1 = \frac{W_1}{W_1 + Y_1 - E_1}, \tag{10.5d}$$

$$f^O_1 = \frac{Y_1 - E_1}{W_1 + Y_1 - E_1}. \tag{10.5e}$$

These weights $f^L_1$ and $f^O_1$, applied to personal income tax, are taxpayer-specific and are determined *without* reference to the deduction scaling factor $\lambda$, the standard allowance or the tax credit. The measurement of the weights requires an assignment of the expense $E_1$ to the relevant income type $(Y_1)$. Where an expense (negative income) item relates to more than one type of income, it is necessary to allocate the expense across the relevant income amounts.

The denominator of the weights $(W_1 + Y_1 - E_1)$ is comprised of flows that establish taxpayer 1's economic income, as opposed to the individual's net income for tax purposes. For practical purposes, the modeler may resort to an accounting measure of net income. The counterpart to this accounting basis at the economywide level is household income on a *National Accounts* basis. Tax provisions relevant to measuring the tax base are *not* taken into account in the measurement of the denominator of the weights. The effect of tax provisions is captured through their impact on reported tax revenues (PIT).

Personal tax raised on a taxpayer's labour income can be expressed as a fraction $(f^L{}_1)$ of personal income tax (see equation 10.5b), or alternatively as a percentage $\tau_1$ of that taxpayer's labor income $W_1$, where $\tau_1$ is *taxpayer 1's average tax rate* on personal income:

$$\tau_1 = \frac{PIT_1}{W_1 + Y_1 - E_1}. \tag{10.5f}$$

*Taxpayer 2*  Modeling taxpayer 2's income tax liability in an analogous fashion we have

$$PIT_2 = t(W_2 + Y_2 - \lambda E_2 - A) - C_2, \tag{10.6a}$$

$$PIT(lab)_2 = f^L{}_2 \cdot PIT_2 = \tau_2 \cdot W_2, \tag{10.6b}$$

$$PIT(oth)_2 = f^O{}_2 \cdot PIT_2 = \tau_2 \cdot (Y_2 - E_2), \tag{10.6c}$$

$$f^L{}_2 = \frac{W_2}{W_2 + Y_2 - E_2}, \tag{10.6d}$$

$$f^O{}_2 = \frac{Y_2 - E_2}{W_2 + Y_2 - E_2}, \tag{10.6e}$$

$$\tau_2 = \frac{PIT_2}{W_2 + Y_2 - E_2}. \tag{10.6f}$$

For each taxpayer, the tax rate $\tau_j$ is an average rate over the taxpayer's labor and other income—in other words, income-specific tax rates for each taxpayer are *not* derived in this framework.[19] However, the rates are taxpayer-specific, with $\tau_j$ reflecting taxpayer j's taxable position. In particular, this rate depends on the *level* of taxpayer j's total taxable income where the tax rate schedule denoted by $t$ is progressive and/or where standard (fixed) allowances are provided. Individual tax rates may also differ across taxpayers depending on the *composition* of income to the extent that personal income tax deductions and/or credits are targeted at (or earned in respect of) different income types, and income composition varies across taxpayers.

In the model the results for taxpayer 1 and taxpayer 2 when compared (i.e., comparing equations 10.5a and 10.6a, and 10.5f and 10.6f) show that the average income tax rates for taxpayer 1 ($\tau_1$) and taxpayer 2 ($\tau_2$) may differ for the following reasons:

· Taxpayer 1 and taxpayer 2 have *different levels of (before-tax) income,* and the personal tax rate structure ($t$) is progressive and/or standard allowances ($A$) are provided, and/or

· Taxpayer 1 and taxpayer 2 have the same (before-tax) income level, but *different income composition,* and different tax payable due to income- or expenditure-specific tax deductions and/or tax credit claims (as denoted by $\lambda E_i$ and $C_i$).

While the approach measures a single average income tax rate for a taxpayer in a single year, the micro data allow one to assess different average tax rates for different taxpayers, and thereby enable notional tax revenue and overall average tax rate estimates for different categories of income that take into account different taxpayer situations.

*Measuring Average Tax Rates on Labor Income* From these *micro data* results an average tax rate on labor income, and an average tax rate on other income can be derived taking into account potentially important taxpayer-level information. For illustrative purposes, consider the measurement of the average tax rate on labor income, which we can denote by $\tau^{L(\text{micro})}$. This rate is determined by adding the taxpayer-level (notional) amounts of personal tax on labor income and dividing by aggregate labor income, as follows:

$$\tau^{L(\text{micro})} = \frac{\tau_1 \cdot W_1 + \tau_2 \cdot W_2}{W_1 + W_2}, \tag{10.7a}$$

where the taxpayer-level personal tax rates are given by

$$\tau_i = \frac{\text{PIT}_i}{W_i + Y_i - E_i}, \qquad i = 1, 2. \tag{10.7b}$$

The point is that the estimate of total tax revenues derived from labor income, appearing in the numerator of the average tax rate calculation (10.7a), is determined using taxpayer-specific (rather than overall) average personal income tax rates. The labor income at the taxpayer-level is weighted using taxpayer-specific tax rates ($\tau_i$).

In contrast, when working with *aggregate data,* as under the implicit tax rate approach, the estimate of total tax revenues derived from labor income is derived by applying a single (overall) taxpayer average personal income tax rate $\tau^{\text{agg}}$, as follows:

$$\tau^{L(\text{impl})} = \frac{\tau^{\text{agg}}(W_1 + W_2)}{W_1 + W_2} = \tau^{\text{agg}} \tag{10.8a}$$

where

$$\tau^{\text{agg}} = \frac{\sum \text{PIT}_i}{\sum(W_i + Y_i - E_i)}. \tag{10.8b}$$

Let us compare the two approaches. The micro-data approach links features of the tax system determining average income tax rates of individual wage earners with the distribution of wage income across taxpayers (similarly for other income). In estimating the notional amount of revenue raised from labor income, the micro-data framework weights labor income at the taxpayer level with taxpayer-specific tax rates. Depending on the distribution of wage income in the economy, and the variation in average tax rates at the taxpayer level, the resulting estimate of the notional amount of tax revenue raised on labor income could differ markedly from that obtained on an overall economywide average tax rate, as under the implicit tax rate approach.

To see this, consider the situation where labor income is concentrated in the hands of taxpayer 1 (with other income in the hands of taxpayer 2), and taxpayer 1's average tax rate $\tau_1$ is lower than that of taxpayer 2 (and thus lower than the overall rate $\tau^{\text{agg}}$). Then weighting labor income by $\tau_1$ would provide a closer approximation of tax revenues raised from labor income than relying on $\tau^{\text{agg}}$. In practice, wage income is dispersed among taxpayers and the importance of using taxpayer-specific rather than overall economywide average tax rates is an empirical question. Yet the use of taxpayer-level data holds out the advantage where such differences are important.

*Analysis by Denmark of Average Effective Tax Rates on Transfer Income*   Work by Denmark analyses how taxpayer-level data can be used to disaggregate personal income tax revenues into notional component parts and derive corresponding average effective tax rates, along the lines set out in the simple framework discussed above. The results are reported in table 10.1. Note that the table shows significant variation in average tax rates across different types of transfer income, indicating that the distribution of transfer income across taxpayers differs depending on the specific type of transfer income. The results also

**Table 10.1**
Average effective tax rates on various types of social transfers: Denmark

| | Average effective tax rate | |
|---|---|---|
| Type of transfer income | Without tax allowances | With tax allowances |
| Social pensions | 29.25 | 29.20 |
| Supplementary pension | 31.46 | 31.38 |
| Civil servants pension | 38.72 | 38.47 |
| Early retirement pension | 31.60 | 30.81 |
| Sickness benefits | 32.29 | 28.25 |
| Parental leave | 28.50 | 22.26 |
| Educational allowance | 20.96 | 20.07 |
| Support, start enterprise | 28.91 | 25.15 |
| Unemployment benefit | 31.98 | 26.49 |
| Early retirement unemployment | 31.46 | 28.31 |
| Low income | 29.12 | 28.57 |

Source: Ministry of Finance, Denmark.

show the relative importance of tax allowances for different taxpayers earning different types of transfer income. For example, tax allowances are shown to have little effect on average effective tax rates on social pensions and low income transfers, while lowering rates on unemployment benefits and sickness benefits by 4 to 5 percentage points.

### 10.2.2 Addressing Progressivity and Income Distribution Effects

Average tax rate measures for labour income may be of policy interest where there are concerns that the tax system is not sufficiently progressive, or more generally does not adequately address income distribution concerns. Such measures may also be of interest where concerns exist that the tax system is creating a large wedge between gross (before-tax) labor costs and the after-tax take-home pay of workers, discouraging labor market participation. However, a representative average tax rate cannot be easily obtained from aggregate data, as the net impact of progressive tax rate structures, tax allowances, and tax credits can differ, sometimes significantly, depending on the gross wage level and household structure.

For example, the effect of a fixed allowance in offsetting tax is relatively more pronounced at low earnings. Tax allowances and credits may be subject to thresholds and have tapering (phase-in and phase-out) provisions, where again the relative importance of such measures depends on gross earnings. Where the average tax rate on labor income varies with gross income, the relevance of an average tax rate derived using aggregate data is less than clear. An analysis of the Austrian data shows that average tax rates on labor income derived from aggregated tax revenue data represent only a narrow range of wage earners. In contrast, micro data can provide a range of effective tax rate calculations of policy interest.

Gathered in Austrian micro data are separate series for taxes assessed on labor income, including wage taxes, (final) income taxes, and social security contributions. While final income tax assessments determine the final income tax burden on labor income, the wage tax statistics (reflecting a prepayment of income tax) offer timely insights into average tax rates on labor income at various wage levels. The figures closely approximate the actual tax burden figures where final assessments required only minimal adjustments, and they have the attractive feature of being available a year before the final income tax data. The wage tax statistics are also compiled separately for employees (table 10.2) and pensioners (table 10.3). This feature is useful for examining the impact of the tax system on employment incentives by taxpayer group (employees) with regard to effective tax rates on current wages (as opposed to pension income taxed as ordinary income). The data show that removing pensioners from the sample sharpens the focus of the exercise, with total wage tax paid by pensioners amounting to over 48 billion ATS in 1999, or roughly 23 percent of total wage tax collected in that year. Moreover effective tax rates are shown to differ between pensioner and employee groups at various income levels.

The average tax rate (ATR) analysis for employees in table 10.2 derives two average tax rate series, one for wage taxes ($\tau^L_I$) and a second for employee social security contributions ($\tau^L_{II}$):

$$\tau^L_I = \frac{WT}{W}, \tag{10.9}$$

$$\tau^L_{II} = \frac{SSC^{ee}}{W}, \tag{10.10}$$

where $WT$ measures wages taxes withheld on wage income, $SSC^{ee}$ measures employee social security contributions, and $W$ measures gross wages and salaries of employees (wages and salaries recorded net of $SSC^{ee}$, plus $SSC^{ee}$). Employer social security contributions and

**Table 10.2**
ATR results for employees based on micro data: Austria, wage tax statistics, 1999

| Gross income | Gross wages and salaries | | | Wage tax | | | | | Social security contributions | | | |
|---|---|---|---|---|---|---|---|---|---|---|---|---|
| 000's ATS | Persons | Million ATS | Per head | Persons | Million ATS | Per head | ATR | DTR | Persons | Million ATS | Per head | ATR |
| 0–50 | 459,915 | 9,727 | 21.1 | 224,916 | 241 | 1.1 | 5.1% | | 341,154 | 1,174 | 3.4 | 16.3% |
| 50–100 | 287,951 | 21,579 | 74.9 | 151,315 | 601 | 4.0 | 5.3% | 5.4% | 269,805 | 3,228 | 12.0 | 16.0% |
| 100–150 | 275,379 | 34,394 | 124.9 | 172,310 | 1,050 | 6.1 | 4.9% | 4.2% | 273,443 | 5,714 | 20.9 | 16.7% |
| 150–200 | 281,780 | 71,736 | 225.7 | 315,526 | 5,217 | 16.5 | 7.3% | 15.6% | 317,212 | 12,482 | 39.3 | 17.4% |
| 250–300 | 372,715 | 102,622 | 275.3 | 371,921 | 9,558 | 25.7 | 9.3% | 18.5% | 372,249 | 17,834 | 47.9 | 17.4% |
| 300–350 | 357,645 | 116,069 | 324.5 | 357,447 | 12,772 | 35.7 | 11.0% | 20.4% | 357,260 | 20,076 | 56.2 | 17.3% |
| 350–400 | 292,265 | 109,239 | 373.8 | 292,161 | 13,556 | 46.4 | 12.4% | 21.7% | 291,954 | 18,728 | 64.1 | 17.2% |
| 400–450 | 215,355 | 91,257 | 423.8 | 215,226 | 12,555 | 58.3 | 13.8% | 23.9% | 215,057 | 15,437 | 71.8 | 16.9% |
| 450–500 | 157,145 | 74,440 | 473.7 | 157,046 | 11,335 | 72.2 | 15.2% | 27.7% | 156,924 | 12,354 | 78.7 | 16.6% |
| 500–600 | 205,798 | 112,314 | 545.7 | 205,558 | 19,535 | 95.0 | 17.4% | 31.7% | 205,346 | 18,133 | 88.3 | 16.2% |
| 600–700 | 119,999 | 77,413 | 645.1 | 119,721 | 15,367 | 128.4 | 19.9% | 33.5% | 119,533 | 11,718 | 98.0 | 15.2% |
| 700–800 | 71,179 | 53,115 | 746.2 | 70,866 | 11,537 | 162.8 | 21.8% | 34.1% | 70,906 | 7,300 | 103.0 | 13.8% |
| 800–900 | 45,304 | 38,358 | 846.7 | 45,101 | 8,852 | 196.3 | 23.2% | 33.3% | 45,078 | 4,797 | 106.4 | 12.6% |
| 900–1,000 | 29,720 | 28,146 | 947.0 | 29,580 | 6,788 | 229.5 | 24.2% | 33.1% | 29,526 | 3,214 | 108.9 | 11.5% |
| 1,000–1,400 | 52,229 | 60,320 | 1,154.9 | 51,865 | 15,705 | 302.8 | 26.2% | 35.3% | 51,768 | 5,815 | 112.3 | 9.7% |
| 1,400–2,100 | 19,944 | 32,982 | 1,653.7 | 19,825 | 9,354 | 471.8 | 28.5% | 33.9% | 19,686 | 2,244 | 114.0 | 6.9% |
| 2,100–2,800 | 4,725 | 11,263 | 2,383.7 | 4,699 | 3,292 | 700.6 | 29.4% | 31.3% | 4,604 | 533 | 115.8 | 4.9% |
| 2,800–3,500 | 1,778 | 5,506 | 3,096.7 | 1,774 | 1,683 | 948.7 | 30.6% | 34.8% | 1,718 | 200 | 116.4 | 3.8% |
| 3,500 & over | 2,207 | 12,764 | 5,783.4 | 2,204 | 4,018 | 1,823.0 | 31.5% | 32.5% | 2,132 | 263 | 123.4 | 2.1% |
| | 3,570,704 | 1,112,660 | 311.6 | 3,071,467 | 165,292 | 53.8 | 17.3% | | 3,426,197 | 169,768 | 49.5 | 15.9% |

Source: Ministry of Finance, Austria.
Note: ATR = average tax rate; DTR = "discrete change" tax rate. ▢ Average income (APW), ▢ Median income, ▢ ATR(agg).

**Table 10.3**
ATR results for pensionners based on micro data: Austria, wage tax statistics, 1999

| Gross income | Gross wages and salaries | | | Wage tax | | | ATR | DTR |
|---|---|---|---|---|---|---|---|---|
| 000's ATS | Persons | Million ATS | Per head | Persons | Million ATS | Per head | | |
| 0–50 | 290,359 | 6,005 | 20.7 | 13,001 | 30 | 2.3 | 11.2% | |
| 50–100 | 257,654 | 19,656 | 76.3 | 18,411 | 85 | 4.6 | 6.1% | 4.2% |
| 100–150 | 422,728 | 51,443 | 121.7 | 83,697 | 259 | 3.1 | 2.5% | −3.4% |
| 150–200 | 264,056 | 45,890 | 173.8 | 240,294 | 2,575 | 10.7 | 6.2% | 14.6% |
| 200–250 | 213,786 | 47,955 | 224.3 | 211,489 | 4,868 | 23.0 | 10.3% | 24.3% |
| 250–300 | 170,819 | 46,733 | 273.6 | 170,228 | 6,102 | 35.8 | 13.1% | 26.0% |
| 300–350 | 123,017 | 39,846 | 323.9 | 122,829 | 6,080 | 49.5 | 15.3% | 27.1% |
| 350–400 | 84,085 | 31,271 | 371.9 | 83,980 | 5,257 | 62.6 | 16.8% | 27.3% |
| 400–450 | 43,562 | 18,403 | 422.5 | 43,508 | 3,334 | 76.6 | 18.1% | 27.8% |
| 450–500 | 29,032 | 13,761 | 474.0 | 29,001 | 2,673 | 92.2 | 19.4% | 30.2% |
| 500–600 | 32,572 | 17,755 | 545.1 | 32,545 | 3,733 | 114.7 | 21.0% | 31.7% |
| 600–700 | 19,453 | 12,551 | 645.2 | 19,438 | 2,861 | 147.2 | 22.8% | 32.5% |
| 700–800 | 12,235 | 9,116 | 745.1 | 12,216 | 2,196 | 179.8 | 24.1% | 32.6% |
| 800–900 | 7,192 | 6,088 | 846.5 | 7,183 | 1,526 | 212.4 | 25.1% | 32.2% |
| 900–1,000 | 5,134 | 4,865 | 947.6 | 5,123 | 1,288 | 251.4 | 26.5% | 38.5% |
| 1,000–1,400 | 8,270 | 9,492 | 1,147.8 | 8,247 | 2,643 | 320.5 | 27.9% | 34.5% |
| 1,400–2,100 | 2,567 | 4,254 | 1,657.2 | 2,563 | 1,207 | 470.9 | 28.4% | 29.5% |
| 2,100–2,800 | 817 | 1,858 | 2,274.2 | 816 | 548 | 671.6 | 29.5% | 32.5% |
| 2,800–3,500 | 382 | 1,184 | 3,099.5 | 380 | 315 | 828.9 | 26.7% | 19.1% |
| 3,500 & over | 530 | 2,970 | 5,603.8 | 529 | 780 | 1,474.5 | 26.3% | 25.8% |
| | **1,988,250** | **391,096** | **196.7** | **1,105,478** | **48,360** | **43.7** | **22.2%** | |

Source: Ministry of Finance, Austria.
Note: ATR = average tax rate; DTR = "discrete change" tax rate. ☐ Average income, ▨ Median income, ▮ ATR(agg).

payroll taxes are not included (although these could be factored in). Instead, the analysis focuses on wage tax and employee social security contribution components of average effective tax rates on labor, and draws out a number of useful observations.[20]

First, the results reveal that a single average tax rate derived using aggregate taxpayer data provides limited tax burden information in the Austrian example, even where the relevant tax revenues on labor income can be isolated (as they can, in this example in the case of the wage tax). In particular, table 10.2 shows that the average tax rate on wage income, derived at an aggregate level for all employees as a group, at 17.3 percent, corresponds to the average tax rate on wages of taxpayers with gross income of roughly 550 thousand ATS. This rate is nearly double that applicable to those with average wage earnings of 300 thousand ATS, and triple the rate applicable to those with gross earnings in the range of 50 to 200 thousand ATS. Given this variability, it is unclear how one should interpret in a policy context the overall figure of 17.3 percent. It would be difficult to compare this estimate of the tax burden on labor with that on capital, given the variability in observed results across income levels.

Rather than generating a single representative value, the micro-data approach solves for average tax rates at various income levels. This range of values allows one to assess how the various Austrian personal tax provisions combine to shape the degree of progressivity in the system. Furthermore average tax rate figures derived from actual tax return data may be helpful in assessing how the tax system has affected employment activity—for example, on labor market participation decisions.[21]

However, it is difficult to interpret a stationary or variable single rate over time derived from aggregate data because of the variability in average tax rates across income levels and because of the sensitivity of the overall rate to the before-tax income distribution. Using microdata tax rate calculations can be made at various income levels and the average tax rates can be associated with corresponding income levels. This may be useful in cases where employment problems tend to be acute for employees at certain earnings levels (e.g., low-paid labor). The micro data allow one to more readily identify differences in effective tax rates over time (and across countries) at various income levels due to differences in tax policy (affecting tax base and statutory rates) compared with differences in before-tax earnings distribution.

Micro data further enable calculations to be made of discrete change tax rates (DTR) that examine how the tax burden changes with discrete increases in gross wage income. These rates are not true marginal rates, as they are measured for discrete rather than unit increases in gross wage income, and do not reflect tax changes arising solely from changes in gross wage income (based on actual tax revenues, the DTR measure does not hold other factors constant).[22] The DTR results for wage income would be useful in addressing the impact of the tax system on work incentives for those already employed who might be considering the net benefits of the additional work effort. The results may be compared with marginal tax rate results derived from a microsimulation model focusing on tax effects resulting from a unit increase in gross wages, holding other factors constant (as in OECD *Taxing Wages*). Where access is limited to aggregate income tax or wage tax revenues, it is not possible to assess effective tax rates at the margin.

Micro data can reveal differences in the tax burden imposed by alternative taxes on wage income at various earnings levels for policy makers who wish to target a particular group of workers for tax relief. To take an example, for employees earning roughly 300 thousand ATS in gross wages, employee social security contributions impose a tax burden roughly twice that imposed by the wage tax. In contrast, for those earning in excess of 600 thousand ATS, the wage tax burden is higher, and increases as wages rise above this mark. Thus reductions in social security contribution rates would favor low- to median-wage earners. While such impacts can be inferred from the statutory provisions relevant to each tax, the availability of micro-based effective tax rates provides the analyst with a useful source of information to assess distributional effects, estimate the fiscal cost, and steer policy decisions.

## 10.3   Assessing Average Tax Rates on Corporate Income

This section focuses on the use of micro data by Belgium and Canada to assess corporate average tax rates, and identifies problems and limitations encountered, when relying on aggregate data. The discussion does not address difficulties in using aggregate data to measure average tax rates on income from capital more generally (covering corporate and shareholder-level taxes), although the findings presented on the corporate side have implications that carry over.

The attention given to average tax rates at the corporate level is motivated in part by the high degree of policy interest in corporate-level tax burdens. For example, in an open economy context, there is interest in examining separately the effective tax rate on corporate profits to address the possible negative impact that taxation may have on (direct) investment incentives. Also there are often concerns captured in the press that corporations are not paying their fair share of tax. The review focuses first on the need to make adjustments in respect of business losses to obtain meaningful average tax rate measures, which requires access to micro data. Such adjustments are shown in the country work to be important. Indeed, the inability to properly account and adjust for losses when relying solely on aggregate *Revenue Statistics* and *National Accounts* data largely explains why implicit tax rate modellers avoid reporting implicit corporate tax rates.[23] The work by Belgium and Canada also highlights the broad set of calculations made possible by micro data, including estimates of average corporate tax rates by sector, asset size, and income strata.

### 10.3.1   Accounting for Business Losses

To properly account for business losses and their tax treatment in the measurement of average tax rates on corporate income is a complicated matter in theory and in practice. One might argue that losses and their tax treatment should be ignored, and attention restricted to the treatment of profitable firms. However, important information relevant to determining the corporate tax burden is lost if the tax treatment of losses is ignored.[24] The issues here include the treatment of unclaimed losses under loss carry-forward rules, and whether or not related firms are taxed on a separate basis or on a group basis, allowing for the losses of one firm to offset taxable income of related companies in the group. Such provisions can significantly affect corporate tax burdens.

When relying on aggregate data, a central problem is that aggregate corporate income tax revenues appearing in the numerator of an average tax rate are reduced by losses incurred in prior years, while the denominator is reduced by losses incurred in the current year. The numerator effect results from loss carry-forward provisions. The denominator effect results from the inclusion of current year losses of current year loss-making firms, offsetting profits of profitable firms in the same year upon aggregation. Thus losses are factored into the numerator and denominator, but the losses are mismatched in the sense that they are in respect of different periods (i.e., prior year versus current year).

This timing problem could be addressed by aggregating numerator amounts (e.g., corporate income tax) over a number of years, and dividing this by an aggregate of denominator amounts (operating surplus of incorporated companies) summed over the same period. The

**Table 10.4**
Corporate ATR implications of relying on macro versus micro data: Example 1

|                                      | Year 1 | Year 2 | Year 3 | Year 4 |
|--------------------------------------|--------|--------|--------|--------|
| *Firm 1*                             |        |        |        |        |
| Profit/loss                          | 20     | 20     | 20     | 20     |
| Taxable profit                       | 20     | 20     | 20     | 20     |
| Tax (@20)                            | 4      | 4      | 4      | 4      |
| *Firm 2*                             |        |        |        |        |
| Profit/loss                          | 0      | −5     | 5      | 10     |
| Cumulative unclaimed losses          | 0      | −5     | −5     | 0      |
| Loss carryforward claim              | 0      | 0      | −5     | 0      |
| Taxable profit                       | 0      | 0      | 0      | 10     |
| Tax (@20)                            | 0      | 0      | 0      | 2      |
| *Macro-data results*                 |        |        |        |        |
| Total tax                            | 4      | 4      | 4      | 6      |
| Total profit                         | 20     | 15     | 25     | 30     |
| ATR(agg)                             | 20%    | 26.67% | 16%    | 20%    |
| *Micro-data results*                 |        |        |        |        |
| Total tax                            | 4      | 4      | 4      | 6      |
| Total adjusted profit                | 20     | 20     | 20     | 30     |
| ATR 1                                | 20%    | 20%    | 20%    | 20%    |
| Total adjusted tax (*no discounting*) | 4     | 3      | 5      | 6      |
| Total profit                         | 20     | 15     | 25     | 30     |
| ATR 2A                               | 20%    | 20%    | 20%    | 20%    |
| Total adjusted tax ($r = 10\%$)      | 4      | 3.09   | 5      | 6      |
| Total profit                         | 20     | 15     | 25     | 30     |
| ATR 2B                               | 20%    | 20.61% | 20%    | 20%    |
| *Discount rate r*                    | 10%    |        |        |        |

longer the aggregation period, generally the smaller is the problem (in relative terms) of any remaining inconsistency in loss treatment. However, policy interest in a multiple-year average tax rate declines for longer aggregation periods.[25] This is particularly the case where tax policy changes have occurred over this period, and one is interested in examining the impact of these changes by consulting the time profile of the effective tax rate on corporations from one year to the next.

Before turning to the work by Belgium and Canada illustrating the flexibility of micro data in accounting for business losses, it is useful to observe some relevant tax figures. Tables 10.4 and 10.5 show the problems of interpretations that rely on aggregate data alone, and how micro data can be used to adjust (denominator) profit figures or alternatively (numerator) tax figures in an average tax rate (ATR) measure for the effects of losses. The assumption is that firms are able to carry losses forward (loss refunds are not provided). Table 10.4 examines

**Table 10.5**
Corporate ATR implications of relying on macro versus micro data: Example 2

|                                      | Year 1 | Year 2 | Year 3 | Year 4 |
|--------------------------------------|--------|--------|--------|--------|
| *Firm 1*                             |        |        |        |        |
| Profit/loss                          | 20     | 20     | 20     | 20     |
| Taxable profit                       | 20     | 20     | 20     | 20     |
| Tax (@20)                            | 4      | 4      | 4      | 4      |
| *Firm 2*                             |        |        |        |        |
| Profit/loss                          | 0      | −5     | 5      | 10     |
| Cumulative unclaimed losses          | 0      | −5     | −5     | 0      |
| Loss carryforward claim              | 0      | 0      | −5     | 0      |
| Taxable profit                       | 0      | 0      | 0      | 10     |
| Tax (@20)                            | 0      | 0      | 0      | 2      |
| *Firm 3*                             |        |        |        |        |
| Profit/loss                          | 0      | −5     | −5     | −5     |
| Cumulative unclaimed losses          | 0      | −5     | −10    | −15    |
| Loss carryforward claim              | 0      | 0      | 0      | 0      |
| Taxable profit                       | 0      | 0      | 0      | 0      |
| Tax (@20)                            | 0      | 0      | 0      | 0      |
| *Macro-data results*                 |        |        |        |        |
| Total tax                            | 4      | 4      | 4      | 6      |
| Total profit                         | 20     | 10     | 20     | 25     |
| ATR(agg)                             | 20%    | 40%    | 20%    | 24%    |
| *Micro-data results*                 |        |        |        |        |
| Total tax                            | 4      | 4      | 4      | 6      |
| Total adjusted profit                | 20     | 20     | 20     | 30     |
| ATR 1A                               | 20%    | 20%    | 20%    | 20%    |
| Total adjusted profit*               | 20     | 20     | 15     | 25     |
| ATR 1B                               | 20%    | 20%    | 27%    | 24%    |
| Total adjusted tax ($r = 10\%$)      | 4      | 3.09   | 5      | 6      |
| Total profit                         | 20     | 10     | 20     | 25     |
| ATR 2                                | 20%    | 30.91% | 25.00% | 24.0%  |
| *Discount rate r*                    | 10%    |        |        |        |

two firms over a four-year period, with each firm subject to an effective corporate income tax rate of 20 percent.[26] Firm 1 is profitable over this period, earning 20 units of profit in each year. Firm 2 begins operations in year 2, and incurs losses in that year, but becomes profitable in year three and is able to carry forward its initial losses to claim against tax in year 3.

Corporate tax burden analysis based on *aggregated* data (shown as macro data) finds an average corporate tax rate ATR(agg) of 26.67 and 16 percent in years 2 and 3. In year 2, with current period losses included in year 2 aggregate (net) profits, but the tax treatment of those losses not factored into the numerator, the effective tax rate is overstated in year 2. In year 3, the effective tax rate at 16 percent is understated due to the year claim for year 2 losses, affecting the numerator, but without those losses factoring into the denominator.

Two types of adjustments to the microdata address the mismatch in the loss treatment in table 10.4. The first approach, with results shown as ATR 1, excludes current year unclaimed losses from the denominator profit measure, and instead reduces the denominator in respect of prior year losses, and in particular, loss carry-forward claims impacting the numerator.[27] In other words, where a firm incurs losses, the losses are accounted for in measuring aggregate corporate profits in the year in which claims are made in respect of those losses. Rather than recognizing the loss of (5) by firm 2 in measuring year 2 aggregate profits, this loss is set off against corporate profits in year 3 when the claim is made for that loss. This yields an ATR value of 20 percent in each year as illustrated in table 10.4.

An alternative approach is to include current-year profits and current-year losses in the denominator (net) profit measure, and to adjust corporate tax revenues in the numerator in respect of future claims on current-year losses. In particular, where losses are realized in a given year, corporate tax revenues for that year are reduced to the present value of future claims on those losses. In the example, the second set of results in table 10.4 (ATR 2A and ATR 2B) adjusts aggregate tax revenues in year 2 to take into account the loss carry-forward claim in year 3 by firm 2 in respect of its losses realized in year 2. In particular, the loss claim in year 3 of 5 units of losses reduces tax in that year by 1 unit (assuming a 20 percent corporate tax rate). Thus, under the adjustment without discounting, aggregate corporate tax receipts (4 units) in year 2 are reduced from 4 to 3 units, yielding an average tax rate of 20 percent.

The second set of results (ATR 2B) takes into account the time value of money, assuming a 10 percent discount rate, and deducts from aggregate corporate tax receipts the present value in year 2 of the loss claim of 5 in year 3. The ATR of 20.61 percent in year 2 reflects the assumption that the tax system does not allow losses to be carried forward with interest (as implicitly assumed in the first set of micro-data results, ATR 2A).

Table 10.5 broadens the analysis by adding a third firm assumed to be in a loss position in each year over the 4-year period. As in table 10.4, the first set of results ATR(agg) illustrate the problems of interpretation created when (unadjusted) aggregated data are used. The next two sets of results are derived using adjusted profits. The ATR 1A results ignore the losses of firm 3, which in the example are never offset in full or in part by the tax system, in measuring corporate profits. The approach can be interpreted as reflecting a benchmark system that denies a loss offset to perpetually loss-making firms. In contrast, the ATR 1B results assume an alternative benchmark, reducing profits in respect of prior year unrelieved losses, regardless of whether loss-making firms eventually become profitable or not.

The ATR 2 results are derived under the alternative loss-adjustment approach of adjusting aggregate corporate tax revenues (rather than aggregate profits) for future claims on current year losses, and assuming a benchmark profit measure that recognizes the losses of all firms. The inability of the loss firm (firm 3) to claim relief for its losses means that aggregate corporate tax receipts would not be adjusted downward for these losses (i.e., the present value of zero relief is zero). The losses do, however, lower aggregate profit, putting upward pressure on the corporate ATR.

The cases examined in tables 10.4 and 10.5 serve to illustrate possible approaches relying on micro data to adjust for business losses. In principle, aggregate corporate tax revenues may be reduced by the present value of future claims (if any) on same period losses, rather than adjusting aggregate corporate profits by the amount of same period claims on prior year losses. A concern that arises under the latter approach is that the results tend to blur the timing of the corporate average tax rate series—that is, the impact of losses on aggregate corporate profits and tax is not recognized until the year(s) in which tax claims are taken. Also realized losses that never get claimed for tax purposes are ignored. However, in practice, the profit-adjustment approach is preferred, as the alternative is difficult to implement even where statutory corporate tax rates remain fixed. Few corporate tax micro models are dynamically structured to provide an account, by firm, of when unutilized losses are eventually claimed (or lost). A manual checking of tax returns and ad hoc adjustments would normally be required, tending to limit the focus to only large firms in the corporate sample.

### Illustrations Based on Micro Data
This section examines the approaches of Belgium and Canada. The micro data used were compiled from tax returns pertaining to measure corporate average tax rates, in particular, domestic corporate income

tax rates on domestic source income.[28] The results are compared and contrasted with findings based on aggregate data. Before turning to the results, it may be useful to look at some of the measurement issues involved.

First, measuring a corporate average tax rate means, in general, dividing (adjusted) corporate tax revenues by an adjusted measure of corporate profits, with a focus in each year on (taxable and nontaxable) firms that are profitable in the year (see the discussion above concerning alternative methods to factor in losses). In principle, the denominator profit measure should reflect economic income at the corporate level. Arguably such a measure is appropriate when assessing fairness and distribution concerns, and also where the measure is used to assess effective tax rates on past investment (as a possible check against forward-looking tax burden measures that ignore tax planning). This benchmark would provide true economic depreciation, corrections for inflation in measuring depreciation and the cost of goods sold (inventory valuation adjustment), and factor in income from the decline in the real value of debt of the nonfinancial sector during periods of inflation. As elaborated below, the profit measures used by Belgium and Canada do not make all of these adjustments. The results nevertheless draw out a number of important considerations, most important, loss effects and variability of corporate ATRs by sectors and firm size.

The implicit tax rate approach to measuring a corporate average tax rate, relying on aggregate data, takes the domestic tax on domestic and foreign-source income as a percentage of the domestic operating surplus of the (domestic) incorporated sector. Corporate operating surplus is a measure of the return to capital employed in the economy, net of depreciation, including returns to debt and equity.[29] As noted above, operating surplus includes current year losses.

The Canadian AETR figures use an adjusted book income figure in the denominator, derived at the micro level for a weighted sample of corporations.[30] Measuring adjusted book income begins with net income as reported in financial statements. This amount is adjusted to arrive at a measure of domestic corporate profit that removes double counting of domestic income, excludes foreign income, factors out corporate tax payments, and adjusts for losses by netting out loss carryforward claims for tax purposes in the current year.[31] Foreign income is excluded in the interest of focusing on domestic tax on domestic source income.[32] No adjustments are made for depreciation. Therefore depreciation claims used for accounting purposes are incorporated in the benchmark profit measure.

Rather than beginning with financial income, the Belgian example takes net taxable income and works backward to arrive at an adjusted benchmark measure of corporate profit. Beginning with net taxable income, corporate profits are measured net of loss carry forward claims without further adjustment.[33] Also, with net taxable income measured net of domestic dividend income, no adjustment is required for these amounts to avoid double counting of domestic profit (with the underlying profit accounted for in the net taxable income of the distributing company). However, to ensure that profits exempted under special tax regimes are accounted for, the exempt profits of qualifying firms are added back.[34] Disallowed expenses (i.e., expenses that reduce economic income but do not qualify for a tax deduction) are subtracted, while tax expenditures are added back.[35] As net taxable income excludes (most) foreign profits, no adjustment is made in for these amounts.[36]

Turning now to the results, figure 10.1 shows the Belgian corporate average tax rate based on micro data, along with other corporate tax rate measures, over the period 1984 to 1998. The results clearly reveal the need to factor in corporate tax base considerations, and not just the statutory corporate rate, in assessing the corporate income tax burden. The progressive narrowing of the discrepancy between the statutory and the average tax rates illustrates a convergence of the actual tax base to the benchmark profit measure in the denominator of the ATR,

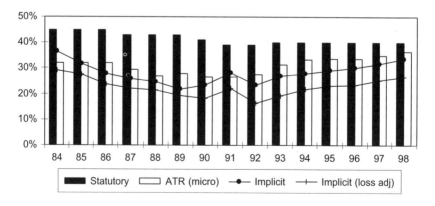

**Figure 10.1**
Corporate tax rate comparison, Belgium, 1984–1998. (Source: Ministry of Finance, Belgium)

with the micro data indicating that this results mainly from a series of tax reform measures that reduced tax expenditures.[37]

Figure 10.1 also shows an implicit corporate tax rate time series derived from aggregate data and an adjusted implicit tax rate series with a loss adjustment that nets out from the denominator (corporate operating surplus) the deduction for losses factored into corporate income tax liabilities in the numerator.[38] In years where significant corporate losses were incurred, the implicit tax rate exceeds the ATR based on micro data (1984 and 1991).

In other years the implicit tax rate is below the micro data ATR. Drawing from the analysis of table 10.4, this suggests that the effect of loss carry-forward claims in the numerator (in years immediately following 1984, and 1991) were more pronounced than the effect of current year losses factoring into the denominator. Another possible explanation is that the *National Accounts* operating surplus measure is significantly broader than corporate operating surplus, for example, due to the inclusion in the *National Accounts* of nontaxable corporations including government enterprises (as indicated by Norway in its work on average effective tax rates on capital). It may also be that corporate profits are not properly consolidated in the *National Accounts*, tending to overstate the true value, as noted by Belgium.

It can also be observed from figure 10.1 that trends in the corporate tax burden may be misrepresented by implicit tax rate figures, particularly for short time intervals. For example, the micro data show that the average tax rate in the corporate sector was essentially unchanged over the three-year period of 1984 to 1986, while the implicit tax rate results show a reduction exceeding 8 percentage points. Similarly the aggregate data suggest that the corporate average tax rate increased by 8 percentage points between 1989 and 1991, while the micro data show a reduction in the corporate tax burden over that period.

A similar finding is evident in figure 10.2 for Canadian corporate average tax rates, which factor in not only corporate income tax but also federal capital taxes (net wealth taxes) on corporations.[39] Results for the last four years (1994 to 1997) show corporate average tax rates when loss-making firms are included in the analysis, as they are under the implicit tax rate approach, with corporate ATRs with loss firms excluded.[40] With loss-making firms included, the figures show a declining average corporate tax burden over the three-year period 1994 to 1996, while the results relying on adjusted profits of profitable firms show an upward trend in the tax burden over this period.

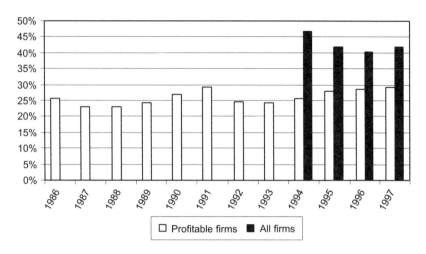

**Figure 10.2**
Canadian corporate ATR, 1986–1997: Implications of loss treatment. (Source: Ministry of Finance, Canada)

### 10.3.2  Measuring Corporate ATRs by Sector and Firm Size

In addition to enabling an adjustment for business losses, micro data also permit disaggregate analyses of corporate tax burdens. A disaggregate approach is useful, for example, where the tax system targets preferential tax treatment to firms engaged in certain business activities, or to firms on the basis of their size. Policy interest naturally arises in observing the impact of the special tax provisions on targeted groups—investment companies in Belgium, and manufacturing and processing companies in Canada are two examples. Additionally the tax systems in both Belgium and Canada provide special tax relief to small firms, and so policy interest arises in comparing the tax burden across companies of different size measured by assets or income.[41]

Even in the absence of targeted measures, there may be interest in assessing the impact of general features of the corporate tax system that affect different industries differently. For example, tax depreciation rules tend to be more important to firms in industries that are relatively capital intensive, while loss treatment tends to matter more to firms in industries exhibiting strong cyclical effects. As the net effect of these and other features of the tax system get captured in disaggregated average tax rates, an incentive exists to construct such rates for firms grouped by industry (and possibly by other criteria, e.g., size or location). The remainder of the chapter reviews findings by Belgium and Canada based on micro data for diverse corporate average tax rates, a diversity that tends to get masked in using aggregate data alone. Certain implications for policy analysis are addressed.

### ATR Results by Sector

Micro-data results by Belgium and Canada reveal significant variation in corporate average tax rates across industries, as illustrated in figures 10.3 and 10.4. As we saw in the analysis provided by Belgium, interpretation of the results by sector requires careful examination of the underlying micro data and an accounting for the impact of special features of corporate tax system.

For example, one striking finding is that in most of the industrial sectors (with the exclusion of the chemical industry, and electricity and water industry) the corporate ATR is found to *exceed* the statutory tax rate. This finding, particularly pronounced for small firms, is traced to disallowed expenses (netted from taxable profits in measuring benchmark profit) that exceed tax expenditures (removed from benchmark profits).

The Belgian analysis gives an insightful interpretation to average tax rates calculated for the industry and retail trade sectors and the other services sector. In particular, the analysis indicates that the actual tax burden on the industry and retail trade sectors is lower than that suggested by the corporate ATRs computed for these sectors. The reason is that part of the actual profits of these sectors is paid out as interest and other deductible charges to related companies where the amounts are received tax free under the Belgian coordination center regime rules. These payments are deductible in measuring tax (numerator) and before-tax profits (denominator) in the calculation of the corporate ATR of the industry and retail trade sectors. The impact of the coordination center rules does not get reflected in the corporate ATRs for these sectors. With coordination centers included in the other services sector, the corporate ATR for this sector is lowered on account of the tax exemption for income from transactions with related companies in the industry and/or retail trade sectors under the coordination regime (i.e., the other services sector corporate ATR would be higher if coordination companies were excluded).

The corporate ATR analysis by Canada reveals the need to distinguish firms by industry when considering trends in the corporate tax burden over time. In particular, when all profitable firms are considered, the

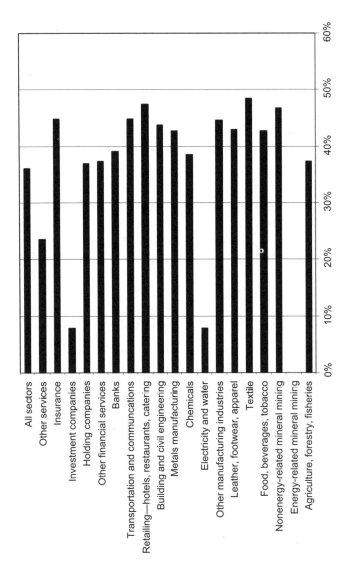

**Figure 10.3**
Belgian corporate ATR by sector, 1998. (Source: Ministry of Finance, Belgium)

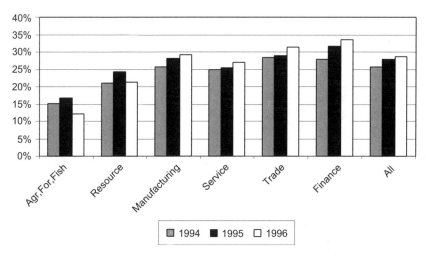

**Figure 10.4**
Canadian corporate ATR by sector. (Source: Ministry of Finance, Canada)

results show an increase in the corporate ATR in 1995 (+2.3 percentage points from 1994), and again in 1996 (+0.5 percentage points). However, the same percentage increases are not found in the manufacturing, service, trade, and finance industries, and the tax burden is shown to decrease in 1996 in the resource sector, and in the agricultural, forestry, and fishing sectors.

### ATR Results by Firm Size

In assessing the tax burden on firms according to their size as measured by assets, Canadian results show variability in corporate ATRs across firms, and over time, not reflected in the aggregate results. For example, profitable firms in the cdn$10 to 50 million asset range are found to have the highest ATR, in the order of roughly 29 to 32 percent, depending on the year, as illustrated in figure 10.5. Small firms with assets less than cdn$1 million are found to have considerably lower ATRs, in the range of 21 to 23 percent, owing mostly a special small business deduction.

Also year-to-year fluctuations in ATRs at the disaggregate level are not always reflected in the aggregate results. For example, while the corporate ATR for all profitable firms shows the corporate ATR increasing by 2.5 percentage points from 1994 to 1995, a 3.6 percentage point increase is found for the most heavily taxed group (in the cdn$10 to 50 million range). For the same group, the corporate ATR falls in

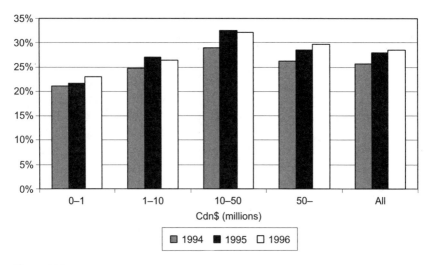

**Figure 10.5**
Canadian corporate ATR by asset size. (Source: Ministry of Finance, Canada)

1996, while the results for all profitable firms show an increase in the corporate ATR in 1996 by over half a percentage point. Similarly the ATRs for firms in the cdn$1 to 10 million asset range is shown to decline by 0.5 percentage points in 1996, while the aggregate data show the ATR increasing by 0.7 percentage points.

The Belgian example takes an alternative approach of grouping firms by gross taxable income strata, and measuring for each income strata, the percentage distribution of firms across different ATR ranges. From this analysis a general profile is evident, as illustrated in figure 10.6. For all of the income strata there is a concentration of firms with ATRs close to zero, and a concentration of firms with ATRs close to the statutory rate. Almost half of the smallest firms (in the fifth stratum with taxable income in the range of 0 to 21,000 euros) are found to have ATRs close to zero. A closer look at the micro data reveals that this can be explained mostly by loss carry-over claims. For larger firms, tax expenditures and the exemption system are found to be more important in bringing ATRs below the statutory rate.

## 10.4  Summary and Conclusions

Relying on tax revenue data to measure average tax rates on labor, capital, and other types of income has the advantage of incorporating

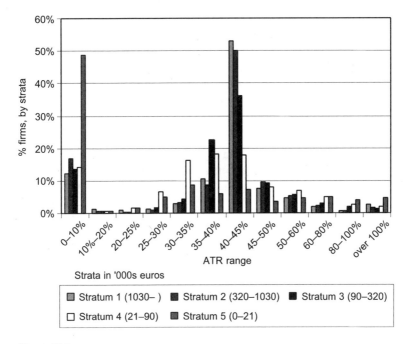

**Figure 10.6**
Belgian corporate ATR dispersion, by gross taxable income strata, 1998. (Source: Ministry of Finance, Belgium)

the net effect of a complex set of factors that determine tax liabilities and are difficult to model.[42] Micro (taxpayer-level) data drawn from tax returns provide values for various entries determining final tax calculations, which can assist in refining measurement techniques. Microdata figures can be (partially) aggregated to cover particular taxpayer groups. The results generated for different taxpayer groups offer insights into divergent tax burdens and in turn help one interpret tax burden trends at the aggregate level, and more generally provide an empirical basis for tax policy analysis.

While a micro-level view (by taxpayer group, or by sector) can address many tax policy-related questions, interest also exists in economywide average tax rates derived, for example, for labour or capital income. This chapter reviewed work by Norway and Denmark examining how micro data can permit more targeted assessments of personal tax revenues imposed on different income types that feed into such measures. In particular, we saw that by isolating taxes that apply to a single income type, and by using taxpayer-specific (rather than economywide) average tax rates to decompose revenues raised by taxes levied on multiple income types, we can measure average tax rates for different categories of income with greater precision.

The work by Belgium and Canada highlights the importance of adjusting for business losses in measuring an economywide corporate average tax rate, with implications for the proper measurement of an economywide average tax rate on income from capital (including both corporate and shareholder-level taxation).[43] The insights are relevant to the wide interest in corporate tax burdens and their effects, and in the general inability of aggregate data to generate a reliable annual corporate average tax rate series. The chapter reviewed a number of possible adjustment techniques relying on micro data, and certain issues encountered with each technique. While not addressed in the chapter, the findings also have implications for the measurement of average tax rates on business or total income of the self-employed.

Most important, the chapter indicated the difficulties in drawing policy conclusions from results based on aggregate data. Effective tax rates tend to vary for different taxpayer groups, sometimes significantly, by taxpayer group. Work by Austria finds significant variation in average tax rates on wage income across wage levels, and this raises a question about the use of a single (implicit) tax rate for a given year based on aggregate data to assess the tax burden of a progressive labor income tax. The chapter argued that the impact of the tax system on labor market participation can be best assessed where one is able to measure average tax rates on labor income at various income levels and for different taxpayer groups.

The chapter also reported a significant variation on average corporate tax rates across firms grouped by industry and firm size. The analyses by Belgium and Canada revealed that economywide results may be misleading indicators of levels and trends in corporate average tax rates for certain groups of firms, emphasizing the need for a disaggregate view to steer policy analysis and decisions.

The chapter provided limited discussion of the use of various micro-based average tax rates to address specific policy questions. Such an analysis is beyond the scope of the question on the extent to which average tax rate results derived from aggregate data can be taken to be representative of the diversity in tax burdens across taxpayer groups and years.

This raises a central issue of the confidentiality of taxpayer information, and the general inability of those outside government to undertake revenue-based average tax rate analysis at the micro level. This is unfortunate (yet understandable), as broader access to micro-level data would accelerate progress in this field. One potentially fruitful area to explore would be to consider what levels of aggregation of taxpayer-level data would be possible that would maintain confidentiality, while supporting revenue-based average tax rate analysis on a disaggregate basis.

## Notes

The author is grateful to Gaëtan Nicodeme and other participants of the CESifo Venice Summer Institute Workshop on Measuring the Tax Burden on Capital and Labour for their comments on an earlier draft. The views expressed here are the author's own and do not necessarily reflect the views of the OECD or its member countries.

1. See chapter 6 of *Tax Burdens—Alternative Measures* for a discussion of the relevance of backward-looking (tax revenue-based) measures to address primarily fairness considerations, in particular, the sharing of tax burdens, and forward-looking (model-based) measures for taxes on capital income relevant to assessing investment incentives.

2. As reported in *Tax Burdens—Alternative Measures*, OECD Tax Policy Studies 2 (2000), and in *Tax Ratios—A Critical Survey*, prepared by Jakob de Haan and Bjorn Volkerink, released as OECD Tax Policy Studies 5 (2001).

3. For a review of the basic implicit tax rate approach, see *Tax Burdens—Alternative Measures*. See also Carey and Tchilinguirian (2001).

4. Under the implicit tax rate approach, total personal income tax on labor (capital) income is estimated as the proportion of aggregate personal income tax that aggregate labor (capital) income is to aggregate personal income.

5. Average tax rates on wage income, which may affect labor market participation decisions, can differ significantly depending on the wage level and household structure (married vs. single, principal vs. secondary earner, with or without children; see OECD *Taxing Wages*). There is evidence that elasticities of labor demand and supply may differ depending on the taxpayer group (e.g., primary earners vs. secondary earners; see R. Blundell 1996).

6. Income may be separated into labor income or capital income. Implicit tax rate analysis generally restricts itself to these two broad income categories (while measuring average tax rates on other taxable events, e.g., consumption). Access to micro data enables measurement of average tax rates on various types (subcategories) of income—for example, on alternative items or groupings of labour income amounts. A broad definition of labor income would include wages and salaries, the labor component of returns to the self-employed, and pension income including social security benefits. Policy analysis may call for effective tax rate measures for more narrow definitions of labor income (e.g., excluding pension income).

7. Ordinary income includes wage and salary income (i.e., fringe benefits), pension/ benefits income, imputed labor income of the self-employed, and capital income (dividends, capital gains, interest, rents, imputed capital income of self-employed business owners, and other forms of capital income) less deductions. A flat 28 percent rate applies to ordinary income in excess of a threshold which varies depending on the household structure (class 1 and class 2). The separate income surtax on gross labour income is imposed at progressive rates with taxable income thresholds and allowances that also depend on the household structure (class 1 or class 2), with no deductions.

8. The revenues from these taxes are aggregated and reported under category 1110 in OECD *Revenue Statistics* ("Taxes on income and profits of individuals").

9. As explained later, micro data yield more precision in estimating the tax imposed in a category/type of income by a broad-based tax.

10. Employee social security contributions are imposed on wage and salary income and pension income, while social security contributions of the self-employed are imposed on pension income and imputed labor income of the self-employed.

11. The income surtax is imposed on wage and salary income, imputed labor income of the self-employed, and pension income.

12. Note that total personal income tax $(OT + S)$ in $(10.2)$ corresponds to category 1100 in the *Revenue Statistics*.

13. In estimating the labor portion of tax on ordinary income, the approach taken in $(10.3a)$—unlike that shown in equation $(10.1a)$—does *not* use taxpayer-level data. As with the implicit tax rate approach, it relies on an overall weight $(w^L)$ rather than on a taxpayer-specific weight. Thus the exercise concentrates on the benefits of isolating the surtax for the purpose of the average tax rate calculation.

14. In measuring $(10.3a)$, the labor component of income from self-employment is measured at the taxpayer level (and then aggregated) by relying on the split of operating surplus of the self-employed into labor and capital components as required for tax purposes. Total labor income in the numerator of equation 10.3b) is measured net of deductions allocated to labor. Ordinary income OY appearing in the denominator of 3b) is measured from tax returns (gross of the class allowance).

15. Such features could include special tax deductions or credits tied to employment income (deductions for travel expenses, earned income tax credits, etc.). Similarly differences in tax burdens on labor income compared with capital income tied to a progressive tax rate structure would be taken into account, unlike in the implicit tax rate approach. If capital income tends to be earned primarily by taxpayers with relatively high average tax rates, tending to increase the average tax rate on capital income relative to labor income, results derived using microdata would account for this, whereas a reliance on aggregated data would not. To take another example, taxpayer-level data can more directly assess features of the tax system that affect the tax burden on income from capital, for example provisions allowing a partial deduction for interest expense on amounts borrowed to generate taxable interest income.

16. An estimate of the average tax rate on wage income may be a better indicator of the tax burden on employment, compared with an average tax rate on labor income broadly defined.

17. The tax rate $t$ can be interpreted as either a flat tax rate or a progressive rate structure applied to the tax base, which is shown in parentheses.

18. For simplicity, we ignore in this illustrative framework, expenses incurred in earning wage income. These expenses can, however, be readily factored in the same way as the expenses in earning other income.

19. As was pointed out at the CESifo conference, an assessment of income-specific rates would be important where one is assessing a marginal (rather than an average) tax rate.

20. The ATR series ($\tau^L_I$ and $\tau^L_{II}$) can be combined to give $\tau^L_{I+II} = [WT + SSC^{ee}]/W$, which more closely aligns with the normal implicit tax rate approach (the Austrian results ignore employer social security contributions and payroll taxes). The combined tax rate $\tau^L_{I+II}$ could be measured using micro data to arrive at the combined tax burden at various wage levels, but the information provided by each series individually would be lost in this aggregation.

21. This may be particularly true where benefit levels for those out of work are not high. Where they are, consideration of the labor market participation decision should factor in benefit and tax impacts of taking up work.

22. The discrete change tax rate on wage income (DTR) series is derived by measuring the change in wage tax per head resulting from a (discrete) increase in gross wages/salaries per head (from one gross income band to the next).

23. The distorting effects (linked to losses) in an implicit tax rate analysis (using aggregate data) are generally more pronounced in measures of the average *corporate* tax rate. These effects, however, also factor in when the average tax rate is measured in income from *capital* (which includes both personal and corporate taxes), since the corporate income tax in the numerator is reduced by losses carried forward and operating surplus in the denominator is reduced by current period losses.

24. In working with micro data, one could use just the average corporate tax rate for profitable companies and include in the numerator an estimate of corporate tax revenues in the absence of loss carryover claims, and in the denominator, current period profits of profitable firms alone. (Note that such an adjustment would not be possible when relying on aggregate *National Accounts* data, as operating surplus in a given year includes the losses of current loss-making firms.) However, in ignoring the losses, one would omit important information relevant to assessing the tax burden of the corporate sector.

25. There are also a number of difficult modeling choices, including the use of a fixed- or moving-average aggregation period and the length and timing of the aggregation period. Arguably the length should reflect the business cycle. However, business cycles do vary over time and across countries, making a uniform aggregation procedure difficult. One could further argue that the aggregation period should take into account the number of years in which losses can be carried over for tax purposes if loss claims are discretionary. This recognizes that where taxpayers delay a loss claim in one year in favor of another claim (e.g., tax credit) under the liberal carry-forward rules, the short aggregation period could overstate the effective tax burden.

26. The effective corporate tax rate of 20 percent can be interpreted as resulting from a statutory corporate tax rate in excess of 20 percent, with tax expenditures (e.g., accelerated depreciation or special tax credits) that lower the effective rate to 20 percent. Alternatively, one could interpret the rate as a statutory corporate income tax rate where such tax expenditures would not be provided.

27. This is the approach followed by Belgium and Canada in their work.

28. An alternative measure would assess net domestic corporate tax on domestic plus foreign-source income of resident firms as a percentage of worldwide income. However, such a measure cannot be easily interpreted, thus limiting its usefulness. Where the home country operates an exemption system, the measure would exclude entirely foreign tax on foreign source income, relevant to fairness, as well as investment and efficiency considerations. Similar problems of interpretation arise where the home country operates a residence-based system, and this is due to difficulties in establishing the amount of foreign tax levied on foreign income.

29. Operating surplus can be measured either gross or net of depreciation of real capital. Although corporate tax could be treated as a percentage of net operating surplus to conform with measures of tax on income, the results across countries would be difficult to compare on account of nonuniform measurement of depreciation in the *National Accounts* across countries.

30. Each year a weighted-sample of profitable corporations is chosen (individual firms included in the sample may vary from one year to the next). The losses are factored into the analysis as prior-year losses of the currently profitable firms (with current year loss claims used to reduce current year aggregate profits).

31. The adjusted book income figure nets out (taxable and nontaxable) dividend receipts both domestic and foreign, foreign branch as well as other (nonbusiness) foreign income, and net equity of affiliates included in financial income. As net financial income is measured net of current income and capital taxes, these amounts are added back to arrive at a before-tax amount. Other adjustments include netting current-period loss claims from book income (including noncapital (business) losses, net capital losses, and farm losses), and adding back charitable donations.

32. The Canadian corporate tax is not imposed on foreign dividends received from the treaty countries. However, the numerator of the Canadian corporate ATR includes some Canadian income tax to the extent that it exceeds foreign tax credits earned on other foreign source income. While, in principle, this tax should be excluded for consistency with the denominator profit measure, the inclusion of this tax does not have a significant impact on the results.

33. As the calculation of before-tax profit begins with net taxable income (already measured net of loss carry-forward claims), no adjustment is necessary for the loss amounts. Also, by focusing on taxable firms, the sample includes firms that are profitable in the given year. As in the Canadian example, losses are factored in by netting loss carry-forward claims from current-year profits.

34. The special regimes include the coordination center, distribution center, and service center regimes.

35. The tax expenditures include special deductions for investment, exempted gifts, and tax relief for additional staff. Of course, profits exempted under special regimes are also added back. These tax expenditures reduce tax liability (and thus factor into the numerator) but do not relate to before-tax economic income.

36. Profits earned in countries with which Belgium has a double tax treaty are tax exempt. Thus these profits are excluded from the denominator (net taxable income) and numerator. Profits earned in countries with which Belgium does not have a double taxation treaty are taxed at one-quarter of the nominal rate. These amounts are included in the denominator, and the resulting tax is included in the numerator. While, in principle,

these amounts should be excluded in a pure domestic corporate ATR measure, their inclusion does not have a significant impact on the results.

37. This includes the elimination over the period of deductible notional withholding taxes (*précomptes fictifs*) on loans and capital contributions to Belgian coordination centers and other amounts.

38. To avoid double counting of losses, it is necessary to exclude current-period losses from current-period operating surplus. Without this adjustment, losses of a firm in year $t$ would be taken into account in year $t$ (through the inclusion in operating surplus of losses of firms in year $t$), and also in subsequent years where previously loss-making firms become taxable and claim a loss carried forward.

39. The inclusion of a tax determined as a percentage of capital stock (or a similar base, as opposed to profit) is appropriate in the measure of a corporate tax paid out of corporate profit. One could argue that this inclusion is suitable only where the resulting rate is used for distribution analysis. When considering the tax consequences of an additional investment, it is desirable to capture the additional capital tax paid as the result of an expanded capital stock. Including capital tax in the numerator of a measure used to assess tax burden on investment may be justified where the aggregate corporate profit is proportional to the aggregate capital stock. Note that the Canadian figures are used in the chapter to address distribution issues.

40. Unlike the profit measure in the denominator of the AETRs computed for the profitable group, the profit measure for the all-firm series does not net out loss carry-forward claims (consistent with the inclusion of loss-making firms).

41. Belgium offers tax relief for supplementary personnel employed in small- and medium-sized enterprises, while Canada targets small firms through its small business deduction.

42. As was pointed out earlier, the tax burden measures that factor in tax liabilities but exclude taxpayer compliance costs understate the true tax burden. Also, measures that rely on financial statements to measure corporate profit may be biased to the extent that profits are manipulated (e.g., overstated).

43. Loss adjustments are also obviously important for analysis at the disaggregate level.

# References

Blundell, R. 1996. Labour supply and taxation. In M. Devereux, ed., *The Economics of Tax Policy*. Oxford: Oxford University Press.

Carey, D., and H. Tchilinguirian. 2000. Average effective tax rates on capital, labour and consumption. OECD Economics Department Working Paper 258.

Mendoza, E., A. Razin, and L. Tesar. 1994. Effective tax rates in macroeconomics: Cross country estimates of tax rates on factor incomes and consumption. NBER Working Paper 4864. September.

OECD. 2000. Tax burdens—Alternative measures. Tax Policy Studies 2.

OECD. 2000. Average effective tax rates—Notes by Canada, Denmark and Norway. Collected papers prepared for the 14–15 November 2000 meeting of Working Party 2 of the OECD Committee on Fiscal Affairs.

OECD. 2001. *National Accounts, 1984–2001*.

OECD. 2001. *Revenue Statistics, 1965–2001*.

OECD. 2001. Tax ratios—A critical survey. Tax Policy Studies 5.

OECD. 2001. Taxing wages.

Rainer, A. 2001. Austrian micro tax data and tax indicators. Mimeo. Prepared for the 12–14 June 2001 meeting of Working Party 2 of the OECD Committee on Fiscal Affairs.

Valenduc, C. 2001. Effective tax rates: The use of micro-data. Mimeo. Prepared for the 12–14 June 2001 meeting of Working Party 2 of the OECD Committee on Fiscal Affairs.

# Index